Ian Copland's comprehensive and meticulously researched study of the role played by the Indian princes, the maharajas and nawabs of South Asia, in the devolution of British colonial power is long overdue. By rehabilitating the princes as subjects of serious historical study, the author demonstrates that, far from being puppets under the control of the British, they were in fact significant actors on the Indian political stage in the inter-war period. He goes on to explain how and why an order so deep-rooted, and outwardly so strong, collapsed so quickly under the successor Congress government in New Delhi. The book will add a new dimension to the political history of late colonial India, and will also impact upon the wider history of the twentieth-century British empire.

Cambridge Studies in Indian History and Society

The princes of India in the endgame of empire, 1917–1947

Cambridge Studies in Indian History and Society 2

Cambridge Studies in Indian History and Society will publish monographs on the history and anthropology of modern India. In addition to its primary scholarly focus, the series will also include work of an interdisciplinary nature which will contribute to contemporary social and cultural debates about Indian history and society. In this way, the series will further the general development of historical and anthropological knowledge and attract a wider readership than that concerned with India alone.

The princes of India in the endgame of empire, 1917–1947

Ian Copland

Monash University

CAMBRIDGE
UNIVERSITY PRESS

Published by the Press Syndicate of the University of Cambridge
The Pitt Building, Trumpington Street, Cambridge CB2 1RP
40 West 20th Street, New York, NY 10011–4211, USA
10 Stamford Road, Oakleigh, Melbourne 3166, Australia

First published 1997

Printed in Great Britain at the University Press, Cambridge

A catalogue record for this book is available from the British Library

Library of Congress cataloguing in publication data

Copland, Ian, 1943–
    The princes of India in the endgame of empire, 1917–1947 / Ian
Copland.
        p.   cm. – Cambridge studies in Indian history and society)
    Includes index.
    ISBN 0 521 57179 0
    1. India–Politics and government–1917–1947. 2. India–Kings and
rulers. 3. India–History–British occupation, 1765–1947.
    I. Title. II. Series.
    DS480.45.C69   1997
    954.03–dc20   96–18313 CIP

ISBN 0 521 57179 0 hardback

Contents

Acknowledgements

In the decade or so that it has taken me to research and write this book, I have benefited from the assistance of many organisations and individuals; indeed, the debts of gratitude that I have accrued over these years are far too many to be listed here in their entirety. Nevertheless I would like to thank, in particular, the following: the governments of India, Punjab, Rajasthan, Madhya Pradesh, Gujarat and Andhra Pradesh for allowing me to work in their archives; the Australian Research Council for funding two trips to India; Monash University, for providing additional financial support and for granting me leave to work overseas; Professor Ravinder Kumar, for allowing me to use the wonderful manuscript collection at the Nehru Memorial Museum and Library; Mrs Sonia Gandhi for giving me permission to consult the Jawaharlal Nehru Papers covering the period 1947–50; Dr David Blake of the Oriental Section of the British Library (or as people in the trade still prefer to call it, the 'IOL') for giving me access to uncatalogued Willingdon Papers; Mr V. K. Juneja of the Bhopal Record Office, both for his professional help, and for his warm hospitality; Mr A. B. Chauhan of the Gujarat State Archives, Baroda, for expediting the paperwork connected with my application; Professor Sharif-al-Mujahid, for making available to me the resources of the Quaid-i-Azam Institute in Karachi; the late Mr Khalid Shamsul Hasan, for allowing me to consult his father's collection of Muslim League documents; Kailash and Shukla Nath, for offering me a place in Delhi that I could call home; Mike Godley, for his unwavering friendship and support; H. H. Mahurdhwaj Sinhji of Dhrangadhra and H. H. Brijraj Singh of Kota, for introducing me to the society of princes; my former mentor, the late Professor Jack Gallagher; and last but not least Professors Anthony Low and Robin Moore, for demonstrating in their many writings that the narrative history of high politics still has an integral place in our craft.

Abbreviations

AISPC	All-India States Peoples' Conference
APSA	Andhra Pradesh State Archives
BRO	National Archives of India, Bhopal Record Office
COM	Committee of Ministers
COP	Chamber of Princes
CR	Crown Representative
CWC	Congress Working Committee
GOI	Government of India
GSAB	Gujarat State Archives, Southern Circle Record Office Baroda
I&B	India and Burma Committee
IAR	Indian Annual Register
IOR	India Office Records
INC	Indian National Congress
ISD	Indian States Delegation
MPSA	Madhya Pradesh State Archives, Bhopal
NAI	National Archives of India
NMML	Nehru Memorial Museum and Library
PC	Durga Das (ed.), *Sardar Patel's Correspondence, 1945–50* (Ahmedabad, 1971–4)
PSA	Punjab State Archives, Patiala
PSO	Private Secretary's Office
PSV	Private sec. to the viceroy
RSAB	Rajasthan State Archives, Bikaner Depositary
RTC	Round Table Conference
SC	Standing Committee
SO	Special Organisation
TOI	*Times of India*
TOP	Nicholas Mansergh (ed.), *Constitutional Relations Between Britain and India: the Transfer of Power* (London, 1970–83)

The major players

Princes

Col. Sir Jey Singh Kachwaha, maharaja of Alwar: b. 1882; acceded 1903; member Indian delegation to League of Nations 1922; member ISD to first RTC; president Sanatan Dharma Sabha; deposed and exiled 1933; d. 1937.

Sir Sayaji Rao Gaekwar III, maharaja of Baroda: b. 1863; acceded 1875; member ISD to first RTC; d. 1939.

Air Vice-Marshal Sir Hamidullah Khan, nawab of Bhopal: b. 1894; M. A. Aligarh; chief secretary Bhopal 1916; acceded 1926; chancellor COP 1931–2 and 1944–7; d. 1960.

General Sir Ganga Singh Rathor, maharaja of Bikaner: b. 1880; acceded 1887; member Imperial War Cabinet 1917; chancellor COP 1921–6; member ISD to first RTC; d. 1943.

Lt.-Gen. Sir Sadul Singh Rathor, maharaja of Bikaner: b. 1902; acceded 1943; d. 1950.

Sir Udaibhan Singh Deo, maharaj-rana of Dholpur: b. 1893; acceded 1912; acting chancellor COP 1936–7; d. 1954.

Major-Gen. Sir Osman Ali Khan, nizam of Hyderabad: b. 1886; acceded 1911; chancellor Aligarh University; Rajpramukh Hyderabad 1950–6; d. 1967.

Major-Gen. Sir Yeshwant Rao Holkar, maharaja of Indore: b. 1908; acceded 1926; member ISD to second RTC; d. 1961.

Lt.-Gen. Sir Hari Singh Dogra, maharaja of Kashmir: b. 1895; involved in 'Mr A' case 1924; acceded 1925; member ISD to first RTC; deposed by GOI 1949; d. 1961.

Lt.-Gen. Sir Digvijaysinhji Jadeja, jam saheb of Nawanagar: b. 1895; acceded 1933; chancellor COP 1937–42; member, Imperial War

Cabinet and Pacific War Council 1942; member Indian delegation to UN 1948–50; d. 1966.

Col. Sir Ranjitsinhji Jadeja, jam saheb of Nawanagar: b. 1872; played cricket for Sussex and England; acceded 1907; member Indian delegation to League of Nations 1921; chancellor COP 1932–3; d. 1933.

Major-Gen. Sir Bhupinder Singh, maharaja of Patiala: b. 1891; acceded 1900; member Imperial War Council 1918; chancellor COP 1926–31, 1932–6 and 1937; subject to inquiry by GOI 1930; d. 1938

Lt.-Gen. Sir Yadavindra Singh, maharaja of Patiala: b. 1913; acceded 1938; president Indian Olympic Association 1938–60; chancellor COP 1947; Rajpramukh Patiala and East Punjab States Union 1948–56; member Indian delegation to UN 1956–7; ambassador to Italy 1965–6; member Punjab Legislative Assembly 1967–8; d. 1974.

Sir Gulab Singh Baghela, maharaja of Rewa: b. 1903; acceded 1918; member ISD to first and second RTCs; investigated by GOI commission of inquiry 1942; exiled 1943; deposed 1945; d. 1950.

Ministers

Sir C. P. Ramaswamy Aiyer: b. 1879; LLB. Madras; member Madras Corporation 1912–16; general secretary INC 1917–18; member Madras LC 1919; held various portfolios including advocate-general, law member and member for Commerce and Industry; member Indian delegation to League of Nations 1928; dewan Travancore 1936–47; d. 1966.

Sir Kailash Narain Haksar: b. 1878; B.A., LLB. Allahabad; private secretary maharaja of Gwalior 1903–12; political member Gwalior 1912–37; joint director Special Organisation of the COP 1929–31; member ISD to all three RTCs; PM Bikaner 1938–9; PM Kashmir 1943–4; d. 1955?

Sir Akbar Hydari: b.1869; B.A. Bombay; various posts Finance Department GOI 1887–1905; accountant-general Hyderabad 1905; secretary Finance Dept. 1907; accountant-general Bombay 1920–1; finance minister Hyderabad 1921–37; member ISD to all three RTCs; chairman COMs 1935–40; president of nizam's Council 1937–40; member for Information and Broadcasting GOI, 1940–1; d. 1941.

Sir Mirza Ismail: b. 1883; B.A. Bangalore; assistant superintendent Police Mysore 1905; private secretary maharaja of Mysore 1923; dewan Mysore 1926–41; member ISD to all three RTCs; PM Jaipur 1941–5; PM Hyderabad 1946–7; d. 1959.

Sir V. T. Krishnamachari: b. 1881; dep. collector Madras 1903; chief revenue officer Cochin 1908–11; under-secretary Madras 1912–22; collector 1922–4; secretary Law Dept. Madras 1924–7; dewan Baroda 1927–45; member ISD to all three RTCs; chairman COMs 1940–4; member Indian delegation to UN 1945; PM Jaipur 1946–8; member Fiscal Commission 1949; member and chairman Planning Commission 1953–60; d. 1964.

Nawab Sir Liaquat Hyat Khan: b. 1887; deputy superintendent Punjab Police 1909; superintendent Police 1919; home secretary Patiala 1923; PM Patiala 1930–40; member ISD to all three RTCs; political adviser Bhopal 1943–5; d. 1948.

Sir Manubhai Mehta: b. 1868; B.A. Bombay; professor Baroda College 1891–9; private secretary maharaja of Baroda 1899–1906; revenue member Baroda 1914–6; dewan Baroda 1916–27; PM Bikaner 1927–34; home minister Gwalior 1937–40; foreign minister Gwalior 1940–6; chairman COMs 1944–6; d. 1946.

K. M. Panikkar: b. 1894; B.A. (Hons.) Oxford; professor Aligarh University 1919–22; editor *Swarajjya*; editor *The Hindustan Times*; political adviser to maharaja of Kashmir 1928; member COP team which briefed the Butler Committee 1928–9; member ISD to first RTC; secretary COP 1931–6; foreign minister Patiala 1933–9; PM Bikaner 1939–48; member Indian delegation to Commonwealth Conference 1945; member Indian delegation to UN 1947–8; ambassador to China 1948–51; Ambassador to Egypt 1951–4; member Indian States Reorganization Commission 1954–6; ambassador to France 1956–9; d. 1963.

Others

Sir Conrad Corfield: b. 1893; assistant commissioner Punjab 1920; assistant private secretary viceroy 1921–2; assistant commissioner Baluchistan 1922–30; assistant resident Hyderabad 1930–2; political agent Rewa 1932–7; joint secretary political department, 1937–9; resident Jaipur 1939–40; AGG Punjab States 1941–5; political adviser to the crown representative 1945–7; d. 1980.

Sir Bertrand Glancy: b. 1882; assistant AGG Rajputana 1915–18; assistant resident Kashmir 1918–21; deputy secretary political department 1921–7; acting political secretary 1928–9; president, Council of State Jaipur 1929–32; AGG Central India 1933; political secretary 1933–7; political adviser to the crown representative 1937–41; governor Punjab 1941–6; d. 1953.

H. A. Gwynne: b. 1865; correspondent for *The Times* and Reuters 1890–1904; editor of the *Standard* 1904–11; editor of the *Morning Post* 1911–37; d. 1950.

V. P. Menon: b. 1894; entered provincial civil service 1914; assistant secretary Reforms Office 1933–4; under secretary 1934–5; deputy secretary 1935–40; joint secretary 1941–2; reforms commissioner 1942–7; secretary states ministry 1947–51; governor of Orissa 1951; d. 1966.

Sir Walter Monckton (Viscount Monckton of Brenchley): b. 1891; B.A. (Hons.) Oxford; called to the Bar 1919; KC 1930; legal adviser to Hyderabad, Bhopal and other states 1933–6 and 1946–8; director-general Ministry of Information 1940–2; member Middle East War Council 1941–2; MP and minister of labour 1951–5; minister of defence 1955–7; chairman Midland Bank 1957–64; chairman Iraq Petroleum Co. 1958–65; d. 1965.

John Hartman Morgan: b. 1896; M.A. London 1896; B.A. (Hons.) Oxford 1900; called to the Bar 1915; leader writer for the *Daily Chronicle* 1901–3 and for the *Manchester Guardian* 1904–5; professor University College London 1915–41; assistant adjutant-general 1919–20; member Inter-Allied Control Commission on Disarmament 1920–3; KC 1926; legal adviser to COP 1934–7; legal adviser American War Crimes Commission 1947–9; d. 1955.

Sir Paul Patrick: b. 1888; B.A. (Oxford); joined India Office 1913; secretary political department 1931–1941; assistant under secretary state for India 1941–7; assistant under secretary state for Commonwealth Relations 1947–9; d. 1975.

Sir Leslie Frederick Scott: b. 1869; B.A. (Hons.) Oxford; called to the Bar 1894; KC 1909; MP 1907–29; legal adviser to COP 1927–31; judge Court of Appeal 1935–48; d. 1950.

Sir John Perronet Thompson: b. 1873; B.A. (Hons.) Cambridge; chief secretary Punjab 1916–21; MLC Punjab 1913–20; member Imperial LC 1918–19; member Reforms Committee 1918; political secretary 1922–7; chief commissioner Delhi 1928–32; member Council of State 1922–32; d. 1935.

William Henderson Wadhams: b. 1873; judge New York District Court 1915–21; based in Paris 1925–35; legal adviser to COP and to Patiala and other states 1935–45; d. 1952.

Sir Francis Vernon Wylie: b. 1891; political agent Tochi 1921–23; acting deputy secretary political department 1923–30; PM Alwar 1933–4; deputy AGG Baluchistan 1935–6; joint secretary political department 1936; resident Jaipur 1936–7; governor C.P. and Berar 1938–40; political adviser to crown representative 1940–1 and 1943–5; Minister at Kabul 1941–3; governor UP 1945–7; d. 1970.

Introduction

Any account of the last days of princely rule will sound incredible today.

K. M. Panikkar, 1977

When India's government-owned international airline was set up in the 1950s, one of the first things its directors had to do was choose a company logo – an arresting icon for its stationery and billboards. It is significant (though not without irony) that among the many resonant national symbols that must have leapt to mind, they hit upon – not a Bengal tiger, or a sacred cow or a *chakra* – but: the salaaming, *pugreed* figure of a king. This was the airline, the caption ran, 'that treats you like a maharaja'. Now the choice of a turbaned prince certainly made good business sense, the figure being a part of India's image abroad and thus easily recognisable to potential tourists. Beyond that, however, the choice reflected another, deeper reality: kings and kingship were, and are, a vital part of India's cultural baggage. In the modern nation-state which is the Republic of India, royalty, in the abstract, remains a rich and potent source of inspiration and political legitimacy.

Yet (and this is the ironical bit) maharajas – as such – no longer exist. Between 1947 and 1949 all 600-odd ruling princes in India were pensioned off and their ancestral domains – the so-called 'princely states' – were submerged in the body politic of the Indian union. Nowadays the few former rulers still alive are just ordinary citizens; while the ex-states survive – if at all – only in attenuated shape as components of larger administrative units. As a practical system of governance monarchy in India has been consigned to the dustbin of history.

By any standards 'integration' (as this process was rather euphemistically dubbed by its architects) represented a major watershed. It swelled the area of the new Indian state by over half a million square miles and its population by nearly 90 millions; redrew the political map of the subcontinent; and overthrew an entire governing order with roots going back to the *Mahabharata* and beyond. Of course there are those who would argue that the princes were ripe for a fall, and that their demise had been

1

long on the cards. But even if one accepts this hypothesis, and pushes the period of princely decline back one, two decades, the point still holds good: their fall was exceedingly rapid. At the end of World War I, the rulers were arguably at the peak of their power – safe under the military umbrella of a British raj imbued with the 'illusion of permanence', venerated by the overwhelming majority of their subjects, admired, even, by many nationalists. Thirty years later they were extinct. By comparison, the fall of the British aristocracy occupied at least a century.[1] No wonder many Indian historians have seen the 'integration' of the states as a 'great ... revolution'.[2]

This book is essentially the story of what happened to the Indian princes during those three decades of rapid – and finally fatal – political change. It seeks to discover both how they were undone, and why; and to determine what, if anything, the rulers could have done to avert the catastrophe which overtook the order in 1948. It is thus, primarily, a study in the diplomacy of the princely courts, or *darbars*, or, to put it another way, an essay in patrimonial politics; but it is also, at a secondary level, a study in imperial politics, for as time went by the *darbars* came more and more to dominate London's strategic thinking about the subcontinent – a trend which culminated in attempts in the 1930s to rope them into an all-India federation as a counterpoint to the electoral power of the Indian National Congress. As allies and clients of the British, the princes were significant players in that frenetic contest between the old world and the new which historians have called the end-game of empire. This is assuredly a grand and important theme; yet it remains a neglected one.

As the premier event in the history of decolonisation in Asia, the transfer of power in India has deservedly attracted much scholarly attention, particularly since the 1970s when the government archives for the period began to be opened. However the vast bulk of this research has focussed on the partition and the establishment of Pakistan, much of the remainder on the imperial debate over decolonisation; very little space has been given to the fate of the states.[3] Similarly, as against the vast aca-

---

[1] David Cannadine in his excellent study of the latter phenomenon nominates the 1880s as the decade when the 'rot' set in. *The Decline and Fall of the British Aristocracy* (New York, 1992), 25–32.

[2] R. C. Majumdar *et al.*, *Struggle For Freedom* (Bombay, 1969), 784. See also R. L. Handa, *History of Freedom Struggle in Princely States* (Delhi, 1968), 6; and William L. Richter, 'Princes in Indian Politics', *Economic and Political Weekly*, 6, 9 (27 Feb. 1971), 538.

[3] Nearly half a century after the event, the most comprehensive survey remains that by one of the principal protagonists, V. P. Menon. However while Menon's *The Story of the Integration of the Indian States* (Bombay, 1961) is remarkably detailed, it is seriously flawed by the author's determination to present himself in a good light.

demic literature that has been produced over the last few decades on 'British' India – that is to say, on the provinces – perhaps a score of books have engaged in a serious way with the history of the two-fifths of the subcontinent that remained outside British rule. And, of these, only three grapple substantially with the issues raised above: Steven Ashton's *British Policy Towards the Indian States*; Barbara Ramusack's *The Princes of India In the Twilight of Empire*; and the volume edited by Robin Jeffrey, *People, Princes and Paramount Power*.[4] How can we claim to have developed a sophisticated historiography of colonial South Asia when the dominant interpretations fail to take so much of the terrain into account?

Yet it is not quite true to say that the princes have been snubbed by history. Whilst they have not yet to any significant extent entered the domain of scholarly inquiry, they have been seized on eagerly by popular writers with an eye to profit. Still perhaps the best-known account of the princes is 'Diwan' Jarmani Dass' *Maharaja*, loosely based on the author's service in Kapurthala and Patiala states during the late 1930s. Packed full of juicy tidbits of royal scandal, real and invented, it has sold more than 100,000 copies.[5] Other examples of the genre are John Lord's *The Maharajas* and Larry Collins and Dominic Lapierre's *Freedom at Midnight*, which, unusually for books on the transfer of power, make the fall of the states a major theme.[6] In addition there is a considerable body of quasi-scholarly literature that sees the rulers as tyrannical despots and the states as unsavoury creations of British imperialism, medieval obstacles in the way of freedom and progress. According to Urmila Phadnis, the British 'upheld an outworn regime which would otherwise have collapsed on itself . . . [but which] compelled the people to lead a life of . . . stagnation, ignorance and apathy'.[7] Of the states in the 1920s S. K. P. Singh writes:

---

[4] S. R. Ashton, *British Policy Towards the Indian States, 1905–1939* (London, 1982); R. Jeffrey (ed.), *People, Princes and Paramount Power: Society and Politics in the Indian Princely States* (Delhi, 1978); Barbara N. Ramusack, *The Princes of India in the Twilight of Empire: Dissolution of a Patron-Client System, 1914–1939* (Colombus, OH., 1978).

[5] Diwan Jarmani Dass, *Maharaja; Lives and Loves of Indian Princes* (Bombay, 1969). Dass was eventually forced out of Patiala by a palace intrigue. Note by Sir Bertrand Glancy, 17 Nov. 1939, IOR R/1/1/3245. When *Maharaja* came out H. H. Harinder Singh of Kapurthala wrote to a friend: 'Yes, the book . . . is quite amusing . . . [but] Of course his ideas on money expendable in millions is completely wrong, because Kapurthala never had 10 lakhs together in their treasury.' Kapurthala to Sir Conrad Corfield 19 Jan. 1970, Corfield Coll., 3.

[6] John Lord, *The Maharajas* (London, 1971); Larry Collins and Dominic Lapierre, *Freedom at Midnight* (London, 1975), especially chapter 7. For an earlier example of this genre, see Kanhayalal Gauba, *H.H., Or The Pathology Of Princes* (Lahore, 1945).

[7] Urmila Phadnis, *Towards the Integration of the Indian States, 1919–1947* (Bombay, 1968), 206.

They [the rulers] were ruthlessly suppressing the exposition of public opinion. Not a day passed without hearing the news of some Maharaja or other issuing *letters* [*sic*] *de cachet* to prohibit public meetings, summarily arresting . . . respectable citizens [and engaging in] wholesale arbitrary confiscation of property and banishment of people from their native land.[8]

The surface assumption here is that the princely states fell prey to an irresistable upsurge of popular outrage and vengeance. But beneath it lies another, which Singh articulates indirectly when he asserts at the end of his book that integration 'revived' the 'traditional unity of our country': namely, that the destruction of the monarchical system was in some mysterious way predestined by the laws of historical evolution.

Aside from the fact that these interpretations are, in many respects, contradictory (it is hard, for instance, to reconcile the characterisation of the maharajas as bejewelled loafers with the picture of them as unremitting despots – despotism presumably calling for at least some expenditure of effort) they are simply not supported by the evidence. To be sure, the princely order in the late colonial period had its share of 'bad' characters. Jey Singh of Alwar, who figures prominently in the early chapters of this narrative, was so orthodox in his religious beliefs that he refused to sit on leather and wore silk gloves lest his fingers inadvertently brushed against anything unclean; but his private life belied the saintly image he cultivated in public. He drank heavily (his flimsy excuse being that Scotch was not one of the substances specifically outlawed in the *Dharmasastras*). Although thrice married, his sexual preference was for young boys and he indulged it brazenly, surrounding himself with a retinue of 'good-looking young men' whom he fondled when fancy took him, even in the presence of guests,[9] and keeping on the payroll a servant whose sole job it was to procure him a steady stream of ball-boys from the local tennis club.[10] Last but not least, Alwar was cruel to the point of sadism. One story has it that when the maharaja became angry with the performance of one of his polo ponies, he poured kerosene over the poor beast and set it alight. Nor did his sadism stop with animals. Denied the son he wanted to secure the succession, he consigned his only daughter, Baijilal, to the care of a common prostitute and was apparently unmoved to learn, some time later, that she had contracted 'congenital syphilis'.[11] The classically

---

[8] S. K. P. Singh, *The Indian Ruling Princes and the National Movement* (New Delhi, 1991), 14–15.

[9] A ruler from a neighbouring state who went to Alwar for a visit in the 1930s was discomforted to find, when he retired for the night, a boy waiting compliantly in his bedroom. Charles Allen and Sharada Dwivedi, *Lives Of the Indian Princes* (London, 1984), 160.   [10] Note by Sir Bertrand Glancy, 31 Aug. 1935, IOR R/1/1/2652.

[11] Sir George Ogilvie, AGG Rajputana, to Sir Bertrand Glancy 15 Feb. 1934, IOR R/1/1/2546.

trained viceroy, Lord Willingdon, dubbed him a modern Caligula. It was no exaggeration. Another prince we shall meet again in these pages, Gulab Singh of Rewa, was, like Alwar, a paedophile, and in the end his passion for adolescent men would drive him to murder;[12] however, his greatest weakness was money and the beautiful things it could buy. Over twenty years Rewa systematically fleeced his state to the tune of at least £2 million. What he did not spend on himself and his palaces, he salted away abroad. Eventually deposed, he left behind him an empty treasury, a demoralised administration and a state lacking even the barest of essential services.[13] Yet a third hard case was Mahabat Rasulkhanji, nawab of Junagadh, who, like Rewa, begrudged spending money on social services for his subjects but thought nothing of squandering two lakhs of rupees on a party and a diamond collar for his favourite pet dog. Yes, the monarchical order was not lacking in depravity. Indeed, a handful of rulers – including Jey Singh toward the end of his life – were probably certifiably insane.

However, truly vicious rulers were rare. The vast majority of the thousand or so who occupied *gaddis* and *masnads* during the period covered by this book – roughly the first half of the twentieth century – were, by and large, a decent bunch. Certainly – as one would expect in such a big sample – most were casual rather than dedicated, plodding rather than brilliant; yet the best of them, who by dint of natural selection tended to provide the leadership for the order, were both intellectually able and hard-working. Hamidullah of Bhopal had a Master's degree from Aligarh University; Mayurdhwaj Sinhji of Dhrangadhra read philosophy at Oxford and later took out a diploma in social anthropology at the same institution. Syed Mohammad of Rampur surprised the American consul-general in Bombay with his assured grasp of 'the complexities of local and international political problems'.[14] As for conscientiousness, Laksman Sinhji, maharawal of Dungapur, thought nothing of spending 'five or six hours every day going through files and cases';[15] while the working day of the ruler of Cutch began summer and winter at 5 a.m. and continued, with a break for lunch, until mid-afternoon. Mayurdhwaj Sinhji spoke for them all when he recalled in conversation with Charles Allen: 'I wanted to be a good and popular ruler, moving in the direction of the ultimate ideal of Ram-Rajya, Rama's kingdom in which there was no injustice.'[16]

Moreover, when it came to politics and diplomacy, some of the nastiest

---

[12] For details, see below chapter 6.
[13] Col. Fisher, resdt. C.I., to Sir Kenneth Fitze 9 Jan. 1942, IOR R/1/1/3812; draft letter, Wavell to king [?] Mar. 1945, IOR R/1/1/4425; and note by G. K. S. Sharma, crown finance officer, 8 May 1946, IOR R/1/1/4245.
[14] Consul-general Bombay to sec. state Washington 15 July 1947, US State Dept. decimal file 845.00/7–1547.   [15] Quoted in Allen and Dwivedi, *Lives*, 310.   [16] *Ibid.*, 311.

rulers proved, paradoxically, the most capable. Jey Singh, perhaps the most immoral of the lot, was articulate, well-read and possessed of a sharp intelligence. A fellow ruler called him 'the cleverest and bravest man in India',[17] while secretary of state E. S. Montagu wrote of him as 'a man of imagination and of industry, of knowledge and of reasoning power'.[18] Likewise, there was grudging admiration among contemporaries for the keen political brain of Maharaja Gulab Singh of Rewa who, it might be added, could never have got away with his long reign of corporate crime if he had been the conventionally stupid prince of romantic fiction: 'a thoroughly wicked ... clever man', was Lord Wavell's astute summation of him.[19] Of course, in the end both Alwar and Rewa were undone by their excesses. But in the interim both men made important contributions to the constitutional debate. The moral here – if we may use the term – is that in the world of politics there is no necessary correlation between ability and goodness.

Thirdly and lastly, the quality of government in a princely state did not hinge solely on the ability and inclination of the ruler. Contrary to popular opinion, the princes did not – could not – rule autocratically in the literal sense; the job was simply too big for any one person. Hence, in practice, it was the quality of the bureaucracy that really mattered – in particular, the calibre of the princes' ministers. And in this regard (because they could afford to hire the best)[20] the states were very well

---

[17] Entry in Yvonne Fitzroy's diary for 28 Mar. 1922, quoted in Iris Butler (ed.), *The Viceroy's Wife: Letters of Alice, Countess of Reading From India, 1921–5* (London, 1969), 71.

[18] E. S. Montagu, *An Indian Diary* (London, 1930), 293 (entry for 1 Mar. 1918). When Reading succeeded to the viceroyalty in 1921, the secretary of state took the trouble to 'commend' Alwar to him, explaining: 'I have come to the conclusion that his eccentricities and defects of character are all thoroughly worth while.' Montagu to Reading 9 Aug. 1921, Reading Coll., 3. Arthur Lothian, who got to know him better than most Englishmen, loathed him as a personality but conceded that he had 'probably the liveliest brain of all the Indian Princes'. Lothian, P. M. Alwar, to AGG Rajputana 19 Apr. 1933, Lothian Coll., 6.   [19] Draft letter from viceroy to king [?] Mar. 1946, IOR R/1/1/4425.

[20] As the princes' public relations man in London, L. F. Rushbrook-Williams earned Rs 2,500 per month; as chief minister of Patiala, Nawab Liaquat Hyat Khan got a monthly stipend of Rs 3000 plus an *inam* worth Rs 51,000 a year for life, and a grant of Rs 1,000 a month for his sons' education in England; as prime minister of Bikaner, Sir Manubhai Mehta drew Rs 5,000 a month, was exempted from customs duty on goods imported for his own use, and got free housing; as constitutional adviser and then chief minister of Travancore, Sir C. P. Ramaswamy Aiyer was paid Rs 6,000 per month but got much more under the counter through various corrupt transactions; by 1945 his total earnings were rumoured to be in the vicinity of 50 lakhs. Rushbrook-Williams to Bhopal 27 Mar. 1930, BRO, Bhopal, Chamber Branch, 22, c-4/9; note by Sir F. Wylie dated 7 Mar. 1941, IOR R/1/1/3660; *The Indian States Reformer*, 8 Feb. 1931; note, n.d., RSA, Bikaner, PM's Office, A 1281–1343 of 1935; memorial by C. N. Madhavan Pillai dated 10 Aug. 1945, encl. in vice-consul Madras to sec. state, Washington, 2 Sept. 1945, US State Dept. decimal file 845.00/10–343. It was indicative of the drawing power of these highly paid jobs that in the mid-1940s two very prominent politicians on opposite sides of the communal divide – H. S. Suhrawady and S. P. Mookherjee – considered pursuing a career in the states.

served. K. M. Panikkar, who worked in Patiala and Bikaner, was the first Indian ever to get a scholarship to Christ Church, only the second after Romesh Dutt to get an Oxford first. Sir C. P. Ramaswamy Aiyer, dewan of Travancore, was thought to be (and not just by himself) 'one of the cleverest men in India'.[21] Of Sir Mirza Ismail, the chief minister successively of Mysore, Jaipur and Hyderabad, the American ambassador in New Delhi wrote effusively: 'I have not . . . met anyone else in India . . . either Indian or European, who is in his class.'[22] Now, it may well be that the employment of highly credentialled outsiders was not, in the long term, a good policy. As foreigners they were often unpopular with the people; and as mercenaries their primary loyalty was to their paymasters, not to any particular *desh*. Arguably, the rulers might have fared better in the denouement of 1947–8 if they had opted for less distinguished but more patriotic servants with roots in the region. Yet, in the short term, the strategy was quite an astute one. Having foreigners as dewans gave the princes a certain leverage over them. Also, it obviated their having to make difficult choices between competing elite communities: for example, Mirza at Mysore helped hold the balance between Brahmins and non-Brahmins; while V. T. Krishnamachari at Baroda was linked neither to the Marathas nor the Gujaratis. Besides, practically to the last,[23] they gave exemplary service. At home they kept the lid on dissent; abroad their forensic skills gave the states a significant diplomatic edge.

Still wearing the scars of their rapid fall from grace and power in 1947–8 – a fall precipitated, to a large extent, by the British crown's abandonment of its allies – the ex-princes feel that they have been betrayed all over again by History. Here is H. H. Mayurdhwaj Sinhji, former maharaja of Dhrangadhra:

I refer you to the period 1942–48, and the transition at the end of it . . . I doubt if any [group] have had such 'a bad press' as they except perhaps the Jews in Germany! One has read so much misrepresentation of the terminal period that one cannot but subscribe to Henry Ford's apothegm that 'History is Bunk'! Accounts of events at which I was myself present have somehow blossomed

[21] Penderel Moon (ed.), *Wavell: The Viceroy's Journal* (London, 1973), 241 (entry for 9 Apr. 1946).

[22] Ambassador to sec. state Washington 13 Jan. 1945, US State Dept. decimal file 845.00/1–1345. In Mirza's case, the hierarchy was reversed: it was the dewan who to all intents and purposes ruled Mysore. During the reign of Krisnarajendra Wodeyar, Mirza had absolute control over the administration. When his successor came to the throne in 1941 he found a situation in which, in effect, 'he was merely presented with a white sheet [of paper] with Sir Mirza Ismail's decisions typed upon it, and asked to sign'. Note of interview between viceroy and maharaja of Mysore 6 Mar. 1941, Mirza Ismail Papers, SF1.

[23] Towards the end, some dewans found it hard to reconcile their obligations to their princely masters with what they saw as a higher duty to their country. This point is addressed in chapter 7 and in the Conclusion.

without regard to fact, and these, whether willful or wishful, are now history. One feels an utter helplessness as if one had been an alien, an outsider. There is, perhaps, no gainsaying that had Ravana triumphed, we would have had a Ravanayana, extolling his virtues and execrating the Aryan aggressors.[24]

The language is emotional; but Dhrangadhra has a point. The maharajas *have* been maligned and marginalised by the historical profession to an absurd degree. It is time the record was put straight.

It goes without saying that this project is likely to raise the hackles of some scholars. For one thing it is about the most privileged of elites – not (at any rate directly) about the life of ordinary men and women. For another it is about high politics and – yes – events. However, any inhibitions I might have had on the score of historiographical fashion were soon erased as I got down to work and began to realise precisely what I had taken on.

First and foremost, there was the sheer scale of the task. As already remarked, the princely states numbered – if one counts all the non-jurisdictionary estates which abounded in Kathiawar and central India – around 600. And collectively they comprised a major slice of the pre-1947 Indian body politic – two-fifths of the area and one-third of the population of the erstwhile Indian Empire excluding Burma. Moreover, many of them were considerable countries in their own right. Kashmir, with an area of 84,000 square miles, was bigger than France; Travancore, with a population in 1921 of over 5 million, had more inhabitants than Portugal or Austria; from the pokey recesses of his Peshi Office, Nizam Osman Ali of Hyderabad presided over a kingdom whose income and expenditure in 1947–8 rivalled Belgium's and exceeded that of twenty member states of the United Nations. On the face of it, the project appeared to call for the re-constitution – in some form – of the modern political histories of several hundreds of separate principalities scattered across a large part of the subcontinent.

Secondly, this was not only a broad canvas: it was an uneven one. References to 'the states' or to 'princely India' suggest a landscape that was, in essential respects, homogenous. Yet, apart from the obvious fact that the states were all monarchies, there was precious little about them that was uniform. As noted above, the biggest ones were comparable to the countries of Europe; but the smallest ones could have fitted into some suburban back yards. Veja-no-ness in Kathiawar, for example, was less than an acre broad, and had a population, in 1921, of 184. Consequently the states' revenue collections, which determined what their *darbars* could

---

[24] H. H. of Dhrangadhra to Dr Hariprasad Shastri 23 Feb. 1983. (I am indebted to the maharaja of Dhrangadhra for this reference.)

Table Intro 1. *Taxation in selected Central Indian states, 1936 (In rupees, annas and paise) (per head)*

Prov./State	Average land tax	Average excise	Average customs rev.	Average rev.
Jaora	8-04-11	0-08-00	0-04-00	12-07-08
Dewas (J)	5-02-04	0-15-05	0-04-07	08-14-06
Nagod	1-13-09	0-02-00	0-02-00	03-06-08
Ajaigarh	4-01-03	0-02-01	0-00-05	04-15-03
Sitamau	3-04-07	0-06-01	0-02-00	06-05-09

Source: Memo by D. B. Tilak, 30 Jan. 1937, App. IV, Federal Papers, Nehru Library, New Delhi, 1.

spend on infrastructure and services, also varied enormously. Indeed as Table Intro 1. shows, taxation levels could be as much as 15 per cent higher or lower even in adjacent states.

Again, by the second decade of the twentieth century, when this narrative begins, some states, such as Gwalior, had already begun to modernise and industrialise. Visiting Gwalior in 1918, Montagu was shown over a bustling new 'industrial city on the site of the old town' complete with cotton and oil mills, a power station and an embryonic machine-tools plant.[25] The state also had sizeable holdings in textile factories and brick kilns in Bombay. Mysore, too, had started to develop rapidly on the strength of its gold deposits at Kolar, the largest in south Asia; while Bhavnagar and Cochin, two coastal states blessed with deep-water harbours, were well on the way to becoming commercial entrepôts. Others, though, remained much as they had been when they first came under British paramountcy. In the remoter parts of Rajputana and central India, female infanticide, *begar*, and agrestic slavery were still commonplace. After visiting Cutch in 1932, Lord Hastings wrote: 'If any European has been here before he hasn't left any traces.'[26] Likewise, while some rulers such as Sayaji Rao of Baroda and Krishnarajendra of Mysore had begun to experiment with new, westernised forms of governance (Mysore by the second decade of the century had a legislative council, a representative assembly, a public service board and a policy of recruitment by competitive examination) others such as the nizam remained firmly wedded to traditional notions of benevolent autocracy: 'This form of rule [Osman

[25] Montagu, *Diary*, 167 (entry for 3 Jan. 1918).
[26] Hastings to Sir Samuel Hoare 29 Feb. 1932, Templewood Coll., 14.

Ali told Lord Reading] suits the genius and temperament of my people and has resulted in peaceful progress and prosperity . . . My subjects are happy and contented and desire no change for they know that day and night I give my personal attention to their well-being.'[27] Yet it was not only ideology which divided the princes; it was also race, religion and upbringing. Proud of their impeccable *kshatriya* ancestry, the Rajput chiefs generally looked down on the *sudra*-descended Maratha princes such as Gwalior and Indore, and the equally plebian Jat-Sikh chiefs of the Punjab such as Patiala. For example, Umaid Singh of Jodhpur preferred to absent himself from the Armistice Day ceremony in London in 1918 – a grave breach of protocol – rather than incur the ignominity of being seated below Patiala. Conversely, Maratha rulers such as the Scindias of Gwalior nursed bitter memories of the Rajputs' role, as allies of the East India Company, in their downfall at the beginning of the nineteenth century;[28] whilst, in their turn, the Maratha states (Kolhapur especially) were held in low regard by their Brahmin-ruled former feudatories, the 'Southern Maratha Jagirs' of Bhor, Aundh, Akalkot, Kurunwad, Miraj and Jamkhandi. Needless to say the same reserve characterised relations between Muslim rulers like Khairpur and Bahawalpur and the mainly Hindu order at large. However even closely related dynasties were not immune from vendettas. As our story opens, Cutch was locked in a bitter dispute with Morvi about the ownership of a slice of the Rann; Dewas Senior with Kolhapur over the former's cruelty towards his wife, sister of the Kolhapur maharaja;[29] Patiala with his Sikh kinsman Nabha over the leadership of the *khalsa*.[30] When, during World War I, the idea of a representative council of princes was first floated, Tukoji Rao of Indore declared himself opposed. 'On account of the differences in the education, training, methods of thought, status and position of the Indian Princes', he averred to one of the scheme's sponsors, Sayaji Rao, 'it would be almost impossible to secure . . . unanimity . . . on any subject placed before the Council.'[31] The claim was exaggerated; yet the fact that it was made at all is indicative of the hurdles which stood in the way of joint

---

[27] Hyderabad to Lord Reading 7 July 1921, Reading Coll., 23.

[28] Sir Michael O'Dwyer, *India As I Knew It, 1885–1925* (London, 1925), 151; Sir Geoffrey de Montmorency, *The Indian States and the Federation* (Cambridge, 1942), 9–10.

[29] This feud culminated in a bizarre midnight flight by the Rajkumar and his young wife by car to Indore, where he sought the protection of the AGG Central India. See E. M. Forster, *The Hill of Devi: Letters From Dewas State Senior* (London, 1953), 163–5; and *The Times of India*, 10 Jan. 1928.

[30] See Barbara N. Ramusack, 'Incident at Nabha: Interaction Between Indian States and British Indian Politics', *Journal of Asian Studies*, 28, 3 (1978), 563–77. E. S. Montagu described the two rulers accurately as 'enemies'. Sec. state to viceroy 27 Oct. 1921, Reading Coll. 10.

[31] Note encl. in Indore to Baroda 21 Oct. 1916, GSAB, Baroda, Pol. Dept., 341, 3.

action by the monarchical order; and which confront the scholar seeking to generalise, sensibly, about it.

Then, as if these complications were not enough, there was the problem posed by the undeniably exotic nature of the subject. At Rampur, guests were likely to be shown the nawab's collection of 200 radio sets, or entertained by his personal jazz band. The jam sahib of Nawanagar thought nothing of shooting a 1,000 brace of partridges in a season; while Ganga Singh of Bikaner and his two sons accounted for 3,300 sand-grouse in one outing in 1925. A large man with even larger appetites, Bhupinder Singh of Patiala was known to eat 25 quail at a sitting, and even on the day of his death managed to consume a 10-egg omelette. Pathologically shy, Nizam Osman Ali's favourite pastimes included taking nude photos of his European guests with hidden cameras, prowling graveyards at night and watching operations in the city hospital; although he still found time now and then to visit the *zenana*, where his 200 wives and concubines were said 'to cumulatively procreate at the rate of one offspring every four months'.[32] The more I read the more challenging the enterprise seemed. How was I to present a rounded account of these eccentric, larger-than-life figures without reducing them to orientalist caricatures?

In the event, fortunately, these conceptual hurdles proved less formidable than expected. For instance, it quickly became apparent that policy and strategy decisions about, and on behalf of the princely order were taken by a relatively small number of *darbars*: the larger, wealthier ones, who spoke from positions of inherent strength; the ones ruled over by lineages of especially exalted status, such as the Sisodias of Udaipur, highest in rank of the Rajput clans;[33] and ones whose voices carried weight by virtue of their ability to speak for a wider community, such as Patiala for the Sikhs: altogether, perhaps a score of states. In addition, a few others procured an influence over the councils of the order by virtue of the forensic skills and political nous of their princes and ministers, Bikaner being the classic example; and these latter tended to become more powerful over time as the order developed institutions to better articulate its opinions on all-India issues – the Chamber of Princes (COP) and the Committee of Ministers (COM). Indeed, with the advent of these bodies, the leadership of the princely order became, to a large degree, self-perpetuating, as office-holders gained in status, confidence and rhetorical power and acquired specialist knowledge not available to the rest of the order. Conversely, while the rank and file no doubt had opinions about

---

[32] Report by Louise Schaffner, US vice-consul, Madras, dated 16 May 1945, US State Dept. decimal file 845.00/8–1645.

[33] The dynasty was said to descend from Rama, the legendary god-king of Ayodhya.

most things, they tended to keep them to themselves and, when it came to taking a vote in the Chamber, to fall in, like the maharaja of Sirohi, with 'whatever the general body of Princes' – in effect the *darbari* oligarchy – decided.[34] In practice, therefore, the project resolved itself into a study – still wide-ranging but obviously much more manageable – of the inter-locking political careers of some thirty *darbari* statesmen, preeminent among them Maharaja Ganga Singh of Bikaner, Maharaja Udaibhan Singh of Dholpur, Maharaja Dijvijaysinhji of Nawanagar, Maharaja Bhupinder Singh of Patiala, Sultana Jahan Begum and Nawab Hamidullah of Bhopal, Mirza Ismail, Panikkar, Sir Akbar Hydari of Hyderabad, Krishnamachari of Baroda, Sir Manubhai Mehta of Bikaner, Liaquat Hyet Khan of Patiala and Sir Kailash Haksar of Gwalior.

Similarly, while it cannot be denied that the states were a diverse collec-tion of societies and their rulers a motley and not always harmonious group, the much-trumpeted notion of an overarching princely order is not entirely wrong. For all their squabbling, the princes had much in common as a class: affluence; privileges that put them above the common law of the land; the status of *khashatriyas*; autocratic power; bloodlines which connected them to gods and mythical heroes and which set them totally apart from ordinary folk. Moreover, while many of them would have had trouble identifying with the concept, everything about the princes' behaviour bespoke a highly developed class-consciousness – not least their custom of referring to each other in public as '*bhai*' (brother). Again, the dynastic elements which sometimes served to divide the order also helped to bind it together. Most princely houses had close kinship connections with at least half a dozen others. In addition some rulers, not linked by blood, developed binding personal friendships based on shared interests – as did Bhupinder Singh of Patiala and Udaibhan Singh of Dholpur, and Hamidullah Khan of Bhopal and Yeshwant Rao of Indore. Whilst generalisations about the princely order in India need to be made cautiously, they *can* be sustained.

As for the problem of stereotyping, I think it becomes less if one draws a distinction between public and private. Of course, the distinction cannot be rigid, if for no other reason than that what the princes did in their bedrooms and on the shooting-range (or were rumoured to do) was an integral part of their public image – a source, incongruously, for part of their charisma: yet, since we are not writing a collective biography of the rulers, this inner world can, with a few exceptions, be safely put to one side. The exceptions, occasions where those private 'excesses' became

---

[34] Maharaja of Sirohi to chancellor COP, 4 Feb. 1935, RSA, Sirohi, Sardar Office, 129 of 1934–5.

matters of public notoriety, and consequently of concern to the government, will be dealt with in their proper place in the narrative.

Which brings me, finally, to the question of method. While this book makes no claim to methodological originality, it does rest on a firm historiographical assumption, namely, that history should not be written backwards. Because the states are gone, it is widely assumed that they were always doomed to destruction by the forces of history; that their demise was inevitable. James Manor asserts categorically that 'by the mid-1930s, the princely order was doomed'.[35] Vanaja Rangaswami thinks that by the 1940s the maharajas were a 'spent force'.[36] Indeed, as noted earlier, there is a clear implication in some nationalistic accounts of the period that the states collapsed in the last resort *because they were monarchies*, an anachronistic form of government which was incapable of survival in the post-colonial era. Now, even on empirical grounds this argument can be contested: for, whereas the Indian princely states collapsed in 1947–8, the order they embodied – monarchy – is still alive and well elsewhere in the Middle East and Asia. For example, the continuing popularity and moral authority enjoyed by the monarchy in Thailand was a major factor in the resolution of the country's constitutional crises of 1957, 1973, 1981 and 1992. Likewise, in Malaysia, sultans very much like the erstwhile rulers of the Indian states and subject during the colonial period to similar forms of British overrule survived the transition to independent nationhood with many of their traditional powers intact; indeed, it was only in the late 1980s that a serious challenge began to be mounted against their right to block legislation and, in the king's case, to declare a state of national emergency. All this, of course, rather begs the question of why the Indian princes should have fared so poorly in the end-game of empire compared with dependent rulers elsewhere in the region. Beyond that, however, the 'inevitability' thesis reflects an alarmingly judgemental approach to the past based on a privileging of present day attitudes and concerns. Of course, it is a truism that all history writing is necessarily influenced by the writer's background; we are all, whether we like it or not, intellectually creatures of our own place and time. Nevertheless, there is a huge difference between suffering 'relativism' as an unwelcome but unavoidable constraint, and vigorously pursuing it as an end in itself – a strategy that can lead to the obscuring or marginalisation of those aspects of the past that do not fit with the writer's preconceptions, or that do not lie squarely on what John Tosh has called the 'assumed trajectory

---

[35] James Manor, 'The Demise of the Princely Order: a Reassessment', in R. Jeffrey (ed.), *People, Princes and Paramount Power: Society and Politics in the Indian Princely States* (Delhi, 1978), 306.
[36] Vanaja Rangaswami, *The Story of Integration: A New Interpretation* (Delhi, 1981), 246.

of historical development'.[37] In a way, all history is the history of 'winners' since winners, by definition, are those who survive to write it. Yet good history should also concern itself with 'losers', and non-survivors, and with what might have been.

Accordingly, in writing this study I have sought to divorce myself from the tyranny of hindsight; to treat the pasts of the princes autonomously, on their own terms. More particularly, the narrative has endeavoured to capture what has been aptly called the frozen moment. I have tried to picture the princes and their advisors as people buffeted by circumstances, people whose plans were often formulated on the run, or in the dark because of lack of knowledge, people struggling valiantly to 'muddle through'.[38] In this respect, though obviously not in others, the book takes something from the 'old-new' genre of 'ethnohistory', which for Lawrence Stone forms part of a broader movement for the 'revival of narrative' as a mainstream historical form.[39]

Here, then, is a study of the Indian princes which is, in many respects, unapologetically revisionist. Starting from the premise that the demise of the princely states is an important topic that has not, so far, received its due from historians, it attempts to re-write the history of decolonisation in India with the princes, for once, not shadowy figures lurking in the wings, but major actors holding centre stage. Nevertheless the project has no partisan agenda. I have no ideological axe to grind with respect to the institution of monarchy, nor have I any desire to whitewash the princes either as men or as politicians. Whatever may be said about the rights and wrongs of the matter, the fact remains that the princely order collapsed, and collapsed in the end quite ignominiously. Prima facie, the rulers (and of course their advisors) must bear a large amount of responsibility for this debacle. It is said that historians should be 'objective', meaning free from bias. So defined objectivity will always be an impossible dream. However, there is another kind of objectivity which is within reach; and that is the objectivity of cultivated detachment. This study seeks neither to condone nor to condemn. Rather, it attempts to say something of what the Indian princes in the early twentieth century were about. It seeks to come to terms with their illusions and fears, their strengths and limitations, their schemes and ambitions; to comprehend the nature of their political struggle and to show why it was ultimately in vain.

---

[37] John Tosh, *The Pursuit of History: Aims, Methods and New Directions in the Study of Modern History* (London, 1984), 122.

[38] My formulation here owes a great deal to Kenneth O. Morgan, 'What is Political History?', *History Today*, 35, 1 (Jan. 1985), 17.

[39] Lawrence Stone, 'The Revival of Narrative: Reflections on the New-Old History', *Past and Present*, 85 (1979), 3–24.

1   The making of Indian India

The essential point is to give the States a formal voice of some kind in the government of India before it is too late . . .

Ganga Singh, maharaja of Bikaner, 1915

Breakwaters in the storm

By the early 1940s the cosy, special relationship between the British crown and the Indian princes which forms the subject of this book had become so much a fact of political life in Delhi and Whitehall that people like Leo Amery, secretary of state in Churchill's wartime coalition government, could speak about it as if it had always existed. In reality, though, the alliance was a twentieth-century creation, a product of circumstance and the fertile imagination of the official mind.

To be sure, the political relationship between the British and the states had deep roots. As early as the 1740s, the East India Company was forging diplomatic ties with Indian kingdoms, and by the second decade of the nineteenth century virtually all the major 'country powers' had been linked to the Company by treaty. What is more, the essential elements of British 'paramountcy' – the system of 'residents' at the princely courts, the regulation of successions, control over the states' foreign affairs – were all laid down in this period. Indeed, by the 1840s, the only big question that still remained to be settled in regard to the states was how many ought to be left intact. As the British raj grew more secure, and as the philosophies of evangelicalism and utilitarianism cast their spell, officials who had once cautiously advocated keeping a ring-fence of friendly states around the Company's territories, now argued forcefully for their extinction on the grounds that native rule – 'oriental despotism' – fell short of the standards of civilisation to which the people of India were entitled. If events had not intervened, the remaining states would probably have suffered the same fate as befell Satara, Jhansi, Nagpur, Awadh and the Punjab between 1848 and 1856 – absorbed into the expanding Indian Empire.

The first of these events and, in retrospect, the critical one, was of course the revolt of 1857. The Great Revolt, as it is aptly known, traumatised officialdom in London and Calcutta with its suddenness, its rapid spread and its ferocity; and their immediate reaction, predictably, was founded on a lust for vengeance. However, once the initial shock had passed and it became clear that the rebellion would not succeed, the Company's senior men on the spot such as the governor-general, Earl Canning, began to look more deeply and analytically into its causes. Out of this post-mortem emerged, firstly, the insight that the policy of territorial expansion had turned a number of peaceable rulers into bitter enemies, and thus could be accounted, as Board of Control president Lord Stanley of Alderley averred in a speech to parliament, a major 'cause' of the late 'disaster'.[1] Secondly, there came an acknowledgement that the princely states as a body had proved remarkably steadfast during the crisis and that their support had helped to turn the tide. Citing particularly the contribution of Gwalior and Hyderabad, Governor-General Earl Canning declared: 'these patches of Native government served as breakwaters in the storm which would otherwise have swept over us in one great wave'.[2] If the surviving princely states had been the raj's salvation in 1857, the government reasoned, so they easily could be again.

The 'Mutiny', then, changed attitudes about the worth of the states as imperial clients; but it also provided, indirectly, a persuasive financial argument against further annexation. While the revolt had been suppressed, the costs had been heavy. In 1858–9 the government's budget deficit was a whopping 14 million lakhs; the following year it was over 9 million. So bleak was the budgetary outlook in 1861 that Calcutta was driven to introduce income tax in a desperate bid to raise revenue. 'Our officers', complained Canning, 'are too few for the work which they have on their hands, and our financial means are not yet equal to the demands upon us.'[3] This was clearly not the time to embark on an aggressive foreign policy which could only lead to new financial burdens on the government.

One problem, however, remained. Canning knew that, while a majority of Indian officials agreed with his conclusions about the states, many – including the redoubtable John Lawrence, who was already being touted as a future governor-general – did not. 'If . . . [my successor] is John Lawrence', he mused unhappily in 1860,

[1] *Hansard*, vol. 157, c. 445–6 (12 Mar. 1860).
[2] Viceroy to sec. state 30 Apr. 1860, IOR, Foreign Letters Received From India, 3, 43A.
[3] Quoted in E. Bell, *The Rajah and Principality of Mysore, With a Letter to the Rt. Hon. Lord Stanley* (London, 1865), 43.

he will go far towards upsetting in a year or two all that I hope to have accomplished in my last three years . . . ; he will not do so by direct means – I can make that very difficult for any man – but by giving a cold shoulder to all measures for increasing the consequence of, and placing trust in, the native chiefs and gentry generally.[4]

Likewise Canning distrusted the fickleness of the politicians in London and fully expected that their new-found affection for the princes to wither once the grim memories of 1857 had dimmed. So he tried to set his vision in concrete. Firstly, he prevailed on the India office to insert in the queen's proclamation of 1 November 1858, issued to mark the transfer of the East India Company's possessions to the crown, a pledge to 'respect the rights, dignity and honour of the native princes as our own'.[5] Thereby he ensured that in an undefined but substantial way, the fate of 600 royal houses in India became bound up with the reputation of another in England. Secondly, he sought – and obtained – London's sanction to convey an assurance to the princes that their dynasties would not be allowed to lapse for want of natural heirs. By the time of his retirement in 1862 some 150 'adoption' *sanads* had been issued – more than enough, he reckoned, to ensure that princely rule in India was safe both from the whims of nature and the ambitions of over-zealous officials.

And he was right! During the ninety-odd years between 1858 and the British departure from the subcontinent in 1947, not one princely state lapsed – and none was annexed. While in British India provinces were created and carved up, the borders of the states stayed frozen in their post-Mutiny mould. No wonder the princes in later years came to look back upon the Canningite settlement as their Magna Charta.

Nevertheless, *darbari* expectations that the states were about to come into their own were quickly shattered. As Canning had predicted, the imperial folk memory of the princes' noble contributions in 1857 dimmed with the effluxion of time; but more seriously the states began to seem a serious obstacle to progress. India in the 1860s was entering into an era of rapid development, fuelled by the demand from English textile factories for new supplies of raw cotton to replace those lost as a result of the Union blockade of the American South. Long-distance trade was growing, and railways were being pushed into the interior to service it. Because the states were widely scattered, especially across the middle of India, many of these lines had of necessity to pass through princely territory and therefore required *darbari* sanction to proceed. This was not

[4] Quoted in *The British Crown and the Indian States: An Outline Sketch Drawn Up On Behalf of the Standing Committee of the Chamber of Princes* (London, 1929), 62.
[5] A. B. Keith, *Speeches and Documents on Indian Policy, 1750–1921* (London, 1922), I, 383–4.

always readily forthcoming. As well, entrepreneurs bridled at having to negotiate, in some parts of the subcontinent, literally dozens of border crossings to get their products to market – a process which cost valuable time and added significantly, thanks to the states' insistence on levying transit duties, to the final cost of the goods.[6] Increasingly, too, the post-Mutiny settlement came under fire from the evangelical fraternity for perpetuating misrule. Was it right, the evangelicals asked, that some of India's people should prosper while others languished in poverty and ignorance and suffered oppression just because they happened to be subjects of a dependent prince? Was the British government not morally obliged to ensure that rulers who owed their power in the last resort to British bayonets did not abuse it? By the end of the decade officials such as General Sir Henry Daly, agent to the governor-general in central India, the foreign secretary Sir Charles Aitchison, and the viceroy Lord Mayo were answering with a resolute 'yes'. 'If we support you in your power', Mayo warned an audience of Rajputana rulers at Jaipur in 1870, 'we expect in return good government.'[7]

The bureaucracy, especially in the India Office, was initially sceptical of this new forward policy. It was felt that Mayo had taken on a commitment he lacked the legal or physical capacity to discharge.[8] Yet in the event the anticipated difficulties did not materialise. For one thing the government's men on the spot, its residents and political agents – for the most part strong-willed, uncorrupt and highly self-confident personalities – proved remarkably adept at persuasion. Meeting them, few *darbaris* could marshal an effective answer to their arrogance and bluster. For another, the policy-makers in Simla found ways of buttressing the position of their agents so that their 'advice' could not be ignored. One way was to exploit the advent of minorities in the states to implement reforms directly through British guardian-administrators. As Table 1.1 shows, such opportunities were relatively plentiful. Another was to compel young princes entering their majority to sign legal documents which bound

---

[6] A journey across a region like Kathiawar, for example, could involve as many as 50 border stops in 120 miles. In the late nineteenth century, transit duties were reckoned, on average, to account for one-third of the market-place cost of goods sold in the Central India political agency.

[7] Speech of 21 Oct. 1870, quoted in *The Times*, 5 Dec. 1870. The title 'viceroy' was added in 1858 to underline the fact that the governor-general was now the personal representative of the sovereign, as well as the head of the government of India. Since relations with the princes came under this latter function, we shall hereafter refer to all incumbents of the office as viceroys.

[8] The political secretary in the India Office, Sir Owen Tudor-Burne, for example, thought that the government had effectively given away the right to intervene in the states by conferring adoption *sanads* on the princes in 1860–2. Minute by Sir O. T. Burne dated 22 Jan. 1875, IOR, Political and Secret Letters to Bombay, 1 (1875–6), 47.

Table 1.1 *Incidence of minorities in the states of Orissa, 1882–1932*

State	Years under minority administration	State	Years under minority administration
Athgarh	14	Khandpura	10
Athwallik	7	Kharaswan	11
Banna	12	Mayurbhanj	16
Baramba	35	Narsinghpur	35
Baud	12	Nayagarh	34
Bonai	23	Nilgiri	20
Daspalla	15	Pal-Lahara	30
Dhenkenal	30	Patna	21
Gangpur	4	Ranakhol	10
Hindo	6	Ranpur	0
Kalahandi	32	Seraikela	0
Keonjhar	21	Talcher	11

Source: Lothian Coll., IOL, File 3.

them to follow the advice of their residents in all important matters, and to retain 'reforms' introduced during the minority period.[9] Another again was to make examples of rulers who defied them. In total, some twelve ruling princes were unceremoniously removed from their thrones in the later nineteenth century for 'crimes' against the queen-empress.

Meanwhile, nagging doubts about the legality of intervention in the princely states were laid to rest by a series of brilliant deductions, based on principles freely borrowed from the English common law, on the part of a group of senior bureaucrats. First, in the early 1870s, Aitchison, the foreign secretary, came up with the notion that the treaties needed to be read with an eye to the circumstances existing when they were drawn up and in the light of the subsequent evolution of the relationship between the states and the crown. Then, in 1877, his successor T. H. Thornton developed the theory of 'usage', which held that any 'long-continued course of [governmental] practice' acquiesced in by the states could be construed as lawful, since acquiescence implied consent.[10] Finally, in the 1890s, C. L. Tupper, chief secretary in the government of the Punjab, and William Lee-Warner, his opposite number in Bombay, contributed the doctrine of *res judicata* which, in its original common law setting, permitted judges to be guided by decisions in previous cases of a precisely

---

[9] See, for example, P. A. Bikaner to Maharaja Bikaner 19 Nov. 1898, quoted in K. M. Panikkar, *His Highness the Maharaja of Bikaner: A Biography* (London, 1937), 56.
[10] Quoted in *Report of the Indian States Committee 1928–1929*, Cmd. 3302 of 1929, para. 41.

similar nature, but which, in its Indian reincarnation, was interpreted to mean that the treaties should be read as a whole, and applied equally to all states.[11] Thanks to these rulings, documents long prized by the *darbars* as bulwarks of their integrity were effectively reduced to mere 'scraps of paper'.[12]

Thus armed, the government of India steadily chipped away at what was left of the sovereignty of its feudatories. Between 1878 and 1886 most of the states were compelled to relinquish control over their post and telegraph networks and to integrate them into the imperial system; in 1879 the salt-manufacturing *darbars* were prohibited from exporting it or except in one or two places from producing it for domestic consumption; and from 1877 the states were gradually deprived of civil and criminal jurisdiction over broad-gauge railways passing through their territory. Bit by bit, too, British Indian currency became legal tender right across the subcontinent and by the end of the century almost all the rulers had been pressured into signing away their right to mint silver and copper coins. Again, after 1879 the states lost the automatic right to employ Europeans; while their freedom to import weapons for the use of their police was steadily curtailed.[13]

Like so many other features of British imperialism in India, intervention in the affairs of the states reached its apogee in the first decade of the new century during the stormy viceroyalty of Lord Curzon (1898–1905). In July 1900 the rulers were informed that they would in future need the permission of the government to travel overseas. In 1902 Curzon personally bullied the nizam into renegotiating the 1860 treaty governing the administration of Berar on more favourable terms;[14] and

[11] William Lee-Warner, *Protected Princes of India* (London, 1893), 39.

[12] A. P. Nicholson, *Scraps of Paper: India's Broken Treaties, the Princes and the Problem* (London, 1930).

[13] The details of these policy changes are documented in K. N. Haksar, 'Fiscal Interrelations of the Indian States and the Empire', *The Asiatic Review*, 24 (1928), 539–43; Haksar, 'The Salt Revenue of the Indian States', *The Asiatic Review*, 25 (1929), 7–16; Nicholson, *Scraps of Paper: The British Crown and the Indian States*; and Appendix 8 to Cabinet Paper RTC 31(2), 'Relations with Indian States', Sept. 1931, IOR L/P&S/13/550.

[14] Under the agreement of 1860, the province of Berar had been placed under a British commissioner and part of its revenues attached to pay off debts incurred by the British-officered Hyderabad Contingent. The new agreement which Curzon wormed out of Osman Ali further integrated the administration of Berar with that of the Central Provinces, and considerably reduced the amount of the Berar surplus which was returned to the Nizam as 'rent'. Worried by adverse press reports, the secretary of state, Lord George Hamilton, asked Curzon for an explanation, but the viceroy was unfazed: 'pray do not think that the Nizam yielded out of personal deference to me, or from weakness, or in alarm', he wrote. 'He yielded in deference to my arguments because he is firmly convinced that I am a friend to him and his State.' Curzon to Hamilton 2 Apr. 1902, quoted in K. R. R. Sastry, *Indian States* (Allahabad, 1941), 176.

in 1903 overhauled the administration of Lord Dufferin's Imperial Service Troop Scheme, making it more efficient but at the same time considerably more expensive for the participating *darbars*. Three rulers – Jhalawar, Panna and Indore – were deposed during his term, which also saw an unprecedented number of states – sixty-three – placed under some form of temporary British control. Scindia of Gwalior told an official shortly after Curzon's departure that 'the tyranny' of his rule had been so unbearable to his fellow princes that 'nothing would have induced them to put up with it [much longer]',[15] while the maharaja of Baroda spoke out angrily against 'the present system of interference and control and needless restriction'.[16] Indeed, according to Ganga Singh of Bikaner, the subject of Curzon was so painful for some princes that merely talking about that epoch was enough to reduce them to tears.[17] Paradoxically, though, one can now see the Curzon viceroyalty as marking the moment when, after decades of indifference, the British began once more to view the Indian states as potentially useful players in the great game of empire.

The romance of the princely courts

Even before that happened, however, imperial perceptions of the states and their dynastic rulers had begun to change in line with wider trends in British thinking about the subcontinent. As the nineteenth century wore on, the British lost much of their earlier confidence about the malleability of Indian society and hence in the feasibility of the Macaulayesque project to turn its peoples into brown Europeans. More and more, Indians seemed uninterested in reformation; increasingly, they came across as eager slaves to caste and custom. Thus, the perception grew that the 'East' – the 'Orient' – was tradition-bound and unchanging, its inhabitants basically uninterested in progress. Likewise, as the British learned more of the complexities of Indian society through the reports of census-takers and local administrators, they became ever more convinced that hierarchy was the axis around which everything turned. The Indians, they decided, had a deep, inbred respect for authority – especially the authority of 'natural' leaders such as landlords, priests and brahmins. 'Politically speaking', opined Lord Lytton, 'the Indian peasantry is an inert mass. If it ever moves at all, it will move, not in obedience to its British benefactors, but to its native chiefs and princes however

---

[15] Lord Minto to Lord Morley 12 Sept. 1907, Morley Coll., IOL, 8.
[16] Sayaji Rao, maharaja of Baroda to Morley, 21 Sept. 1906, Stanley Rice (ed.), *Selected Letters of H.H. Sayaji Rao of Baroda* (Baroda, 1936), 2, 631.
[17] Minute by Bikaner, 1915, quoted in Panikkar, *Bikaner*, 164.

tyrannical they may be.'[18] These understandings suggested to men like Lytton that a policy of conciliating the social arbiters would do more to bolster the security of British dominion than one of 'mere' good government.

At first, understandably enough, the prospect of giving up, or at any rate toning down the civilising mission was viewed with considerable regret and distaste; but, necessity being the mother of invention, it was not long before the British began to find things to admire in the very social traits they had hitherto regarded as a cause for despair. Thus, the unrepentant East became translated, by gradual degrees, into the 'mysterious' East – a repository of ancient traditions sanctified by time, colourful rites, majestic spectacle and arcane knowledge. Where, as in the cities of Bombay and Calcutta, actuality in the shape of a burgeoning westernised middle class challenged this romantic construction, it was neatly marginalised by the skilful penmanship of scholar-administrators such as William Wilson Hunter, Henry Maine and Alfred Lyall who, in their pioneering ethnographic accounts, projected a picture of Indian society which privileged the traditional, the rustic and the martial over the urban and modern.[19] By the end of the nineteenth century there was a clear sense, best articulated perhaps in the stories of Kipling, that the 'real' India was to be found not in the developing cities, but in the still predominantly unaltered countryside and on its unruly tribal frontiers.[20]

Much has been written about the reasons for this sea-change in British attitudes to India. For our purposes, however, causes are less pertinent than consequences. As will be readily apparent, the princely states fitted the emerging imperial stereotype perfectly. They seemed, at least to the untutored gaze of English romantics, immensely old. Speaking in the House of Commons in 1876, Benjamin Disraeli declared that some of the princes sat on thrones which were in being 'when England was a Roman

---

[18] Lytton to Disraeli 11 May 1876, quoted in Lady Betty Balfour, *Personal and Literary Letters of the Earl of Lytton* (London, 1906), II, 21.

[19] Sir William Wilson Hunter, *The India of the Queen and Other Essays*, ed. Lady Hunter (London, 1903); Henry Sumner Maine, *Village Communities in the East and West* (London, 1871); Alfred Lyall, *Asiatic Studies: Religious and Social* (London, 1907); and Sir Mortimer Durand, *Life of the Right Hon. Sir Alfred Comyn Lyall* (London, 1913). Hunter was a senior Bengal civilian, Maine a law member of the government of India, Lyall successively governor-general's agent in Rajputana and foreign secretary under Lytton. For an older but still useful overview of these developments see Francis G. Hutchins, *The Illusion of Permanence: British Imperialism in India* (Princeton, NJ, 1967), ch. 8.

[20] On Kipling's contribution to this emerging ideology see especially Lewis D. Wurgaft, *The Imperial Imagination: Magic and Myth in Kipling's India* (Middletown, CT, 1983). Amongst other examples of the genre: Lt.-Gen. Sir G. Macmunn, *The Martial Races of India* (London, n.d.); J. D. Rees, *The Real India* (London, 1908); S. J. Thomson, *The Silent India: Being Tales and Sketches of the Masses* (Edinburgh, 1913); and *The Real Indian People: Being More Tales and Sketches of the Masses* (Edinburgh, 1914).

province';[21] while Alfred Lyall argued in his influential *Asiatic Studies* that, far from being trumped up oriental despotisms as James Mill and other previous writers on the subject had argued, the Rajput states, at least, represented, in their clan-based polity, a direct link with the Hindu kingdoms of the pre-Muslim conquest period. What is more, the states reeked of that now much-prized essence, 'tradition'. The rulers' pedigrees proclaimed them to be descendants of the very god-kings whose valour was celebrated in the *Ramayana* and the *Mahabharata*,[22] while the institutions and practices of the princely courts – the highly ritualised audiences, or *darbars*, the giving of *khilats* and the receiving of *nazars*,[23] the royal processions, the reliance on astrologers, the palace intrigues and the *zenana* entertainments – spoke of a world which had not much changed in centuries and which, in its essential elements, went back to the very 'dawn of history'.[24]

Again, in these and other respects, the states and their courts offered rich pickings to Europeans looking for pageantry and spectacle. Visiting Alwar with her husband, the viceroy, in 1909, Lady Minto was quite dazzled by the magnificence of their reception, and afterwards wrote in her diary of 'the wonders of these Native States which open up to Westerners an unbelievable pageant of Eastern magnificence'.[25] And to judge from the *Times of India*'s coverage of Lord Irwin's viceregal visit in 1929, the theatre of princely pomp was equally dazzling in Kolhapur. When Lord Irwin arrived he was met at the railway station by a squad of the maharaja's crack camel corps in 'red riding coats, orange breeches and indigo pagris', a massed band of kettle-drummers and a veritable zoo of royal animals including 'elaborately painted elephants, camels, greyhounds' and ten pet cheetahs 'with silken bandages over their eyes'. After a formal exchange of greetings, Irwin was conveyed to the palace atop what the *Times* claimed was 'the largest elephant in India', ensconced in 'a canopied howdah made of gold and ornamented with coloured lights'.

[21] Quoted in B. S. Cohn, 'Representing Authority In Victorian England', in Eric Hobsbawm and Terence Ranger, (eds.), *The Invention Of Tradition* (Cambridge, 1992), 184.

[22] Alwar, for example, believed that 'My family is descended from the Suriya [Sun] Dynasty, the oldest in existence, coming down to Raghu, after whom the dynasty is called Raghuvanshi, in which Shri Rama took incarnation.' 'Epistle to Rama', forwarded in Jai Singh's petition to the king 20 Oct. 1933, IOR L/PO/91.

[23] A *khilat* was literally, and sometimes actually, a robe; but other artefacts were also given. The giving of *khilats* was designed to bind the recipient to the ruler. *Nazars* were gifts from subjects or subordinate princes. They were usually, though not invariably, in coin.

[24] Speech by the maharaja of Bikaner to the Ladies Carlton Club, London, 29 May 1935, *The Asiatic Review*, 31 (Jan.–Oct. 1935), 447.

[25] Mary, Countess of Minto, *India Minto and Morley 1905–1910* (London, 1934), 339. (Diary entry for 26 Oct. 1909.)

Later still, at a public *darbar*, ladies of the *zenana* attired in gold-threaded silk saris watched through 'nebulous curtains' as the members of the court, resplendent in 'Vivid sashes and pagris and jewelled swords', waited their turn to pay homage to the viceroy. To visit the states, the *Times* correspondent concluded approvingly, was to come face to face with 'the full blaze of oriental pageantry'.[26]

Finally, the princes appeared to be quintessential 'natural' leaders. As *kshatriya*-kings, purportedly descended from the gods, their status was of the highest and their legitimacy in the eyes of Indian society unquestionable. Moreover, they were apparently held in high regard by their subjects. Of the nawab of Palanpur, his resident reported: 'there is no doubt that he is much beloved of his subjects and that they are happy and contented under his rule'.[27] Visiting Dholpur, Arthur Lothian was struck by the way the maharana was pursued in public by excited crowds of subjects 'shout[ing] his praises'.[28] 'If any tourist . . . wishes to enter into the political ideas of the people of India', wrote Sir Theodore Morison,

let him accompany the Rajah on his evening ride. From the gateway of the fort, the Rajah's elephant, in long housings of velvet and cloth of gold, comes shuffling down the steep declivity; on his back, in a silver howdah, sits the Rajah, laden with barbaric pearl and gold; behind him clatter his kinsmen and retainers on brightly caparisoned horses . . . As the cavalcade winds down the narrow streets the men pick up their swords and hurry forward; the women and children rush to the doors of their houses, and all the people gaze upon their prince with an expression of almost ecstatic delight; as the elephant passes, each man puts one hand to the ground and shouts 'Maharaj Ram Ram'.[29]

And the princes fitted the bill, too, on a personal level. They seemed to the British to epitomise all the martial virtues. They came of warrior stock, they rode, they hunted. Of the maharaja of Idar and sometime regent of Jodhpur, Pertab Singh, Lord Hardinge recalled: 'His courage was extraordinary and he did not know what fear meant. He excelled as the best pig-sticker in India, but he had been trained to fight a boar on foot with only a knife in his hand . . . He was of Spartan simplicity . . . truly a white man among Indians.'[30] As to their appearance, many of the rulers from this period looked like characters straight out of the *Arabian Nights*, at once fierce and outlandish, proud and patriarchal; yet to the romantic spirits in the government of India this merely added to their glamour.

---

[26] The *Times of India*, 19 Nov. 1929.
[27] Lt.-Col. Hyde-Cates to acting chief sec. Bombay, 16 July 1907, quoted in Ian Copland, *The British Raj and the Indian Princes: Paramountcy in Western India 1857–1930* (Bombay, 1982), 39.   [28] Sir Arthur Lothian, *Kingdoms of Yesterday* (London, 1951), 170.
[29] Theodore Morison, *Imperial Rule In India* (Westminster, 1899), 48–9.
[30] Lord Hardinge of Penshurst, *My Indian Years, 1910–1916* (London, 1948), 34.

None of these perceptions sprouted overnight; the change in attitudes was a very gradual one. However, by the beginning of the twentieth century a new orthodoxy, conservative and romantic, was developing. Indeed, by the outbreak of World War I it had developed to the point where some officials were willing to make heretical comparisons between the British system of governance and the 'native' one. One was the Aligarh stalwart Sir Theodore Morison, another Sir George Clarke, governor of Bombay, a third Harcourt Butler, chief commissioner of Awadh and subsequently political secretary under Minto. As Butler put it in a 'handing-over note' to his successor, 'We have much to learn from Native States':

The indigenous system of government is a loose despotic system tempered by corruption, which does not press hard on the daily lives of the people and relies for its sanctions on occasional severe punishments of erring and offending individuals. Our system is a scientific system which presses steadily on the people in their daily lives, controls them, regulates their actions, attempts to be preventive and through its hordes of subordinates makes itself everywhere felt. The advancing Native States generally adopt our methods, because it is easy to get good men of their own school with modern training . . . But he would be a bold man who said that our system was always the better.[31]

It was always, perhaps, a minority view: but after 1909 and still more after 1919, it won many converts among that hard core of officials opposed to the parliamentary direction of the reforms process.

Yet, much as the British tried to pretend otherwise, all the while the gap between perception and reality was widening. As we noted in the Introduction, some of the larger states, by the early twentieth century, had started to modernise, indeed to introduce representative institutions. Conversely, thirty years of constant imperial surveillance and pressure had sapped much of the energy, much of the *raison d'être*, from the old *darbari* system. Once upon a time the princes had fought to protect their subjects; now any fighting that was necessary was done for them by the Indian Army, leaving them with only the hunting-range to patrol. Once too, the rulers had exercised total control over their states; but now had to take advice from outsiders. The outer shell remained, complete with all the ceremonial trappings of the 'theatre state'; but the life-blood, the inner substance, had long departed.[32] Indeed, by the end of the century

---

[31] 'Handing Over Note', 1910, quoted in Terence Creagh-Coen, *The Indian Political Service: A Study In Indirect Rule* (London, 1971), 17.

[32] The term is borrowed from Clifford Geerz who, however, would say that ceremonial was integral, not peripheral, to the workings of the dynastic Asian state. See his *Negara: The Theatre State in Nineteenth Century Bali* (Princeton, NJ, 1980). See also Nicholas Dirks, *The Hollow Crown: Ethnohistory of an Indian Kingdom* (Cambridge, 1987). Paradoxically,

even the ceremonial was no longer entirely genuine, being an amalgam of old traditions and new ones borrowed from abroad, such as the gun-salute, orders of knighthood, coats-of-arms and honour-guards. In the states, as in England, invented traditions provided an illusion of stability and continuity in a period of rapid social change and helped to mask the real decline of monarchical power.[33]

If the states had altered so too had the princes. A half-century of systematic indoctrination by private tutors and three decades of English public school education at 'chiefs' colleges', supplemented in some cases by educative trips abroad, had helped to fashion a generation of rulers who bore little resemblance to the imperial stereotype and whose life-styles were, in many cases, far from traditional. Having discovered cricket, Ranjitsinhji of Nawanagar stayed on to play for Sussex and in the later years of his life spent more time at his country property at Staines, on the Thames, than in his capital. Another cricketing prince, the nawab of Pataudi, complained ingenuously to his political agent that his 'English upbringing' made it hard for him to interpret the 'complexities of the ori-ental mind';[34] while Raja Martanda of Pudukkottai was pithily described by his resident as a 'coloured European gentleman with entirely European tastes'.[35] Baroda and Kapurthala both kept European mis-tresses, and Pudukkottai braved convention by marrying, in 1915, one Molly Fink of Melbourne. When Lord Mountbatten first visited Rampur, he thought the palace resembled a New York hotel. Kapurthala's was a replica of the Petit Palace in the Champs-Elysées. 'Personal rule is good if it is according to Oriental tradition', declaimed a critic, 'but today these Princes have no oriental tradition.'[36] It was an over-statement, but only just.

However, if this new hybrid strain of Indian rulers did not altogether fit the stereotype, their lack of taboos in regard to interdining, their familiar-ity with the outside world, above all their command of the English lan-guage, made them more accessible; by the end of the century British dignitaries were queueing up to stalk tigers in Alwar and shoot sand-grouse in Bikaner. In turn, easier intercourse opened the door to a

administration in the states tended to become more centralised in the late nineteenth century as *darbars* increased their power, with British help, over truculent nobles; yet this only made them, in Lyall's terms, less authentic. See Robert W. Stern, *The Cat and the Lion: Jaipur State in the British Raj* (Leiden, 1988).

[33] See David Cannadine, 'The Context, Performance and Meaning of Ritual: The British Monarchy and the "Invention of Tradition", c. 1820–1977', in Hobsbawm and Ranger, *The Invention of Tradition*, esp. 102–8.

[34] Note by P. A. Punjab Hill States, encl. in resdt., Punjab to pol. adviser, 29 Feb. 1940, IOR, R/1/29/2227.   [35] Quoted in Dirks, *Hollow Crown*, 391.

[36] B. Das (Orissa) speaking on the Princes' Protection Bill, 8 Sept. 1933, *Legislative Assembly Debates*, VI, 4.

genuine meeting of minds, to a sharing of experience, to friendship. By the end of their stay at Viceregal Lodge the Mintos counted the maharaja of Bikaner among their personal circle;[37] while Minto's successor Hardinge regarded Madho Rao Scindia of Gwalior as 'one of my best friends in India'.[38] Moreover, despite their surface westernisation, the new breed of rulers remained in close touch with their dynastic legacy and its real and invented traditions; when required, they had no trouble in reproducing the prescribed rhetoric about the states being repositories of 'ancient culture, oriental traditions and ideals'.[39] So, when the raj found itself in the midst of another major crisis, and again in need of stout allies, they turned, not to the 'authentic', old-worldly princes like Fateh Singh of Jodhpur, but to their 'modern' cousins, who, knowing something of the conventions of western political discourse, could be counted on to give an effective performance when wheeled out on the public stage.

The politics of counterpoise

The second great imperial crisis of the nineteenth century – the challenge of nationalism – arose in the 1890s; but, unlike that of 1857, it arrived, not suddenly but stealthily. Nationalism in the form of a political ideology began to manifest itself in the big presidency cities around the middle of the century, but its transformation into an all-India phenomenon occupied another twenty years, and even then looked far from threatening to the raj, the flagship of the patriotic movement, the Indian National Congress (INC), being noted during its early years for its respectability and deference to authority. Indeed, so weak and meek did the INC appear to the incoming Lord Curzon that he confidently predicted, in 1900, that his viceroyalty would see the organisation's demise.

However, even as Curzon spoke, other forces were gathering strength inside and outside the Congress network. In Poona, former capital of the eighteenth century Maratha Empire, mass meetings were staged under the banner of the Maratha hero Shivaji to condemn imperial plague and famine measures. In Calcutta and Dhaka, university students poured on to the streets to vent their displeasure at Curzon's interference in the governance of the university and to protest his planned partition of Bengal, effected in 1905. Later, a campaign was started to boycott English cloth and to encourage people to buy and wear home-grown, *swadeshi* garments. But mass agitation was not the sum of the

---

[37] Minto, *India Minto and Morley*, 298 (Journal entry, 15 May 1909).
[38] Hardinge, *My Indian Years*, 35.
[39] Address by maharaja of Indore read to the second session of the RTC, 18 Nov. 1931, B. S. Moonje Papers, subject file 18.

government's worries. During the 1890s, a hard core of nationalists turned to violence, and with each passing year attacks on British officials and their families became more commonplace. In 1908, for example, there were over twenty separate incidents including seven murders.[40] At the same time, uncertain whether to deplore the use of violence or applaud the patriotism which lay behind it, the 'Moderates' began to lose their grip on the Congress to younger and more outspoken men such as Bal Gangadhar Tilak from Maharashtra, Lala Lajpat Rai from the Punjab, and Aurobindo Ghosh from Bengal. For these men the notion that India's destiny lay within the British Empire was repugnant; they wanted and demanded unqualified independence.

Faced with terrorism and mass agitation for the first time, the government's complacency crumbled. Although it maintained a façade of dour imperturbability throughout the crisis, by winter 1906–7 it was secretly very concerned, especially at the seeming capitulation of the moderates. 'The Moderates are frightened, or shocked or amazed', noted Harcourt Butler.[41] Fearing that the moderate party was no longer able or willing to take on the 'extremists', the British sought to find a 'counterpoise to Congress aims' elsewhere, among other conservative interest groups.[42] One outcome of this reassessment was a *rapprochement* with the Muslims; another a proposal to cultivate and politicise for imperial purposes the Indian princes.

In the circumstances in which the British found themselves in 1907–8, playing the princely card was an obvious tactic. For one thing the princes could be relied on. Their attachment to the throne had never wavered, even in the gloomiest days of Curzonist paternalism, and since Curzon's departure the budding friendship between the more outgoing rajas and their British overlords noted in the previous section had blossomed. For another, with the significant but sole exception of the gaekwar of Baroda, Sayaji Rao,[43] the rulers were as one with the government as regards the extremists. The maharaja of Benares described the Bengali students taking part in the anti-partition struggle as 'knaves' who had no real

[40] James Campbell Ker, *Political Trouble in India, 1907–1917* (repr., Delhi, 1973), 451–7. For a general account of these events see Amales Tripathi, *The Extremist Challenge in India Between 1890 and 1910* (Bombay, 1967).

[41] Butler to Dunlop Smith, private sec. to the viceroy, 1 Dec. 1907; Martin Gilbert, *Servant of India: A Study of Imperial Rule From 1905 to 1910 as Told Through the Correspondence and Diaries of Sir James Dunlop Smith* (London, 1966), 97. See also Sir George Clark, gov. of Bombay to John Morley, sec. state for India, 10 and 31 July 1908, Morley Coll., 42C.

[42] Minto to Morley 28 May 1906, Morley Coll., 1.

[43] On Sayaji Rao's brushes with authority see Ian Copland, 'The Dilemmas of a Ruling Prince: Maharaja Sayaji Rao Gaekwar and "Sedition"', in P. Robb and D. Taylor (eds.), *Rule, Protest, Identity: Aspects of Modern South Asia* (London, 1978), 28–48; and Charles W. Nuckolls, 'The Durbar Incident', *Modern Asian Studies*, 24, 3 (1990), 529–59.

conception of patriotism.[44] Hira Singh, raja of Nabha, dubbed Arya Samajists 'troublemakers with a canker in their hearts'.[45]

Moreover, as collaborators the rulers carried considerable clout. Generally held in high esteem by their own subjects, the *darbars* also had their share of admirers among nationalists and progressives in British India. In a period when independence for the provinces was still merely a distant dream, the states, as 'existing specimen[s] of Indian sovereignty',[46] exercised a strong sentimental hold on the hearts and minds of many Indians, while the advanced programmes of education and social reform in place in states such as Travancore and Baroda were seized on as evidence that Indians really were competent to rule themselves. Speaking from personal knowledge as a one-time dewan of Baroda, Congress president and champion of good government Romesh Chandra Dutt affirmed that no part of the subcontinent was better governed than the 'States ruled by their own Princes'.[47] Similar tributes were registered by other nationalist leaders including Annie Besant and Mahomed Ali. Finally, the princes commanded a great deal of influence among certain sections of the political elite by virtue of their extensive patronage of good causes, in particular by their endowment of temples and educational trusts. Patiala, Mysore, Jodhpur, and Kashmir were major benefactors of M. M. Malaviya's Hindu university foundation; the nizam and the begum of Bhopal gave several *lakhs* to the new Muslim University at Aligarh; Sangli, Bhor and other western Indian *darbars* were patrons of the Deccan Education Society; Patiala and Nabha gave money to the Sikh Khalsa College at Lahore; and Bikaner became a large benefactor after the War of the Servants of Hindu Society and Gandhi's Hindi Prachar campaign on behalf of untouchables.[48] The leverage this gave the princes was made abundantly clear in 1910 when Annie Besant, who had taken advantage of her position as head of the Benares-based Hindu Central College to criticise the racist conduct in India of her countrymen, was compelled to retract her 'offensive' remarks after the college's major donor, the maharaja of Benares, threatened to cancel his subscription and lobby

[44] Benares to Dunlop Smith 29 May 1907, Gilbert, *Servant of India*, 86.
[45] Note by Dunlop Smith on interview between Nabha and Lord Minto, 29 June 1906, *ibid*, 48.
[46] Speech by S. Satyamurthi to the All-Parties Conference, Calcutta, 1 Jan. 1929, *ToI*, 2 Jan. 1929, 10.
[47] Romesh Dutt, *Economic History of India in the Victorian Age, From the Accession of Queen Victoria in 1837 to the Commencement of the Twentieth Century* (London, 1903), 32.
[48] For details see Ramusack, *Princes*, 50; K. M. Panikkar, *An Autobiography* (Madras, 1977), 86; chief sec. to account.-gen., 22 Oct. 1929, RSA, Bikaner, PM's Office, A 672–682 of 1927; Seth Jamnalal Bajaj to maharaja of Bikaner 12 Aug 1935, Seth Jamnalal Bajaj Papers; and maharaja of Patiala to Sir Sunder Singh Majithia 26 Sept. 1937, Sunder Singh Majithia Papers, subject file 27.

other rulers to do the same.[49] From almost every angle the princes looked a good bet.

When the imperial summons eventually went out, in the form of a circular letter of August 1909 from Minto, asking the states to advise on the best way of dealing with 'sedition', it evoked a set of responses at once so effusively loyalist and authoritarian as to be almost embarrassing: for instance, the sage advice from the regent of Jodhpur, Pertab Singh, that the only effective way of curbing dissent was 'much chili, then hanging'.[50] However, in the majority of cases the rulers did not simply limit themselves to words, but replied also with action against radicals in their own states. Jaipur and Gwalior suppressed liberal newspapers, the raja of Sangli prohibited its high school students from attending Shivaji festivals, Junagadh outlawed the local *swadeshi* campaign, the Kashmir *darbar* clamped down on public meetings, the maharaja of Patiala took issue with the Arya Samaj, and Kolhapur launched what one nationalist newspaper called a 'reign of terror' against prominent Brahmins.[51] Watching these proceedings from Simla the foreign secretary felt more than ever that the raj and the states were destined to be partners. 'I want to keep them wholeheartedly on our side', he wrote to his mother, 'because they are our only real support.'[52]

Nevertheless, while the concept of a close, on-going working relationship with the princely states was an appealing one, Butler and Minto knew that the support of the rulers could not simply be taken for granted, no matter how far their interests coincided with those of the raj. Accordingly, the two men considered how they could reward the chiefs by giving them what they so clearly wanted more than anything – autonomy in their internal affairs. But the policy of *laissez-faire*, as it came to be called, was not wholly based on pragmatism. The viceroy believed strongly that, given the home government's determination to introduce constitutional reforms in the provinces, in order to appease the raj's critics, they were morally bound to grant a corresponding boon to its most faithful allies. As well, Minto and Butler were persuaded by the gaekwar's argument that a looser leash on the princes would improve, rather than retard, the standard of their administrations.[53]

---

[49] M. N. Das, *India Under Minto and Morley* (Oxford, 1964), 29.

[50] Minto, *India*, 363 (Journal entry dated 21 Dec. 1909). For other replies see *The Pioneer*, 14 Nov. 1909.

[51] For details see Ian Copland, 'The Maharaja of Kolhapur and the Non-Brahmin Movement 1902–1910', *Modern Asian Studies*, 7, 2 (1973), 209–25; and Ramusack, *Princes*, 36–7.

[52] Butler to his mother 15 Dec. 1909, Butler Coll., 7. See also Butler's note dated 11 Mar. 1909, NAI, F&P, Confdl.B, Intl.A, 1911, 3.

[53] Speech by maharaja of Baroda at viceregal reception, Baroda, 15 Nov. 1909, Minto, *India*, 351.

The *laissez-faire* policy was launched on 1 November 1909 with a speech by Minto at Udaipur, significantly one of the most old-fashioned and backward of the major states. Its key passage went as follows:

I have always been opposed to anything like pressure on Durbars with a view to introducing British methods of administration. I have preferred that reforms should emanate from Durbars themselves and grow up in harmony with the traditions of the State. It is not the only object to aim at [and] though the encouragement of it must be attractive to keen and able Political Officers and it is not unnatural that the temptation to further it should, for example, appeal strongly to those who are temporarily in charge of the administration of a state during a minority . . . I cannot but think that Political Officers will do wisely to accept the general system of administration to which the Chief and his people have been accustomed.[54]

Meanwhile Butler, at Minto's suggestion, went to work on a new code of practice for political officers. The result of these labours, the *Political Department Manual*, was issued confidentially to all residencies in 1910. It exhorted the men on the spot to place themselves figuratively in the princes' shoes and to try to appreciate their point of view; warned them against offering gratuitous advice; urged them at all times to uphold the dignity of the *darbars*; and advised them, in a phrase that came to sum up the document, to 'leave well alone', adding that unilateral interference should be reserved for cases where misrule had reached 'a pitch which violates the elementary laws of civilisation'.[55]

The *laissez-faire* revolution did not happen overnight. Old habits die hard, and senior politicals especially found it very difficult mentally to adjust to a system which greatly curtailed their power. As we shall see in chapter 2, Minto's decree was still meeting resistance in the late 1920s. Yet 'revolution' it undoubtedly was. Princes everywhere hailed the Udaipur speech as ushering in a new era in relations with the raj. In the words of the nawab of Palanpur, 'like schoolboys we got a holiday when Lord Minto at Udaipur declared the non-intervention policy'.[56] A corner had been turned – and there would be no going back. Nevertheless the watershed changes which occurred in political practice during Minto's term were not accompanied, as Butler and others had hoped, by the development of permanent structures and institutions for tapping the princely goodwill generated by the Udaipur declaration and channelling it

[54] C. H. Philips (ed.), *The Evolution of India and Pakistan, 1858–1947: Select Documents* (London, 1962), 427. The speech was drafted by Minto's private secretary, Dunlop Smith, while the viceregal party were en route from Delhi. Dunlop Smith to Minto 18 Oct. 1909, Gilbert, *Servant of India*, 198.

[55] A full text of the Introduction to the *Manual*, from which these quotes are taken, may be found in IOR L/P&S/13/550.

[56] Palanpur to maharaja of Patiala 5 Aug. 1931, Keyes Coll., 31.

in imperially beneficial directions. Borrowing the idea from Lytton, who had proposed it in the 1870s, Minto initially considered setting up a princely advisory council, or, alternatively, appointing selected rulers to sit in a council of notables with *zamindars* and other landed magnates from British India. Such a forum, meeting annually for one or two weeks, would be a good way, he told the secretary of state, to meet his government's twin objectives of 'recognizing the loyalty of [the] Ruling Chiefs and enlisting their interest in Imperial affairs'.[57] But the suggestion of a princely 'upper house' elicited little enthusiasm in London, Morley fearing that it might give the rulers ideas beyond their station, and, taking the hint, Minto decided that it might be 'wiser to drop it'.[58] Similarly, high hopes were aroused in *darbari* circles in 1913, by the announcement by Minto's successor, Hardinge, that he proposed to call a conference of rulers at New Delhi to seek their opinions on issues of common interest; however in the event, neither the 1913 conference nor its sequel in January 1914 lived up to their promise. Debate was confined to set speeches on the one subject of the future of the chiefs' colleges, and tightly controlled by officials from the political department. Much disappointed, for he was a man bubbling with ideas, Ganga Singh of Bikaner put it to Hardinge after the second conclave that it was high time the states were given a proper and permanent role in the counsels of the imperial government, and suggested, as a first step towards this goal, that in future the princes should be consulted before bills touching their interests were introduced into the imperial legislative council. However the viceroy dismissed the maharaja's proposal as so much 'rubbish'. Like his political secretary, John Wood, Hardinge doubted that the princes would ever become part of the 'regular machinery of government'.[59] For all the raj's brave rhetoric about partnership, old notions of subordinate isolation continued down to 1914 to drive policy. It would take yet another external crisis – in this case a major European war – to push the government into making the structural changes which princes such as Bikaner were starting to demand.

The tides of war

British overrule had weakened the *darbari* polity in a number of ways. Yet if the states were no longer crucibles of a vigorous and wholly authentic

---

[57] Minto to Morley 12 Aug. 1908, Minto, *India Minto and Morley*, 214. The history of this proposal can be followed in Syed Razi Wasti, *Lord Minto and the Indian Nationalist Movement 1905 to 1910* (London, 1964), 155–9.
[58] Minto to Morley 5 Dec. 1908, quoted in Wasti, *Lord Minto*, 159.
[59] Hardinge to Wood, 19 Jan. 1914 and Wood to Hardinge 21 Jan. 1914, quoted in Ashton, *British Policy*, 48.

political culture, neither were they simply Geertzian theatre-states – hollow crowns in Nicholas Dirks' crisp but overly dramatic metaphor.[60] The sedition crisis of the early twentieth century showed that the states were still capable of dealing effectively with domestic dissent; the war of 1914–18 showed that they had the resources and expertise to make a valuable imperial contribution also at the all-India and even at the international level.

To a greater extent than perhaps any other social group in the country, the princes stood out in their support for the war effort. Some dozen regiments of states' Imperial Service Troops saw service in France or the Middle East, while the maharajas of Bikaner, Nawanagar and Idar, the raja of Akalkot and the nawabs of Loharu and Sachin all spent time at the battlefront. As well, the states gave generously of money and munitions. Tiny Sangli donated Rs 75,000 directly to war funds and invested five lakhs in war bonds; Nawanagar contributed the equivalent of half a year's revenue from the public fisc and the jam saheb another £21,000 out of his own pocket; Bikaner in 1916 gave the equivalent of his 'entire Privy Purse allowance for one year'; Rewa offered his entire hoard of jewels.[61] At the same time the rulers helped out on the propaganda front, lending their names to recruitment drives and weighing in on the government's side against elements opposed to the war on ideological grounds. For instance, in 1914 Hardinge asked the nizam as the *de facto* leader of India's Sunni Muslim community to try to get his co-religionists to ignore the *fatwa* issued by the Ottoman *khalif* calling for a holy war; Osman Ali obliged with a formal proclamation of his own urging them to fight instead on the Allied side. All this, needless to say, put the princes very much in the raj's good books; more importantly, it gained them a lifelong friend and patron at Buckingham Palace. When Lord Chelmsford succeeded Hardinge as viceroy in 1916, George V advised him to visit the rulers regularly, and to heed their advice. Later, hearing that Scindia and Bikaner had been 'cruelly slandered' by the 'malicious tongues' of certain officials 'in responsible places', the king made it clear to Chelmsford that he expected this smear campaign against his friends to

---

[60] The problem with Dirks' thesis, at least as applied to the colonial period, is that it rests on evidence drawn from a fairly atypical state. Pudukkottai was small, well away from the princely geographical mainstream, and ruled in the late nineteenth and early twentieth century by a very westernised prince short on ability and commitment.

[61] Copland, *British Raj*, 243n; Ramusack, *Princes*, 38–9; Hardinge, *My Indian Years*, 103; Roland Wild, *The Biography of Colonel His Highness Shri Sir Ranjitsinhji Vibhaji, Maharaja Jam Saheb of Nawanagar* (London, 1934), 174, 182; Bikaner to Chelmsford 19 May 1916 and Jaisalmer to resdt., W. Rajputana 16 Nov. 1916, Chelmsford Coll., 17; NAI, F&P, Intl. B, Feb. 1917, 32–42.

be stamped out.[62] Although never again wielded so openly, royal influence remained a constant and important element in the relationship between the government and the princes throughout George V's reign, lending it both glamour and stability.

Yet, while the princes' contribution to the war effort was warmly welcomed – and with the coming of peace well rewarded by the government[63] – it was need rather than gratitude that finally pushed the British into taking the leap in the dark which John Morley had contemplated and rejected in 1908. Politically, India in 1914 was fairly quiescent, but the economic by-products of the domestic war effort – rising prices for foodgrains, cloth and sugar, acute shortages of essential household products such as kerosene, higher taxes and charges – generated a groundswell of discontent which in Bengal and the Punjab spilled over into a renewed spate of terrorist violence. Meanwhile, as noted above, feelings among the country's Muslims were inflamed by Turkey's entry into the war on the side of Germany, by the Khalif's *fatwa*, and after 1916 by growing anxiety about the fate of the Islamic holy places in Palestine. This was followed, also in 1916, by the negotiation at Lucknow of a pact between the Muslim League and the INC which bound the two bodies to pursue a common constitutional strategy, thereby greatly weakening the capacity of the raj to keep order by playing off its opponents. Finally, the Allies' war propaganda about 'subject' minorities and 'self-determination' fuelled hopes among the Indian middle class that major constitutional concessions were in the wind.[64] Facing its most serious challenge since the Bengal anti-partition agitation, the government turned, as in 1905–8, to its powerful friends for help. This time, however, the Muslims were unavailable. In their absence, the spotlight fell squarely on the aristocracy.

As we have seen, members of the princely community had already come to the party in numerous ways – assisting the war effort materially, and politically via recruitment drives and patriotic speeches. And collaboration of this type was further encouraged after 1916 by the appointment of selected rulers to governmental bodies responsible for war planning and propaganda. However by this stage it was clear to the

---

[62] Chelmsford to king 17 July 1916, sec. state to viceroy 7 Aug. 1916, encl. letter from king, Lord Stamfordham, private sec. to George V, to Chelmsford 22 Aug. 1916 and Stamfordham to Chelmsford 1 Aug. 1917, Chelmsford Coll., 1.

[63] At the end of the war a number of princes received enhancements to their gun-salutes, while the nizam was granted the title of 'Faithful Ally of the British Government' by George V.

[64] The picture is presented in more detail in Judith M. Brown, 'War and the Colonial Relationship: Britain, India and the War of 1914–18', in D. C. Ellinwood and S. D. Pradhan (eds.), *India and World War I* (Delhi, 1978), 19–48; and Brown, *Modern India: The Origins of an Asian Democracy* (Delhi, 1985), ch. 4.

government that isolated acts of princely munificence would no longer suffice by themselves to win the battle for the hearts and minds of the masses; that what was really required was some *collective* manifestation of princely loyalty, properly focussed and orchestrated. This train of thought led Chelmsford, as it had Minto, to contemplate the creation of a permanent constitutional structure for the articulation of princely opinion. But whereas Minto's idea had been an entirely British one, Chelmsford's owed at least as much to *darbari* initiatives. In 1915 Bikaner had argued that the war offered an 'opportune moment' for the states to request the government to begin removing 'disabilities which to them have been extremely discouraging and disheartening'.[65] Others, notably Sayaji Rao of Baroda and Ranjitsinhji of Nawanagar, were quick to jump on the bandwagon.

In adopting this strategy the princes were in substantial agreement about what they wanted. First, they expected due recognition for their war services, preferably by the award, as in 1858, of land grants. (Bikaner thought territory captured from Germany in East Africa might be usefully employed for this purpose.)[66] Second, they wanted discussions with the government on the reform of political practice. It appeared to the princes that, the policy of *laissez-faire* notwithstanding, officials in the political department remained wedded to nineteenth century values; that the dominant tendency was still to denigrate the rulers as individuals and to regard their treaties as 'obsolete'. At best they hoped that some of their lost rights might be restored; at worst they wanted guarantees that no further encroachments were contemplated. Thirdly, as a long-term goal, the rulers wanted the practice of consultation initiated by Hardinge greatly extended. They wanted their views heard, and not only on paramountcy issues; to be treated, in Ganga Singh's plaintive and revealing phrase, 'as *somebodies* in the . . . Indian Empire'.[67] Early drafts of the princely programme advocated annual conferences at Delhi; but later versions went well beyond this to advocate the setting up of permanent machinery for the exchange of opinions and ideas between the states and British India.[68]

Chelmsford felt somewhat uncomfortable with many of these demands. As a total package the princes' programme seemed to him excessive, unrealistic and even slightly arrogant. Yet with the political

---

[65] Quoted in Panikkar, *Bikaner*, 166–7.
[66] Chelmsford to Chamberlain 1 Mar. 1917, Chelmsford Coll., 3.
[67] Note by Bikaner dated [?] Aug. 1915, encl. in Bikaner to Chelmsford 16 Apr. 1916, Chelmsford Coll., 17.
[68] Note by Baroda encl. in his circular letter of 10 Nov. 1917, GSAB, Pol. Dept., Section 341, file 31.

situation what it was, he could not afford to alienate the rulers or pass up a chance to bind them more closely to the government. He decided, therefore, to try to meet them half way by taking up their proposal for a resurrection of the conference format. For one thing, another conference at Delhi would allow the chiefs to get better acquainted and, if necessary, to let off steam; for another, the presence at the imperial capital of a clutch of rulers and retainers resplendent in their finery had the potential to win the government some valuable propaganda points with the public. In the event, however, the conference of November 1916 did much more than just boost morale. Unexpectedly, and in stark contrast with the proto-types of 1913–14, it proved highly successful as a talkfest and as a work-shop for resolving problems. All this led Wood and Chelmsford to think that the experiment should be repeated, perhaps annually. As the political secretary put it in a memorandum which Chelmsford sent on to London:

such gatherings . . . are of the greatest value to the Viceroy and the Political Department. Discussion with . . . representative Chiefs . . . ensures that the Chiefs' views are adequately put foward . . . and save[s] Government from the errors resulting from a misconception of their attitudes. These Conferences act more-over as a safety-valve through which minor grievances find a harmless vent, and tend to prevent subterranean communications behind the backs of Political Officers. . . . The old practice of . . . 'subordinate isolation' . . . is now, owing to the greater facilities of communication and the spread of education impossible to maintain, and it is recognised on all hands that the collective goodwill and support of the Ruling Chiefs is an Imperial asset of incalculable value. If the growing demand for collective discussion is disregarded, we run the risk of alienating the sympathies of those whose support is most worth having.[69]

To their chagrin however, the secretary of state Austen Chamberlain gave the idea of regular conferences a cool reception. Already, he averred, the rulers were exhibiting a dangerous 'tendency to meddle with the affairs of British India'; 'collected at Simla', they could easily end up becoming 'tools of the Opposition'.[70] Pressed, Chamberlain agreed to sanction a further conference in 1917: but only as a special case and with the proviso that any resolutions were forwarded to him in advance for vetting.[71]

In part, this was simply the knee-jerk reaction of an old-fashioned con-

[69] Minute by J. B. Wood dated 27 May 1916, NAI, F&P, Secret Intl., July 1916, 29.
[70] Chamberlain to Chelmsford 24 Nov. 1916, Chelmsford Coll., 2.
[71] In the event, Chamberlain seized on the new minority rules which had been drawn up by a subcommittee chaired by Wood to meet the objections expressed by princes at the 1916 conference, taking issue especially with the clause that said that rulers, on their majority, should have the right to disallow any measures introduced by the interim regime with which they disagreed. While approving the resolution as a whole, he ordered the veto pro-vision excised. sec. state to GOI 27 Apr. 1917, NAI, Secret Intl., Aug. 1918, 1–11.

servative who liked things to stay the same. But it was also coloured by Chamberlain's growing suspicions about the maharaja of Bikaner's political agenda. Late in 1916 Ganga Singh started to buy into the current political debate in a way which appeared to put him firmly in the nationalist camp. Addressing a meeting of the Empire Parliamentary Association in London, Ganga Singh said that he thought India was ripe for 'further political . . . advance', and that the moderates' demand for dominion status within the British Empire was 'perfectly reasonable'. Afterwards, he elaborated his views in a note for Chamberlain, penned at the latter's request. The note stressed:

1 The extreme importance – indeed, the vital necessity – of a formal and authoritative official declaration being made by the British Government at the earliest possible opportunity to the effect that self-government within the British Empire is the ultimate object and goal of British rule in India.
2 The advisability of inaugurating, on liberal and sympathetic lines, further political reforms in the constitution and function of the Provincial Legislative Councils as well as in the Imperial Legislative Council in British India.
3 The desirability of greater autonomy being granted to the Government of India as well as to the Provincial Governments. . .[72]

While there was nothing in this manifesto which had not already been said openly by others, including members of Lionel Curtis' *Round Table* group, nationalist sentiments coming from the mouth of a ruling prince struck a raw nerve. Chamberlain resolved to teach the upstart maharaja a lesson he would not forget.

Fortunately for the princes, he did not get the chance. Chamberlain was forced out of the ministry in the summer of 1917 over the Mesopotamian scandal, and was replaced by his under-secretary, Edwin Montagu, a liberal romantic sympathetic to the princely order and to the aspirations of the Indian middle class. In August 1917 Montagu sought, and secured, the cabinet's authorisation for such an announcement. Read out in the House of Commons on the 20th and immediately wired to India, the 'Montagu declaration' pledged that, henceforward, British policy in India would be directed at 'the gradual development of self-governing institutions';[73] further, it stated that Montagu himself would visit India that winter to draw up, in concert with the viceroy, and in consultation with interested parties representing a broad cross-section of Indian political life, concrete recommendations for a limited devolution of power.

[72] Note dated 17 Apr. 1917, quoted in Panikkar, *Bikaner*, 174–86.
[73] *Parliamentary Debates*, House of Commons, 5th series, 97, c. 1695–6 (20 Aug. 1917). It is curious that none of the many historians who have written about the Montagu Declaration and the ensuing reforms appear to be aware of the striking similarity of the declaration to Bikaner's note, which Montagu would undoubtedly have seen.

The declaration raised hopes in many quarters in India, but in none more so than among the chiefs, for in Edwin Montagu, who was already familiar to many of them from a previous tour in the winter of 1912–13, the princes reckoned they had acquired a true friend at court. Sensing that their hour of opportunity had come and determined to make the most of it, the leading lights of the monarchical fraternity met at Delhi in November, shortly before Montagu's scheduled arrival, and elected an *ad hoc* 'committee of four' consisting of Bikaner, Ranjitsinhji of Nawanagar, Bhupinder Singh of Patiala and Jey Singh of Alwar, to draft a common set of proposals to put before the secretary of state.

Montagu did not disappoint. He encouraged the rulers to come to him with their troubles, spent much of his spare time in their company and listened with approval to their plans, many of which, fortuitously, coincided with his own. After his initial meeting with the princes' deputation in New Delhi on 11 November he wrote in his diary: 'the Native States as a body ought now to have some approximation to self-government'; and the following day he wrote out a list of the structural changes that appeared to be required to bring this about – the establishment of a council of princes, the appointment of selected princes as advisers to the political secretary, the full separation of the political from the foreign department (in which, Montagu believed, the bad traditions of the past still lingered), the abolition of extraneous intermediaries between the rulers and the centre.[74] But it was the maharaja of Alwar who really caught Montagu's ear. The more he talked to Jey Singh, the more impressed he was with 'this man's intelligence'. 'Alwar', he wrote after one especially 'entrancing' meeting over breakfast early in the new year, 'has given me so many new ideas and his power of organisation is so splendid that I like to talk things over with him.'[75] When the maharaja presented him with a book he had written on the problem of the states, the secretary of state devoured it avidly. In this way, Jey Singh, who did not possess anything like the international reputation of the other committee members and who indeed was not particularly admired by his brother princes, came to play a dominant role in the process of debate and consultation from which emerged the 1918 Montagu–Chelmsford report.

However, the rulers had a much harder time getting their own act together. Right from the start several small-minded princes, jealous of the limelight being captured by a cosy circle of what were merely middle-ranked monarchs, resolved to oppose anything with which Bikaner,

[74] Montagu, *Diary*, 20–21 (entries for 11, 12 Nov. 1917).
[75] *Ibid.*, 245, 297 (entries for 5 Feb. and 2 Mar. 1918).

Patiala and company were associated.[76] Yet these difficulties were over-shadowed by a much more fundamental, and potentially more serious, tussle over ideology which came to a head at a summit meeting of rulers, dewans, and invited guests (political secretary John Wood, S. P. Sinha, M. M. Malaviya, Lionel Curtis, Srinivasa Sastri, Ali Imam and C. Y. Chintamani)[77] at Patiala over the pre-Christmas 1917 period. While it was generally agreed that the states deserved to be rewarded for 'their whole-hearted and ungrudging co-operation' in the war and for 'the part they [had] played in the past in the consolidation of British rule',[78] and that, given Delhi's proclaimed goal of 'responsible Government of the people by the people', the states had a legitimate claim both for the restoration of their 'obliterated' sovereign rights, and for a broader 'emancipation from the restrictions and obligations imposed by the treaties' as reinterpreted through the distorting prism of 'usage', and whilst, too, there was a consensus that the princes deserved, as 'natural leaders' with a god-given capacity to detect 'the innermost thoughts of the [Indian] people', to 'be taken much more seriously' as politicians and awarded a 'defined share in the administration of the country',[79] the dele-gates at Patiala could not agree about what form the states' participation in the all-India political domain should take. The more 'liberal' *darbars* – Baroda, Mysore and Gwalior – were keen to see something along the lines of the gaekwar's scheme described above, that is to say, a princely 'seat' in the viceroy's executive council plus representation for the states in an imperial or 'federal' second house. The majority of delegates, however, found this conception unacceptable. They disliked the idea of a mixed chamber in which the states would in all probability constitute a voting minority; they feared that the *darbars*' participation in a formal, organic federation would be construed by the provincial politicians as a 'tacit recognition' of the right of the Delhi government to poke its nose into their affairs; last but not least, they demurred at the notion that 'one from amongst their . . . Order' should have to 'sit with other Ordinary Members of Council' – in other words, in the company of commoners.[80]

---

[76] For example, Maharaja Ripudaman Singh of Nabha, a long-standing rival of Patiala's in the Sikh community, launched in January 1918 a scathing attack on the 'secret machina-tions' of the committee of four. Ramusack, *Princes*, 82.

[77] Curtis we have met. The others were moderate politicians from the newly formed National Liberal Federation.

[78] Note by Abdul Hamid, dewan of Kapurthala, n.d., GSAB, Baroda, Pol. Dept., section 341, file 38.

[79] Introduction to note by Committee of Four by Kailash Haksar, pol. member, Gwalior, dated 10 Dec. 1917; and note by V. D. Satghare, pol. sec. Baroda, dated 8 Jan. 1918, GSAB, Baroda, Pol. Dept., section 341, file 33.

[80] Note by the Committee of Four dated 10 Dec. 1917, GSAB, Baroda, Pol. Dept., section 341, file 33.

This viewpoint, in turn, attracted strong behind-the-scenes backing from certain hard-line officials present at the meeting, who thought to use the princes to derail the reforms bandwagon. One was Sir Michael O'Dwyer, the maverick lieutenant-governor of the Punjab, who had already marked himself out as a bitter opponent of the policy of *laissez-faire*; another his chief secretary, Sir John Thompson, an unreconstructed Punjab paternalist whose diary includes the revealing notation, next to Montagu's name: 'Knave'.[81] Wood may have been a third.[82] Nevertheless, encouraged by Malaviya, Sastri and Chintamani, the liberal *dewans* continued to press for the adoption of their more sweeping scheme. At this point the conference degenerated into a slanging match, with three delegations – from Kashmir, Hyderabad and Indore – threatening to walk out unless the liberals' scheme was rejected root and branch.

For the first, though not by any means for the last time, a split in the ranks of the princes threatened; but this calamity was averted, temporarily at least, by some fancy footwork on the part of another of the invited guests, Sir Ali Imam, a high court judge from Bihar. Before the summit Ali had discussed the notion of the states playing a more formal part in the governance of the Indian empire with M. A. Jinnah, generally acknowledged to be the sharpest constitutional lawyer of his day, and Jinnah – uneasy as Ali was about formal princely representation in the legislature – had proposed, as a fallback arrangement, the creation of a 'joint committee of reference' to advise the government on the potential impact of legislation before it was introduced into the council. This compromise position Ali now hawked around the summit, and so persuasively that the liberals, while not convinced that Ali's scheme would give the states the effective voice in high quarters that their own had been designed to secure, could find no strong reason to oppose it. As Baroda's Manubhai Mehta confessed to his master the maharaja afterwards, 'Sir M. Visesvaraya [of Mysore] and myself had [such] an uphill battle in dispelling groundless apprehensions, we had to yield on the point of a Federal Chamber or Upper House.'[83] Thus, when it was time for the committee of four to table its report, which it did on 4 February 1918, it was able to present a document incorporating, to all intents and purposes, the agreed demands of a united order. Meanwhile, an effervescent Montagu had been hard at work assuaging Chelmsford's fears about the princely agenda. By the time the committee's report arrived, he had pretty much got the viceroy on side.

---

[81] Diary entry for 1 May 1919, Thompson Coll., 12; and see also Thompson to pol. sec., GOI, 28 Dec. 1917, NAI, F&P, Secret Intl., Feb. 1918, 28–34; and O'Dwyer, *India As I Knew It*, 155.

[82] This, at any rate, was Montagu's opinion. See his *Diary*, 232–3 (entry for 30 Jan. 1918).

[83] Mehta to Baroda 11 Jan. 1918, GSAB, Baroda, Pol. Dept., section 341, file 33.

The eloquence of the report did the rest. Five months later the princes' main demands were included, with only one substantial change,[84] in the joint recommendations on constitutional reform forwarded by Montagu and Chelmsford to the British government.

Connaught's pledge

Now, at last, the campaign launched by Bikaner in 1914 began to bear fruit. In September 1919, following further face-to-face talks with the princes at Delhi in January, a joint working party of rulers, dewans and officials was formed to scrutinise existing political procedure in the light of the accumulated complaints of the *darbars*, and to identify such general principles as could be abstracted from the states' treaties and engagements. Its interim report, submitted to another rulers' conference in November, drew from Chelmsford the frank admission that 'the treaty position has been affected and that a body of usage, in some cases arbitrary . . . has insensibly come into being'.[85] Further inquiries were promised. Meanwhile, discussions were initiated on the recommendation in the joint report that no ruling prince should be set aside, or heir-apparent to a throne removed from the line of succession, without the relevant issues being first examined by an independent commission. At the princes' request, the commission procedure was made optional. Finally, the rulers got their long-desired council. In 1919, as part of its post-war reform package, London established by royal warrant a 120-seat 'Chamber of Princes' to advise the viceroy on all 'questions affecting Indian States generally or which are of concern either to the Empire as a whole or to British India and the States in common'.[86] The Chamber was to meet, at least once a year, at the capital. Although under the general control of the viceroy, it was to have its own elected president or chancellor, and was at liberty to develop its own rules of business. Between sessions a six-man standing committee, also elected, was to help the chancellor make the princes' views known to the government.

The Chamber of Princes (COPs) was launched with glittering ceremonial at the Red Fort on 9 and 10 February 1921 – the Diwan-i-Am palace

---

[84] The *Joint Report* left the door open for deliberations between the Council of State and the proposed Chamber of Princes on matters of imperial or all-India interest, but balked at the Committee of Four's suggestion for a standing 'committee of reference' to be composed of nominees of the two chambers.

[85] Speech of 3 Nov. 1919, *Indian Annual Register*, 1920, 89. Eventually some twenty-three points of dispute were identified as requiring modification. These were referred in November to a reconstituted Codification Committee. The twenty-three points are listed in Phadnis, *Towards Integration*, Appendix III, 217–18.

[86] Constitution of the Chamber of Princes, NAI, F&P, Secret Reforms, June 1920, 11–16.

decked out for the occasion with cloth-of-gold and two huge gilded thrones for the guests of honour, Chelmsford and the duke of Connaught representing the king-emperor. Indeed, so effective was the pageantry created for the opening, that the *Times of India* reporter covering it was moved to opine that if the builder of the Fort, Shah Jahan himself, had been a 'ghostly witness' of the proceedings, he would 'have recollected sadly to his own disadvantage between the condition of our day and those of his'.[87] But while the pageantry was rather more than window-dressing, symbolising as it did the conventional wisdom that the princes were the living heirs to an ancient and splendid Indian ruling tradition, it was the presence of the king's cousin, and the personal message from George V that he carried in his pocket, that made the ceremony significant. 'The King's desire', declared Connaught, 'is that every breath of suspicion or misunderstanding should be dissipated', and with that object in mind 'His Majesty now invites Your Highnesses, in the fullness of his confidence, to take a larger [role] . . . in the political development of your Motherland.' The duke's words filled the hearts of the assembled princes with pride and hope, but it was the king's own words, which the duke now proceeded to quote, which fixed the moment forever in their minds. Recalling that, years before, his grandmother had taken a pledge 'to maintain unimpaired the privileges, rights and dignities of the Princes of India', the king-emperor continued: 'The Princes may rest assured that this pledge remains inviolate and inviolable.'[88] It was a brief, almost terse announcement; yet for the eagerly expectant princely audience, craning forward in their plush seats so as not to miss one royal syllable, it was enough. Publicly, solemnly, the British monarchy had committed itself to their protection – indeed, had dedicated itself to their welfare. Moreover, since the king spoke as a constitutional monarch, it was evident that his invitation to them to take on a larger part of the burden of all-India governance was no empty rhetoric, that it reflected also the thinking of his ministers, that an offer of imperial partnership had been extended to them. Afterwards the standing committee of the COP pinpointed February 1921 as ushering in 'a new era . . . in the relations between the Government of India and the States'.[89] It was, in retrospect, much more than that; it was, in fact, the high-water mark of the relationship between the princes and the British crown, a mark that over the next three decades would be sometimes approached, but never surpassed.

By 1921 the imperial compact with the princes looked set in stone.

---

[87] *The Times of India*, 10 Feb. 1921.   [88] Quoted in *The Times*, 8 Feb. 1921.
[89] Special Directorate of the Chamber of Princes, *The British Crown and the Indian States*, 97.

Now we can see, with the wisdom that distance confers, that from the very start it was fatally compromised and weakened by the British government's failure to grasp that it was based on an illusion. In forming a partnership with the rulers, the British believed, to paraphrase a witty U.P.-*wallah*, that they were calling up the 'old' world of the states to redress the balance of the 'new' nationalist world of the provinces.[90] However the 'old' India summoned up between 1906 and 1921 was neither truly old, nor, despite the widespread perception that the states were the quintessential, the 'Indian India', wholly an indigenous creation. By the early years of the twentieth century, such obstacles to social and political intercourse between the states and the provinces as still existed were fast breaking down. Even the most backward states were beginning to feel the winds of change. By clinging to an anachronistic image of the states as a separate, Indian India, the British not only turned a blind eye on reality, but missed the seemingly obvious point that calling up the old world to offset the new necessarily involved a greater interaction between them, and the likelihood that the states would become increasingly 'contaminated' by the larger and more aggressive political culture of the provinces. In 1921 the fiction could still, with a bit of effort on the part of the British and their princely clients, be maintained. But, like an unwanted intruder, reality lurked just offstage, awaiting the moment when the princes realised – as they were bound eventually to do – that the key to their salvation lay in throwing down the artificial geographical barriers imposed by British paramountcy and embracing the turbulent world beyond.

[90] Morris to Meston 24 Sept. 1917, quoted in D. A. Low, *Eclipse of Empire* (Cambridge, 1991). The same aphorism appears, unacknowledged, in Sir A. Rumbold, *Watershed in India 1914–1922* (London, 1979), 114.

2   The shackles of paramountcy

Paramountcy must remain paramount . . .

The Indian States Committee, March 1929

The new order questioned

The first two decades of the twentieth century had been singularly good ones for the Indian princes. In 1900 the *darbars* had been isolated from one another and from British India, firmly under the bureaucratic thumb of the political department, a butt for Curzon's paternalist rhetoric; by 1921 they had emerged from the shadows into the sunlight as acknowledged partners of the British raj, no longer scorned but lauded as repositories of tradition and loyalty and political wisdom. Mere onlookers twenty years before, they had become the 'steady goal-keepers in the great Indian game'.[1]

By comparison, the decade of the 1920s was laden with disappointments. To some extent the princes brought this on themselves by aiming too high. Buoyed with success, and relishing their new sense of empowerment, the rulers were primed, as it were, for disillusionment. Yet the main reason why the 1920s proved such a testing time for the Indian states was that the political environment, so benevolent from 1916 to 1921, suddenly became a lot more hostile. Why was this?

On one level, the transformation can be explained with reference to three significant departures from high office in Delhi and London. The first of these changes, chronologically, took place at viceregal lodge, where the mild, patrician Chelmsford gave way in 1921 to the Jewish advocate Lord Reading – the first ennobled commoner to hold the viceroyalty since John Lawrence in the 1860s. Understandably, perhaps, this self-made man found it hard to warm to an order which reeked of snobbishness and inherited privilege, and though not lacking in charm,

---

[1] Speech by Sir Walter Lawrence at the English-Speaking Union, Dartmouth, 10 Jan. 1929, quoted in *TOI*, 29 Jan. 1929, 8.

he rarely used it in their company, preferring a demeanour which the princes charitably described as judicial. The second change involved the key post of political secretary. Tired and jaded after seven hectic years in the job, and not overly keen to serve under Reading, whom he suspected of being out of sympathy with his ideas, Sir John Wood asked to be transferred to an undemanding residency, and Reading, with unconcealed relief, agreed. Meanwhile, the question had arisen of what to do with Sir John Thompson, the chief secretary of the Punjab, who had been given extended leave to shield him from nationalist attacks over his role in coordinating the province-wide repression which followed on the heels of the Amritsar Massacre of April 1919. Convinced that Thompson could not go back to the Punjab, Reading put him into the political department. Thompson was furious, believing himself to have been the victim of a 'gross injustice', and told the home member Sir William Vincent that he regarded his new posting as 'more or less the end of my career'.[2] However he was an able official, and a hard worker, and Reading was impressed by his industry. In 1923, to the chagrin of many career officers in the department, he was appointed to act in place of Wood. Thus the government of India acquired a political secretary who lacked first-hand experience of the states, who carried a sizeable chip on his shoulder, and who, as a disciple of Sir Michael O'Dwyer, was openly opposed to the whole thrust of the 1919 reforms. The third change, perhaps the most crucial, involved Montagu. In March 1922, the secretary of state was forced to resign after a clash with Lloyd George over Britain's policy towards Turkey. To mark his departure, the princes took the unprecedented step of hosting a valedictory dinner for him in London; significantly, the incoming secretary Lord Peel chose not to attend. Two years later the return of the Tories to office saw the control of Indian affairs pass to Lord Birkenhead, whose stated policy of 'reaction to weakness and surrender'[3] encompassed troublesome princes quite as much as it did seditious nationalists.

On another, deeper level, however, the change in official policy reflected a growing British disenchantment with the new corporate princely culture which had grown up as a result of the liberalisation of political practice – a culture most conspicuously embodied in the COP. Designed to be the showpiece of the new order, the Chamber never matched the expectation of its founders. At the first session, in November 1921, only 30 princes were present out of the 109 who were entitled to seats, and down to the mid-1920s attendance rarely exceeded 45. Moreover, the early sessions generated little real debate, most of the

[2] Diary entry, 14 May 1921, Thompson Coll., 16.
[3] Birkenhead to Reading 21 Jan. 1925, Reading (Private) Coll., 100.

participants being content, whether from lack of facility in English, or natural diffidence, or ingrained caution, to read from prepared speeches on anodyne topics. Even Alwar, who was one of the few to thrive in these new surroundings, admitted in 1924 that 'we have not [yet] arrived at that stage in respect of powers of oratory or of debate where we can throw open the galleries to the public and the press during our discussions'.[4] The British, increasingly, were convinced that they never would, and that the Chamber was destined to remain 'nothing more than an academic debating society'.[5]

Another aspect of the COP that gave rise to official concern was its transparent unrepresentativeness. Even before the Chamber was inaugurated several of the major states indicated that they would not be participating. Hyderabad, hyper-conscious of its premier position in the monarchical pecking-order, was one: 'I see no reason why the present system which has existed for considerably over a century . . . should be disturbed', wrote the nizam emphatically in 1917, 'I should not like any question affecting my State being determined on the advice of other ruling princes or their representatives.'[6] Another non-starter was Mysore, the second-ranked state, deterred by its distance from Delhi and by its dissatisfaction with the constitution and powers of the Chamber. As we have seen, Mysore had all along favoured a broader-based assembly drawn equally from the states and the provinces.[7] Yet another absentee was Udaipur, the leading Rajput principality, like Hyderabad sensitive on the score of status.[8] And Holkar of Indore, too, stayed out, fearful that his Maratha ancestry and 'want of education' would make him the target of Rajput condescension.[9] This left the Chamber with only two 21–gun rulers, Baroda and Gwalior – the one enfeebled by chronic illness and the other handicapped by an unwarranted, but nonetheless acute sense of

[4] 'Note on Giving Publicity to Chamber Proceedings' dated 9 May 1927, RSA, Alwar, P[rivate] S[ecretary's] O[ffice], 112 of 1927.

[5] Note by A. N. L. Gates, resdt. Jaipur, encl. in Gates to pol. sec. 22 Apr. 1927, IOR R/1/1/1686.

[6] Note by Hyderabad dated 1 Dec. 1917, GSAB, Baroda, Pol. Dept., section 341, file 31; and *Proceedings of the Conference of Ruling Princes*, 507. The nizam's *khilafat* scheme was hatched in the context of Kemal Attaturk's abolition of the Turkish monarchy in 1922. As a first step towards realising this ambition, in 1924 he arranged for his heir apparent to be married to the ex-sultan's eldest daughter. See resdt. Hyderabad to pol. sec. 19 May 1933, IOR L/P&S/13/541.

[7] Note by Maharaja Krishnaraja Wadiyar dated 3 Jan. 1918, GSAB, Baroda, Pol. Dept., section 341, file 33.

[8] R. A. E. Benn, offg. AGG, Rajputana, to pol. sec. 23 June 1920, NAI, F&P, Reforms A, Sept. 1920, 45–51.

[9] Wood to PSV 1 Nov. 1916, Chelmsford Coll., 17; note by Wood on conversation with Indore, 23 June 1920, and note dated Sept. 1920, NAI, F&P, Reforms A, Sept. 1920, 45–51.

Table 2.1 *Membership of the Standing Committee of the Chamber of Princes, 1921–1926*

State	Salute (in guns)	Total attendance (in days)	Membership (in years)
Gwalior	21	19	4
Kashmir	19	13	1
Bhopal	19	4	1
Bikaner	17	28	6 (5*a*)
Cutch	17	13	3
Patiala	17	23	6 (1*a*)
Alwar	15	28	4
Dholpur	15	28	3
Jhalawar	13	18	1
Nawanagar	13	12	6
Palanpur	13	20	2
Sangli	9	28	2

Notes:
a Indicates as chancellor
Source: India Office note, Mar. 1931, IOR L/P&S/13/545.

social inferiority *vis-à-vis* the quintessentially blue-blooded Rajputs[10] – as founder members.

Thus, almost by default, the COP came to be dominated, as Table 2.1 shows, by a group of middle-sized, mainly Rajput rulers whose states were situated within relatively easy travelling distance by motor car from Delhi, who were fluent in English, who had acquired political skills in forums such as the wartime chiefs' conferences, and who, in the last resort, had little to lose and much to gain by moving into a wider political arena: Alwar, Dholpur, Nawanagar, Palanpur, Cutch, Rewa, Sangli, and, above all, Bikaner and Patiala. This may have been a just outcome, given the preeminent part these rulers, Bikaner especially, had played in the creation of the Chamber, but in the eyes of the government it stamped the nascent organisation as a rump parliament. 'Looking at the effective membership of the Chamber', wrote an India Office official, 'it may be said to represent in the main only the "middle class" states . . . whose activities are known to be resented and feared by many of the smaller States and to be viewed with dislike by some of the leading

---

[10] Years before Harcourt Butler had observed that when Scindia went riding with Rajput rulers such as Alwar, he kept a discrete two lengths distance behind them. Butler to his mother 18 Feb. 1909, Butler Coll., 7.

Princes.'[11] Reading agreed. The Chamber, he believed, would continue to struggle for influence until 'a considerable number of princes from different groups of States [condescended to] take a genuine . . . interest' in its proceedings.[12]

However, the government's main concern was not the Chamber's future, limited as that seemed to be, but the behaviour of its members. One of the presumptions behind the new order had been that it would make the princes more contented and thus more compliant; but to Delhi's puzzlement – and irritation – they remained restless, fractious and on the face of it no more warmly disposed toward officialdom than before. Throughout the 1920s reports flooded into headquarters from residents that the princes were avoiding them, ignoring their advice, going over their heads to Delhi. One officer wrote feelingly that if the trend continued he would soon be reduced to a 'mere Post Office'.[13] Some of these reports also suggested that the princes were meddling in politics more than was good for them, or the raj; while others lamented their rudeness and want of respect. After a meeting with the chancellor in April 1926, Thompson wrote in his diary: 'Bikaner was as usual ungracious and offensive.'[14] In the same vein the agent to the governor-general in Central India, Colonel Heale, complained that he had been deliberately snubbed by Nawab Hamidullah Khan of Bhopal. (Spurning ceremony, Bhopal had 'received' him in shirt sleeves on a tennis court.) Did these criticisms reflect a substantive change, or were they merely products of bruised egos and paranoia?

Actually, it was a bit of both. With confidence born of experience, some of the princes were indeed becoming more assertive – and none more so than Ganga Singh. War hero, signatory of the Treaty of Versailles, Ganga Singh could not resist playing the elder statesman and giving the British the benefit of his accumulated wisdom. At his first interview with Reading, in April 1921, he ventured to tell the viceroy what was wrong with his political department, then had the presumption to solicit his 'protection should anything happen in consequence'.[15] Later he suggested to Reading that 'A Round Table Conference with a selected number of Princes' might enable him to better understand their 'difficulties, hopes, and aspirations'.[16] This, too, implied that the viceroy was incapable of reaching a sensible conclusion on the states unaided. But

---

[11] India Office note on 'The Chamber of Princes' dated 6 Mar. 1931, IOR L/P&S/13/545. The rather limited composition of the ruling elite of the Chamber has been remarked on before, notably by Ramusack, *The Princes of India*, pp. 119–22 and 133–8.

[12] Speech of 25 Jan. 1926, RSA, Alwar, PSO, 99 of 1926.

[13] K. S. Fitze, P.A. Baghelkhand, to sec. AGG, C.I., 20 Apr. 1927, IOR R/1/1/1686.

[14] Diary entry, 1 Apr. 1926, Thompson Coll., 20.

[15] Bikaner to Reading 5/7 July 1924, Reading Coll., 26.

[16] Bikaner to Reading 18 May 1922, Reading Coll., 24.

Bikaner did not just confine himself to offering general advice; he sought to intervene in particular cases, flouting the understanding that the Chamber should not involve itself in the internal affairs of member states. For instance, in 1921 he tried to mediate in a dispute over the Jaipur succession; and in 1923 offered to take up the nizam's case for the retrocession of Berar (of which more later) with the government. Moreover, though an impressive performer in public, Ganga Singh did not always present well in face-to-face encounters. Big man that he was, his personal manner tended to be brusque and abrasive, and like all princes he was highly protective of his *izzat*, almost walking out on a state dinner for the Prince of Wales when he discovered that he had been seated below Patiala. Yet the British were equally, if not more, at fault. If the political department had been less blinkered, if the viceroy and his political agents had been less concerned with ritual and show and more with the vitality of the monarchical order, they might have detected in this assertive behaviour indications of an emerging political maturity among their putative allies. For example, when Hamidullah was asked why he had not arranged a formal *darbar* for Colonel Heale as required by protocol, he explained that he had been trying to do things 'in the European way' – in other words, in the modern way.[17] Instead, Delhi chose to interpret it as insubordination. As many commentators on colonialism have observed, European officials in the 'East' typically used family metaphors to characterise their relationship to those they governed. Like caring but stern fathers, the British residents agents in the Indian states were made deeply uneasy by any signs of 'youthful' independence on the part of their princely 'children'.

By the early 1920s, therefore, it was clear to the political department that a fundamental problem had arisen in the raj's relationship with the princes. They saw an order overdosed on grandeur, out of control. Yet, for all their dislike of Bikaner, they suspected that the 'problem' was not, at heart, one of personalities, but of policies and structures – that its roots lay in the system of *laissez-faire* which they had inherited from their predecessors. Thus, determined as they were to put the princely 'malcontents' like Bikaner and Patiala in their place,[18] Reading and Thompson knew they would have to cut deeper if the canker that had sprouted in the heart of the imperial system was to be destroyed. They would have to cut right down to the bone. They would have to dismantle much of the new order that had been built up since 1909. 'He is coming round to the view',

---

[17] Bhopal to Heale 10 May 1930, IOR R/1/1/1943. Earlier Bikaner was accused by Thompson of snubbing the AGG Rajputana at a reception for the prince of Wales. Diary entry 19 Dec. 1921, Thompson Coll., 11.

[18] Reading to Montagu 25 Oct. 1921, Reading Coll., 3.

Thompson noted after an interview with Reading in November 1922, 'that we have carried the policy of non-interference too far.'[19]

The new order qualified

The first intimation to the *darbars* that a new spirit had taken up residence in the political department came when Reading, out of the blue and without prior consultation, announced that the Press Act of 1910, on which the princes had come to rely as a defence against unwanted propaganda and blackmail, would be repealed. Naturally anxious, but still at this stage ignorant of the viceroy's wider agenda, the princes through Alwar urged Reading to enact alternative legislation, arguing that 'they were entitled to such protection under their treaties'.[20] But he remained unconvinced, and only retreated from this intractable position when the India Office threatened, in the absence of new legislation, to advise the king to disallow the repeal of the Press Act. Thus, while the promulgation of the Princes' Protection Act of September 1922 was warmly welcomed by the rulers (it did, after all, give them what they wanted), the suspicion remained that Reading had not acted out of genuine concern for their welfare.[21]

In the meantime, too, other evidence had started to pile up. Although the regular talks between the standing committee and the political department on treaty rights and political practice which had been fore-shadowed in the Montford report continued, the atmosphere became less cordial, standoffs more common. When the princes put forward the tentative suggestion that the states be allowed to exercise civil and criminal jurisdiction over mainline railways passing through their territories, it was met with what Bikaner described as a 'wall of departmental prejudice'. Similarly, Reading refused to be drawn on the *darbars'* request for a judicial inquiry into the erosion of their treaty rights. Then, in 1922, the government actually back-tracked on a previous commitment when it ruled, again without bothering to seek the views of the standing committee, that the 1920 convention that princes threatened with deposition should have the right to have their case arbitrated by an independent commission of inquiry had been designed to apply only to the rulers of

---

[19] Diary entry, 1 Nov. 1922, Thompson Coll., 16.

[20] Reading to Montagu 21 July 1921, Reading Coll., 3.

[21] Failing to pass the imperial legislative assembly, the bill had to be certified by the viceroy, the first time this power was used during the Montford period. Partly because of this, the Princes' Protection Act came to be seen as a major pillar of the raj's alliance with the princes, which, considering Reading's reservations about it, was something of an ironic outcome.

'major' states. This was followed, in 1924, by the announcement that, with the exception of the Kathiawar agency, the planned transfer of states under the control of the provincial governments to the direct control of the government of India had been postponed indefinitely.[22]

These developments – or more accurately non-developments – left the Chamber's leaders feeling bewildered and betrayed. However, it was the government's vigorous re-assertion of its paramountcy powers that really brought home to them how much things had changed in New Delhi. Having reached the conclusion that the rulers had been given too much rein, that the paramount power was slipping in its duty of care towards the states' subjects, Reading and Thompson moved quickly to purge the political department of slackers and incompetents. One of the first to go was Sir Lennox Russell, who was compelled to take early retirement from the Hyderabad residency after it came to light that he had, for years, been letting the nizam see copies of confidential letters and telegrams from the political secretary and the viceroy.[23] Another casualty was Charles Minchin, agent to the governor-general in the Punjab, who was felt to be too close to Patiala; a third, the elderly and ailing Sir John Wood, forced out after he unwittingly placed the heir apparent to the throne of Kashmir, Hari Singh, in the clutches of a nest of pimps and blackmailers. At the same time, orders went out that residents were to keep their eyes and ears open, and to report regularly on the efficiency and probity of the *darbars* falling within their jurisdiction. Nevertheless, these changes were but a preliminary, a means to a larger end. What Reading and Thompson really wanted to do was to change the policy. And for that they needed a pretext – a reason to come down heavily on one or more of the 'pushier' princes in a way that would permanently change the rules on intervention. Such an opportunity soon presented itself, in the shape of three notable acts of princely indiscretion.

The first of these involved the Punjab state of Nabha, ruled by Maharaja Ripudaman Singh. Locked in a fierce tussle with Bhupinder Singh of

[22] The princes under the control of local governments had argued for centralisation both on grounds of status and in the belief that they would get a better deal from Delhi than from a more hard-line adminstration such as that in Bombay. This argument had been accepted by Montagu and Chelmsford, but was bitterly opposed by the local governments, especially Bombay under Sir George Lloyd. See Copland, *The British Raj*, 250–62. In the event the Deccan states were not transferred until 1933, the Bengal, Orissa and Madras states until 1936. Likewise, the retention of the AGG-ship in Rajputana was in part due to a vigorous rearguard campaign by the incumbent officer, Sir Robert Holland.

[23] As a parting shot, Russell suggested to his superiors that the Hyderabad residency had become redundant and should be abolished as an economy measure. For a brief pen-picture of this eccentric man, see K. P. S. Menon, *Many Worlds* (London, 1965), 81 (Menon was then a junior officer in the residency).

Patiala for the leadership of the Sikh *panth*, Ripudaman Singh had thrown in his lot with the anti-British Akali movement, and this in itself made him a marked man in the eyes of the political department; but proof of seditious activity was lacking. Moreover, for all his desire to cut the princes down to size, Reading was inhibited by his lawyer's training. He noted nervously: 'Nabha's sanad gives him special protection against interference.' It also seemed to the viceroy that, although Ripudaman was not much liked by the other chiefs, 'he might, on a point like this, get a good deal of support'.[24] Nevertheless, further ammunition was soon to hand. For some time stories had been circulating of kidnapping and mistreatment of prisoners; and in 1922 the revelation that a British subject named Malak had been unlawfully detained in Nabha put the matter beyond doubt. This gave the viceroy the authority he needed. Without waiting for Ripudaman's consent, Reading appointed a commission of inquiry, under Justice Stewart, to investigate the Malak case and other allegations against the *darbar*; and when Stewart's report came in, every bit as damning in its indictment of Ripudaman as Delhi had expected, the viceroy used it to mount a case for the maharaja's deposition. 'The whole story', he informed the secretary of state smugly, 'will reflect the greatest discredit upon Nabha and cannot but have an adverse effect upon the public mind in relation to the autocratic rule of the princes.'[25] Peel, though, felt that a lesser penalty would be more fitting. Accordingly, in June 1923, Nabha was told in a letter from the viceroy that he would be allowed to keep his title and salute so long as he paid Patiala 50 lakhs compensation, left the state, and promised to step down from the *gaddi* once his son was of age. But the document had a sting in its tail. Ripudaman was warned that the terms were not negotiable, that failure to sign would be treated as an act of rebellion 'for which I might be shot'. Chastened by this prospect, the maharaja wrote a letter agreeing to the government's conditions and gave it to one of his employees, an Irishman named O'Grady, to take to the governor-general's agent at Lahore – only to regret his decision a few hours later. But by then O'Grady was well away. On 8 July, the AGG arrived at Nabha with a detachment of troops, and the following day Ripudaman Singh was sent off under escort to Dehra Dun.[26]

---

[24] Viceroy to sec. state 16 Dec. 1921, Reading Coll., 10.

[25] Reading to Peel 7 June 1923, Reading Coll., 6.

[26] Nabha to Reading 14 Dec. 1923, Reading Coll., 25. For an extended discussion of this episode, which focusses on the increasing interpenetration of princely and provincial politics during the 1920s, see Ramusack, 'Incident at Nabha', 563–77. After Ripudaman Singh was deposed, militant Akalis launched a violent agitation to have him restored. Dozens were killed and hundreds imprisoned. Richard G. Fox sees this, controversially, as part of a 'Third Sikh War' against British colonialism. *Lions of the Punjab: Culture in the Making* (Berkeley, 1985), 87–93.

The second incident was equally dramatic and, since the protagonist, Holkar of Indore, was a major prince, offered even more grist to the government's mill. In January 1925, some British army officers strolling through the posh Bombay suburb of Malabar Hill noticed a girl being dragged, struggling, into the back seat of a car. They intervened, released the girl, and summoned the police. The trail led first to the house of a rich Muslim merchant named Bawla, where the girl, Mumtaz, had been living. The police found Bawla lying in a pool of blood, murdered by the girl's abductors. Subsequently, it was learned that before coming to Bombay Mumtaz had been a palace dancer at Indore, a favourite of Maharaja Tukoji Rao Holkar. Circumstantial evidence, and the confessions of several of the accused, pointed to the abduction, if not indeed the murder, having been done on the orders of the palace. 'That the object of the plot was to capture Mumtaz and bring her [back] to the Maharaja', Reading later told the king, 'would seem beyond question.'[27] Believing that the government had a *prima facie* case, the viceroy offered Holkar a commission of inquiry under the resolution of 1920; though he doubted whether a prince as jealous of his *izzat* as Tukoji Rao had shown himself to be throughout his reign would accept. His judgement proved correct. 'Rightly or wrongly', wrote Holkar by way of reply, 'I have all along adhered to the belief that neither on the analogy of International Law nor as a matter resting upon treaty is a prince of my position liable to be tried.'[28] Having sealed his fate, Tukoji Rao preempted the inevitable order for his deposition by abdicating in favour of his son.

It was, however, the nizam, the premier ruler, who presented Reading and Thompson with their *cause célèbre*. As remarked in the previous chapter, the touchstone in relations between Hyderabad and the government of India had long been the status of Berar, a Hyderabadi province assigned to the Company in 1853 in settlement of arrears owed to the British for the upkeep of the Hyderabad Contingent; and in 1919 this smouldering issue again burst into life when, as part of the princes' log of post-war demands, Osman Ali revived his father's claim to full sovereignty over the province. Now, insofar as the nizam's goal was the complete recovery of Berar, this was always going to be a tough assignment. From the British viewpoint the Berar issue had been settled – permanently – by Curzon in 1902. Nevertheless, from the standpoint of 'absolute justice',[29] Osman Ali had a good case in seeking to have the

---

[27] Reading to the king 25 Feb. 1925, Reading Coll., 1.
[28] Indore to AGG Central India 26 Feb. 1926, quoted in J. Coatman (ed.), *India in 1925–26* (Calcutta, 1926), 215.
[29] Speech by nizam to Hyderabad legislative council, 1919, *Indian Annual Register*, 1920, 192.

question reopened. Quite apart from the lingering suspicion (shared privately by some British officials such as Wood) that Curzon had obtained Nizam Mahbub Ali's consent to the 'agreement' of 1902 by duress, the large and increasing surplus which Berar returned to the CP every year made a mockery of the 25 lakhs annual rental that had been paid to Hyderabad since 1860. If Osman Ali had forsaken his claim for retrocession in favour of a more modest claim for an upward revision of the financial aspects of the 1902 agreement, and if he and his minister, Sir Ali Imam,[30] had acted more diplomatically, Hyderabad might well have prevailed.

In the event the claim was hopelessly mishandled. First, encouraged in his quest by Wood and Montagu, and eager to demonstrate that he was worth the Rs1000 a day the nizam was paying him, Sir Ali got off on the wrong foot with Reading by marching into the viceroy's study and threatening to make public Hyderabad's 'incontrovertible evidence' of Curzon's sharp practice unless a joint commission of inquiry was granted. White-faced with suppressed rage, Reading thumped his hand on the table and announced that the interview was over; at which point, according to Thompson, the Hyderabad minister 'almost collapsed, and the V[iceroy] had to send for water to revive him'.[31] Then, after Delhi had formally rejected the Hyderabad claim, the nizam tried to challenge the constitutionality of the government's action, arguing that:

The refusal to entertain an Ally's claim or proposal stands on a different footing from a 'decision' which signifies a constitutionally binding force which in the circumstances of the case is not applicable. The rejection by His Majesty's Government of my claim to the restoration of the Berars can only be a fact expressing its views but it cannot impose upon me or my House any obligation to treat the subject as closed or regard the claim as barred for all time.[32]

This arrogant and needlessly provocative letter, another example of Sir Ali's handiwork, converted what had been a minor bilateral quarrel into a major issue of principle carrying implications for the entire system of paramountcy.

Coincidentally, the viceroy was already preparing to tackle the nizam on the score of misgovernment. Since taking over from Russell in 1925, the new Hyderabad resident, Sir William Barton, had unearthed a morass of corruption, nepotism, arbitrary decision-making, illegal exactions and confiscations, and general inefficiency so deep and so entrenched that

---

[30] The same man who had saved the day at the 1917 Patiala conference. In between times the Bihari lawyer had served on the viceroy's executive council, and gained a knighthood.
[31] Diary entry 28 Mar. 1922, Thompson Coll., 16.
[32] Nizam to Reading 20 Sept. 1925, quoted in Adrian Sever (ed.), *Documents and Speeches on the Indian Princely States* (Delhi, 1985), II, 414.

initially the authorities found his reports hard to credit. Yet prior to receiving Osman Ali's letter, Reading had been disinclined, despite Thompson's prodding, to make a personal example of the nizam. Damning as it was, the evidence had not seemed to him sufficient to justify a public humbling of the premier state and of a ruler whom George V was known to admire. Now, he did not hesitate. He had all the evidence he needed. In March 1926, in what was, fittingly, the last important act of his viceroyalty, Reading dispatched a long letter to Osman Ali which was simultaneously published, for all the rulers to see, in the government *Gazette*. 'The sovereignty of the British Crown', it began,

is supreme in India, and therefore no Ruler of any Indian State can justifiably claim to negotiate with the British Government on an equal footing. Its supremacy is not based only on Treaties and Engagements but exists independently of them, and quite apart from its prerogative in matters relating to Foreign Affairs and policies, it is the right and duty of the British Government . . . to preserve peace and good order throughout India . . . .

It went on:

The right of the British Government to intervene in the internal affairs of Indian States is another instance of the consequences necessarily involved in the supremacy of the British Crown . . . the internal, no less than the external, security which the ruling Princes enjoy is due ultimately to the protecting power of the British Government and where Imperial interests are concerned, or the general welfare of the people of a State is seriously and grievously affected by the action of its Government, it is with the Paramount Power that the ultimate responsibility of taking remedial action, if necessary, must lie. The varying degrees of internal sovereignty which the rulers enjoy are all subject to the due exercise by the Paramount Power of this responsibility.[33]

This was at once hailed, and has ever since been recognised, as the classic statement of the doctrine of unfettered paramountcy. Then, in July 1926, after Reading's departure but in consonance with directions he had drawn up, the nizam was handed an ultimatum like that given to Nabha three years earlier: delegate all executive power to a council whose members would serve at Delhi's pleasure, or abdicate.[34] Outwardly contrite but inwardly seething, Osman Ali signed the necessary orders, bringing to a close the first, tumultuous phase of his long reign.

However if the government's 1926 intervention in Hyderabad ended one crisis, it laid the seeds for another; for contrary to Reading and Thompson's expectations, the princely order did not crumble before the

---

[33] Quoted in Government of India *White Paper*, Appendix I.
[34] For details of these arrangements see, I. F. S. Copland, 'The Hyderabad (Berar) Agreement of 1933: A Case Study in Anglo-Indian Diplomacy', *The Journal of Imperial and Commonwealth History*, 6 (1978), 285.

implicit warning contained in the viceroy's letter. For six years they had watched the systematic destruction of the post-war edifice built by Montagu and Chelmsford. They had seen – and felt – the shackles of paramountcy being tightened. Now, in the aftermath of the Indore and Hyderabad coups, the rulers' anger with the government became tinged with desperation. There was a general feeling that the time had come to make a stand, 'for the British Government to be warned' that princely loyalty could no longer be taken for granted.[35] It was no more a question of whether, but of when, and how. Reading and Thompson had found the princely order unorganised and divided; unwittingly, they had transformed it into a militant pressure-group.

The demand for an inquiry

Nevertheless, it would be wrong to lay the blame for this breakdown of relations entirely on the shoulders of Reading and Thompson. While the revival of paramountcy may have been the issue that served to bring matters to boiling point, it was not the only one on which the princes and the raj had a different view. For instance, there were large disagreements over fiscal policy. Since most states were landlocked, they had to import goods through British India. These goods were charged imperial customs duty. Thus, indirectly, the states contributed every year a considerable amount to the government of India's coffers – at least 5½ *crores* for most of the 1920s. Yet they received not a paise remuneration in return. This, the *darbars* believed, represented a denial of natural justice and flouted 'the elementary principle of economics, that the revenue derived from any taxation is the due of the Government whose subjects consume the commodities taxed'.[36] Furthermore, the states objected to paying a tax that, insofar as it added to the cost of imported articles, raised the local cost of living and thus imposed a financial burden on the states' people, which in turn reduced their capacity to pay the domestic taxes necessary to fund social services and development. Thirdly, the *darbars* resented being subject to what was, increasingly, a protective tariff. Previously minimal, the level of duty had been lifted sharply in 1916 as a war measure, and was raised again after 1922 on the recommendations of the Fiscal Commission.[37] While the princes had not minded contributing to

[35] Note by Maqbool Mahmud, P. M. Alwar, dated 7 Feb. 1928, RSA, Alwar, PSO, 121–I of 1927–8.

[36] Memo No. 3 from chancellor, COP dated 10 Mar. 1928, RSA, Sirohi, Sardar Office, serial 103, file 36. It was also, arguably, at variance with the 1921 Barcelona Convention on trade.

[37] Between 1890 and 1930, the government of India's receipts from sea customs increased ninety-fold.

the cost of the war, they cavilled at subsidising indirectly a programme of hot-house industrialisation which, given the states' much smaller manufacturing base, was going to bring them little commercial benefit.

Additionally, the states felt short-changed by Delhi in regard to its excise policy, its control over the exchange rate, and its management of post offices and mainline railways. Like the imperial sea customs duty, the salt tax fell on consumers in the states no less than it did on those in British India, and again, a very substantial figure was involved; after deducting the compensation paid to the one-time salt-manufacturing states, the Standing Committee reckoned that the states altogether contributed at least 90 lakhs to the imperial treasury under this head. Likewise, they calculated that imperial excises on liquor, kerosene and petrol, cost them collectively some 39 lakhs a year in revenue. Ironically, one of the losers from this system was 'Muslim' Bhopal, which, though it had a policy of prohibition, was unable to enforce it rigorously because of the non-cooperation of the imperial authorities, who permitted alcohol to be freely sold at cantonments and railway stations within the state. The *darbars* also felt they were entitled to a return from profitable imperial services such as the railway and the post office which were patronised by their subjects. For example, the Standing Committee calculated that even if the states' people, on a per capita basis, used the imperial railway system only 85 per cent as frequently as people from the provinces, they were still owed a refund of at least 120 lakhs a year. There was concern, too, about the efficiency of some of the 'nationalised' services, such as the post office, which the states were forced to use but which lay outside their control. Finally, the states believed they were penalised by the government of India's control over the currency: which yielded it a profit from the minting of coins, and enabled it to manipulate the sterling exchange rate to the advantage of British India.

Of course these claims on the part of the princes did not go unanswered. Most commonly it was argued that the subsidies which the states paid in this way were a fair recompense for the fact that they got their defence, in effect, for free. As an official in the political department noted in 1926, 'The answer to this is that . . . the States are specially favoured in other ways in comparison with the provinces . . . notably in not paying a proportionate share of the cost of defence.'[38] However the princes vigorously contested this argument, holding that they had already contributed

---

[38] Note by G. F. Turner dated 18 Oct. 1926, IOR L/P&S/13/573. Another official calculated that, allowing for the tribute paid by some states and the cost of the upkeep of the Imperial Service Troops maintained by others, their total direct contribution was in the vicinity of £2 million, way short of the £8 million that it cost to defend the one-third of the subcontinent under their control. Note by H. W. Garrett dated 26 Oct. 1926, *ibid.*

much to the 'general peace and security' of the subcontinent by sub-
mitting to the paramountcy of the crown, by paying tribute, and by ceding
territories whose value had multiplied over time. More to the point, the
princes did not believe that the benefits they received from the protection
of the raj were worth anything like the 10 *crores* a year which its fiscal policies cost them.[39]

Nevertheless, even as they counted the financial burden, the *darbars*
were aware that the heart of the problem was their declining influence
over the decision-making apparatus of the imperial government. Lacking
a member in council, the political department had never been particularly
effective in standing up for the states' interests when they clashed with
those of the provinces, but under the decentralised Montford constitution the department's voice carried even less weight in provincial matters.
Moreover, the reforms had put elected Indians, for the first time, in
charge of a range of portfolios. This had made policy-making much more
subservient to powerful elements outside the bureaucracy, elements committed to the overriding goal of provincial development. The states' case
had suffered accordingly. As Bhupinder Singh told a meeting of the East
India Association in London in 1928, 'in a great variety of directions . . .
we have found ourselves most deeply and vitally affected by policies in the
framing of which we had no hand'.[40] Thus, when in the mid-1920s the
darbars took stock of their situation and looked for ways to improve it,
they focussed not only on the hammer of paramountcy but also the anvil
of the Montford constitution which effectively denied them a voice in
matters of common interest. Baroda's Manubhai Mehta spoke for many
when he declared, bluntly, at a summit at Bikaner in July 1924: 'The only
effective way of safeguarding the financial interests of States to which the
Indian Legislature is often callous, is to secure representation of the
States in the Legislature . . . This leads to the idea of Federation and [the]
redistribution of British India and Indian States into [new federal]
Units.'[41]

The other main circumstance which bore on the princes' decision to go
on the offensive was the outcome of the 1926 chancellorial elections.
Down to 1926 Ganga Singh had monopolised the office of chancellor,

---

[39] *The British Crown and the Indian States*, 213. The Standing Committee's advisers tabu-
lated these costs (in the form of contributions to the imperial fisc) as follows: sea customs,
706 lakhs; salt, 93 lakhs; railways, 120 lakhs; currency and mints, 86 lakhs; and excise, 39
lakhs – a grand total of 1,044 lakhs or 10.44 *crores* of rupees.

[40] Speech of 23 July 1928, quoted in K. M. Panikkar, *The Indian Princes in Council: A Record
of the Chancellorship of His Highness the Maharaja of Patiala 1926–1931 and 1933–1936*
(London, 1936), 11–12.

[41] Notes prepared by Sir M. Mehta at informal conference of states, Bikaner, 14 July 1924,
GSAB, Baroda, Pol. Dept., section 341, file 48.

winning easily in four successive contests. Others such as Jey Singh had
aspirations to leadership, but none possessed Bikaner's dazzling
combination of seniority, experience, kinship ties,[42] and influential
friends in England. However by the mid-twenties the maharaja's hegemony over the Chamber no longer went unchallenged. The younger
rulers, particularly, were increasingly critical of Bikaner's manner, which
had become more abrasive with the passage of time. As twenty-year-old
Gulab Singh of Rewa told Thompson, 'Bikaner is impossible unless one
is prepared to kowtow to him.'[43] Increasingly, too, there was a feeling that
Bikaner had not delivered the goods; that as the princes' elected leader he
could and should have done more to protect them from the depredations
of Thompson and Reading. But it was not until Bhupinder Singh of
Patiala, who as a Jat Sikh envied Bikaner his superior Rajput status and
hated him for flaunting it, and who still burned with the memory of a
Ganga Singh snub eight years previously,[44] announced his candidacy for
the job, that this simmering unrest came to the boil. For, unlike the other
aspirants on the Standing Committee, Bhupinder Singh was a popular
and charismatic figure.

Sensing that Bikaner was no longer invulnerable, Patiala spent the pre-
Christmas 1925 period doing something which had never been done
before in the Chamber: actively canvassing votes. Belatedly, Bikaner's
supporters began to do likewise. However, when it became apparent that
the numbers lay with Patiala, Ganga Singh withdrew from the contest,
ostensibly to 'let some other Prince have a chance'.[45] Ranjitsinhji, suffering a recurrence of the asthma which had plagued him since his cricketing
days, followed suit. With these influential princes out of the running
Bhupinder Singh was easily able to out-point the perennially unpopular
Jey Singh. However, Patiala's success carried a hefty price-tag for the
princely order. In any event his elevation would have aroused expectations of change. But Bhupinder Singh had not merely allowed these to
form; he had encouraged them. In his campaigning, he had gone out of
his way to present himself as a fresh face, and as the harbinger of bold new
policies. Specifically he had promised to rejuvenate the Chamber and,

---

[42] Bikaner was brother-in-law to the maharao of Cutch and an uncle to the maharaja of
Kota. More distant ties connected him also to the houses of Jodhpur, Kishengarh, Bundi
and Sirohi. This kinship network almost guaranteed him a block of Rajput votes.

[43] Thompson diary, entry dated 9 Aug. 1926, Thompson Coll., 20.

[44] Patiala tried, repeatedly, to assert a claim to Rajput ancestry, but as late as the 1930s none
of the important Rajput rulers were prepared to contract marriages with his family.
Bikaner rubbed this in by invariably addressing him, patronisingly, as his 'elder brother'.
In 1918, Ganga Singh very conspicuously absented himself from a dinner held to cele-
brate Patiala's appointment to the Imperial War Council.

[45] Bikaner to Manubhai Mehta 9 Oct. 1925, GSAB, Baroda, Pol. Dept., section 341, file 50.

through it, the fortunes of its members. That was understood to mean that he would take on the government over paramountcy.

But there was more. To the extent that Patiala, by virtue of these dynamics, was committed to a 'reformist' agenda, his hand was greatly strengthened by the election of two new members to the Standing Committee: Maharaja Hari Singh of Kashmir and Nawab Hamidullah Khan of Bhopal. Both were young (31 and 32 respectively), able and articulate. And both, by the standards of their order, were politically liberal. Indeed Hamidullah's credentials – a close connection with Muhammad Ali, going back to the time when the *maulana* had been his personal tutor, another with M. A. Ansari, who doubled as the family doctor, a third, through his private secretary Shuaib Qureshi, with Gandhi – put him squarely in the nationalist camp.[46] More to the point, both princes nursed a grudge against the political department: Hari Singh, because of its role in the 'Mr A' scandal of 1924, which had seen the then heir-apparent's name and reputation assailed in the English law courts;[47] and Hamidullah, because of its dogged opposition to his succession on the dubious technical ground that he wasn't his mother, the begum's, eldest surviving son.[48] The ever-suspicious Thompson had them pegged as yet another pair of potential trouble-makers. For once, he was absolutely right.

[46] Shuaib had served as Gandhi's secretary for a short time in 1922, and later edited *Young India* before taking service in Bhopal. At a luncheon party in viceregal lodge in 1932 Bhopal was heard to proclaim loudly that he would leave if the then vicereine did not stop making disparaging remarks about Gandhi. Memo by Kanji Dwarkadas dated 28 Jan. 1945, encl. in US consul-gen. Bombay to sec. state Washington 10 Apr. 1047, US state dept. decimal file 845.00/4–1047. As late as the 1940s, Hari Singh was recognised by Lord Wavell as having 'liberal ideas' – though by this time his liberalism had been overlaid by a world-weary cynicism. Wavell to Lord Pethick-Lawrence 16 Oct. 1945, IOR L/PO/10/22.

[47] A frequent visitor to Europe, Hari Singh became involved in a clandestine affair with an English 'widow' named Mrs Robinson. Unfortunately the so-called Mrs Robinson was in fact the wife of a London bookmaker, hired by a gang led by the prince's own ADC Captain Arthur who, as we saw earlier, had been recommended to him by the resident Sir John Wood. One night, as the couple relaxed in bed in a Paris hotel room, a gang member burst in and demanded £125,000 in hush money. Hari Singh paid up, but then instructed his bank to stop the cheque. Undeterred, Robinson sued the bank for the recovery of the money; only to be prosecuted in turn for blackmail. At the request of the government, the presiding judge in the blackmail trial allowed Hari Singh to give evidence under the pseudonym 'Mr A'. However while the English press respected the suppression order, newspapers in France and America showed no such restraint, and the full story soon became common knowledge – to Hari Singh's vast humiliation – in India.

[48] The political department based its objection on the fact that succession in Bhopal had always followed the principle of primogeniture; this assumption turned out, after lengthy enquiries, to be false. But it took a special trip to England by the elderly begum, and a discreet word from the king, to get the matter resolved. Even then, Thompson remained unhappy, describing the decision as a 'triumph of evil'. Lord Stamfordham to Reading 8 Oct. 1925, Reading Coll., 1; Reading to Birkenhead 30 Mar. 1926, Reading (Private) Coll., 100; Thompson diary [coded] entry dated 12 Jan. 1926, Thompson Coll., 20.

Nevertheless, whilst resolved on action, the princes were initially unsure about when and how they should act. When they first met to consider their options, prior to the January 1926 Chamber session, there was considerable support, especially among the younger *darbaris* present, for the proposition 'that a delegation should go to the Viceroy and ask him to app[oint] a new Pol[itical] Sec[retary] before the new Viceroy came. One said they had Thompson sahib's knife always at their throats.'[49] Other delegates, however, thought that it would be prudent to await the arrival of the new viceroy who was expected to be Lord Irwin, a junior minister in the Baldwin Conservative cabinet. Rumour had it that Irwin was a decent, sympathetic type. Eventually, this view prevailed; in the event, it proved a wise choice.

Irwin came to India without fixed preconceptions, but with an impeccable pedigree. As he pointed out to the rulers in his opening speech to the Chamber in November 1926, it was his grandfather, Sir Charles Wood, who, as secretary of state in the 1860s, had signed the dispatch authorising the grant to them of adoption *sanads*. What is more, Irwin was a natural diplomat. He had a patrician's dignified bearing and manners, and an easy, unassuming charm. In stark contrast to his predecessor, he had a way of putting visitors at their ease. Right from the start, the princes saw him as a person of 'unquestioned all-round goodness, sympathy and kindness'[50] – a person in whom they could confide. Moreover, by happy coincidence, Irwin's arrival was closely followed by the retirement of John Thompson, which paved the way for the promotion of a crop of younger, more moderate officials headed by Charles Watson and Bertrand Glancy, who took over as secretary and deputy-secretary respectively. These men had cut their teeth on the Butlerian bible, and they were strong supporters of the policy of *laissez-faire*. Thus, when the Standing Committee approached Irwin in November 1926 with a request for a summit on paramountcy and the states' relations with British India, no objection was raised by the viceroy's departmental advisers, as it certainly would have been if Thompson had still been in charge. 'How different in tone', observed Jey Singh after the meeting, 'from Thompsonian tyranny.'[51]

The Chamber's preparations for the summit were made easier by organisational changes introduced by the new chancellor. First he set up a permanent secretariat in rented premises at 8 Underhill Road, New Delhi. Next, mindful of the Chamber's parlous financial situation, he

---

[49] Thompson diary, entry dated 30 Jan. 1926, Thompson Coll., 20. What passed in these meetings was supposed to be confidential, but rarely remained so.
[50] Dholpur to Sir Samuel Hoare, 3 Nov. 1932, IOR L/PO/92.
[51] Marginal note by Alwar on letter from Glancy dated 14 July 1928, RSA, Alwar, PSO, file 117 of 1928.

persuaded the Standing Committee to authorise a levy on the membership (initially set at Rs1,000 per head for five years, but later reduced to Rs 800 for three years) and to establish a voluntary fighting fund to meet legal and other expenses associated with the Chamber's campaign for an inquiry. Third, Patiala pepped up the Chamber's policy-making machinery by instituting the practice of holding regular Standing Committee meetings at Underhill Road and encouraging the members of the Chamber, and ministers from both Chamber and non-Chamber states, to meet informally twice yearly at Delhi (before the annual sessions in February and November) to exchange views about matters of mutual concern.

Meanwhile, the more substantive work of preparing for the conference was assigned to a special committee of princes and ministers which met at Bikaner in August 1926 and again at Patiala in February 1927. First, the committee looked to the requirements of the princely order, and quickly identified four as paramount: guaranteed security against 'aggression or revolt'; the removal of all remaining restrictions on internal sovereignty; 'an adequate voice' in matters of joint concern with British India; and the right to have relations with foreign states. However, when the committee went on to consider how these goals should be pursued, it found itself, like its predecessor in 1917, in two minds. On the one hand, there was widespread support, particularly among the princely members of the committee but also, notably, from newcomer Laurence Rushbrook-Williams, a former director of the Central Bureau of Information who had recently been appointed foreign minister of Patiala, for what might be termed a 'defensive' strategy. This strategy aimed, broadly, at extracting firm 'undertakings' from the government. Specifically, it called for the 'appointment of an independent Committee of Enquiry' headed by 'a distinguished English statesman of weight and standing' 'of the type of Lord Ronaldshay', and containing 'an eminent jurist in international law', and 'an economist and financier of repute', to review the operation of paramountcy.[52]

On the other hand, the ministers on the committee, Rushbrook-Williams excepted, leaned strongly towards the view that in the longer term the states could only survive the challenge of 'advancing Democracy' if the rulers stopped relying exclusively on the British and learned to help themselves. Accordingly, they pressed for what could be

---

[52] *Ibid.*; and minutes of conference of princes and ministers at Patiala, 14–19 Feb. 1927, GSAB, Baroda, Pol. Dept., section 341, file 23. Bikaner wanted the enquiry committee broadened to include a ruling prince, a representative of the India Office, a political officer and 'some ministers', but was persuaded that this would rob it of any pretence to being independent.

called an 'offensive' strategy. This strategy aimed, first, at building bridges with the provinces. It envisaged the princes cultivating journalists, seeking out and attempting to 'make political friends of certain desirable and leading Indian statesmen', and endeavouring through private channels and public speeches to convince the people of British India that the *darbars* were 'sympathetic and not hostile to their legitimate political aspirations'. It also foresaw, in the longer term, the forging of organic links with the provinces. Secondly, the offensive strategy looked to domestic reform to strengthen the bonds between the princes and their subjects. 'The States must gradually reform their own methods of Administration and make it more popular, responsible and representative', urged Mehta.[53] You must 'take your subjects with you', opined Bhavnagar's Prabhashankar Pattani.[54] Specifically, the authors of the offensive strategy urged the Standing Committee to 'work out a . . . programme of development and nation-building', with the object of ensuring that, within five years, all the Chamber's member governments incorporated all the basic features of the modern bureaucratic state including an independent judiciary and security of tenure for public servants.[55]

There was, in fact, a basic contradiction between these two approaches. In the first, the emphasis was on imperial guarantees. This assumed a continued British supremacy in the subcontinent. In the second, the stress lay on political solutions, both internal and external. The clear presumption here was that, at some stage, the *darbars* would have to give up their imperial client status. Indeed the defensive strategy was self-contradictory, in that it called, simultaneously, for the emasculation of paramountcy (no more interference by the political department in the states' internal affairs) and its maintenance as a defence against revolution. In effect the committee's prescription was like a cart drawn by two horses pulling in opposite directions.

Nevertheless, although the Chamber's policy-makers must have been aware of the inherent tensions in the 'Patiala programme', they chose to ignore them. When the special committee's final report was tabled for the Standing Committee's consideration in late February 1927, it was adopted, contradictions and all, without amendment. 'The farsighted Princes', enthused the chancellor after the meeting, 'have, luckily, read

---

[53] Notes prepared by Mehta during a conference at Bikaner, 14 July 1924, GSAB, Baroda, Pol. Dept., section 341, file 48. Unfortunately we do not have a record of what was said in committee by Mehta in 1927, but all the indications are that it was of a piece with what he said at Bikaner three years earlier.

[54] K. K. Pillai to Mehta 12 July 1928, reporting an earlier conversation with Pattani, RSA, Bikaner, PM's Office, Nos. 286–311 of 1929.

[55] Report of the Committee of Ministers [?] Feb. 1927, GSAB, Baroda, Pol. Dept., section 341, file 23.

the sign[s] of the times and have addressed themselves to averting the impending crisis.'[56]

But Patiala's jubilation proved premature. When the membership at large learned what had been decided on their behalf, particularly as regards reform, dissenting voices were raised, particularly in central India, a region which had long felt itself to have been overlooked by the COP in the matter of representation on the Standing Committee, and which included many of the more backward states. 'I must frankly confess', wrote Yadvendra Singh of Panna,

that I believe that Western methods are not necessarily the best that can be devised to suit our environments or that their adoption is invariably beneficial. In fact I hold that their indiscriminant adoption may be positively harmful . . . I believe that the administration of Indian States should continue to be . . . based upon our ancient customs . . . tradition and culture and above all on the teachings of our ancient Dharma Shastras which are best suited to the temperaments and environments of our people.[57]

Soon the Standing Committee had a backwoods revolt on its hands, fanned, for his own self-interested purposes, by Bikaner. But Patiala held firm, refusing to heed Bikaner's call to postpone the meeting with Irwin, and subsequently the chancellor managed to persuade the chief rebel, Gulab Singh of Rewa, to drop his public agitation against the official package in exchange for the offer of a place on the Chamber team – an offer he failed, in the end, to take up. Thus, when the Simla conference finally got underway, on schedule, on 5 May, Patiala was able to pass himself off as the leader of a united delegation committed to a single set of agreed demands.

Irwin was impressed: not only with the princely party's apparent unanimity, but also with its sincerity and with the thoroughness of its preparation. Therefore, while he had severe reservations about the Standing Committee's call for an inquiry (he dreaded, for one thing, the impact it would have on his already heavy workload, and he did not believe the enquiry would actually solve anything), the viceroy did not feel able to deny them their request; and after taking advice from Watson and Glancy he formally requested the secretary of state to set up the machinery.

The India Office, predictably, were sceptical. Surely, mused Birkenhead, the 'sort of findings that would most completely allay the Princes' apprehensions would be likely only to increase the difficulties of the path ahead' and 'hamper very seriously the conduct of current relations with

[56] Chancellor's circular letter dated 27 Feb. 1927, RSA, Alwar, PSO, file 110 of 1927.
[57] Panna to Patiala 28 Mar. 1927, BRO, Bhopal, Chamber Section, 11, 48/1 of 1927.

the States'? However, like Irwin, the London officials found it hard to refuse loyal allies. Something needed to be done, they conceded, 'merely for the sake of the Princes' peace of mind'.[58] Accordingly, in October 1927, Birkenhead gave the go-ahead for the inquiry. A few weeks later he announced in parliament that the recently retired governor of the United Provinces, Sir Harcourt Butler, had accepted the chairmanship of a three-man committee to 'report upon the relationship between the Paramount Power and the Indian States' and to 'inquire into the financial and economic relations between British India and the States.'[59]

The princes on the Standing Committee received this news with relief and jubilation. Not only had they got their inquiry, but everything about the published terms of reference suggested that it would be a *pukka* and a fair one. The nomination of Butler – 'a very old and true friend', as Jey Singh reminded his colleagues[60] – confirmed that impression. At long last, it seemed that the tide had turned.

Hope extinguished, hope revived

Having spent seven months preparing for the round table conference with Lord Irwin, the COP now had just twelve months to ready itself for the Butler Committee which was due to arrive in India to take evidence sometime during the winter of 1928–9. It was a tall order. Essentially, the Standing Committee had in that time to arrange for, and brief, legal counsel, collect documentation from member states on alleged abuses of paramountcy and infractions of treaty rights, assemble its submission, and put the resultant 'case' to the membership for its approval. Patiala's advisers, led by Rushbrook, told him flatly that the deadline could not be met with the Chamber's existing resources, and that a new 'whole-time organisation' was needed to handle the Butler 'account'. This, they warned, would be expensive. Nevertheless, the chancellor did not flinch. He put the proposition to the Standing Committee and, with its backing, to the full membership at the February 1928 session of the Chamber. Such was Bhupinder Singh's eloquence (and so optimistic were the princes that the Butler inquiry would deliver) that the meeting agreed, not only to the establishment of a new full-time body (dubbed the Special Organisation) but to the creation of a Special Fund to finance it. Patiala, Kashmir and Bhopai all pledged 5 lakhs, Jodhpur 2, Bikaner and Cutch 1½, and Alwar and Nawanagar 1 each. With this injection of cash, the

---

[58] Birkenhead to Irwin 15 Dec. 1927, Irwin Coll., 2; and Sir Arthur Hirtzel, under-sec. state, to Butler, 25 Nov. 1926, Butler Coll., 59.
[59] Quoted in *Report of the Indian States Committee 1928–1929* (London, 1929).
[60] Speech to COP, 27 Feb. 1930, RSA, Alwar, PSO, file 19–IV of 1926.

Special Organisation's annual budget soon approached 18 lakhs, far more than had been spent by the Chamber as a whole in all the previous nine years of its existence.

Did the princes realise what they had brought into being? It is doubtful. For one thing, they were not told, in February 1928, that the joint directors of the new body were to get the viceregal sum of Rs 8,000 per month for their pains; or, indeed, who the recipients of this largesse would be. For another, it is probable that not even the Standing Committee – not even Patiala – anticipated what the Special Organisation's activities would cost the Chamber over the next five years. In the event, the Standing Committee chose to entrust the running of the new executive arm of the Chamber to the scholarly, urbane Kashmiri Brahmin *dewan* of Gwalior, Kailash Haksar, and, more controversially, to the new boy from Patiala, Rushbrook-Williams (which drew from the latter's friend, Frank Brown of *The Times*, the wry comment that Rushbrook seemed to be 'the kind of man who always falls on his feet').[61] Did the COP, nonetheless, get value for its money? Let us see.

The first task which Rushbrook and Haksar undertook – even before the Special Organisation had been fully commissioned – was to secure the services of a reputable English barrister, knowledgeable in the area of international law, to represent the Chamber before the Butler Committee. Arriving in London in the summer of 1927, the two emissaries headed to the chambers of Coward, Chance and Company, solicitors, who had been recommended by a former chief justice of Allahabad, Sir Grimwood Mears; and on their advice, the job of leading counsel was offered to Sir John Simon, the junior's job to Donald Somervell. However, having already accepted the chairmanship of the Statutory Commission, Simon was forced, reluctantly, to pass up 'the biggest fee I have ever seen in my professional life'.[62] And so the brief ended up not with a Liberal MP, but with a Conservative; a privy councillor, and a former solicitor-general, the Right Honourable Sir Leslie Scott, KC, who, as well as being an eminent jurist, had the added advantage of being a personal friend of the secretary of state, an association which dated back to the time they were members of the same law firm in Liverpool. Scott, too, was attracted by the fee; but he was also excited by the legal issues that the brief raised and by the political challenge that it represented. Indeed, it seemed to Rushbrook and Haksar that they had secured, not merely an able lawyer, but a staunch friend and a thorough convert.[63] Accordingly,

---

[61] Sir Frank Brown to Mirza Ismail 25 Feb. 1956, Mirza Ismail Papers.
[62] Sir John Simon, *Retrospect* (London, 1952), 145.
[63] 'Report on the Haksar-Rushbrook-Williams Mission', n.d., RSA, Alwar, PSO, file 121–I of 1927–8.

it was arranged that Scott should visit India before Christmas to meet the princes, access relevant documents, and familiarise himself with the local political situation.

This accomplished, the Rushbrook–Haksar partnership got to work on the politicians and the press: 'we decided to pool at an early date', they recalled later, 'all our private influence in official, political, social and press circles, so that we could mobilise that influence for the service of Their Highnesses'. They cultivated journalists; through the good offices of an old school-chum of Rushbrook's, they gained the ear of Frank Brown, the editor of *The Times*; Rushbrook's wife helped them to meet socially with a number of Conservative MPs and stalwarts of the party organisation; and Haksar's old friend Sir Stanley Reed assisted with introductions to other people in public life; last but not least, the two men threw lavish private dinner parties at their suite in the Ritz for 'all the senior officials' of the India Office. Precisely how much benefit the princes got from the £29,000 which was spent in this way down to 1931 is difficult to say. Certainly, they got very little joy from Sir Michael O'Dwyer or from Lord Reading.[64] Nevertheless, the states received unprecedented publicity during this period, much of it favourable, and through this, many more politicians were made aware of the states' grievances. It is reasonable to suppose that at least some of them became converts.[65]

In the first instance, however, it was the Butler Committee which had to be persuaded, and from this point of view the Standing Committee were immeasurably reassured by the arrival in April of Leslie Scott, replete with a closely argued twenty-page opinion. Scott quite bowled over the chancellor with his charm and erudition; and his passionate conviction, which the opinion appeared to support, that the states had a watertight case,[66] proved infectious. Eventually, even the ever-suspicious Jey Singh was forced to admit that Scott's arguments looked unshakeable. Yet, soon after this things began to go wrong. It had been expected that

---

[64] Reading to Irwin 8 Aug. 1928, Reading (Private) Coll., 107.

[65] Haksar to Bhopal 1 May 1931, BRO, Bhopal, Chamber Section, 45, S-3/44 of 1931–3; Rushbrook to Bhopal 18 May 1931, BRO, Bhopal, Chamber Section, 22, C-11/9 of 1931–3; and 'Report on the Haksar–Rushbrook-Williams Mission'. About £59,000 was sent to Rushbrook in London between 1928 and 1931, of which £30,000 went on legal fees to the Chamber's solicitors. As well as the extensive press coverage, several monographs dealing with the princes' situation were published in London between 1928 and 1930. Perhaps the most influential of these was A. P. Nicholson's aforementioned *Scraps of Paper*, copies of which, according to the author, were bought by 'more than half the members of the . . . Conservative Cabinet'. Nicholson to Mehta 10 Jan. 1931, RSA, Bikaner, PM's Office, A 513–628 of 1931.

[66] After visiting a number of states Scott was 'more than ever convinced of the strength of our case'. Patiala to Sirohi 1 Apr. 1928, RSA, Sirohi, Sadar Office, serial 103, file 36.

the big non-Chamber states – in particular Mysore, Baroda and Hyderabad – would agree to be represented by the Chamber's legal team and help to defray the heavy expenses involved; but none would countenance Scott. Simultaneously, a number of the Chamber's members let it be known that they were less than excited about the prospect of paying for the services of a high-flying (and somewhat controversial) English lawyer, especially as they had not been consulted in advance about his appointment. As a consequence, promised donations to the Special Fund did not eventuate and by June the Chamber found itself staring down the barrel of bankruptcy. On the verge of panic, Patiala appealed to the other members of the Standing Committee to come to the rescue: 'We have to raise three and a third lakhs before end June and two and a half lakhs in August', he wired Alwar. 'I am doing all I can . . . but hope my dearest Dada will consent help whole Order in this great crisis.'[67] This flattery generated some money, but not enough, and in the end Bhupinder Singh had to negotiate an interest-bearing loan from Nawanagar to cover the balance of Scott's £60,000 fee. Then, when it came to actually preparing the case, the Special Organisation experienced great difficulty prising records out of the *darbars* – some of whom had no proper archives – and indeed in getting the princes to respond to the questionnaire it circulated asking for their opinion on the substantive issues which were before the inquiry. When the Butler Committee arrived at Delhi, on 14 January 1928, it found the Chamber still in the throes of assembling its evidence. An embarrassed chancellor was forced to ask for more time, and was greatly relieved when Butler agreed to let the princes defer the presentation of their case until his Committee returned to London in the summer.

However the real trouble began when the contributing members of the COP learned what Scott proposed to say to the Butler Committee on their behalf. After perusing material supplied to him in London by Haksar and Rushbrook, Scott decided that all the rights and obligations of the rulers as British allies were defined essentially by their treaties and engagements, and that the oft-invoked rubric of 'paramountcy' did not endow the viceroy or his political agents 'with any general discretionary right to interfere with the internal sovereignty of the states'.[68] Now this was very good news to those twenty-odd states – including, one might note, five out of seven members of the Standing Committee – whose treaties contained an unambiguous guarantee of internal independence. It was cold comfort to those large states – such as Mysore and Baroda –

---

[67] Patiala to Alwar [?] June 1928, quoted in circular letter from Alwar dated 15 July 1928, RSA, Sirohi, Sadar Office, serial 103, file 38.
[68] A later version of this Opinion, dated 24 July, may be read as Appendix III to the *Report of the Indian States Committee*.

whose treaties gave the government an equally unambiguous right to intervene, or to the overwhelming majority of small states which possessed no treaty at all. Yet in the end it was not so much Scott's opinion on the treaties which condemned him in the eyes of the rank and file, so much as the manifesto he drafted while he was in India summarising his ideas on the constitutional changes required to entrench the sovereign rights he had identified as belonging to the princes. In this manifesto (which bore the cryptic appellation 'Document 4'), Scott proposed, first, the creation of an executive 'States Council', comprising three princes nominated by the Chamber, two English politicians nominated by the crown, and the political secretary, to advise the viceroy on paramountcy questions and to 'thrash out', in concert with the governor-general's council, questions of common concern to the states and the provinces on their 'merits'. Secondly, Scott suggested the setting up of a common supreme court of 'unquestioned competence and impartiality', to deal with justiciable disputes.[69] While these proposals were similar to ones that had been made before, particularly at the time of Montagu's visit in 1917–18, the more liberal *darbars* were alarmed by their narrow and backward-looking character; in particular, by their failure to encompass any mechanism for bringing the states into closer contact with the central or provincial legislatures. It appeared to them (correctly, as it turned out) that Scott was trying to use the princes to further his party's anti-nationalist agenda.

Scenting trouble, the chancellor tried to ward it off by inviting selected rulers to meet Scott at Patiala on 28 March, and, when few bothered to show, by calling a general princes' conference at Bombay on 19 April. But hardly had invitations gone out than Document 4 was leaked to the press, apparently by a prince on the Standing Committee. Comment from British India was even more acerbic than the rulers' comments had been; and Irwin observed caustically that it looked like Scott 'has got his head badly turned either by the size of the fee he hopes to extract from the princes or by the feeling that he has been called upon by a wise providence to save the Indian Empire'.[70] And the conference was not a success. Several Kathiawar states, led by Junagadh, walked out; in the end the Standing Committee was forced to disclaim responsibility for the scheme, which of course did not please Scott.

Nevertheless, such was Scott's magnetism, that the chancellor, and to a lesser extent the Standing Committee, refused to heed the danger signals. Thus, when Butler's report was presented to parliament in March 1929,

[69] Memo encl. in chancellor's circular letter dated 27 Feb. 1928, RSA, Sirohi, Sadar Office, serial 103, file 36.   [70] Irwin to Geoffrey Dawson 21 July 1928, Irwin Coll., 18.

its findings came as a nasty shock to the Chamber's leaders. To be sure, the *Report of the Indian States Committee* did have some good news for them: for instance, it fully endorsed the rulers' assertion that their relations were with the crown, not the government of India, and could not therefore be transferred, without their consent, to 'a new government in British India responsible to an Indian legislature'. However it gave short shrift to Scott's opinion that the powers of paramountcy were defined by what was said in the treaties. 'We cannot agree', wrote the Butler Committee, 'that usage is in any way sterile. Usage has shaped and developed the relationship between the Paramount Power and the States from the earliest times . . . in all cases usage and sufferance have operated to determine questions on which the treaties, engagements and sanads are silent'. More controversially still, the *Report* appeared to qualify the previously unchallenged thesis that the paramount power had an obligation to protect its clients against attempts to overthrow them, or to substitute another form of government. If, it read, there was 'a widespread demand for [constitutional] change' in a state, the latter would be obliged 'to suggest such measures as would satisfy this demand'.[71] Even the political department, which, not surprisingly, was pleased with the bulk of the Butler report, was alarmed by the implications of a doctrine which, as it rightly observed, pushed 'the theory of paramountcy beyond any hitherto accepted limit'.[72]

What had gone wrong? Afterwards, Scott declared the Committee's proceedings to have been a farce, and while this sounds like the whinge of a loser, there is some substance in the claim. The Special Organisation was refused permission to consult records kept in the political department; Scott was denied access to confidential copies of Tupper's *Indian Political Practice* and the manuscript of a more recent, unpublished study of a similar kind by the former AGG Rajputana, Sir Robert Holland; evidence introduced by the princes from documentation supplied by the *darbars* was excluded from the Committee's report; and Scott was refused leave to cross-examine witnesses, which prevented the Chamber from contesting the government's submission. Last but not least, the Committee was carefully primed by the Political Department to return a favourable verdict.[73]

---

[71] *Report of the Indian States Committee*, paras. 58, 40, 57 and 50.
[72] Govt. India to sec. state 13 Sept. 1930, IOR L/P&S/13/550. And see also Irwin to Butler 21 Mar. 1929, Butler Coll., 85.
[73] Worried by Butler's reputation as the author of the *laissez-faire* policy, Birkenhead instructed the viceroy to ensure that the Committee were 'carefully incensed' with the government's views before it started work. Birkenhead to Irwin 15 Dec. 1927, Irwin Coll., 2.

Inevitably, though (and, in the main, justifiably) it was Scott who bore the brunt of the princes' disappointment and anger. At a general conference of princes and ministers in June 1929, called to decide what response the COP should make to Butler's *Report*, several rulers led by Bikaner claimed that the English lawyer had, to all intents and purposes, defrauded the Chamber of a large sum of money.[74] Others concurred with Prabhashankar Pattani that the whole thrust of the Special Organisation's campaign had been misdirected, that instead of attacking paramountcy, the states would be better served pursuing 'good government' and 'redress[ing] . . . grievances' and looking to 'the contentedness of our people'.[75] Others again declared that they could no longer support a strategy which threatened to bring them into collision with their British suzerains and protectors. Despite a spirited defence of the Special Organisation's work in England by Rushbrook, who had flown out from London specially for the meeting, Scott's plan for a published critique of the Butler *Report* and an appeal to the Privy Council never even got to a vote. As he observed testily, 'my draft ultimatum [was] put in the waste-paper basket'.[76] Instead, the conference assigned the task of preparing a formal response to the Butler report to a subcommittee headed by Bikaner, his fiercest critic. A few days later, when the Standing Committee met Irwin at Guneshkhind, Bikaner assured the viceroy that the princes had learned their lesson and were now agreed that all 'the unsatisfactory questions . . . at issue between the British authorities and the States and between the States and British India' should be 'solved by . . . recourse to frank and friendly negotiations, rather than by any legal steps or by any caucus or non-cooperation'.[77]

Bedridden in Patiala with fever, Bhupinder Singh watched with ever-deepening despair the unravelling of his grand design. Publicly he held his peace; privately he agreed with his colleague and sometime friend Alwar that the princely order was facing an 'acute crisis'.[78]

However, just when things were looking at their grimmest, the tide of events began, unexpectedly, to turn the rulers' way. In particular, two things happened. First, the nizam, who for ten years had steadfastly refused to have anything to do with the Chamber, wrote to Patiala soliciting the chancellor's help to rid him of the 'constant interference on the part of the Government of India in my purely private and family affairs', which Osman Ali believed was turning his two sons against him. To have

[74] Note dated 2 July 1930, AP 47/10/42(33A).
[75] Pattani to Patiala 4 May 1929, RSA, Sirohi, Sadar Office, serial 103, file 36.
[76] Memo dated [?] 1931, PSA, COP, 37 (21) of 1931.
[77] Quoted in *The Times*, 22 Oct. 1929.
[78] Note by Alwar's private sec. dated 24 Dec. 1929, RSA, Alwar, PSO, file 121–I of 1927–8.

been addressed at all by the premier ruler in India was something of a coup for the status-conscious Bhupinder Singh; but, better still, the nizam's letter also hinted that rewards of a more substantial kind, such as financial support for the Chamber's campaign, would be forthcoming if Patiala agreed to put in a good word with Lord Irwin.[79] Bhupinder Singh promised to do everything within his power; and early in December Hyderabad made the first of several large donations to the Special Organisation Fund.

The second thing which rescued the princes from despair was the Irwin Declaration of October 1929. A conciliator, for all his Tory pedigree, Irwin had realised that only a bold initiative would deter Congress from its intention, outlined at its Calcutta session of December 1928, to embark on a campaign of civil disobedience if India was not granted 'Dominion Status' – in effect internal self-government – within the year. With this in mind he had persuaded a very unwilling Sir John Simon to 'suggest', by means of an exchange of letters with the prime minister, Ramsay Macdonald, that a meeting of all interested parties, including the princes, be called to discuss the question of constitutional reform in the context of the still-to-be-written report of the Statutory Commission; and that the Statutory Commission's terms of reference should be widened to allow it to make recommendations for the states as well as for the provinces. On 31 October this correspondence was published in London. Simultaneously, the viceroy announced in India that a Round Table Conference (RTC) would take place in London towards the end of 1930, adding that it was the understanding of the government that Dominion Status was the logical and inevitable goal of the process of devolution begun by Montagu in 1917.

The Standing Committee greeted the viceroy's announcement with jubilation, for they saw it, rightly, as offering them the chance of another hearing – this time at the highest political level – on their claims for autonomy. 'Far from feeling any apprehensions', declared Ganga Singh, 'the Princes . . . welcome the proposed Round Table Conference as it will finally set at rest all doubts [about their sovereignty] and . . . clarify the position of the States within the Empire.'[80] Against all the odds, opportunity had knocked for the *darbars* a second time.

---

[79] Hyderabad to Patiala 28 Oct. 1929 and Feb. 24 1930, Gwynne Coll., 8.
[80] Speech at informal conference of rulers and ministers, Feb. 1930, RSA, Bundi, English Records, serial 876, file C 38/IV.

3   A vision splendid

The transcendental merit of this constitution is that it provides for one government for the whole of India . . . It is the Vision Splendid [that] many dreamt of; [but] none hoped to realise in their own days.

The Times of India, 5 March 1931

Flirtations with nationalists

Historians of colonial India have generally glossed over the long and complicated saga of all-India federation: partly, one suspects, *because* it was long and complicated, but also because, as we shall see in chapter 5, this grandest of imperial projects had finally to be abandoned. We need not spend too much time on this episode, the argument runs, since federation, at least in the form in which it was conceived in 1930, was doomed from the start. There are several problems with this view, however. For one thing, it represents a victory for smug hindsight. For another, it significantly underrates how close the federal scheme of 1930, embodied in the India Act of 1935, came to being implemented (before the outbreak of war in 1939 forced the project to be shelved). For a third, it overlooks the fatal impact of the 'failure' of federation on the compact between the princes and their British overlords. Last but not least, it ignores a significant strand in the politics of the 1930s, for this was one time – and perhaps the only time – that the princes occupied the front of the Indian political stage, and had an opportunity to shape their own destiny. How this position of advantage came about, and how it was utilised by the rulers, forms the central theme of this chapter.

Needless to say, the princes were greatly flattered and excited by their invitation to the London RTC. But few of them, in late 1929, gave much thought to the big constitutional issues that the conference was supposed to address, being much more interested in the possibilities which the summit held out for a reopening of the debate on paramountcy.[1]

---

[1] Circular from chancellor dated 27/28 Aug. 1930, PSA, COP, 36 (9) of 1929.

Nevertheless, by year's end there was general recognition in the *darbari* camp that success at the RTC, even in the narrow terms defined by the chancellor, would require detailed forward planning, perhaps even negotiations beforehand with other interested parties. Only Ganga Singh, irascibly, urged the contrary benefits of a free hand. In December 1929, without, it would seem, informing his colleagues, Bhupinder Singh called on Sir Leslie Scott in London and told 'that distinguished lawyer that the Princes would like him to help us [in preparing for the Conference] and that he might consider himself as engaged'.[2] Simultaneously, he authorised the directors of the Special Organisation to take whatever steps they considered necessary to ensure that the states delegation arrived in London properly prepared and in a strong position to negotiate.

In the absence of Rushbrook (who had returned to London to liaise with Scott), this task fell principally to Kailash Haksar, the sagacious minister from Gwalior, and he took full advantage of the opportunity to shape the planning process in ways congenial to his liberal disposition. Firstly, aware that disunity could be fatal to the princes' chances of achieving their goal, he sought, and received, the chancellor's authorisation to sound out Sir Mirza Ismail, the dewan of Mysore, and Sir Akbar Hydari, the finance minister and *de facto* foreign minister of Hyderabad, with a view to forging a common front between the two powerful and wealthy southern states and the COP in advance of the London summit. These overtures were rewarded when for the first time ever both Hyderabad and Mysore sent observers to the Chamber session in Delhi. Meanwhile, at Haksar's suggestion, Bhupinder Singh went to work on Osman Ali and tried to persuade his new friend, in return for continued diplomatic support at Delhi, to throw in his lot with the Chamber once and for all. 'Whatever may be said in respect to the policy of detachment from the Chamber which your Government have unfortunately pursued', he wrote somewhat daringly in April 1930, 'it cannot divest Your Exalted Highness of your responsibilities as the head of the Princely Order.'[3] Osman Ali declined to join the Chamber formally – citing the same reasons he had advanced against the move in 1917 – but he agreed to send Hydari north for further talks with the COP's advisers and to continue to subsidise its operations. Secondly, Haksar persuaded the chancellor of the desirability of sounding out other Indian political groups, not excluding the Congress, to see whether an alliance could be forged in that quarter too. 'There is reason to believe', he informed Akbar Hydari, 'that by quite honest negotiations the representatives of certain sections in British India . . . can be made to support

[2] *Ibid.*   [3] Patiala to Nizam 8 Apr. 1930, PSA, COP, 36 (10) of 1929.

the Princes' claims.'[4] What is more, to the horror of Rushbrook and Scott, who heard about this development too late to nip it in the bud, he got Patiala to agree that the princes should publicly back the nationalist demand, as formulated at the All-Parties Convention of 1928, for an early constitutional advance towards dominion status.

That Haksar wanted an alliance between the princes and the nationalists is not surprising, for he himself had deep roots in the latter camp. As well as being Sir Tej Bahadur Sapru's brother-in-law, he was a close relative of Shiv Narain Haksar, secretary of the Delhi DCC, and his circle in Gwalior included a number of fiercely chauvinistic Maratha irredentists, with links to the Bombay Congress. At least one British official thought him 'an out and out Swarajist'.[5] Much more remarkable (at least on the surface) is the way his scheme was accepted, virtually without demur, by the rulers. 'I think I have induced the Princes not to come in the way of British India's advance', a gleeful Haksar informed Sapru at the end of 1929.[6] His hunch was correct. In January the plan received the assent of the Standing Committee and the following month it was formally endorsed by the full membership at a general conference in Delhi prior to the COP's annual session. What possessed the 'autocratic' princes to support such a radical initiative?

To some extent – not to put too fine a point on it – they were taken in by the artfully deceitful pen of Haksar's brilliant new Malayali deputy K. M. Panikkar, a graduate of Oxford, Sorbonne and the Middle Temple, who had caught the director's attention with a timely book on the relations of the states with the government of India. Panikkar shared Haksar's broad political views and like him had nationalist credentials. Immediately after graduating from Oxford he had edited the Madras *Swarajjya* newspaper, and helped Gandhi diffuse the Akali *gurudwara* agitation in the Punjab; later he had taken part in the Vaikom temple *satyagraha* in his home state of Travancore. Yet he was also very ambitious; liked rubbing shoulders with the powerful; and was attracted by the perks of princely service: 'a fixed residence, freedom from financial worry, facilities for the proper

---

[4] Haksar to Hydari 3 Feb. 1930, AP R/1/47/10/48.

[5] Memo by Sir M. Coatman [Nov.] 1930, Reading Coll., 56 E (1).

[6] Haksar to Sapru [?] Nov. 1929, Sapru Papers, G 2142, 6/7. One of the first converts was Ranjitsinhji of Nawanagar. When the Labour secretary of state, Wedgewood-Benn, met him for the first time in October 1929, he 'found him far from a die-hard opponent to the political development of British India . . . I gathered that the Jam Saheb and most of those with whom he is associated have a good deal of sympathy with the Moderate Politicians in British India; and he committed himself to the view that a clear declaration by the Governor-General as to the goal of British policy . . . would greatly help in clearing away the suspicion that the British are not entirely sincere in their professions of a desire for India's political advancement.' Wedgewood-Benn to Irwin, 24 Oct. 1929, Irwin Collection, 4.

education of . . . [his] children'.[7] Accordingly, tired of journalism and uninterested in practising law, he had joined the Chamber. Nevertheless, Panikkar's inner loyalties remained divided. Thus, when Haksar asked him to draft a memorandum for the Standing Committee canvassing the advantages to the states of a *rapprochement* with the nationalists, he needed no second bidding.[8]

In the main, though, it would be fair to say that the princes went along with the Haksar scheme because they were willing to be convinced. For all their defence of privilege and the imperial connection, the rulers cared deeply for their country and its traditions. 'Adamant as I am in my loyalty to the Crown, so adamant am I in my patriotism and love for my country and religion', declared Jey Singh of Alwar.[9] 'I personally have always held it to be the first duty of an Indian prince that he should also be an Indian Nationalist', affirmed Hamidullah of Bhopal.[10] When Haksar showed them how they could contribute, in a practical way, to India's reemergence as a strong, proud and independent member of the community of nations, his message struck a chord. Moreover, the idea of working closely on this national project with politicians from the provinces did not faze them, because they had long been doing it – intermittently, since 1917, and on a fairly regular basis since the mid-1920s. In the autumn of 1928, for example, M. R. Jayakar and other 'British Indian friends' had held talks in Bikaner during the maharaja's forty-eighth birthday celebrations; the following February, Bikaner and Kashmir had joined the elder Nehru, Jinnah, Malaviyya and Sir Abdul Qaiyum at a working tea-party hosted by Vithalbhai Patel, the Congress Party leader in the Central Legislative Assembly; and in August 1929, the Standing Committee had conferred, at Motilal Nehru's invitation, with a delegation from the All-Parties Convention.[11] As for the notion of working

---

[7] Panikkar, *Autobiography*, 70. Conservative MP Robert Stopford, who met Panikkar during the RTC, said of him: 'he is an able young man who is determined to get on at all costs'. Stopford to the marquess of Zetland 30 Nov. 1931, Stopford Coll., 7.

[8] Unfortunately the memorandum itself cannot be traced; but its arguments were reproduced in the longer version which Panikkar wrote 'in a month' early in 1930 and which was afterwards published, under the joint authorship of Panikkar and Haksar, as *Federal India*. See K.M. Panikkar, *An Autobiography* (Madras, 1977), 83–4.

[9] 'My Epistle to Rama', encl. in Alwar to the king 20 Oct. 1933, IOR L/PO/91.

[10] Speech by Bhopal at the RTC, 15 Jan. 1931, quoted in *The Times of India*, 17 Jan. 1931, 14.

[11] The personnel of the Committee were Motilal Nehru, M. R. Jayakar, M. M. Malaviyya, Sir Tej Bahadur Sapru, Sir Ali Imam (of Berar fame), S. Satyamurthi, Sardar Sardul Singh, M. A. Ansari, Ramchandra Rao and Manilal Kothari. However the meeting, like the All-Parties Convention and its *Report*, was overtaken by the march of events leading to the Congress' decision in December 1929 to launch civil disobedience. This saved the rulers from an awkward situation, because the Nehru *Report* contained some features that they disliked; and they would never have agreed to confer with Kothari, a state subject. See Bhopal to Patiala 6 Sept. 1929, Cutch to Patiala 27 Sept. 1929, and aide-mémoire by chancellor dated [?] Oct. 1929, PSA, COP, 36 (11) of 1929.

alongside the Congress, such reservations as the princes harboured about its political aims for British India were offset by their admiration for the philosophy and social programme of the party's *de facto* leader, the Porbandar-born M. K. Gandhi, and by the fact that Congress had repeatedly made plain its belief that the issue of the constitutional future of the states was one solely for the rulers and their subjects to resolve.[12]

In the event, though, Congress ruled itself out of the equation by deciding, at Lahore in December 1929, to withdraw from the constitutional process and commence a campaign of civil disobedience against the raj with the object of forcing Whitehall to concede *purna swaraj*, or full responsible government. At first, Haksar saw this as a setback to his plans and was very disappointed. On further reflection, though, it occurred to the Special Organisation director that the elimination of the Congress from the field of potential allies might be a blessing in disguise – and so it proved. For one thing, it helped to ease the apprehensions of the conservative princes toward the nationalist programme. For another, the Congress' decision to absent itself from the RTC gave the rulers additional room to manoeuvre, since, by raising the political heat, it increased the chances of a governmental compromise with the moderates on dominion status.[13] Moreover there is some circumstantial evidence that several of the *darbars* – certainly Bhavnagar and Bikaner – were sufficiently impressed by the mass mobilisation and disciplined mass action which followed Gandhi's Salt March to Dandi in March 1930, to want to keep their options open in case the unthinkable actually happened and the British were compelled to withdraw.[14]

So, first the Standing Committee and then the COP at large, took up

---

[12] In her presidential address to the 40th session of the Congress at Cawnpore in 1925, Sarojini Naidu (herself a native of Hyderabad) declared: 'let not the princes believe for a moment that we want to crush them by any subtlety or device, hidden or covert . . . And let them feel that some day when we have the great federation of free India, the Indian states will come in as an integral unit of Greater India working on the same basis of democratic freedom with the people of [British] India.' Quoted in S. H. Patil, *The Congress Party and Princely States* (Bombay, 1981), 18. The policy towards the states between the wars is discussed in Ian Copland, 'Congress Paternalism: The "High Command" and the Struggle for Freedom in Princely India', in Jim Masselos (ed.), *Struggling and Ruling: The Indian National Congress 1885–1985* (New Delhi, 1987), 121–40; and Barbara Ramusack, 'Congress and the People's Movement in Princely India: Ambivalence in Strategy and Organization', in Richard Sisson and Stanley Wolpert, *Congress and Indian Nationalism* (Berkeley, 1988), 377–403.   [13] Haksar to Hydari 3 Feb. 1930, AP R/1/47/10/48.

[14] Bhavnagar's Prabhashankar Pattani went out of his way to visit Gandhi's *ashram* at Sabarmati on the eve of the Salt March, and Bikaner later criticised the government publicly for its draconian handling of peaceful protesters. According to the government's spies, Ganga Singh told the Standing Committee that 'he was convinced Great Britain was down and out and that they had better make terms with the Hindu leaders'. Sir G. Schuster to Irwin, 7 Nov. 1930, Irwin Coll., 19.

the challenge spelled out in the Haksar plan. During the winter, several highly placed princes made public statements supporting the national demand for dominion status,[15] while others, such as Ranjitsinhji of Nawanagar, made their sympathies clear to the new Labour government in London.[16] Meanwhile, feelers were put out to the politicians, and in March more formal conversations were held with a cross-section of moderates including Malaviyya, Muhammad Ali, Jayakar, Jinnah, Sir C. P. Ramaswamy Aiyer and Sir Muhammad Shafi. By the end of February, Haksar had received 'personal assurances from the leading lights of these groups, of supporting the demands of the Princes'.[17] Much encouraged, the rulers deputed Haksar and Sir Manubhai Mehta, the dewan of Bikaner, to continue this dialogue over the summer. However, just as the princes were congratulating themselves on having stitched up a foolproof arrangement which would ensure their success at the RTC, the threads of this ambitious creation began, slowly but surely, to unravel.

The first thing that took the wind out of Haksar's and Patiala's sails was the nizam's decision to severely curtail his association with the Chamber. Miserly with his own finances, Osman Ali was worried by the reports that were beginning to appear in the press about Bhupinder Singh's reckless extravagance, and he began to have serious doubts, too, about the expenses which were being run up – partly with Hyderabad money – by the Special Organisation. But the main cause of his about-face was the skilful propaganda fed to him by the new British resident in Hyderabad, Sir Terence Keyes. Like others in the political department, Keyes was anxious about the radical direction the Chamber was taking under the influence of Kailash Haksar. However, in making his pitch to the nizam, Keyes made a point of emphasising Haksar's connection with 'the so-called Maratha movement',[18] with its irredentist designs on the Marathi-speaking districts of the central provinces, Berar and – by implication – Hyderabad. Haksar, he assured Osman Ali, was a 'most bitter Brahmin' obsessed with a desire to avenge the 'disappearance of the Brahmin power of the Peshwas' of Poona by creating 'blocks' of independent Hindu-ruled states 'with a strong Brahmin flavour in their policy'.[19] This was not total subterfuge, for

---

[15] e.g., Kashmir's press statement, 2 Nov. 1929, quoted in the *Times of India*, 4 Nov. 1929.

[16] The Labour foreign secretary, Wedgewood-Benn, came away from his first interview with Nawanagar with the impression that 'the Jam Saheb and most of those with whom he is associated have a good deal of sympathy with the Moderate Politicians in British India'. Wedgewood-Benn to Irwin, 24 Oct. 1929, Irwin Coll., 4.

[17] Memo, n.d., in 'Explanation of Item 11 on the Informal Agenda', RSA, Bundi, English Records, serial 876, file C 38/IV.

[18] Keyes to Barton [?] Sept. 1930, Keyes Collection, 28.

[19] As described in Keyes to Bray 21 July 1930, Keyes Coll., 28; and Keyes to Pol. Sec., 15 Apr. 1930, IOR L/P&S/13/548.

Keyes genuinely believed in the importance of Hyderabad as a Deccani stronghold of Muslim power and culture. But it was deliberately designed to inflame Osman Ali's ingrained fear and distrust of organised Hinduism – and it worked. In April 1930, the nizam told the chancellor that he was discontinuing his contribution of Rs50,000 a year to the Special Organisation Fund on the grounds that it was being used for other than the purposes originally agreed on; and in July he informed the Standing Committee that Hyderabad would be sending a separate delegation to London.

However, the most crippling blows to the Chamber's plans came from the government of India. As we have seen, Lord Irwin had grown to regard the princes with a certain affection, and in this spirit had successfully pressed the matter of their representation at the RTC on the cabinet. But the viceroy liked his princes pliant, and he found the COP's new political orientation disconcerting. The problem, he told the secretary of state, was that the chiefs had become 'obsessed with the hope and desire of eliminating paramountcy when they come to [the] round table conference', adding that he believed that the directors of the Special Organisation were 'largely responsible for stirring up feeling in this matter'.[20] Eager to nip this scheme in the bud, Irwin took a deliberately hard line when he addressed the Chamber at its annual session in February 1930, flatly rejecting Bikaner's motion that the Standing Committee should be consulted by the government in all cases where intervention in a state's internal affairs was contemplated. Then, when he met the Standing Committee at Simla in July to finalise arrangements for London, he informed them that the government intended to adopt almost all of the recommendations of the Butler report, and that none of the matters dealt with in the report would be permitted to be raised at the RTC.[21] Their 'carefully thought out strategical plan' in ruins, the shell-shocked princes left Simla more than half-convinced that the trip to London was now an empty exercise.

That it all turned out so differently was due, once again, primarily to the imagination, foresight and political acumen of Haksar and Panikkar. Guessing that the government might try to thwart the princes' plans, the two friends sat down after the 1930 Chamber session and reassessed the states' options at the RTC on the assumption that paramountcy was off

[20] Viceroy to sec. state 16 Mar. 1930, IOR L/P&S/13/557.
[21] Minutes of conference at Viceregal Lodge, Simla, 14/15 July 1930, IOR L/P&S/13/557. To soften the blow, Irwin agreed, as a special favour, to request the secretary of state to allow the princes, while in London, to lay their complaints before him at a private meeting at the India Office. See note by Paul Patrick, pol. sec., India Office, dated 27 Nov. 1930, L/PO/93.

the agenda. Was there another way, they asked themselves, that the states could secure their political goals? The answer came almost immediately: by joining an autonomous all-India federation. Federation was a practicable goal. It entailed, so far as the states were concerned, little risk, since central legislative and executive authority already affected them *de facto* via the mechanism of paramountcy; on the other hand, participation in a federation would release the *darbars* from their current subservience to the centre, both in matters of common concern and in respect of paramountcy. Encroachments on the states' domestic freedom of action such as had taken place since 1919 would 'not be possible' if there was a federal legislature and a federal court. As for the dreaded Political Department, this would simply wither away, for once a federation was in place, all matters pertaining to the administration of the states would be 'automatically excluded from the sphere of Paramountcy'. Finally, federation would allow the princes to widen their horizons, extend their power and enhance their prestige and status.[22]

The more Haksar and Panikkar thought about it, the more they were convinced that 'from the standpoint of the Indian States themselves, federation was the one course by which they could achieve the aims which they had so long had in view'.[23] Now, all they had to do was sell their splendid vision to the rulers.

The federal solution

The two bureaucrats never for a moment imagined that this was going to be an easy task. While the idea of all-India federation had been around for at least a decade[24] and had been canvassed on several occasions by Haksar himself, it was still a novel concept and one which had few supporters. For instance, when Haksar had raised it with the Standing Committee in 1927, he had been told that the idea was 'out of the question'.[25] However, this time around it was not so much the body of princes who proved obstructive but one in particular – the chancellor – ironically a prince whose support Haksar and Panikkar had counted on. To be sure,

[22] Note by Haksar dated [?] Sept. 1930, PSA, COP, file 36 (9) of 1929; memo by Haksar on 'Federalism' prepared for meeting of ISD on 25 Oct. 1930, PSA, COP, file 37 (21) of 1931; Haksar to Sapru 5 Oct. 1932, Sapru Papers, 6/7, G 2142.

[23] Confdl. memo No. 2, n.d., RSA, Sirohi, Sadar Office, file 127 of 1931.

[24] See above, pp.39–40; draft note by Alwar [?] 1918, GSAB, Baroda, Pol. Dept., section 341, file 33; letter from Sir Albion Banerji, foreign minister Kashmir, to *The Times*, 17 Nov. 1926; and D. V. Gundappa, 'The Indian States Committee: A Note On Its Terms of Reference and Their Implications' [1928], Jayakar Papers, 81 (1).

[25] Note of meeting between Alwar and the AGG Rajputana, Col. Ogilvie, 12 Feb. 1928, RSA, Alwar, PSO, 121–I of 1927–8.

Bhupinder Singh's main concern had always been the elimination of paramountcy rather than the building of bridges with British India; nevertheless, it is doubtful whether his opposition would have reached the heights that it did, had it not been for certain changes which occurred in his domestic circumstances and, as a consequence of this, in his relations with the government of India.

The event which triggered this mid-reign crisis was an unbridled personal attack on him by the extremist wing of the Sikh Akali Dal, aided and abetted by the newly formed All-India States Peoples' Conference and its local affiliate, the Punjab Riasti Praja Mandal. In February 1930, an AISPC-appointed five-man 'enquiry committee' headed by the respected Liberal politician C. Y. Chintamani, published a pamphlet called, unambiguously, *Indictment of Patiala*, accusing the maharaja of having instigated the murder of at least one of his subjects, of having condoned 'Inhuman tortures, illegal arrests, confinements and confiscations', of having misappropriated public funds for private ends, and of causing girls to be abducted from the Pahari Hills and confined, for immoral purposes, in his *zenana*.[26] Miraculously, these embarrassing allegations did not cost Patiala a fifth term as chancellor, although it was a close-run thing, but with the RTC coming up the maharaja felt constrained to try to clear his name. Accordingly, in May 1930, he took the bold but risky step of inviting the government to conduct an official inquiry. Delhi, in turn, placed the matter in the hands of the new AGG Punjab, J. A. O. Fitzpatrick.

As an ally of the king and head of the COP, Bhupinder Singh expected a friendly hearing – and he got one. Fitzpatrick agreed to the maharaja's request to take evidence *in camera* and refused to give governmental protection to witnesses testifying against the *darbar*. He also declined to allow Patiala to be cross-examined. On 4 August Simla announced, on the basis of the AGG's report, that they were satisfied that the charges against Patiala were the 'outcome of a deliberate conspiracy' by 'revolutionary' elements to destabilise the maharaja's rule.[27] Nevertheless, Bhupinder Singh did not escape unscathed. At the conclusion of the enquiry the political secretary, Watson, called Patiala in and gave him a stern lecture about his lax morals and spendthrift habits. If things continued on their present course, the maharaja was told, he would be dealt with as the nizam had been in 1926.[28] After such a dressing down, and with the

---

[26] The pamphlet was entitled, unambiguously, *Indictment of Patiala*. When he saw the published version Chintamani was so appalled that he publicly dissociated himself from it. See *Indian Annual Register*, 1930, I, 506–20.

[27] Quoted in Reginald Reynolds, *The White Sahibs* (London, 1930), 398. See also viceroy to sec. state 2 Apr. 1930, Irwin Coll., 5; and note by Wilberforce-Bell dated 19 July 1930, IOR R/1/1/1917(1).   [28] Note by Irwin dated 5 Aug. 1930, IOR R/1/1/2024.

threat of intervention hanging over his head, Patiala would have been very anxious to keep in the government's good books. But there may have been more. Fitzpatrick was an arch Tory, a 'diehard' before the term had gained the notoriety it was to do over the next decade. He distrusted most nationalists, regarded the Congress as a thoroughly wicked organisation, and thought the British government's conciliatory policy, as embodied in the Irwin Declaration, a recipe for disaster. Unlike his colleague Keyes, he supported totally the continued separation of the 'two Indias'.[29] We know that Fitzpatrick saw Patiala privately several times during and after the inquiry. As well as telling Patiala to mend his manners, did the AGG hint that the Chamber's political leanings too were a matter for regret in Delhi? Did he suggest that Bhupinder Singh cool the Special Organisation's ardour for a federation with the nationalist-dominated provinces? The official record (naturally enough) is silent, but Patiala's erratic behaviour that summer and autumn indicates that pressure was applied – and that Bhupinder Singh buckled under it.

At any rate, when Haksar and Panikkar came to the chancellor with their idea in advance of the Simla conference with the viceroy (remembering that at this point the Standing Committee still believed they would be able to raise their grievances on paramountcy in London) he cavalierly dismissed it as an exercise in star-gazing; and later censured Haksar for trying to hijack the agenda for the conference with a federalist position paper on 'machinery for dealing with matters of common concern' with the provinces.[30] Ironically, despite these precautions on Patiala's part, the subject of federation was raised at Simla – by Irwin, who wanted to test the water. However the Standing Committee and the ministers representing the non-Chamber states gave it short shrift. As the Hyderabad delegation informed the nizam, 'all [the] States including Mysore are at present opposed to any commitment for immediate [entry] . . . into Federation'.[31]

Patiala persisted in this stonewalling approach during the autumn and indeed right up to the eve of the RTC; but it was not his only tactic. Realising that he could not keep the lid on federation talk indefinitely, and aware that some of the ministers, if not yet the princes, were starting to take it seriously, he tried to stack the states' delegation to London with men he thought he could control. Back in February, it had been decided in consultation with the government that ten places at the RTC should go

[29] Little of this is spelled out in black and white, but the gist can be deduced from a close reading of Fitzpatrick's reports, e.g. to Wilberforce-Bell, dep. sec. Pol. Dept. 4 Aug. 1930, IOR R/1/1/2024.   [30] Note by Patiala dated [?] June 1930, PSA, COP, 36 (10) of 1929.
[31] Akbar Hydari, Charles Chevenix-Trench, Mahdi Yar Jung and Amin Jung to Nizam (teleg.), 11 July 1930, Keyes Coll., 28.

to representatives of the states. In March, Patiala presented the Standing Committee with a draft ticket which included only two ministers, and none from the big non-Chamber states. There was uproar. Sensing that the numbers were against him, Patiala volunteered to expand his list to include Manubhai Mehta from Bikaner, a minister from Baroda, and the raja of Sangli (another Bikaner supporter) as a representative of the small states. This compromise was accepted, whereupon a new list was drawn up with the ministers ranked in order of preference; yet somehow during the process of retyping in the chancellor's office, Rushbrook-Williams' name came to be inserted above that of Mehta, while that of the Baroda minister got left out altogether.[32] On 6 May, without alerting his colleagues on the Standing Committee or seeking their authorisation, Bhupinder Singh submitted this revised list to Lord Irwin.

It was a bold throw, and Patiala almost got away with it. According to Keyes, the political secretary had 'practically agreed' to exclude all non-Chamber states from the delegation by the time news of Patiala's machinations filtered south;[33] likewise Irwin initially seems to have been unfazed by Patiala's omission of Sangli and Mehta. However, not for the first or last time, Bhupinder Singh's plans were wrecked by some resolute action on the part of the wily Bikaner. Ganga Singh did not yet fully perceive what lay behind Patiala's conduct. He attributed it mainly 'to His Highness' personal jealousy and unfriendliness towards me'.[34] But he understood clearly enough that the chancellor's team was unrepresentative and he resolved that it should not stand. On 28 May he cabled the chancellor from Bombay demanding an explanation for his behaviour; and on 2 June, Bhopal, at Ganga Singh's instigation, upbraided Patiala for presuming to exclude Mehta, a minister 'possessing intimate knowledge of our affairs'.[35] Stalling for time, Patiala delayed answering these communications for nearly a month, and then merely restated his arguments for giving preference to Haksar and Rushbrook. But Bikaner was not to be put off. On 6 July he wrote separately to Mirza Ismail and Akbar Hydari explaining what had happened, bucketing Patiala's leadership of the COP and soliciting their support for a united approach to the viceroy:

His Highness the Maharaja of Patiala has . . . yet to favour his colleagues of the Standing Committee . . . with the reasons, necessity, urgency, and, above all, his authority for his having, as Chancellor of the Chamber of Princes, addressed his tentative reply to the Viceroy . . . containing proposals, widely differing from the

[32] Note by Bikaner dated 2 July 1930, encl. in Bikaner to Hydari 6 July 1930, AP R/1/47/10/42(33A).   [33] Keyes to Barton [?] Sept. 1930, Keyes Coll., 28.
[34] Circular letter from Bikaner dated 4/7 Aug. 1931, RSA, Alwar, PSO, file 156 of 1931.
[35] Bhopal to Patiala 2 June 1930, PSA, COP, 36(10) of 1929.

view and proposals of the . . . Standing Committee, and made on the Chancellor's own account and without reference to his colleagues . . .

I have heard adverse criticisms of late, and expressions of definite views that – in spite of the established practices of the last fourteen years . . . if things develop along certain lines, the Chancellor might, in days to come, assume the functions and role of a 'dictator' instead of – what has all along been intended – to his working under the Chamber and with the Standing Committee.[36]

Hydari and Mirza were not much bothered about Patiala's alleged dictatorial tendencies – their states not being members of the Chamber – but they were alarmed at the possibility that they might be excluded from the Indian States Delegation (ISD) to London. Both approached Irwin on the matter. Meanwhile, Bikaner himself had managed to get the ear of the political secretary, Watson. This combined initiative resulted in a suggestion from the viceroy to the chancellor that he might wish to 'revise' his list. Of course it was an offer he could not refuse. Nevertheless Patiala managed to preserve something of his ticket by persuading the viceroy to expand the ISD by two, which allowed him to include both Mehta and Sangli while keeping his own core of loyalists intact.[37] Thanks to this compromise, the states' team that arrived in London at the beginning of October included only two pro-federationists among the rulers (Bhopal and the gaekwar), and was deeply divided on both regional and ideological lines.

By this time, however, Haksar and Panikkar had gained two very powerful converts in the shape of Hyderabad and Mysore. It will be remembered that the resident at Hyderabad, Sir Terence Keyes, was a fierce opponent of the Chamber and especially of its Special Organisation. Paradoxically, though, Keyes was also an ardent federationist. Like most British officials of his day and class (such as Fitzpatrick) he was afraid of real democracy, or as he put it, the 'principle of counting heads'; however, as an imperialist of somewhat broader vision than his colleague in the Punjab, Keyes understood the need for managed political change and saw the states with their 'indigenous' character and 'high measure of sovereignty' as providing an essential stabilising element in any reformed Indian constitution. To Keyes an all-India federation offered the British a 'chance of . . . neutralising all the disruptive forces that exist in India', of shoring up the raj.[38] Thus, with 'a plan for India almost clear cut' in his

---

[36] Note by Bikaner dated 2 July 1930, encl. in Bikaner to Hydari, 6 July 1930, AP R/1/47/10/42(33A) See also Bikaner to Mirza Ismail 6 July 1930, *ibid.*

[37] The final team was Patiala, Bikaner, Baroda, Kashmir, Alwar, Bhopal, Rewa, Sangli, Akbar Hydari representing Hyderabad, Mirza Ismail representing Mysore, Kailash Haksar and Manubhai Mehta. Panikkar went too as secretary, but he did not have a seat at the table.

[38] Note by Keyes encl. in letter to Irwin 2 July 1930, Keyes Coll., 28; and Keyes to Sir Philip [Chetwode] 1 July 1931, Keyes Coll., 29.

mind,[39] the resident launched a private and wholly unauthorised crusade to convert the Hyderabad *darbar* to the cause of federation. As before, he played on the nizam's fears, sketching for Osman Ali a dire scenario of what could easily befall Hyderabad once the provinces got their autonomy. At very least, he predicted, it was likely that, free of British control, the provincial politicians would lend their backing to local insurgency movements; at worst, there could be 'frequent military demonstrations within India and, in the end . . . regular civil wars'. However, the keynote of his pitch to the nizam was that the ruler possessed the power, by a stroke of the pen, to secure his future against the hostile forces arraigned against it. Inside a federation, enthused Keyes, the state would be protected by constitutional guarantees of 'mutual non-interference' and by its voting power in the federal executive and legislature, which would give it 'the same say' in formulating policy as 'any of the major Provinces'.[40] This was powerful, persuasive stuff, and by midsummer Keyes felt he had the nizam in his pocket. He was later to claim Osman Ali as his earliest 'convert to Federation'.[41]

However Keyes struck trouble when, in advance of the Simla summit, he put his proposals formally to the Hyderabad executive council. Although the veteran president Sir Kishen Pershad and the finance minister, Hydari, were both initially receptive, the powerful English revenue minister, Sir Richard Trench, taking his cue from the recently published Simon report, believed that the needs of the states could be satisfied by the creation of an advisory 'Council for Greater India' such as the Standing Committee had envisaged back in 1927.[42] Then Hydari got cold feet. As already noted, the finance minister had long been an admirer of Gandhi and the Congress. Indeed, by his own reckoning this was the main reason why an otherwise distinguished career had not yet attracted imperial recognition.[43] As well, he had connections with Congress through his daughter, who was a paid up member of the party, through his lawyer cousin, Abbas Tyabji, and through his community, the Khojas of Bombay city. Thus, when Congress launched civil disobedience early in 1930 Hydari found himself pulled between conflicting loyalties, and this dilemma became more acute in the early summer when, during a break

---

[39] Keyes to Frederick Oliver 24 Nov. 1930, Keyes Coll., 28.
[40] Keyes to Hyderabad 30 June 1930, Keyes Coll., 28.
[41] Keyes to Lothian 30 Aug. 1931, Keyes Coll., 29.
[42] Notes by Sir Richard Chevenix-Trench dated 27 June 1930, AP R/1/47/10/8 and 3 July 1930, AP R/1/47/10/52. Earlier Keyes had thought that he had 'brought the Council round to my point of view'. Keyes to Watson 14 June 1930, IOR L/P&S/13/666, he was mistaken.
[43] Keyes believed a promised CIE in 1919 had been withdrawn after he 'played up to Gandhi and Jinnah'. Keyes to Watson 10 Mar. 1931, IOR L/P&S/13/548.

on a business trip to Bombay, he visited the Congress hospital where his daughter was working as a volunteer, and saw the victims of police *lathi* charges laid out in gory testimony to the severity of governmental repression. Even before this, Hydari may have absorbed something of the official Congress opposition to the RTC; but after Bombay his hostility was overt. 'Hydari's last visit to Bombay', exploded Keyes, 'has frightened the wits out of that chicken-hearted little creature.'[44] Soon after this Keyes learned to his sorrow that the Hyderabad delegation at Simla had joined with the other states in putting federation on the back-burner.

A lesser man might have capitulated; but Keyes was a fighter. Even as the four-man Hyderabad contingent for London left early in August to take ship at Bombay, he convinced Osman Ali to rewrite their instructions in a more purposeful vein, and drove at high speed to Bombay to deliver them personally into Hydari's hands. Not surprisingly he found the finance minister 'reproachful' at this intrusion, and still looking to appease the Congress. Yet things were to change dramatically as the S.S. *Narkunda* with its 'cargo of delegates'[45] left Bombay behind and sailed west across the Arabian Sea. Perhaps it was, as Keyes afterwards maintained, the force of his personal appeal at Bombay which wrought the transformation; or perhaps it was the ensuing voyage: the bracing sea air and the good company and the leisurely pace of shipboard life, which allowed ample time for discussion and reflection. But whatever it was, the effect on Hydari was remarkable. By the time the ship got to Aden he had reached agreement with Mirza Ismail of Mysore and Sir Tej Bahadur Sapru on the basics of a plan whereby the states, led by Hyderabad, would offer to join a reformed, Westminster-style federal government. As another member of the company, the government of India's Sir George Schuster recollected:

My voyage home proved to be of some significance because I had, as fellow passengers, a delegation from the Indian States led [*sic*] by Sir Akbar Hydari. On our first days [out] he started conversations with me about certain plans which he intended to put forward on behalf of the Indian Princes – plans for an All-Indian Federation . . . These ideas seemed to me of such significance that I took the occasion of our normal stop at Aden to telephone to the Viceroy. He agreed with me about the importance of this new initiative and asked me to send him a full report and also to get Hydari to produce a written statement of his general plan.[46]

This was not the last time the Hyderabad minister would surprise his colleagues by a sudden change of direction. Indeed, Hydari's ability to trim

[44] Keyes to Cunningham 5 July 1930, Keyes Coll., 28.
[45] Keyes to PSV 16 Nov. 1932, Keyes Coll., 30.
[46] George Schuster, *Private Work and Public Causes: A Personal Record 1881–1978* (Cambridge, 1979), 105.

his sails to the prevailing political wind became a trademark of his career. But none of his later shifts had quite the same consequences as this one, for in retrospect it can fairly be said that Hydari's conversion on the sea-road to Aden marked the moment when all-India federation became practical politics.

Nevertheless, selling federation to the ISD proved a long and thorny business. When the delegation assembled for the first of five preliminary meetings at St James' Palace on 11 October 1930 they were handed copies of a note by Haksar which posed a series of hypothetical questions. One of these read: 'What should be the attitude of the Delegation if any scheme of Federal Government for the whole of India is put foward?'[47] However no-one wanted to bite the bullet – either then or at the second meeting a fortnight later. According to the official minutes, 'The sense of the meeting was that it is not practicable to have an all-India scheme ready at the present stage, nor is it necessary for the States to put forward such a scheme.'[48] Indeed as late as the end of October, just two weeks before the RTC was due to start, it would seem that the princes of the Chamber group had still 'not . . . faced squarely the issue of federation'.[49]

As before, the diffidence of the princely contingent stemmed mainly from natural caution. Conservatives like Gulab Singh of Rewa were convinced that federation would 'lead to democratization in the States and [institutionalised] aggression from the young nationalism of British India',[50] and if Tory MP Robert Stopford is to be believed, these intransigents received plenty of encouragement from elements within the India Office;[51] conversely, moderates such as Sangli and Kashmir, while sympathetic to the principle of association, were dubious about the practicalities. Besides, the princes assembled in London were serious men acutely conscious of their responsibilities, as dynastic rulers, to their subjects and heirs; they were not about to be hurried into making critical decisions about the future of their patrimony. Nevertheless, the selling of federation to the princes was made harder than it should have been by the failure of the pro-federationist ministers to pull together. Comparing notes in London, Haksar, Hydari and Mirza found that while they agreed on the need for a federal structure, they had very different conceptions of what was involved and differing motivations for wanting to build one: and arguments soon broke out over the optimum size of the federal legislature, whether it should be uni- or bi-cameral, and whether the princes'

---

[47] Note by Haksar [?] Oct. 1930, PSA, COP, file 37 (21) of 1931.
[48] Minutes of the second meeting of the ISD, 27 Oct. 1930, PSA, COP, file 37 (20) of 1931.
[49] Memo by Patrick dated 31 Oct. 1930, IOR L/P&S/13/547.
[50] Note by Rewa circulated to ISD [?] Nov. 1930, IOR L/PO/93.
[51] Note by Stopford on discussion with Panikkar 25 Nov. 1930, Stopford Coll., 9.

representatives should be allowed to vote on legislation which did not directly concern their states.[52] And these differences of opinion were sharpened by personal rivalries and animosities which, if anything, grew more pronounced as opening day approached. According to John Coatman, an adviser to the Liberal Party delegation, 'Mirza Ismail is very angry with the Northern Princes . . . he thinks that they do not want to do real business and he says that if necessary he will commit Mysore, Travancore and Cochin to a real plan of federation and let the others do what they please about it.'[53] Likewise, the fact that Mirza and Hydari were distantly related did not stop them from falling out over the latter's unconcealed urge to turn the Conference into a vehicle for his personal advancement. Hydari 'is desperately jealous of Mirza', observed Keyes, as he watched his goal of a south Indian combination fade away.[54] And Hydari's own bargaining position was not improved by the nizam's advice to Patiala to 'be careful in dealing with the members of the Hyderabad delegation' on the ground that they were 'traitors and . . . servants of the Government of India'.[55]

Slowly, however, the intensive lobbying and frenetic shuttle diplomacy of the pro-federation ministers (and especially of the suave Panikkar) began to bear fruit. As regards the princes, what had at first seemed strange and threatening began to appear, as the mechanics of federalism were explained to them by the ministers, logical and compelling, particularly as Haksar and Panikkar were careful, in outlining the options available to the ISD, to 'emphasize all the sweets and omit . . . [all] the sacrifices'.[56] Once the seed of understanding had been planted by this clever propaganda, peer-group pressure, and the dynamics of daily close confinement over a period of weeks in an environment far from home, and thus mildly disorientating, all helped to bring it to fruition. Meanwhile, bit by bit, with Sapru and Jayakar acting as go-betweens,[57] a deal with the British Indian delegation was stitched up, and on 2 November it was presented to the full ISD for ratification. A few days later Harry Haig, the government of India's special observer at the RTC, wired Delhi with the news that the 'States as a whole are considering seriously the possibilities of some immediate federal union with

---

[52] K. N. Haksar and K. M. Panikkar, *Federal India* (London, 1930), 150; note by Hydari dated 2 Oct. 1930, IOR L/P&S/13/548; and memo. by Paul Patrick dated 31 Oct. 1930, IOR L/P&S/13/547.   [53] Memo by Coatman [?] Nov. 1930, Reading Coll., 56E (1).

[54] Keyes to Todhunter 17 Nov. 1930, Keyes Coll., 28.

[55] Nizam to Patiala 1 Oct. 1930, Gwynne Coll., 8.

[56] Note by Stopford on conversation with Panikkar, 25 Nov. 1930, Stopford Coll., 9.

[57] On Sapru's role see D. A. Low, 'Sir Tej Bahadur Sapru and the First Round-Table Conference', in Low (ed.), *Soundings in Modern South Asian History* (London, 1968), 294–329.

British India', adding that if this was true it 'would largely transform Central problem and open up considerations not discussed by Government of India.'[58] Nevertheless it was was not until 10 November, only hours before the Conference was due to begin, that the text of the speeches to be given by the states' delegates on opening day were finally approved.[59] Thus, even though the government had an indication of what to expect, many of the other delegates, and the members of the press and others watching proceedings in the public gallery, were stunned when first, Ganga Singh of Bikaner, and then, in turn, Sayaji Rao of Baroda, Hari Singh of Kashmir, Akbar Hydari of Hyderabad and Mirza Ismail of Mysore announced, in response to a carefully orchestrated 'invitation' from the British Indian delegation, that they were ready and willing to join an all-India federation occupying 'a position of honour and equality in the British Commonwealth of Nations'.[60] Keyes spoke for many when he dubbed the first day's events at St James' Palace a 'miracle'.[61]

The princes' astonishing offer made them instant celebrities, which further strengthened their emotional commitment to the cause which they had taken up. But the real beneficiaries of the initiative were the British cabinet, who, having set up the RTC in the expectation that it would provide them with a ready-made solution to the Indian problem, had begun to think, with Robert Stopford, that, what with the Hindu–Muslim antagonism in the Indian camp and the antipathy of the majority Conservative and Liberal delegations, still smarting over Macdonald's treatment of Simon, towards the idea of responsible government at the centre, the experiment was going to end ignominiously in 'dismal failure'.[62] Coming like a bolt from the blue, the princes' offer to make a federal compact with the provinces, in the words of Bhopal's political secretary, 'revolutionised the position',[63] for it made it possible for the Liberals, and saner elements among the Tories, to contemplate limited central responsibility in the knowledge that the princes would be there to restrain the more rampant nationalists. As the astute UP governor Malcolm Hailey put it, in a letter to Irwin: 'if we could obtain a Federal assembly in which they [the states] were well represented, and in which the Viceroy would have a wide nomination in order to discharge his responsibilities to Parliament, then we should all of us be prepared to go

[58] Sec. of state to viceroy 7 Nov. 1930, Irwin Coll., 5.
[59] Minutes of 5th meeting of ISD, 10 Nov. 1930, PSA, COP, 37 (20) of 1931.
[60] Speech by Kashmir at RTC, 12 Nov. 1930, *IAR* 1930, II, 280.
[61] Keyes to Todhunter 17 Nov. 1930, Keyes Coll., 28.
[62] Diary entry, 9 Nov. 1930, Stopford Coll., 2.
[63] Note dated 21 Nov. 1930, BRO, Bhopal, Chamber Section, file 12, 3/15 of 1930.

much further in the way of responsible Government than we should if matters . . . [had been left to take] their ordinary [course]'.[64]

The transformation in the situation was not instantaneous, for it took time for the parties to assimilate all the implications of the princely offer, and longer still for those on the Right to bring themselves to act on them. But gradually, beginning with the Labour Party, whose mouthpiece the *Manchester Guardian* had been intensively briefed by Haksar, the dominoes fell. Prior to 10 November, the leader of the Liberal delegation Lord Reading, whose reputation as an Indian expert made him a crucial player, had been staunchly opposed to dominion status. Caught off-guard like everyone else by the states' initiative, he invited Mirza Ismail next day to afternoon tea at his town house in Curzon Street, and asked him whether the princes 'were really serious'.[65] Assured that they were, Reading called a meeting of his delegation and told them that it was his considered opinion that 'the whole situation had been changed by the attitude towards Federation adopted by the Princes and the other Indian delegates to the Conference'.[66] The princes were 'ag[ains]t separation' and 'ag[ains]t Bolshevism and Communism', he added emphatically, seemingly forgetful of his own disparaging assessment of their political leanings only a few years previously.[67] Reading's, and the Liberal Party's conversion to the cause of all-India federation in turn put pressure on the Conservatives to follow suit, since it had already been agreed that the two delegations would coordinate their approach. And a short time later they did so, although it took several stormy meetings, and a lot of frenetic back-stairs lobbying, before the opposition leader Stanley Baldwin and the Tories' spokesman on India Sir Samuel Hoare were able to persuade the majority of the party to accompany them on the road to reform.[68]

This did not in itself guarantee that everything at this first session of the RTC would go smoothly. During its nine weeks of deliberations, the conference experienced numerous standoffs and deadlocks, not least in respect of the communal problem and the Muslim demand for weighted representation in the legislature; while the Federal Structure Committee, appointed to make recommendations on the mechanics of all-India federation, went through a period of drift until it was pulled into line by its able and sagacious chairman, Lord Sankey. However, by December, the

---

[64] Hailey to Irwin 14 Nov. 1930, Irwin Coll., 19.
[65] Sir Mirza Ismail, *My Public Life: Recollections and Reflections* (London, 1954), 64.
[66] Minutes of meeting of the Liberal Delegation 19 Nov. 1930, Reading Coll., 56G.
[67] *Ibid.*
[68] Coatman to Irwin, 21 Nov. 1930, Irwin Collection, 19. A minority of Tories led by Winston Churchill, who resigned from the shadow cabinet in January 1931, refused to accept the new line. They became the 'Diehards'. See below, chapter 4.

crucial hurdle – the question of dominion status – had been cleared, and Prime Minister Ramsay Macdonald was able to wind up the proceedings on 19 January on a note of well-founded optimism. Thanks to the courageous and daring offer by the princes it appeared that, at long last, the British had found a practicable way out of their Indian dilemma.

The parting of the ways

The ISD arrived home at the end of January 1931 feeling well pleased with themselves: and with good reason. To all intents and purposes 'the Indian States [now] held the future of India . . . in the hollow of their hands'.[69] Wrapped in euphoria, they never doubted for a moment that they would be able to persuade the rest of the princely order to endorse the bold commitment that they had made.[70]

However, when the delegation members finally got round to consulting their constituencies they found, to their consternation, little enthusiasm for the federal idea. A public meeting called by Mirza to explain the implications of federation to Mysoreans drew only a meagre audience; while a questionnaire distributed to the 109 members of the COP elicited just 55 responses, of which 9 were downright hostile and others lukewarm. Similarly, Akbar Hydari's efforts to sell the idea in Hyderabad were vitiated by the indifference of the nizam (who seems to have quickly repented his promises on the subject to Keyes), by his low social standing, as a *ghair-mulki*, in the eyes of the hereditary Hyderabad aristocracy, and by his enemies' apprehension that the international prestige he had gained in London might prompt Osman Ali to make him president of the executive council.[71] What is more, the opposition proved hard to shift. Despite the best efforts of the Standing Committee and its southern allies, anti-federation sentiment grew steadily. By April the new chancellor, Hamidullah Khan of Bhopal, belatedly realised he had a major problem on his hands.

[69] 'Policy Pursued By Indian States Delegation At The Round Table Conference', Confdl. memo No. 2, n.d., by Kailash Haksar, RSA, Sirohi, Sadar Office, file 127 of 1931.

[70] So confident were Haksar and Panikkar, that on reaching India they at once approached Sapru and Jayakar about forming a new all-India Centre Party. One of their first steps towards this end was to investigate the purchase of a daily newspaper to act as a party mouthpiece. Both the ailing *Daily Mail* of Bombay and the equally straitened *Pioneer* of Allahabad were approached in this context. See Sapru to Jayakar 8 Apr. 1931, Jayakar Papers, 454; note by Haksar dated 27 Apr. 1931, BRO, Bhopal, Chamber Section, 50, C-2/55 of 1931–3; and Sapru to Bikaner 13 June 1931, Sapru Papers, 24, G 2150.

[71] Keyes to Watson 10 Mar. 1931, IOR L/P&S/13/548. Although he had worked in Hyderabad for over a decade, Hydari, born in Bombay, remained to the inner circle at court an outsider. On Hyderabadi nativist chauvenism see Karen Leonard, 'The Mulki–Non-Mulki Conflict' in Jeffrey, *People, Princes and Paramount Power*, 65–106.

Why did a scheme of all-India federation which appeared to hold out such glittering prospects for the princely order generate so much alarm? In 1931, the most important and vocal critics of the ISD's federal scheme were the conservative Rajput rulers from central India led by Gulab Singh of Rewa and Udaibhan Singh of Dholpur – basically the same group which had tried to subvert the Chamber's push for reform in 1927. Fervent autocrats all (a political officer once remarked, only half in jest, that Udaibhan's views on divine right would have made Charles I blush), Rewa, Dholpur and company did not want to be associated, even marginally, with democracy, and believed that federation would inevitably result in the subordination of the states to 'the rule of the united majority from British India, who are republicans at heart'.[72] However, while their passion and sincerity made them opponents to be reckoned with, the conservative hard-liners were too few to pose a real threat to the acceptance of the scheme by the princely order. More dangerous by far, because it potentially involved a large majority of the order, was the attitude of the rulers of the small, 'second and third class' states who, at first apparently indifferent, began, from the time of the annual COP session in February 1931, to display increasing signs of unease.

Again, monarchical values underpinned this negative response; but on the whole this group were less worried by the ideological implications of federation than by what it might mean for the survival of their states as independent entities. As we have seen, one of the mooted attractions of the federation idea was that it would give the states a voice at the centre, and thereby a means of protection from the rampant politicians in the provinces. But that scenario depended on them obtaining a seat in at least one of the two projected federal houses; unrepresented, a state would have no voice and its interests would be entirely at the mercy of others. Thus, from the start most rulers made individual representation in the legislature a 'condition precedent' for their acceptance of the scheme.[73] However it was apparent that, even to accommodate all the 109 states eligible to sit in the COP, several criteria would need to be met. First, the legislature would need to be very big; second, at least one house (presumably the upper) would have to be, like the Australian Senate, a 'states house', representative of the units of the federation rather than of ordinary citizens; third, there would need to be approximate parity of representation as between the states collectively and British India. Accordingly when, early in 1931, the government called for submissions on the seats

---

[72] Dholpur to Sir Samuel Hoare 3 Nov. 1932, Templewood Coll., 17.
[73] Danta and Wankaner to Bhopal (draft) 4 Aug. 1931, RSA, Sirohi, Sadar Office, file 127 of 1931;

question, the ISD put forward a proposal for a nominated upper house of 250 seats, half reserved for the states, and a partly elected, partly nominated lower house of 350 seats apportioned as between the states and the provinces in the ratio 40:60 – that is to say broadly along population lines.[74]

However the claim was advanced without much conviction. The ministers from the big states, Hydari and Mirza, had all along believed that a select upper house composed of between 60 and 100 'efficient men with a sense of responsibility'[75] (men, no doubt, such as themselves) would provide the strongest guarantee of the rights of the states within the federal structure; and while Ganga Singh and Hamidullah did not share their preference, they got a clear impression from their talks with the government and the moderate politicians that when the RTC resumed its business it was likely to opt for an upper house of around 150. 'If you have only 150 [seats]', wrote Bikaner anxiously, 'I do not quite know how we are going to fit in [all our] . . . members.'[76] As this unwelcome news spread, more and more of the Chamber's members came to believe, with the yuvaraj of Limbdi, that all-India federation would lead to the 'extinction of a large majority of the States as substantive units'.[77] Confused, angry and fearful for their future, these rulers needed only a leader with flair and authority to show them the way. In June 1931 the hour and the man came together in the ample shape of the maharaja of Patiala.

The foundations of Bhupinder Singh's defection were laid at the RTC. Patiala went to London confident that his machinations had brought the federation brushfire under control. But sea-air euphoria, the indefatigable lobbying of Haksar and Panikkar and the flaws in his own character conspired against him. Brilliant when it came to grasping the large picture, Bhupinder Singh was much less at home in the world of detail, especially when the details were of an arcane constitutional nature; and while a rousing speaker when occasion demanded, he was less effective as a debater of issues. Last but not least, he was an essentially fun-loving man and therefore easily distracted. Thus, once the ISD got down to serious work, Patiala's intellectual limitations were sorely exposed, and he found himself – the man supposedly calling the shots – increasingly pushed aside by more agile performers. After a week of this, pique got the

---

[74] Haksar to Fitze 9 July 1931, IOR L/P&S/13/547. These recommendations were based on the princes' replies to the aforementioned questionnaire. See note by Haksar, n.d., PSA, COP, file 113 (8) of 1931.

[75] Speech by Hydari at informal meeting at Delhi, 20 Mar. 1931, quoted in viceroy to sec. of state 23 Mar. 1931, IOR L/P&S/13/547.

[76] Circular letter dated 10 July 1931, RSA, Alwar, PSO, file 156 of 1931.

[77] Note by the Yuvaraj of Limbdi dated 28 June 1931, PSA, COP, file 29 (14) of 1931.

better of him and he retired, on the pretext of a sore throat, to the sanctuary of his top-floor suite at the Hyde Park Hotel; and shortly afterwards left for Paris. In his absence Bikaner spoke first for the princes, completing the chancellor's humiliation.

At this point, with Patiala at his most vulnerable, Leslie Scott reappeared on the scene determined to undercut the princes' support for the federal scheme which he saw as potentially dangerous for the states and possibly fatal for British imperial interests in the subcontinent. As a shrewd operator, however, Scott did not attack the federal concept directly, but rather sought to play on the rulers' paranoia about paramountcy, reminding the ISD that the slate had not yet been wiped clean:

If they [the princes] are controlled by an undefined and unlimited paramountcy, if they are subject to unknown 'residuary' powers, as claimed by the Government of India, they are not free men, and the part which they can play in the moulding of the future constitution will be rendered to a great extent ineffective . . .

I believe the Princes have drifted into a position of great danger in regard to . . . their sovereign rights. Unless they take very strong action immediately, utilising the opportunity afforded them by the Round Table Conference, I fear, indeed I feel practically certain, that they will be finally defeated in the long battle for the definition of Paramountcy . . . I think the present opportunity is the last they will ever get.

Urging that the 'next few days' were critical, if the 'fatal' mistakes which had been made by the Standing Committee since the Simla conference were to be put right, Scott proposed that the ISD should forward to Macdonald, as chairman of the RTC, a 'carefully worded diplomatic letter' demanding a judicial inquiry into paramountcy and making it plain that if the request was refused, they would have no alternative but to withdraw from the Conference and hold the government responsible for the breakdown.[78]

Tabling this unwelcome missive at the ISDs next meeting at St James' Palace, Panikkar and Haksar strenuously counselled the delegation against heeding 'a lawyer-cum-politician's opinion' intended to dupe the princes into being 'used as levers and handles for a retrograde policy'.[79] But Rushbrook-Williams argued forcefully in Scott's defence;[80] and Patiala, sensing an opportunity to recapture lost ground, rushed back from Paris and into the fray with a barrage of 'veiled references and insin-

[78] Memo. by Scott encl. in letter to Haksar, 18 Nov. 1930, PSA, COP, file 37 (21) of 1931.
[79] Note by sec., ISD, n.d., AP R/1/47/10/42; and memo. by Haksar [?] Oct. 1930, PSA, COP, file 37 (21) of 1931.
[80] Panikkar to Bhopal 4 June 1931, BRO, Bhopal, Chamber Section. file 22, C-4/9 of 1932–3. For Rushbrook-Williams' views on the Scott strategy, see note by Patrick dated 22 Nov. 1930, L/PO/93.

uations' to the disloyalty which had been displayed in his absence by some members of the delegation.[81] Unexpectedly the pro-federationists found themselves on the defensive and Ganga Singh was forced, in an attempt to defuse the situation, to insert some pious references to paramountcy in his speech of 17 November.

However, Scott, as we have seen, was now widely distrusted in the princely camp as a man who failed to deliver on his promises, while Bhupinder Singh's erratic behaviour over the previous months had undermined his authority over the Standing Committee. Although their combined call for a stand on paramountcy struck a chord, especially with the princely members, the ISD decisively rejected Scott's plea for an ultimatum on the subject, condemning it as a reckless strategy born of desperation; and in the end Ganga Singh managed to prevail on the princes to keep their gripes about the political department for the private meeting with the secretary of state which had been set up by Irwin. Defeated yet again by his old adversary, suffused with 'impotent rage at seeing others succeeding him and taking the lead',[82] Patiala announced on 18 November 1930 that he was vacating the chancellorship because of ill-health.

Time, though, is a great healer, particularly of emotional wounds, and within weeks Bhupinder Singh had convinced himself that his decision to step down had been premature, and unnecessary. Moreover, he yearned to get even, and that was harder to do from the sidelines. Accordingly, soon after his return to India, Patiala reentered political life with something like his old zest and flair. First, he started a whisper campaign designed to discredit his fellow members of the ISD, putting it about, through one of his associates, that Bikaner had been 'conspiring with the British Indian seditionists and agitators' and that Hamidullah of Bhopal was embroiled in an anti-Hindu conspiracy.[83] Then he announced his candidacy for the chancellorship. But fate had one more shock in store for the embattled maharaja, for when election day came round the princes went, not for experience but youth, in the shape of Hamidullah of Bhopal. Indeed, such was the swing against him that Patiala was very nearly eliminated in the ballot for the Standing Committee, getting in only on a countback after a tie for last place with the lowly raja of Sangli. Apparently the electorate had been swayed by Bhupinder Singh's lacklustre performance at the RTC, and by the persistent rumours that some of the money collected to finance the Special Organisation's work in

[81] Bikaner to Irwin 27 Nov. 1930, Irwin Coll., 19.
[82] Interview with Bikaner in *The Times of India*, 23 June 1931.
[83] Circular letter from Bikaner, 4/7 Aug. 1931, RSA, Alwar, PSO, file 156 of 1931.

England had been hived off to service Patiala's mushrooming debts.[84] Rejected by his old constituency, which broadly speaking had consisted of princes committed to change, Bhupinder Singh looked around for another, and found it in the growing body of rulers anxious to preserve the constitutional *status quo*.

Nevertheless, Patiala's decision to raise the anti-federation standard was not, as Bikaner scornfully asserted, just 'an electioneering stunt pure and simple'.[85] Behind it lay a mixture of motives, and not all were entirely self-serving. For one thing, Bhupinder Singh had come to share many of the doubts and reservations of his constituents about the ISD's scheme. He feared the competitiveness of a parliamentary system and worried, like Rewa, that the states' representatives would be swamped by the nationalist hordes from the provinces. He dreaded what it might cost. Following Scott, he deplored the scheme's lack of safeguards for princely rights and its failure to confront the challenge of paramountcy, which, on the face of it, would 'continue to be exercised by the representatives of the Crown in the same unreasonable manner as before'. Looking down the track he foresaw 'inevitable interference by the federal legislature and the federal executive not only in respect of federalised subjects but also in matters outside the scope of the federal constitution'.[86] For another, Patiala seems to have been influenced by the consideration that the scheme had not yet won the support of the Congress. As we have seen, Bhupinder Singh had always believed in talking to the enemy. After the civil disobedience movement was suspended in March 1931 he resumed this dialogue, writing, amongst others, to Bhulabhai Desai and Jawaharlal Nehru. He was told, unequivocally, that the princes' participation in an all-Indian federation of the sort which had been proposed in London would not be in the national interest.[87] Finding himself, quite fortuitously, in agreement with the Congress leaders on this matter, Bhupinder Singh thought he saw a good way to win some influential and much-needed backing in his long-running fight with the Akalis for hegemony over the Sikh *panth*.

Moreover, there are strong indications that Patiala's revolt against federation was encouraged, and perhaps even facilitated, by elements within the government of India. With the exception of Irwin and a few of his senior officers such as Haig and Hailey and of course Keyes at Hyderabad, the news of the federal compact was received coolly by the

---

[84] Haksar to Bhopal 1 May 1931, BRO, Bhopal, Chamber Section, file 45 S-3/44 of 1931–3.
[85] Bikaner interview in *The Times of India*, 23 June 1931.
[86] Circular letter from Patiala [13] June 1931, PSA, COP, file 29 (14) of 1931.
[87] Desai to Patiala 28 Aug. 1931, Bhulabhai Desai Papers; and Nehru to Patiala 16 Sept. 1931, Jawaharlal Nehru Papers, 81/4779.

Indian bureaucrats. Many British serving officers in India shared the Die-hards' view that central responsibility, even with the promised safeguards, was incompatible with the maintenance of Britain's imperial position in the subcontinent; and senior members of the government disliked the fact that Whitehall had given the go-ahead to all-India federation without consultation and in spite of Delhi's clear preference, enunciated in its dis-patch of September 1930, for a more limited type of reform along the lines of that suggested in the Simon *Report*.[88] As for the politicals, federa-tion threatened not only their own lucrative jobs but also, more distantly, their romantic vision of the princely kingdoms as preserves of order and continuity in a changing world – for they too gave the *darbars* little chance of surviving in a democratic environment. Acting secretary Bertrand Glancy was quite sincere when he opined that federation would prove 'fatal to the States'.[89] Moreover, these attitudes seem to have infected the incoming viceroy Lord Willingdon, who succeeded Irwin in 1931, having previously governed both Bombay and Madras earlier in the century. 'I have [all along] thought it very odd and very undesirable for the Princes to tumble into a [commitment to] Federation', he wrote to the new secre-tary of state, Samuel Hoare, early in 1932.[90]

Yet, the question remains: did the government of India confine its opposition to federation to the realm of argument, or did it actually try to sabotage the scheme by warning off the rulers? Needless to say, there are no directives about it on file, and Willingdon's private papers disclose no covert activities on the part of the viceroy. The only direct evidence of official pressure that I have been able to discover is in the papers of Colonel Frederick Bailey, who was at that time AGG in Central India.[91] Yet at the time rumours abounded. Conservative MP J. C. Davidson, who was in Delhi during the winter of 1931–2, believed that the viceroy was up to his neck in it: 'the fact is', he informed Hoare in March 1932, 'Willingdon has all along been opposed to Federation and only a few days ago advised Travancore to stay out.'[92] Haksar, likewise, believed that political officers had received firm orders to 'keep the States under their influence out of the Federation', on pain of being passed over for

[88] Lord Lothian to Hoare 30 Apr. 1932, Templewood Coll., 14. This may have been the source of finance member Sir George Schuster's reported opposition, which sits uneasily with Schuster's liberalism. B. L. Mitter to Jayakar, 7 Apr. 1931, Jayakar Papers, file 407 (2).

[89] Note by B. J. Glancy dated 18 Jan. 1933, IOR l/P&S/13/888. See also his note dated 15 May 1927, IOR R/1/1/1668(1).

[90] Willingdon to Hoare 27 Mar. 1932, Templewood Coll., 5. See also Sir R. Glancy to Findlater Stewart, 28 Mar. 1932, Findlater Stewart Coll., 11.

[91] Bailey to Rewa 3 Oct. 1931, Bailey Coll., 293.

[92] Davidson to Hoare 24 Mar. 1932, Templewood Coll., 14.

promotion;[93] while Keyes claimed he had evidence that the political department was 'trying to frighten the States out of Federation by harping on the financial strings'.[94] Did this pressure extend, specifically, to Patiala?

Again, conclusive evidence is lacking. However we do have, courtesy of the local correspondent of the *Indian Daily Mail* the intriguing snippet of information that Patiala and his political officer, Fitzpatrick, spent a lot of time in each other's company in Simla in the early part of June 1931. According to the correspondent, this encounter was no coincidence, but was set up by Fitzpatrick, whose die-hard political views have already been noted, so that he could discreetly assist Bhupinder Singh plan his attack on the ISD scheme.[95] Ordinarily, one does not give much credence to newspaper gossip. But this particular allegation seems plausible. As we know, Bhupinder Singh owed Fitzpatrick a favour; secondly, the memorandum with which Patiala launched his campaign bears the unmistakable stamp of being written by a native English speaker; thirdly, and perhaps most tellingly, the campaign began just days after the aforesaid Simla encounter.

On 10 June *The Statesman* of Calcutta carried a front page story that Patiala had put himself at the head of 'a revolt' that was being organised by princes against the proposals made at the RTC. Assuming a beatup, the chancellor at once cabled the maharaja seeking a denial of the allegation,[96] to be told ingenuously by Patiala that he had simply written a 'note' 'to clearly illustrate the genuine dangers and pitfalls which we may encounter if we blindfoldedly accept the principle of Federation under the present circumstances'.[97] Now seriously alarmed, Bhopal begged Bhupinder Singh not to circulate the document at least until the Standing Committee had had a chance to examine it. But his words fell on deaf ears. On 13 June Patiala's note – actually a five-page memorandum – was sent under a covering letter to all members of the Chamber and three days later it was released to the press. The revolt foreshadowed by the *Statesman* had begun.

[93] Haksar to Sapru 18 Feb. 1933, Sapru Papers, 6/7, G2142. Haksar nominated McKenzie's elevation from the Jaipur residency to Hyderabad in 1933 and the accelerated promotion of the then secretary to the resident of Mysore, Corfield, as cases in point. On the other hand, Keyes certainly believed that his advocacy of federation did him no good: 'one is so ignored by the Secretariat', he wrote in November 1932, 'that I can't flatter myself that my services are really of any further use'. Keyes to Sir R. Glancy 6 Nov. 1932, Keyes Coll., 30.   [94] Keyes to Sir M. Gwyer 6 Mar. 1932, Keyes Coll., 31.
[95] *Indian Daily Mail*, 16 June 1931.
[96] Bhopal to Patiala 11 June 1931, PSA, COP, file 29 (14) of 1931.
[97] Patiala to Bhopal 12 June 1931, PSA, COP, file 29 (14) of 1931.

Daunting discoveries

Patiala hoped that his memorandum of 13 June 1931 would help to cement the widespread but fragmented opposition to the ISD in advance of the general meeting of princes and ministers, set down for the end of the month in Bombay, which had been called by the chancellor to decide the Chamber's approach to the second session of the RTC. He was not disappointed. Within the week the nawab of Rampur had made public his opposition to federation. The nawab of Bahawalpur, the yuvaraj of Limbdi, the maharao of Cutch, the nawab of Sachin, the prime minister of Indore, Sir S. M. Bapna, Pattani of Bhavnagar and the maharaja of Talcher on behalf of the Orissa states quickly followed suit as did, quite unexpectedly, the raja of Sangli. Although Haksar tried to make light of these defections,[98] the opening day of the Bombay conference, when Bikaner and Bhopal came in for sustained and sometimes vitriolic criticism from the floor, showed that Patiala had found a winning recipe. It was plain, even to Willingdon, that the new chancellor had become 'terribly unpopular'.[99]

Belatedly realising that they had a real fight on their hands, the Standing Committee launched a vigorous counter-attack. In a 'Note on the Implications of Federation' circulated to COP members, Hamidullah reiterated the ISD's claim that federation would eliminate existing 'encroachment[s] on the authority of the States' and challenged Bhupinder Singh's assertion that in a federal assembly the representatives of the states and British India would naturally 'be ranged against each other', predicting that 'voting would be more likely to be along .. regional' lines.[100] Using similar arguments, the jam sahib of Nawanagar tried to drum up support in Western India.[101] More crudely, that canny street-fighter Ganga Singh put it about that the 'Patiala clique' were acting at the bidding of the officials[102] and in a desire to protect themselves, and their states, from parliamentary scrutiny:

if His Highness of Patiala and his associates . . . of his school of thought only took a little more trouble and did something practical and substantial to ensure the happiness, prosperity and contentment of the peoples of their States . . . and if

---

[98] Haksar to Sapru 2 June 1931, Sapru Papers, 6/7, G2142; and Haksar to Bhopal 11 June 1931, BRO, Bhopal, Chamber Section, file 84, A-6/48 of 1931–3.

[99] Lord Willingdon to his son 31 July 1931, Willingdon Coll. Characteristically, the viceroy could not resist pointing out the fact to Bhopal. Willingdon to Bhopal 10 Aug. 1931, IOR L/P&S/13/549.

[100] Memo by chancellor dated 12 May 1931, RSA, Alwar, PSO, file 156 of 1931.

[101] Circular letter from Nawanagar, 19 July 1931, PSA, COP, file 29 (14) of 1931.

[102] Bikaner to Bhopal 13 July 1931, BRO, Bhopal, Chamber Section, file 47, H-2/52 of 1931–3.

they will again, where called for, put their own houses in order, then they would not feel so alarmed by the claims valid and invalid of Paramountcy, or by the rising tide of democracy. . . . No Ruler, no Government or Ministers . . . can forever oppose legitimate popular demands . . . for the essentials of good Government in their territories. If all Rulers would pay attention to their duties and responsibilities . . . the present day position of the States would be far happier and brighter and their claims would . . . be rendered . . . irresistible.[103]

More public and hard-hitting than anything previously seen in the decorous precincts of the COP, this propaganda blitz managed to slow Patiala's momentum. At the June conference in Bombay, the raja of Baria had been 'decidedly in a mood of unfriendliness' towards the ISD, but three weeks later he had 'become a resolved and discerning convert'.[104] Similar indications of support came in from the rulers of Banswarra and Tripura. Nevertheless, the core of Bhupinder Singh's support amongst the smaller states remained staunch, and in a dramatic show of strength on the eve of the ISD's departure for London to attend the second sitting of the RTC, he mobilised thirty states under his banner at Bombay. With this backing, Bhupinder Singh was able to demand two places on the delegation for his faction, one of which went, at the expense of Haksar, to his chief minister, Nawab Liaquat Hyat Khan, brother of the future Unionist Party premier of the Punjab,[105] the other to his cousin Udaibhan Singh of Dholpur. Of course he could have chosen to go himself; but with the bitter memories of the previous winter still fresh in his mind, Patiala was happy on this occasion to let others claim the limelight while he pulled the strings.[106]

Already powerful, Patiala's position was further strengthened by developments at the second RTC, which appeared to confirm his assertions about the perils of federation for the states. In July 1931 all-India federation was still a nebulous concept, open to differing interpretations; by the conclusion of the second session in late November a finite constitutional structure had begun to emerge – and for the princes the picture had some ominous features. For instance, the tendency in Sankey's Federal

---

[103] Circular letter from Bikaner, 9 Aug. 1931, RSA, Alwar, PSO, file 156 of 1931.
[104] Bikaner to Bhopal 15 July 1931, BRO, Bhopal, Chamber Section, file 47, H-2/52 of 1931–3.
[105] In London Paul Patrick concluded that Haksar 'had rather dropped in the estimation of the Chamber'. Minute dated 20 May 1931, IOR L/P&S/13/546.
[106] This was certainly a correct assumption in the case with Liaquat; but the upright and highly principled Udaibhan went to London convinced that he was his own man. As he wrote just before his departure, he saw himself as acting 'with an absolute selfless motive and an honest heart'. Circular letter [4] Sept. 1931, RSA, Bundi, English Records, Serial No. 896, file C-70/A. On the other hand, Patiala may have been counting on Dholpur's reputation for integrity to absolve him of any accusation of double-dealing.

Structure Committee was for the category of federal subjects to be progressively widened to include such matters as the regulation of labour in
mines and factories, the control of epidemic diseases and interstate
migration; and there was also talk of a list of 'fundamental federal rights'
which it would be incumbent on each federating unit to enforce in the
areas under its jurisdiction. Again, the ISD were disturbed to find, as the
FSC's deliberations progressed, that they had a different conception from
most of the British Indian delegates as to what was entailed in making a
subject 'federal'. Even when it came to the subject of communications,
which all parties accepted as falling within the federal sphere, the states
were reluctant to concede the federal government an executive role. It
was the 'desire of the Indian States', opined Hydari, 'that the actual
administration of State Railways should be in their own hands' – and the
same applied to post offices, sanitation and the gathering of statistics.[107]
Last but not least, it concerned the ISD that their friends among the
British Indian delegates increasingly favoured the federal government
taking over the central role performed by the existing government of
India. 'Their object', declared an agitated Hydari, 'is to preserve under a
federal facade what, so far as British India is concerned, will be a Unitary
Government.'[108] This was far from what, in November 1930, the princes
had imagined they were bringing into being.

Another worrying aspect of the emerging picture, particularly from the
rulers' perspective, was the ability of the proposed federal constitution to
safeguard their prerogatives. When they first raised this issue, the princes
were told to look to the protection of the federal court; but this recourse
was of limited utility because it applied only to rights of sovereignty which
had been federalised. As far as their dynastic rights were concerned, it
appeared that they would have to continue to rely on the reserve powers
of the crown. The question was, would the crown in the person of the
viceroy be willing or able under the new arrangements to discharge this
responsibility as it had done in the past? The princes had serious doubts.
'I could never agree to Hyderabad entering the Federation', wrote Mir
Osman Ali, 'unless the Viceroy, as representative of the Crown, were
invested, separately from the Federal Government, with the authority and
material power to implement the treaties between the States and the
Crown.'[109] And their apprehensions were redoubled by the appearance,
early in 1932, of the interim report of Lord Sankey's Committee. The
Sankey report spoke of a 'transition period' after which the crown in India

---

[107] Speech by Hydari to the RTC Consultative Committee, Delhi, 1 Mar. 1932, Moonje
Papers, Subject File 19 (2).   [108] Hydari to Keyes 11 May 1931, Keyes Coll., 28.
[109] Hyderabad to Willingdon 1 Aug. 1931, IOR L/P&S/13/541.

would be effectively the king advised by the ministers of his federal government. This opened up the nightmarish prospect, for the states, of the king being obliged to appoint a native-born governor-general.[110]

The second round of deliberations in London also heightened the states' fears about their chances of surviving in a party-controlled federal legislature. Against the ISD's wishes, the FSC came down on the side of fixed terms for members of the federal upper house, thereby shattering the princes' expectations that they would be able to keep their representatives on a tight rein through the threat of recall. And, despite a fervent plea from Bikaner through his prime minister, Manubhai Mehta,[111] the FSC came down in its third and final report in favour of a moderately sized upper house of 200, with just 40 per cent of the seats reserved for the states. The raja of Morvi at once registered his 'great alarm' in a cable to Sankey, while Rajpipla warned that the FSC's decision would 'have [a] most prejudicial effect upon entry of the states into federation'.[112] Similar cries of outrage emanated from Jhalawar, Cambay, Udaipur, Baria, Balasinor, Lunawada, Sant, Bansda, Danta, Sachin, Dharampur and Mudhol.

Conversely, though, one aspect of the federal puzzle caused concern not because it had become clearer but because it remained, in Rewa's words, cloaked in 'dark shadows'.[113] This was the fiscal aspect. As we have seen, the *darbars* believed themselves, with some justification, to have been penalised by the government of India's tax policies; thus one of the potentially attractive things about federation was the knowledge that it would make the existing tax-sharing arrangements between the provinces and the states redundant. However the states wanted a firm assurance, in advance, that any such revision would be, at the very least, revenue neutral. As Sir Sukdeo Prasad, the chief minister of Udaipur, put it, his master the maharana would not enter any federation if it meant 'exposing his dear subjects . . . to extra taxation'.[114] More particularly the *darbars* sought an 'assurance of the solvency of the Federation', and a guarantee that they would not be required to bail out the indebted provinces, whose financial position had been badly eroded by the plunge in agricultural prices associated with the world depression. This they did not get, although 'our representatives held their

[110] On this prospect see the Opinion of the Hyderabad solicitors encl. in Coward, Chance and Co. to Hydari 29 July 1932, Keyes Coll., 30.
[111] Speech by Sir Manubhai Mehta, PM of Bikaner, 28 Nov. 1932, Moonje Papers, Subject File 19 (1).
[112] Morvi to Sankey 20 Nov. 1931, and Rajpipla to Sankey 21 Nov. 1931, IOR L/P&S/13/547.
[113] Speech by Rewa at Simla meeting with the viceroy, 21 Sept. 1932, IOR L/P&S/13/550.
[114] Note encl. in Prasad to resdt. Mewar 4 Apr. 1932, IOR L/P&S/13/547.

ground firmly'.[115] The rulers were also disturbed to learn that the expert committee under the chairmanship of British MP John Davidson, appointed at the end of the second RTC to work out the fine details of a provincial-state financial settlement, did not have to stay within the generous guidelines drawn up by Hydari's Federal Finance SubCommittee, and had the right to make alternative suggestions. 'It seems to me', reflected Robert Stopford, 'that British India is asking the States to take a leap in the dark, and that when the States find after federation that the burden is greater than they expected, there will be a lot of trouble.'[116] As the counter-arguments against federation began to stack up, several important *darbars* moved across into the opposition camp, including Kolhapur[117] and the Rajputana big three of Udaipur, Jodhpur and Jaipur.

Meanwhile, taking advantage of the fact that both Bikaner and Bhopal were out of the country, Patiala increased the pressure on some of the smaller states which had not yet committed themselves to either side. Weekly bulletins were issued to friendly states spurring their ministers on to greater efforts; 'selected workers' were sent out to make new converts and 'confidentially . . . to canvass support for His Highness for [the] chancellorship'; and regular press statements were issued summarising the latest unpromising developments at the RTC in order to show how everything seemed 'to swing towards [a] greater need for safeguards'.[118] There were even plans for a three-week propaganda tour by the maharaja of north and central India, though these had to be put on hold when Bhupinder Singh came down with a recurrence of fever. Gradually, too, this campaign started to have an effect, with several of the major Kathiawar princes, led by the jam sahib, deciding to switch sides at a meeting at Jamnagar early in the new year. With the numbers continuing to drift Patiala's way, Jayakar begged Bikaner to redouble his efforts, especially in regard to the smaller states.[119] But by this stage even the redoubtable Ganga Singh had begun to wonder whether federation was a saleable product. Willingdon found him, in November 1931, after the maharaja's return from London, looking jaded and 'weakened very considerably in his enthusiasm for the Princes entering a Federal scheme'.[120] Only

[115] Bulletin No. 5 from Bhopal dated 15 Oct. 1931, RSA, Sirohi, Sadar Office, file 127 of 1931.   [116] Stopford to Lord Peel, 16 Oct. 1931, Stopford Coll., 7.

[117] Kolhapur's motives were mixed. Apprehensive about the direction the federal scheme was taking, the maharaja was also miffed that his dewan, Surve, had not been included in the ISD.

[118] Note by R. C. Khanna, personal sec. to Patiala, dated 31 Dec. 1931, PSA, COP, file 31 (23) of 1931; and Patiala to Sachin 2 Aug. 1931, PSA, COP, file 29 (14) of 1931.

[119] Jayakar to Bikaner 28 Dec. 1931, Jayakar Papers, 455. See also Panikkar, *Indian Princes in Council*, 67.   [120] Willingdon to Hoare 30 Nov. 1931, Templewood Coll., 5.

Hydari, who by this stage had well and truly put his career on the federation line, remained staunchly, even defiantly, optimistic.[121]

It was in London, though, that the success of Patiala's revolt against
federation excited perhaps the greatest dismay. The National government
which took office in Britain in August 1931, although Tory dominated,
remained wedded to the Round Table process and more generally to the
goal of Indian reform. No less than its predecessor, it was committed to
making a dominion status constitution, with all that that entailed in the
way of central responsibility. However, as Willingdon quickly discovered
when he suggested to the incoming secretary of state, Samuel Hoare, that
the government might find it easier to win across the board political
support for its proposals if it settled for a more limited 'British Indian
Federal Scheme',[122] the Conservatives had no intention of proceeding
down the central responsibility road without the states. All along, they
had counted on the prospect of the princes or their nominees playing a
stabilising role in the federal legislature. As Hoare testily reminded the
viceroy:

The Government and I are pledged at every turn to the All-India Federation . . .
Over and over again we have emphasised this fact in public and particularly in the
Parliamentary debates. So far as I myself am concerned I could not have made the
Conservatives move at all without this condition and if it had not been made per-
sistently clear in the last Parliamentary debate we should have had [no more than]
20 Conservatives supporting the Government.[123]

With a section of the Tory back-bench already in revolt over India, the
last thing the secretary of state needed was the princes to defect too. Yet
by the end of the second RTC it had become as obvious to him as to
Willingdon that the rulers' enthusiasm for federation was waning. 'I have
been terribly depressed', he confided to the viceroy, 'by the individual
talks I have had with almost all the members of the Conference and particularly with the Princes, for I have found that we have scarcely a friend
among them . . . I have been really horrified by the impression that these
talks have left upon me.'[124]

Faced with a situation that looked more desperate with each passing
day, Hoare was ready to consider almost any expedient that would keep
the princes solid. As early as September 1931, he put it to Willingdon that

---

[121] Some of Hydari's critics thought his good humour might have had a lot to do with the
delights of the conference social round. See Sarojini Naidu's comments on one of his
and Lady Hydari's lavish London dinner parties in her letter to Padmaja Naidu, 1 Dec.
1931, Padmaja Naidu Papers.
[122] Willingdon to Hoare 17 Jan. 1932, Templewood Coll., 5.
[123] Hoare to Willingdon 28 Jan. 1932, Templewood Coll., 1.
[124] Hoare to Willingdon 2 Oct. 1931, Templewood Coll., 1. And see also Willingdon to
Hoare 30 Nov. 1931, *ibid*, 5.

it was 'very desirable' that the princes' anxiety on the score of paramountcy should be laid to rest, adding that he himself was 'prepared to go
further' than any of his predecessors in the direction of defining occasions
for intervention and taking advice from other rulers about the form of
intervention.[125] Getting no joy, he tried again in October, asking the
viceroy if he could 'go someway to meet the Princes' demands' – if not on
paramountcy, then at least 'in smaller things'. For example, would the
government of India be prepared to reconsider the proposed merger of
the Gwalior and Bhopal agencies, which had 'terribly upset' the young
chancellor?[126] Could it see its way clear to satisfy Mysore on its demand
for a reduction in its tribute? Or Baroda with regard to the gaekwar's
claim to suzerainty over the states of Gujarat? Or Hyderabad on the
Berars? 'It is most important that the Nizam should enter the
Federation', the secretary of state added emphatically, 'and any decision
that will be likely to keep him out must at all costs be avoided.'[127]

Dutifully Willingdon agreed to refer the matters raised to the political
department; but this did not suit Hoare at all. Like others, he strongly suspected that the department had all along deliberately stonewalled on
federation and would continue to do so. With the princes due to pro-
nounce on the Sankey scheme at the next Chamber session, scheduled for
March 1932, the drift away from all-India federation had to be arrested
quickly, before the trickle became a flood. So he tried another tack. Surely
the viceroy had some personal influence with the rulers? Could he not
twist a few arms?

it does seem to me vital that even if we cannot get a definite 'yes' out of them at the
meeting of the Chamber of Princes, we should certainly refuse to take a 'no' from
them. I feel sure that you will not let them say 'no', and if it looks as though they
are getting ready to make a negative answer may I ask if you could get the
Chamber adjourned, or anyhow something done that would prevent the door
being closed? If the door is closed, it will have a disastrous reaction here.[128]

Willingdon was sceptical, but he agreed to try. As the princes and ministers gathered in Delhi, the British cabinet held its collective breath.

The Delhi Pact

By the end of 1931 the maharaja of Patiala had split the princely order
down the middle; and it seemed only a matter of time before the Patiala
anti-federation juggernaut went on to crush its remaining opponents. Yet,

[125] Sec. state to GOI 9 and 18 Sept. 1931, IOR L/P&S/13/550.
[126] Hoare to Willingdon 2 Oct. 1931, Templewood Coll., 1.
[127] Minute by Hoare dated 14 Feb. 1932, IOR L/P&S/13/541.
[128] Hoare to Willingdon 3 Mar. 1932, Templewood Coll., 1.

to Bhupinder Singh's increasing frustration, final victory eluded him. No matter how much he pleaded, reasoned and intrigued, he was unable to capture the states that really mattered – the major states. Hyderabad, Mysore, Baroda and Gwalior remained impervious to his overtures; and Travancore, which, as a maritime state with a generous customs convention, had always been regarded as an unlikely candidate for federation, started to take a more positive line under its new constitutional adviser, the able and forthright former Congressman[129] and law member in the Madras government, Sir C. P. Ramaswamy Aiyer. As the time for the annual gathering of the princes neared, it was apparent that while Bikaner and Bhopal were well beaten, Patiala and Dholpur did not have sufficient support to carry the body of the princes against their opposition.

Meanwhile, members of Bhupinder Singh's group unexpectedly found themselves under renewed attack – not this time from the Standing Committee and the ISD, but from the government. As promised, Willingdon came to the party with a forceful speech on the benefits of federation to the states in his annual speech to the Chamber and, more tellingly still, with an informal late night appeal to two dozen key rulers on the eve of the plenary session. He may also have tried to sway Patiala directly with the offer of a knighthood for his prime minister and a re-think on the vexed question of his salute.[130] And the viceroy's efforts were supplemented by the covert canvassing of J. C. Davidson's Federal Finance Committee which had been asked unofficially by Hoare to rally the 'doubters and wobblers'.[131] The committee reached Bombay on 29 January 1932 and spent three hectic weeks touring, in which time it visited nearly all the important states. Afterwards Davidson claimed, probably correctly, to have pulled several leading *darbars* back into line.[132]

---

[129] C. P. Ramaswamy Aiyer served as Congress general secretary under Annie Besant during 1917–18. But he left the party when it went over to a policy of non-cooperation in 1920 and, though a Brahmin, joined the Justice Party government in 1923 as advocate-general and later law member, for which labours he was awarded a CIE. This occasioned a satirical comment from the young editor of *Swarajjya*, K. M. Panikkar – something about 'opportunists'. Sir C. P. was not amused, and when he moved to Travancore he set about undermining Panikkar's position in the COP. For three years the two men never spoke.

[130] The allegation is contained in a letter from the *Morning Post*'s India correspondent, N. Madhava Rao. Rao claims to have been shown a handwritten note from the viceroy offering the concessions mentioned. He is not, it must be said, a reliable source; nevertheless an approach of the kind alleged would not have been beyond Willingdon, especially in the circumstances. Madhava Rao to Gwynne 7 Jan. 1935, Gwynne Coll., 3.

[131] Hoare to Davidson 16 Feb. 1932, Templewood Coll., 14. The other members of the team were Lord Hastings, Sir Maurice Gwyer and Paul Patrick of the India Office, and Major-General Hutchinson. Only Hutchinson was not a firm supporter of the federal ideal.

[132] e.g., Rewa and Alwar. Davidson to Sir S. Hoare 6 Mar. 1932, Templewood Coll., 14. Davidson's assessment of his impact on the princes was not shared by the Political Department. See Sir Louis Kershaw to Findlater Stewart 25 Mar. 1932, Findlater Stewart Coll., 11. But then, the Delhi bureaucrats did not like 'meddling' outsiders.

However, while this last-minute intervention certainly helped to arrest the drift away from federation, it did not seriously weaken the Patiala–Dholpur camp. Bhupinder Singh and his clique continued to command the numbers, at least among the Chamber states, raising the distinct possibility that the COP would split permanently at Delhi, or worse, self-destruct. No ruler or minister on either side seriously wanted this to happen. Moreover there was always a chance that the government, under pressure from British India, might decide to go ahead with the reforms without the states, or to impose, in concert with the provincial parties, a settlement which infringed the states' vital interests: such as Ramsay MacDonald had already threatened to do in the matter of seat allocation if the rulers did not come up with an acceptable scheme of their own by April 1932. Again, this was a risk that no-one wanted to take. By March Hamidullah and Ganga Singh had reached the sober conclusion that they must try to reach an accommodation with the dissidents.

Yet, for all that *Realpolitik* now called the tune, reconciliation would have been difficult had not Patiala and Dholpur chosen, in an attempt to conciliate the large states, to modify their opposition to the concept of all-India federation. Hitherto, they had maintained that the states would be safer staying out of the scheme altogether; but now, resigned to the fact that a quota of *darbars* were bent on joining regardless, they focussed on what they saw as the deficiencies of the Sankey proposals and tried to win the Chamber's support for an alternative scheme, framed by Prabhashankar Pattani with help from Alwar's erstwhile adviser Mir Maqbool Mahmud, which they dubbed 'confederation'. Confederation, as the name suggests, was built around the principle of collective participation by the states at the federal level. Instead of joining individually, as provided for in the RTC model, they would join as a block and return their representatives through the agency of an intervening electoral college, based perhaps on the existing COP. As well, it envisaged a small, preferably unicameral, legislature and a weak federal government funded entirely from indirect taxes and confined to only a few functions of a clearly all-India nature (such as foreign affairs, defence and communications). To be sure, this was a very different conception to the one that the ISD had helped to fashion, but Bhopal and Bikaner thought they saw in it at least a basis for negotiation. And they were also sensible to the scheme's obvious appeal to the constituency whose votes would ultimately decide the issue. Because it preserved the states as separate, autonomous entities, and avoided the awkward issues of dual nationality and allegiance, because it appeared to give the *darbars* a better chance of keeping a tight rein over their representatives and preventing 'hasty or ill-conceived opinions' being expressed in the legislature on their behalf, because it meant that the states' quota of seats would always be filled,[133] above all, because it solved the intractable problem of finding room in the federal houses for 200 and more states,[134] confederation spoke eloquently and reassuringly to the rulers of the smaller states who held the balance of power in the Chamber. Much as they found aspects of the scheme unpalatable, Bhopal and Bikaner recognised that Patiala had hit on a winning formula. When the young rana of Jhalawar, acting as a go-between, suggested an early meeting between the two factions to discuss how confederation could be reconciled with the RTC scheme, the chancellor accepted with alacrity. The meeting was duly fixed for 11 March at Patiala's residence in the capital.

Bikaner, Bhopal and Patiala had not met face to face since February 1931, and there was a brief moment of awkwardness. Then Ganga Singh broke the ice by embracing his younger adversary. 'My dearest bhai', he exclaimed feelingly. Bhupinder Singh reciprocated the compliment by touching the feet of his 'elder brother'. Honour satisfied and personal relations reestablished, the rest proved relatively easy, and by the end of the first day a broad working arrangement between the two sides (immediately dubbed the 'Delhi Pact') had been negotiated. Firstly, on the political side, it was decided that both Bhopal and Patiala would step aside from the upcoming contest for the chancellorship in favour of the jam sahib, and that Hamidullah and Ganga Singh would support Bhupinder Singh's reelection in 1933. Secondly, on the constitutional side, it was agreed that Sir C. P. Ramaswamy Aiyer should be asked to convene a representative committee of ministers to investigate the merits of the confederation plan and otherwise to suggest what additional safeguards for the states needed to be incorporated in the official Sankey scheme.[135]

When news of this deal leaked out there was much grumbling from Patiala's supporters, and according to Ganga Singh strenuous efforts were made before and during the March Chamber session by the Dholpurites to 'persuade Patiala . . . [to] resile from position agreed to

[133] One of the drawbacks of the Sankey scheme from the princes' point of view was that there was no mechanism for apportioning their seats among the participating states. This meant that unless all the states joined at the start (an unlikely eventuality) the dominance of the provinces would be exaggerated beyond even the 60:40 weighting in the upper house which the ISD had reluctantly accepted as their due.

[134] Joint memo by Indore, Dholpur, Liaquat Hyat Khan and Prabhashankar Pattani dated 30 Nov. 1931, Sir Maurice Gwyer and A. Appadorai (eds.), *Speeches and Documents on the Indian Constitution 1921–47*, II (London, 1957), 751–2. See also speeches by Indore and Dholpur to the Second RTC, 28 and 30 Nov. 1931, Moonje Papers, subject files 18 and 20 (2).

[135] Bikaner to Bhopal 17 Mar. 1932, and Bikaner to Patiala 19 Mar. 1932, BRO, Bhopal, Chamber Section, file 47, H-2/52 of 1931–3.

with us'.[136] Indeed, when Ranjitsinhji of Nawanagar, now advised by Rushbrook, announced out of the blue on the sixth day that he had 'joined hands' with Hyderabad to press for a unicameral legislature, there was a moment when it looked as if the whole carefully crafted edifice put together by the Aiyer committee might come crashing down in ruins. However the day – and the plan – was saved by a heroic and impassioned speech from Bhupinder Singh, who had by this time fully recovered his earlier poise and panache, and by some quietly effective work by Willingdon and Davidson behind the scenes.[137] By the 28th Haksar felt cautiously optimistic about the outcome,[138] and when the vote was finally taken, on 1 April, there was in fact a fairly convincing majority for the Standing Committee's motion. 'The Princes . . . have nearly killed me with all the work they've given me', Willingdon informed his son, 'but it's been worthwhile, for they are now definitely committed to Federation.'[139]

The adoption of the Delhi Pact by the COP was, without doubt, a personal triumph for its architects, Bikaner and Patiala, and it signalled a resumption of their dual hegemony over the organisation which had been on the wane since the late 1920s. Ranjitsinhji might have donned the mantle of chancellor, but the understanding within the Standing Committee was that he would do what it dictated; and with Hamidullah gone into voluntary retirement, there was no-one on the Committee capable of standing up to a Bikaner–Patiala combination. As for the Chamber at large, the only remaining danger there – from small states resentful of their marginalisation – was dexterously defused by the new Standing Committee's offer of full Chamber membership to Mayurbhanj, the leading light of the Orissa group, and its setting up of a sub-committee of the Chamber to vet the claims of twenty-one other contenders. Formidable as rivals, Bhupinder and Ganga Singh made a pretty unstoppable team.

However, was the denouement at Delhi also a victory for federation, as Willingdon and others like Jayakar presumed?[140] While historians cannot read minds, and must make do with the imperfect prism of the written record, there seems little doubt that the princely leaders interpreted the resolution of 1 April as a resolution to federate; and the fact that the new

---

[136] Bikaner to Bhopal 17 Mar. 1932, BRO, Bhopal, Chamber Section, file 47, H-2/52 of 1931–3. It was a measure of the strength of feelings on both sides that the 1932 session ran for an unprecedented ten days, some sessions lasting until late into the night.

[137] Davidson to Hoare 31 Mar. 1932, Templewood Coll., 14.

[138] Haksar to Sapru 13 Mar. 1932, Sapru Papers, 6/7, G2142.

[139] Willingdon to his son 5 Apr. 1932, Willingdon Coll..

[140] Jayakar to Polak 1 Apr. 1932, Jayakar Papers, file 407 (2).

Standing Committee immediately opened negotiations to purchase a controlling interest in *The Pioneer* newspaper as a propaganda vehicle for federation and as a future mouthpiece for the proposed Centre Party demonstrates, I suggest, that their intentions in this regard were genuine.[141] But what *kind* of federation was it that the princes intended to enter? The Aiyer committee made it clear that its endorsement of federation was subject to a number of *sine qua nons*, namely: that the states obtained sufficient seats in the upper house to provide for individual membership for all members of the Chamber; that their treaty rights remained unimpaired; that the authority of the federal government was confined to subjects specifically assigned to it by member states; and that there was a guaranteed right of secession. These *sine qua nons* were subsequently spelled out in a manifesto called 'Document A'. Further, the ministers' committee held that the princes should not federate unless certain specified safeguards were incorporated in the constitution. In a separate memorandum, designated 'Document B', it listed seventeen such safeguards. They included:

1 Any amendment to the constitution to require the assent of two-thirds of the members of the federal legislature and separate ratification by three-quarters of the members representing the states.
2 The federation to have no concern with the form of government in the states or the method of electing the states' representatives.
5 Bills opposed by two-thirds of the states' representatives to be referred to the federal court.
6 The constitution to contain a clause absolutely guaranteeing India's continued connection with Britain.
7 No discrimination between units of the federation to be permitted.
8 The states to enter federation by way of treaties with the Crown; these to be beyond the purview of the federal court.
9 The federal legislature to have no cognisance of the states' internal affairs.

---

[141] The deal was that the princes would put up 2 lakhs, and landowning interests from the UP another 2 lakhs. The princes, however, were to get overall editorial control, and an executive committee consisting of Haksar, Manubhai Mehta, Liaquat Hyat Khan and V. T. Krishnamachari, the new dewan of Baroda, was set up to police this. Rampur contributed Rs 15,000, Jaipur, Alwar, Bhopal, Bikaner, Kashmir, Mayurbhanj and Patiala contributed Rs 10,000, Tehri-Garhwal, Bhavnagar, Cochin, Cutch, Travancore, Nawanagar, and Benares Rs 5,000, Morvi Rs 2,000 and Wankaner Rs 1,000. Hydari had offered Rs 25,000 on behalf of Hyderabad, but the nizam refused to pay. This left a shortfall of Rs 77,000, which the Chamber had to meet by way of a loan. See Haksar to Sapru 3 Apr. 1932, Sapru Papers, 6/7 G2142, Sapru to Jayakar 17 Apr. 1932, Jayakar Papers, file 407 (2), Nawanagar to Patiala 17 May 1932 and Desmond Young, *Pioneer* staff, to I. M. Stephens, 24 Dec. 1934, NAI, Home (Pol.), file 33/4/35 of 1935.

13 Federal laws to have no application in states until they were re-enacted as state laws.[142]

While friends of the states tried to make light of these reservations, Sapru, for example, insisting in a letter to Sankey that they were not fundamentally 'inconsistent with the broad features of the federal form of government',[143] others – Sankey and most of the officials in the newly created reforms department of the government of India included – thought differently. It was outrageous, declared reforms commissioner J. M. Dunnett, that the states should seek to prevent the organic growth of the federation by negotiating treaties of accession with the crown which would preclude all possibility of amendment.[144]

Thus, despite its surface unambiguity, the Delhi Pact did not really clarify the attitude of the *darbars* on federation in a way satisfactory to its supporters. On the one hand, it read like an endorsement of the states' participation in the federal scheme; on the other, it seemed to be saying that the princes would join an all-India federation only on very special and limited terms, terms which raised questions both about the viability of such a union and, indirectly, about the rulers' motives for putting this list of *sine qua nons* forward. Was it just a negotiating position, or did they really expect the government and the parties in British India to accept them, or most of them? Or, alternatively, was this uncompromising position adopted precisely because it was sure to be rejected? Were the states trying to find a blame-free exit from the obligations they had entered into in November 1930 – obligations they now regretted? Was the Delhi resolution just a complex April Fool's Day charade? Such questions were to be posed repeatedly in Britain and India over the next decade. But in the meantime, the government felt obliged, for the lack of a viable alternative, to put the best gloss it could on the Delhi outcome. As the India Office's Richard Glancy remarked, voicing a widely held official view, 'We are none of us, I should imagine, convinced that [federation] . . . will work, but we . . . are pledged to try the experiment.'[145]

No longer quite the vision splendid it had seemed in 1930, federation

---

[142] 'Note Summarising Conclusions of the Meeting of Princes and Ministers, Patiala House, March 1932', PSA, COP, file 29 (7) of 1932. Bikaner, who tried unsuccessfully to have the list trimmed, remarked wryly after the vote had been taken to the Udaipur minister Sir Sukdeo Prasad, one of the strongest hard-liners: 'Old man, after all you have had your rice cooked.' Prasad to resdt. Mewar 4 Apr. 1932, IOR L/P&S/13/547. Nevertheless it was not a total defeat because some – Hydari, for example – would have preferred an even tougher list of conditions.

[143] Sapru to Sankey 10 Apr. 1932, Jayakar Papers, file 456.

[144] Memo dated 29 Feb. 1932, IOR L/P&S/13/604.

[145] Glancy to Sir F. Stewart 29 Feb. 1932, Findlater Stewart Coll., 11.

still commanded the formal allegiance of the Indian princes; but there were signs that their commitment was beginning to weaken. For the enemies of federation in the British Conservative party this was an encouraging development.

4   The princes and the Diehards

Over here, we who know the position realise the pressure that is brought upon you, but I beg of you and the Princes to stand firm and reject publicly and emphatically the Federal Scheme. I am quite convinced that if you do so, your order will be saved.

H. A. Gwynne to the maharaja of Dewas Junior, 8 February 1934

The courtship Of Nawanagar

Winston Churchill's resignation from the Conservative Party shadow cabinet in January 1931 owed more than a little to his contempt for the party leader Stanley Baldwin, whose job he coveted. As the newspaper baron Lord Rothermere noted in a congratulatory letter, 'you have really got your foot this time on the ladder that quite soon leads to the Premiership'.[1] However, while conveniently paving the way for a future leadership challenge, Churchill's retreat to the back-bench was not just about improving his own political prospects; it was also about policy. Churchill, like Rothermere, resented what he saw as the Baldwinite Conservative Party's downgrading of empire commitments in favour of an insular, Britain-first strategy. In particular he deplored Baldwin's decision, at the RTC, to associate the party with Labour's policy of Indian reform.

Of course, Churchill's attitudes on India were extreme and in many ways outdated, more reflective of the 1890s (when he had gone there as a young war correspondent) than of the 1930s. Yet they were by no means unique. Many in the Tory parliamentary party thought as he did: in the Commons, people like Henry Page-Croft, a decorated World War I general, J. S. Courtauld, a scion of one of Britain's most powerful industrial families, and Sir Reginald Craddock, a former governor of UP: in the Lords, Tory stalwarts like the former Bombay governor Lord Lloyd, the

---

[1] Rothermere to Churchill 31 Jan. 1931, quoted in Martin Gilbert, *Winston S. Churchill*, V (London, 1981), 254.

marquess of Salisbury, the duke of Argyll, the earl of Kenmare, the duke of Westminster, and Viscount FitzAlan of Derwent, a former viceroy of Ireland. Altogether, about eighty MPs were sympathetic to the Churchillian or 'Diehard' position on India – almost enough to sway the outcome of a close division. Moreover, the Diehard group was stronger than its parliamentary numbers indicated. It enjoyed considerable public support. A substantial section of the press – including Lord Beaverbrook's *Daily Express* and Rothermere's *Daily Mail* – were friendly, as were organisations such as the India Empire Society, the Primrose League and Beaverbrook's 173,000-strong United Empire Party. As well, the Diehards could count on a loyal following in the Conservative constituency associations which performed the important task of selecting the party's candidates for election. This was especially so in the economically troubled north and in the 'home counties' where, as the *Morning Post*'s editor H. T. Gwynne reminded Austen Chamberlain, 'nearly every Conservative [member had] . . . some relative [working] in India'.[2] As we shall see, this grass-roots support almost carried Churchill to victory at the party annual conference in 1934.

However it soon became apparent to the Diehards that they were never going to win a straight vote on Indian reform on the floor of the House. In the December 1931 debate, for example, only 41 Tory MPs crossed the floor in the Commons, and 43 in the Lords – this at a time when the Conservative-dominated National government enjoyed an unprecedented majority of 430. So they concocted, with input from *Post* editor Gwynne and advice from Leslie Scott and Rushbrook-Williams, a plan to defeat the dreaded RTC scheme by wrecking federation.

The rationale of the Diehard scheme was simple. Without the states, it was unlikely that the government would dare to grant central responsibility. But even if they went ahead, and the reform package passed into legislation, the federal part of the new constitution could not, according to the Sankey proposals, become operative until a majority of the states had acceded; this, in effect, gave the rulers a veto on the whole scheme. All the Diehards had to do was persuade the princes to shy off. In the light of the Delhi Pact's formidable array of *sine qua nons*, and the evidence of disaffection contained in Patiala's manifesto of June 1931, they considered this an eminently attainable objective. Nevertheless, whilst the Diehards were sure they were on to a good thing, they remained uneasy about a strategy which placed the fate of their campaign (and, indirectly, perhaps the fate of the Indian Empire) so squarely in the hands of a group known for its volatility and, of course, vulnerable to governmental pressure.

[2] Gwynne to Austen Chamberlain 3 Oct. 1933, Gwynne Coll., 1.

Accordingly, they resorted to some discreet pressure of their own. Overtures were made to Rushbrook-Williams, now foreign minister of Nawanagar, and Leslie Scott. Both agreed to help, Rushbrook's enthusiasm perhaps whetted by the offer of a safe seat at the next general election.[3] Meanwhile, *Morning Post* editor H. T. Gwynne had unearthed another potential intermediary in the person of the paper's Indian correspondent N. Madhava Rao, who persuaded Gwynne that he was not only on friendly terms with Patiala but had enough 'dirt' on the maharaja to purchase his cooperation. Later, through Madhava Rao, yet another 'agent' was recruited: the Punjabi Oxford-educated chief minister of Jhalawar Mir Maqbool Mahmud, whose taste for elegant clothes and elegant women had made him, too, an intimate of Patiala's circle. To protect himself and his parliamentary associates, Gwynne devised a code for telegraphic communication between England and India, in which 'Perkins' stood for Willingdon, 'Gray' for Hoare, 'Moradabad' for Patiala, 'Lahore' for Panna, 'University' for the COP and 'lecture' for federation. It was all rather like something out of a John Buchan novel; yet we should not be too scornful or dismissive. The intrigue was an audacious one, mounted in deadly earnest. And it almost succeeded.

Apparently ignorant of the real balance of power in the COP and seemingly oblivious to the fact that the Chamber was itself only one element in a larger political configuration, the Diehards made their first pitch to the titular leader of the princely order, the new chancellor, Ranjitsinhji. Yet as things turned out it was a shrewd move. For one thing, 'Ranji' in 1932 was ripe for plucking. Although a signatory of the Delhi Pact, he had never been an ardent federationist, and he was one of those at Delhi who had pushed for additional safeguards beyond those recommended by the ministers.[4] Moreover, a series of domestic setbacks had soured Ranji's relations with the government. Since the reimposition of the Viramgam customs cordon in 1927, Nawanagar had contributed at least £1.5 million to Delhi's coffers by way of customs duty for no measurable return, and had also suffered indirectly from the resulting fall-off in transit trade. Three times the jam sahib had asked the secretary of state to submit the case to arbitration, and three times his appeal had been rejected on the advice of the government of India. Likewise, his persistent appeals to the viceroy for a revision of his salute which stood at a lowly

---

[3] See, for example, Willingdon to his son, 26 Mar. 1933, Willingdon Coll., though on this matter Willingdon cannot be counted a reliable witness. At any rate, Rushbrook did not get into parliament. Instead, in 1935 he entered the Colonial Office and afterwards pursued a journalistic career with the BBC and *The Times*.

[4] Nawanagar to Keyes 21 Mar. 1932, Keyes Coll., 31; and address by Sir Philip Cadell to the East India Association, 16 Oct. 1933, *The Asiatic Review*, 32 (1935), 4.

thirteen guns – four less than Bikaner and Patiala commanded – had fallen on deaf ears. For another thing, Nawanagar defied expectations that he would be a lame-duck chancellor. Right from the start, he made it clear that he wanted to put his own stamp on the COP. Eager to lead, Ranjitsinhji was only too glad of the advice that Rushbrook was only too ready to offer.[5]

The first hint of this new agenda came in April 1932, when in a letter to Bhopal the jam sahib declared himself opposed to the Standing Committee's decision to buy into *The Pioneer* newspaper on the grounds that it would not greatly enhance the states' cause and would provide the provincial politicians with an excuse to pry into the princes' private affairs.[6] However Ranjitsinhji's break with existing COP policy only became total after he left for England in May, ostensibly to avoid the heat of the summer. Soon after his arrival, he learned that his fourth appeal over the port case had been rejected by the government. Still smarting from this blow, he went to see Leslie Scott, who put it to him that the safe-guards which the government planned to insert in the constitution were 'likely to be paper safeguards only', that the only sure protection for the states was 'an absolute right of appeal, not only as against the new Federal Government, but also as against the crown itself, to a suitably-constituted judicial tribunal', and that the rulers were 'in a position of great strategic advantage' to make good such a claim.[7] Two days later, on 5 July, Ranjitsinhji put out another circular, again written by his foreign minister, containing the blunt message that the princes were 'not willing to federate', regardless of the shape of the new constitution, until the 'doctrine of paramountcy' was replaced by the 'doctrine of the sanctity of treaties'.[8]

Recognising the handiwork, Bikaner and Patiala implored the chancellor (in the latter's case rather hypocritically) not to allow himself to become a tool of narrow sectional interests. Seeking to appease, the jam sahib offered to re-draft the letter to read that the princes shared a 'definite assumption' that the paramountcy issue would be settled prior to the start of federation, but the Standing Committee found this formulation

---

[5] Ranjitsinhji was naturally shy, and this trait was exacerbated after 1915 by a hunting accident which left him blinded in one eye; by 1932 he was 60, and suffering from chronic bronchitis and lumbago. Recently, new light has been shed on Ranjitsinhji's chequered relationship with the government of India by the detailed researches of John McLeod. See John Edmond McLeod, 'The Western India States Agency 1916–1947', Ph.D. thesis, University of Toronto, 1993.

[6] Nawanagar to Bhopal [?] Apr. 1932, BRO, Bhopal, Chamber Section, file 17, P-115 of 1931–3. Additionally, Nawanagar questioned the financial viability of the paper whose price had fallen by four lakhs since it was first offered to the princes in 1928.

[7] Rushbrook-Williams to Mehdi Yar Jung, 8 and 22 July 1932, AP R/1/47/10/105.

[8] Quoted in Willingdon to Hoare 10 July 1932, Templewood Coll., 5.

equally unacceptable, and said so.[9] Then, in late August, the chancellor received a blunt (he thought rude) missive, jointly signed by Bikaner and Bhopal, warning him to have 'no truck with Sir Leslie Scott'. Furious beyond measure, he at once got Rushbrook to draft a further circular, reiterating his stand on paramountcy. This was dispatched, like the others, to members of the Chamber; but this time copies were also sent to the secretary of state and the viceroy. 'The Jam Sahib, I am afraid, has got into the hands of that horrid little fellow Rushbrook-Williams,' surmised Willingdon shrewdly.[10]

Caught out by the suddenness of Ranji's action, the Standing Committee and its allies hastened to limit the damage. Bikaner, Bhopal and Patiala sent personal cables repudiating the chancellor to Willingdon and Hoare; Haksar wrote independently to the viceroy's private secretary, Mieville, an old friend; in England to prepare the ground for the ISD in advance of the third RTC, Panikkar outlined the official COP position in a press-release, and conveyed a formal reprimand, in person, to the chancellor.[11] Now it was Ranjitsinhji's turn to be taken aback. An official censure! Could it be true? As the awful reality sank in, Ranji's shame and fury mounted, and Panikkar, who was no more than the messenger but had been painted by Rushbrook as the instigator of the Standing Committee's rebuff, had to endure a blistering harangue that lasted the better part of an hour. For months afterward, the Chamber secretary could not bring himself to speak to his nominal boss.[12] Yet beyond venting his anger there was little Ranji could do, because under the COP constitution the chancellor was bound to comply with the Standing Committee's directives. He agreed, grudgingly, to issue no more circulars without permission and in September left for the French resort town of Aix-les-Bains to lick his wounds. Later in the year, in a speech evidently aimed at the Diehards, he apologised for having 'failed to do more for England'.[13] Much cheered, Haksar wrote to Sapru: the rulers 'are playing a straight game . . . No, you need not worry about the Princes.'[14]

The Standing Committee, too, were pleased by the jam sahib's backdown; and they were also heartened by the release in July of Davidson's long-awaited report on the states' financial claims pursuant to federation. The *Report* held that, in so far as the states' tributes to the crown were of a

---

[9] India Office note dated 5 July 1932, and Dholpur to Jam Sahib 23 July 1932, L/PO/92.
[10] Willingdon to Hoare 12 Sept. 1932, Templewood Coll., 6.
[11] Haksar to Sapru 4 Sept. 1932, Sapru Papers. 6/7, G2142; and Panikkar, *Autobiography*, 89.
[12] Wild, *Ranji:* 293; and Panikkar, *Autobiography*, 89.   [13] Quoted in Wild, *Ranji*, 293.
[14] Haksar to Sapru 4 Sept. 1932, Sapru Papers, 6/7, G2142.

'feudal' nature, they should be phased out *pari passu* with income tax payments from the provinces but in any case within twenty years of the commencement of federation; and that immediate relief be given to states whose contributions under this head exceeded 5 per cent of their total revenues. Again, like the Federal Finance SubCommittee of the RTC, the Davidson Committee accepted that the states should not be required to pay twice for the privilege of protection – given that they were already contributing substantially to the central fisc by way of sea-customs. Thirdly, it found that four states – Gwalior, Hyderabad, Indore and Sangli – were entitled to cash credits on account of ceded territories. Fourthly, as regards immunities, it attempted to sweeten the pill by recommending the lifting, after federation, of existing restrictions on the manufacture of salt for local consumption in Cutch and Kathiawar, and an arrangement whereby the maritime states would be allowed to continue to keep the duties paid on goods imported through their ports for local consumption and inland states to continue to levy transit duties.[15]

However, just when it appeared 'that . . . the pro-Federation Princes were getting stronger',[16] Willingdon undid most of his earlier good work, and that of the Davidson Committee, by launching an ill-judged and ham-fisted assault on the COP. As we have seen, Willingdon had never been much of a fan of the Chamber; and now, ironically, he saw it as posing a threat to the success of the federation cause to which he had become a reluctant convert. Like the Hyderabad resident Keyes, he believed some of the Chamber heavyweights were privately sympathetic to the Congress, which was once again in rebellion against the government; he resented the way the COP had made its endorsement of the federal scheme conditional on a shopping-list of safeguards; and he feared the consequences of the Chamber's dogged insistence on a large federal legislature. Correctly identifying Bikaner and Patiala as the major architects of this policy, Willingdon set out to 'break up the Bikaner Party' by stitching together a counter-combination of what his commander-in-chief accurately described as the 'States that really count'[17] – that is, the big 19–gunners.

It was all really a matter of numbers. If 80 seats in the upper house went to the states, the two dozen 17–21-gunners would be entitled, his advisers

[15] *Report of the Indian States Enquiry Committee (Financial) 1932* (Calcutta, 1932), 161, 163.
[16] Sapru to Jayakar 30 Aug. 1932 relating an interview with the Viceroy at Simla, Jayakar Papers, 450.
[17] Sir Philip Chetwode to Irwin, 11 Sept. 1932, quoted in F. W. F. Smith, second earl of Birkenhead, *Halifax* (London, 1965), 327–8. Aware of some unease at the India Office with regard to Simla's big states strategy, Chetwode went on to say that 'people in England do not understand that Bikaner, Bhopal, Alwar, and other talking folk, are of very little account in the real India'.

Table 4.1 *Anticipated financial adjustments consequent on federation, July 1932 (in Rupees)*

| State/Region | Credits | | | Debits | | |
	Tribute	Territory	Salt	Customs	Posts	Balance
Bhopal	1,61,290				51,180	+1,10,110
Indore	1,11,214	41,214			35,000	+1,87,000
Dhar	18,602				3,000	+15,602
Cochin	2,00,000		4,66,576	12,57,000		−15,26,576
Mysore	24,00,000				5,57,000	+18,93,000
Mandi	1,00,000		27,000			+73,000
Bundi	40,000		3,200			+36,000
Jaipur	4,00,000		4,10,000			−10,937
Udaipur	2,00,000		1,57,812			+42,188
Kathiawar	7,00,000		7,00,000	120,00,000		−120,00,000
Baroda		23,00,000	40,000	3,80,000	65,000	+17,95,000

Source: IOR, L/P&S/13/590.

informed him, to at least 54 on the basis of population. It followed therefore that the adherence of all, or even most, of this group would give the government the majority it needed to inaugurate federation. In mid-August Willingdon tried out his plan on the India Office and found that they too were eager to mobilise the 'great Princes . . . against the Chamber . . . as soon as possible'.[18] He then sounded out some of the bigger states to see if the India Office's perception, that Mysore, Travancore, Baroda and possibly Hyderabad, all intended to federate,[19] was correct. It was. Hyderabad's only major prerequisites, it appeared, were a small legislature and a minimum of eight seats in the upper house,[20] Travancore's a limited moratorium on sea-customs and five upper house seats, Mysore's and Baroda's an equitable financial settlement. Confident that he could persuade Whitehall to agree to these terms, the viceroy now applied himself to driving a wedge between them and the coterie of middle-sized states which controlled the Standing Committee of the COP.

Willingdon's opening gambit was to commend to London a reforms department scheme for basing the allocation of plural seats in the upper house not on the salute table but on the 'size and material importance of

[18] Minute by Findlater Stewart dated 15 Aug. 1932, IOR L/PO/92. Hoare added the marginal note: 'I agree'.
[19] Gwyer to Findlater Stewart, 19 Mar. 1932, Findlater Stewart Coll., 11.
[20] Proceedings of 68th meeting of the Hyderabad ERC, 13 July 1932, AP R/1/47/10/155.

the States concerned'.[21] This gave a very obvious boost to the electoral aspirations of the big six. Next, when it came time to draw up the guest list for the Simla conference on paramountcy he had offered to host during the marathon Delhi meeting in March, when he was still pursuing a conciliatory line towards the Chamber, he made a special point of inviting the ministers of Baroda, Mysore, Travancore and Hyderabad, even though the meeting was supposed to be with the Standing Committee only.[22] But these were preliminaries. It was at the Simla summit itself that Willingdon's divide-and-rule strategy really got into gear. In the midst of his opening address, he suddenly produced a copy of the jam sahib's letter of 31 August and, turning to where the princes were seated, demanded: 'do Your Highnesses agree with His Highness the Chancellor that I should be relieved of my duties as Viceroy [so] . . . that you [can] . . . have discussions over my head?' Then, having encouraged Bhopal in private conversation to think that the government was prepared to meet the Chamber at least half way on the vexed question of arbitration in justiciable disputes between the states and the crown, he arranged for the political secretary, Watson, to raise objections to the proposed procedure, thereby making Bhopal look foolish in the eyes of his colleagues. So transparent had Willingdon's strategy become by this stage, that a smirking Mahdi Yar Jung of Hyderabad leaned across to Panikkar and whispered, 'this [summit] might be considered the funeral of the Chamber of Princes'.[23]

Moreover, in that this strategy had a purpose beyond satisfying Willingdon's desire to exact revenge for the trouble the COP had caused him, it proved remarkably successful. On the second day, Hamidullah opened the debate by restating what he thought was the generally accepted position on paramountcy after federation: that in federal matters, the crown would have no jurisdiction beyond what was provided for in the constitution. But Akbar Hydari, who spoke second, disputed this. Emboldened by Willingdon's opening remarks, he asserted that Hyderabad wanted paramountcy to remain paramount, with the crown armed with sufficient power, including military power, to uphold the treaties with the states. As soon as Hydari had finished Hamidullah

---

[21] GOI to sec. state 29 Oct. 1932, IOR L/P&S/13/647.

[22] This followed hard on the heels of the government of India's decision to ignore the Standing Committee's recommendations as regards princely representation on the Indian Sandhurst Committee and the Road Conference, 'on the ground that the Chamber of Princes did not represent some important States'. Draft letter from Bhopal to Willingdon, n.d., BRO, Bhopal, Chamber Section, file 77, C-117 of 1931–3.

[23] Report by Panikkar on the Simla conference dated 24 Oct. 1932, BRO, Bhopal, Chamber Section, file 17–P-115 of 1932; and Haksar to Sapru 5 Oct. 1932, Sapru Papers, 6/7, G2142.

jumped to his feet and, fixing the Hyderabad minister with a withering stare, asked him if this meant that the nizam accepted the propositions contained in Reading's letter of 1926. Taken unawares, Hydari mumbled something about 'certain unfortunate generalities'; then, fully ten minutes later, taking advantage of a lull in the discussion, he interjected, 'I desire to state that Hyderabad does not accept Lord Reading's letter.' At this, a titter went round the room. For the rest of the day Sir Akbar said little, but wore an expression which made it plain that he did not intend to forget or forgive the nawab of Bhopal's indiscretion. Nevertheless, others picked up on the Hydari theme. The princes were ultimately the beneficiaries of an unfettered viceregal discretion, declared Rewa's Gulab Singh; in political relations it was the 'human touch' that counted. To Haksar's disgust these sentiments were echoed by Sir C. P. Ramaswamy Aiyer, 'the Viceroy's darling', and other ministers. Willingdon could hardly wait to share his joy with London. As he told Butler, 'there was evident a regular revolt ag[ain]st the domination of Bikaner and Bhopal, wh[i]c[h] was most satisfactory from our point of view'.[24]

In the event, the Standing Committee came away with one modest gain to compensate for their humiliation: an agreement in principle with regard to the settlement of justiciable disputes. However, even this was filched from them after technical objections were raised in Whitehall to the wording of the formula. Outraged, Hamidullah told Willingdon that all bets were off, and that the states would not enter federation until the paramountcy issue was settled to their satisfaction – a position virtually identical to that taken up by the chancellor in his letter of 31 August.[25] Hearing of this through Rushbrook, the Diehards were understandably cock-a-hoop. Hoare, too, recognised the danger and told the viceroy to start mending bridges. But it was too late. His credibility with the Chamber had been irreparably compromised.

Ranji and the White Paper

The task of promoting the safeguards agreed upon by the princes at the third and final session of the RTC, which began in November 1932, fell by default to Patiala's Liaquat Hyat Khan, Bikaner's Manubhai Mehta and newcomer Oudh Narain of Bhopal, for they were the only members of the ISD fully committed to the Delhi Pact. Inevitably, the battle was an

---

[24] Willingdon to Butler 1 Oct. 1932, Butler Coll., 54. See also Watson to Paul Patrick 14 Nov. 1932, and GOI to Sec. State 25 Oct. 1932, IOR L/P&S/13/550.
[25] Haksar to Sapru 5 Oct. 1932, Sapru Papers, 6/7, G2142.

uphill one. Nevertheless, by dint of much hard work behind the scenes, meticulously documented in their twice- and thrice-weekly confidential reports to Patiala, Liaquat and Mehta managed to score some useful points. Starting first with the ISD, they managed, 'in spite of the attitude of some of our friends', to get the Delhi Pact adopted, with minor modifications, as a common basis for negotiation by the princely team.[26] Then, turning to the British, they made some headway in gaining official backing for the confederation principle. Last but not least, Manubhai succeeded in wringing several important concessions from the Federal Finance Subcommittee of the conference, notably an endorsement of the Davidson Committee's recommendations on compensation for federating states in respect of tributes and ceded territories,[27] and a decision that the states should not be liable for direct federal taxation. Only on the vexed seats issue, did they fail to make any impression on the British Indian delegates.

However these considerable achievements were to a large extent nullified by the re-emergence from Parisian seclusion of a very angry jam sahib, whose opposition to the federal scheme had if anything hardened since the summer in the light of the poor financial return which, as Table 4.1 shows, the maritime Kathiawar states stood to receive under Davidson's formula. Asserting his right as chancellor, Ranjitsinhji took charge of the ISD's policy meetings at the Metropole Hotel. From this position of vantage, he at once invited Leslie Scott to attend as an observer (in direct defiance of the Standing Committee's instructions that he should have nothing further to do, officially, with the English lawyer),[28] and repeatedly pressed for an ultimatum on paramountcy. He got nowhere, but prevented others from turning the debate into more constructive channels, with the result that after two weeks the ministers from the large states stopped attending and started caucusing separately. Then, for a time, Ranji appeared to behave, Scott too making himself useful by helping to re-draft the Chamber's submission to the RTC on confederation. But this turnabout was purely tactical. Privately, Scott's advice to the chancellor was that the states' best defence against the 'dangers of aggressive democratisation by British India inside the

---

[26] Liaquat to Patiala 9 Dec. 1932, PSA, COP, file 38 (47) of 1932.

[27] Significantly, however, the FFS cavilled at Davidson's suggestion that the maritime states should be compensated for the extinction of their customs rights – even though they recognised that their decision might force these states to stay out. 'Memo. on Federal Finance For JSC', n.d., Reading Coll., 55C.

[28] The Standing Committee eventually agreed that Scott could attend, but repudiated any financial obligation to him. Haksar to Sapru 5 Oct.1932, Sapru Papers, 6/7, G2142. This meant that the jam sahib had to pay the tab. As he was still owed more than a lakh by the Chamber in respect of earlier advances for legal fees, he was not pleased.

Federation' lay in 'the united abstention of all'.[29] In mid-December, as the conference was winding up, Ranjitsinhji preached this message in an interview with Reuters news agency. Shortly afterwards he cabled the Standing Committee asking to be released from his mandate to support the Delhi Pact. In January dissent became open revolt, when forty Gujarat rulers voted at Jamnagar to reject federation root and branch. As the date for the annual COP session in March 1933 drew near, the Standing Committee prayed that the British government's promised white paper outlining its preferred reform package, would be generous to the states.

Fortunately, it was. Although broadly based on proposals contained in the final report of the RTC, it represented, from the states' point of view, a substantial improvement on the conference draft. First, it raised the states' share of upper house seats from 90 to 100, a number which guaranteed most medium-sized Chamber states an individual place. Second, it varied the financial formula agreed upon at the RTC to confine the states' fiscal liabilities to the payment of corporation tax, and that to be progressively phased in over ten years. Third, it substantially strengthened the 'crown element' in the constitution by giving the governor-general a 'special responsibility' 'for the protection of the rights of any Indian State' in the event that these were threatened by the federation. Fourth, it excised all mention of 'fundamental rights' on the plea that a federal constitution should be a compact between units, not between rulers and subjects.

Noting these changes, Liaquat and Mehta in a report for the Standing Committee, pronounced the white paper largely free of the 'lurking snares or pitfalls' which had dogged the original scheme. They gave it their strong endorsement. Further, the two ministers urged the princes to do the same. Once, they conceded, it had been possible for the states to exist in splendid isolation under the protective umbrella of the political department. But the latter would have limited power in a federal India and its protection was no longer needed 'when self-reliance is at our command'. With 100/260 seats in the upper house and 125/375 in the lower house at their disposal, they held 'the balance of power in their own hands'. However the favourable reception awarded the white paper by the ministers (and more guardedly, by the Standing Committee)[30] was not shared by Ranjitsinhji. Ignoring the positives, the chancellor noted that eight out of the seventeen *sine qua nons* embodied in 'Document A' had

---

[29] Memo by Scott and Rushbrook-Williams for Nawanagar dated 8 Dec. 1932, IOR L/P&S/13/668.
[30] See memo by Bhopal dated 23 Mar. 1933, BRO, Bhopal, Chamber Section, file 36, D-5/146 of 1932.

still to be achieved. These were 'important points discussed by the Princes at . . . the Round Table Conference and consistently pressed by them as essential'. Under the circumstances, he could 'not advise our Order to join an All-India Federation'.[31] The challenge was on.

Alerted to the danger by the demeanour of his parliamentary opponents, Hoare sought, as in 1932, to sway the outcome of the vote, urging Willingdon to get his political officers to push federation in their agencies, and pleading with him to speed up negotiations over Berar (which appeared to have been stalled by Sir Terence Keyes' 'notorious' antipathy towards Hydari) in the hope of extracting a vote of confidence from Hyderabad.[32] Again, the viceroy promised to do what he could to ensure a favourable outcome at the Chamber meeting and to make sure that Hydari was 'kept on his perch'.[33] But again he was unable to hold out any guarantees beyond, perhaps, staving off a 'definite break from Federation'.[34] No less than the Standing Committee, Hoare awaited the opening of the COP session on Monday 20 March 1933 with considerable anxiety. No one, however, had any inkling of the bizarre sequence of events that was to follow.

The first shock came on the fourth, penultimate day of the session, during the chancellor's report to the Chamber. Reading from a text penned for him by Rushbrook, Ranjitsinhji began by addressing the ministers' report. Ignoring its conclusions, he stated that it 'had convinced him that the present scheme was dangerous to the States and the British connection'. Then, he turned to the white paper scheme itself and, mischievously citing as his major authority the eminent constitutional lawyer Berriedale Keith, delivered what the viceroy afterwards called, without exaggeration, a 'violent attack' on the whole principle of all-India federation. The government, declared Ranji,

are relying upon Indian States with their essentially monarchic politics to contribute the necessary elements of stability and experience . . . For my own part, I feel that it is very unfortunate that the realisation of British Indian political ambitions should have been made contingent upon the acceptance of a particular type of Federation by the Indian States, and I do not see that there is any logical connection between these two matters . . . the centralising tendencies to which all Federations inevitably give rise will so operate as to increase the power of the Centre at the expense of the States . . . I cannot help feeling that the constitution as it has emerged from the White Paper will inevitably work as to destroy the very principle of Indian Kingship.[35]

---

[31] Note by Nawanagar dated 20 Mar. 1933, PSA, COP, file 37 (39) of 1933.
[32] Hoare to Willingdon 10 Feb. 1933, Templewood Coll., 3.
[33] Willingdon to Hoare 20 Feb. 1933, Templewood Coll., 6.
[34] Viceroy to sec. state 9 Feb. 1933, IOR, L/P&S/13/668.
[35] Speech of 24 Mar. 1933, *IAR*, 1933, I, 478–9.

There was supposed to be much more in this Diehard vein; but at that moment an enraged Lord Willingdon, well aware that the jam sahib's rhetoric came straight out of the mouth of 'that d—d little scoundrel Rushbrook Williams',[36] stood up and ruled the chancellor out of order – something which had never happened before in the eleven-year history of the Chamber. An ashen-faced jam sahib sank slowly to his seat, folded up his speech, and spent the rest of the day staring fixedly into space.

However, far from stifling criticism of the federal scheme, Willingdon's crude and tactless intervention only intensified it. Bhupinder Singh who spoke next, conscious of the approaching election for the chancellorship and wanting to maximise his vote, praised the ministers for their efforts but pointedly stopped short of endorsing their report. There was a need, he felt, for further safeguards. Most of the princes who followed him expressed similar reservations. Sensing a mounting groundswell in their favour, Rushbrook, Maqbool Mahmud and Madhava Rao (in town ostensibly to cover the session for the *Morning Post*) spent much of that evening scurrying back and forth between the Chamber secretariat and the Imperial Hotel canvassing votes. 'They are fighting like cats and dogs', wrote the viceroy condescendingly in a note to his son.[37]

But it was on the final day, Friday 26 March, that the drama reached its climax. Wounded and bent on revenge, the chancellor commenced hostilities by using the budget debate to mount a scathing attack on the Chamber secretary, his *bête noire* Panikkar, accusing the urbane southerner of disloyalty, graft and financial mismanagement. At once, a chorus of demands for Panikkar's dismissal erupted from the floor. Patiala loyally jumped to his protégé's defence, but for once even Bhupinder Singh's powerful voice went unheeded. During the luncheon adjournment a bemused Panikkar was informed by the chancellor that he was out of a job.[38] Shaken by these ominous developments, the Standing Committee met over lunch and hurriedly drafted an amended resolution to put to the meeting, commending the general thrust of the white paper scheme, but tying the entry of the states to the 'inclusion in the Constitution and treaties of accession of essential safeguards' – by implication the safeguards itemised in Document B. But the Nawanagar camp trumped this ace by moving from the floor a further amendment making accession to the federation conditional on an 'equitable and satisfactory settlement of the . . . problem' of paramountcy – the old Leslie Scott formula. To the Standing Committee's dismay, *both* amendments were carried,

---

[36] Willingdon to Butler 28 Mar. 1933, Butler Coll., 54.
[37] Willingdon to his son 26 Mar. 1933, Willingdon Coll.
[38] Panikkar, *Autobiography*, 89–91; and Panikkar to Nawanagar 21 Mar. 1933, BRO, Bhopal, Chamber Section, file D-2/18 of 1931–3.

Ranjitsinhji ruling from the chair, in virtually his last act as chancellor, that they were not contradictory.[39] Watching this scenario unfold, Willingdon put on a brave face. 'We shall probably be able', he informed the secretary of state, 'to proceed on the assumption that they have never been passed and base [our] hopes . . . on individual negotiations with a considerable number of more important States who . . . appear not unfavourable to the scheme.'[40] But Churchill and his supporters were ecstatic.

Following the federation debate, the princes went through the motions of an election. With Nawanagar having previously declared himself a non-starter on the grounds of deteriorating health, the ballot for the chancellorship was won easily by Bhupinder Singh over the ever-hopeful Jey Singh of Alwar, by twenty-nine votes to four. Significantly, though, six out of ten places on the enlarged Standing Committee went to Nawanagar supporters: Sangli, Jhalawar, Panna, Bahawalpur, Rampur and Dholpur, who secured the coveted position of pro-chancellor.[41] Moreover, while Ranjitsinhji was now effectively retired, he remained a beacon of dissent, and Rushbrook had high hopes of making propaganda capital out of the celebrations planned at Jamnagar to mark the silver jubilee of the maharaja's reign. They did not eventuate – at least in the way he and his mentors had intended – for just ten days after leaving Delhi, Ranji collapsed and died from heart failure. Yet the Diehards managed to turn even this unexpected (and for most of them, sincerely tragic) occurrence to good account, by representing the jam sahib's death as being 'very closely connected' to 'Willingdon's public rudeness and rebuke' to him during the COP meeting.[42] Having already attained a kind of apotheosis in Delhi, Ranji now became, courtesy of the *Morning Post*, an enduring martyr to the Diehard cause.

Nevertheless, while the March 1933 session of the Chamber gave the Diehards the result they had been seeking, it was won at considerable cost to the organisation's prestige. Kolhapur, fed up with being consistently passed over for a place on the Standing Committee, walked out on Day Four, declaring that he would have nothing further to do with the Chamber.[43] Following the debacle on the Friday afternoon, Bhopal and Jodhpur did the same. By the end of the month Kashmir, Travancore,

[39] *The Indian States Gazette*, 3 (4), Apr. 1933, 7.
[40] Viceroy to sec. state 26 Mar. 1933, IOR L/P&S/13/668.
[41] Patiala to Bhopal 25 Mar. 1933, BRO, Bhopal, Chamber Section, file 77, C-117 of 1931–3.
[42] E. G. S. Churchill to Gwynne 12 July 1934, Gwynne Coll., 9; and see also M. Birdwood to the duchess of Atholl 9 Feb. 1934, Atholl Coll., 6. The broken heart hypothesis is also canvassed by Ranjitsinhji's biographer. See Wild, *Ranji*, 308–11.
[43] Kashmir to Nawanagar 23 Mar. 1933, IOR L/P&S/13/668.

Rampur and Kapurthala had all tendered their resignations. By 1933 the Diehards had acquired a significant degree of influence over the Chamber's policy; but they were still a long way from winning the battle for the allegiance of the princely order.

The courtship of Patiala

Seemingly unaware of the credibility crisis which had overtaken the COP, the Diehards pressed on with their campaign, focussing, now, on Bhupinder Singh. On the face of it, winning over Patiala looked a difficult assignment. Publicly, the new chancellor remained – as he had been for over a year – a firm supporter of federation with appropriate safeguards. As he told Liaquat, who had begun to wonder, 'insisting on adequate safeguards . . . do[es] not mean opposing federation'.[44] Moreover, Bhupinder Singh was said to be highly strung and susceptible to 'attacks' of nerves. He had a reputation for wilting under pressure. Could he be trusted, the Diehards wondered, if the going got tough?

Yet, hard task or not, the Diehards had no choice but to make the attempt. As chancellor, Patiala held the keys to the COP. Indeed by the summer of 1933, the subborning of Patiala had become a priority because of developments in the joint select committee (JSC) set up in April 1933 to frame parliament's response to the white paper. After the fracas at Delhi, the Diehards had anticipated turning the JSC into a witch-hunt against the federal scheme; but when the suggestion was put by Sir Michael O'Dwyer to Liaquat and Mehta, as the official representatives of the Chamber, that the Delhi resolutions showed that the princes had gone cold on federation, the point was vigorously denied. The Diehards did not believe that the ministers' interpretation truly reflected Chamber policy, but it was damaging to have such views aired publicly by its delegates. They needed Liaquat and Mehta silenced, and Patiala had the authority to do it.

Fortunately for the Diehards, Patiala was not quite the honest broker he pretended to be. Although during the recent past he had aligned himself with the government and the Standing Committee, this public posture was not underpinned by a genuine conversion to the federal cause. Unlike Haksar and Panikkar he was not driven by noble dreams of national renaissance. He remained, as he had been almost from the start, wary of the scheme's implications for his autonomy and anxious about its cost. And he was bitterly disappointed that Liaquat had been unable to persuade the RTC Franchise Committee to award Patiala more than two

---

[44] Patiala to Liaquat 1 July 1933, PSA, COP, file 38 (42) of 1933.

seats in the federal upper house – a poor return, he felt, for 'all the services of my State and my ancestors for the King-Emperor and [the] British cause of over [a] century and [a] quarter'.[45] Moreover, while Bhupinder Singh had gone along since 1932 with the government's wishes on federation, his relations with Delhi had never been easy and in 1933 they began once again to deteriorate. When his friend Fitzpatrick retired as AGG Punjab at the end of the year, the maharaja sought permission to appoint him as his prime minister; but was curtly informed that the employment of ex-political officers was 'not in accordance with the policy of Government'[46] – a very strict interpretation of a rule that had been bent before and would be again. He became embroiled, as president of the Indian Cricket Association, in a public quarrel with its patron Lord Willingdon; and earned the undying enmity of both viceroy and vicereine by recounting a lewd joke about Lady Willingdon in the wrong company. Meanwhile the *darbar* had got into a standoff with the political department over the state's massive debts, estimated at over 140 lakhs and rising. The maharaja was compelled to take on the retiring accountant-general, Sir Frederick Gauntlett, as his finance minister and to agree to a plan of austerities. Bhupinder Singh was, as always, fearful of the government's coercive power, but he had little reason to do it any favours.

But if Patiala was vulnerable, Maqbool and Madhava Rao made the most of his vulnerability. First, they encouraged Bhupinder Singh to take a strong line on paramountcy, knowing this to be an issue on which the government was particularly averse to compromise. Next, they played up to the maharaja's vanity by suggesting that the JSC was heading for an impasse which only his charismatic presence could resolve.[47] Thirdly, unable to persuade Whitehall to issue an invitation to Patiala, they stoked Bhupinder Singh's festering doubts about the loyalty of Liaquat (who for his part had still not forgiven the maharaja for his *volte face* at Delhi) by sending back slanted reports of the minister's activities in London which carried the veiled imputation that the failure of the India Office to move on the matter of the maharaja's invitation was mainly Liaquat's doing. Within weeks of this covert campaign being initiated, Patiala was assuring 'Conservative friends' in London that his 'views [on federation] were not necessarily those of the Chamber'.[48] And by the end of the summer he had virtually made up his mind to replace Liaquat as dewan.[49]

[45] Patiala to Madhava Rao [?] 1933, Atholl Coll., 6.
[46] Willingdon to Patiala 6 May 1934, IOR R/1/1/2569.
[47] Lord Lloyd to Maqbool 2 June 1933; and Maqbool to Patiala 17 June 1933, PSA, COP, file 38 (44) of 1938.
[48] Maqbool to Patiala 24 June 1933, PSA, COP, file 38 (44) of 1933.
[49] Thus the aforementioned approach to the government about Fitzpatrick.

Nevertheless, Madhava Rao felt that his editor, Gwynne, or some other leading Conservative, should come out to India over the winter to stiffen the maharaja's resolve. Gwynne declined; but he liked the idea of a Diehard mission. He sought volunteers and funds. Eventually the task was entrusted to Viscount Lymington from the Lords, and Jack Courtauld, a director of the *Post*, from the Commons, with the duke of Westminster underwriting their costs.[50] The delegation arrived at Bombay on 8 March and proceeded by stages to Patiala.

Apart from bolstering Patiala's resistance to governmental pressure, the mission hoped to talk him and others into making public their private reservations about federation. To this end, they requested the maharaja to set up a meeting with his friends. Dholpur, Panna and Jhalawar came, while Bahawalpur indicated that he would support whatever move was decided upon. After preliminaries, Madhava Rao presented the princes with a draft letter to the press which made it plain that they reserved the right to stand out of federation unless the JSC made substantial beneficial changes to the white paper. With hardly a demur, the four rulers present signed it, Bahawalpur adding his signature later. But that was not the only success achieved by the mission. Lymington and Courtauld came away with potentially damning information about the subtle coercion which had been applied to wavering states by the government of India. In addition, they extracted from the princes an offer to take the Diehard message back to their constituencies, Dholpur undertaking to canvass the central Indian states, Patiala promising to send agents to Kathiawar and Rajputana. At the end of the mission a very satisfied Jack Courtauld concluded: 'Through Patiala, Dholpur and Bahawalpur, we expect to get the support of nearly 80 out of 104 Princes in the Chamber to reject Federation.'[51]

Nevertheless, the very success of the mission underlined the necessity of further contact. According to Madhava Rao, the mission's movements had been shadowed by the CID and their phones tapped. Bhupinder Singh had been told that Delhi was planning 'retaliatory measures against him'. 'Unless you are here', wrote the *Post* correspondent, 'you cannot imagine . . . what . . . terror they are passing [through].'[52] Even before Lymington and Courtauld had left India, he was urging his editor to send

---

[50] Hoare to Willingdon 1 Feb. 1934, Templewood Coll., 4; Madhava Rao to B. S. Moonje 5 Feb. 1934, NAI, Home (Pol.) file 84/34 of 1934; and Gwynne to Lymington 6 Feb. 1934, Gwynne to Courtauld (draft) 7 Feb. 1934, and Gwynne to Westminster 30 May 1934, Gwynne Coll., 7. Originally three MPs were due to go, but Lord Clive dropped out at the last moment, frightened off, Gwynne thought, by the government.
[51] Memo. by Courtauld, n.d., Gwynne Coll., 7.
[52] Madhava Rao to Gwynne 9 Apr. 1934, Gwynne Coll., 2.

a second mission to consolidate the bridgehead which they had carved out. By May his tone had become frantic. 'If the second party does not reach India by mid-June at the latest we shall collapse . . . For God's sake don't let us down.'[53]

Not surprisingly, none of the Diehard's elderly leaders was keen to visit India in mid-summer; but Gwynne managed to put together a scratch team consisting of the *Post*'s Edward Russell and Captain Spencer Churchill, Winston's cousin. The mission left London by air on 9 June, reached Karachi on the 14th, and Chail, Patiala's summer seat, four days later, where they were joined for talks by Dholpur and Indore. Then followed a whirlwind 5,700-mile tour of state capitals, including Mysore and Hyderabad, which left Russell and Madhava Rao exhausted and Churchill hospitalised in Poona, but which garnered additional compromising evidence of governmental coercion and further cemented the connections which had been forged in April. Churchill returned home convinced that 'Patiala and his group' were now 'definitely' committed to an anti-federation line.[54] This appraisal encouraged Winston Churchill and forty other Diehard MPs to write in July 1934 an open letter to the princes promising them their steadfast support 'against any attempt to encroach upon' their rights and privileges.[55]

It still remained to be seen whether Patiala could deliver a solid 'no' vote when it came time for the COP to assess its position on federation in the light of the JSC's recommendations. Yet, here again, events smiled on the Diehard cause. Firstly, the JSC took an unexpectedly critical line on the White Paper. Princely reservations on federal jurisdiction were attacked on the grounds that they would make the federation a 'sham'.[56] Likewise, the JSC gave strong indications that it was preparing to recommend a reversion to the small upper house (80 seat) model of the first RTC – this after the *darbars* had received strong indications from the political department that their quota of upper house seats was going to be raised from 100 to 104.[57] Secondly, the snail-like pace of the JSC's deliberations, which dragged on over nearly eighteen long months, added greatly to the rulers' nervousness, while the somewhat closed-shop atmosphere which prevailed in the committee left the Indian delegates

[53] Madhava Rao to Gwynne 16 May 1934, Gwynne Coll., 2.

[54] 'Report of the Tour of Capt. Spencer-Churchill and Edward Russell, 14 June–3 July 1934', Gwynne Coll., 9.

[55] The letter can be read in IOR L/PO/92; the signatories are listed in an enclosure to a letter from Willingdon to Hoare 9 Dec. 1934, Templewood Coll., 8.

[56] The phrase was Lord Lytton's. See Hoare to Willingdon 9 Feb. 1934, Templewood Coll., 4.

[57] Note of discussions at the India Office dated 24 Jan. 1934, viceroy to sec. state 26 Jan. 1934, and viceroy to sec. state 3 May 1934, IOR L/P&S/13/651.

(including the ministers from the states) feeling cut off and alienated from the constitution-making process. To make matters worse, the sittings of the JSC coincided with a period of unprecedented upheaval in the domestic life of the states, with Kashmir, Alwar, Bharatpur, Bahawalpur, Kapurthala and Jind all experiencing major agrarian revolts and bloody communal clashes.[58] These convulsions were in themselves distracting and unsettling. What was more, they occasioned, in two cases, heavy-handed exercises of British paramountcy. In 1932 Hari Singh of Kashmir was subjected to an imperial inquiry and made to take on an English ICS officer as his prime minister. In 1934 Jey Singh of Alwar was deposed and sent into exile. Jey Singh had not been a popular member of the order, but he had been a respected one and an intimate of the COP's governing circle since its inception. Rightly or wrongly, his removal was widely seen as another calculated Willingdonian assault on the prestige of the Chamber. However it was the role played in several of the movements by *jathas* or bands of volunteers belonging to outside organisations, such as the Hindu Mahasabha and the Majlis-i-Ahrar of Lahore, that did the greatest psychological damage, for it made the rulers realise how dependant they had become for their protection on the sheltering umbrella of British paramountcy – an umbrella that would vanish once they entered the federation.

Always sensitive to the changing moods of his constituents, Bhupinder Singh sensed that some of them were having second thoughts and campaigned accordingly. But the pro-federation forces were not idle either. Early in 1934, the Aga Khan went on the road to promote federation in Rajputana and the Punjab; at Patiala, Liaquat did what he could to nullify the intrigues of Maqbool and Madhava Rao; Akbar Hydari sounded out Baroda's V. T. Krishnamachari, Mirza and Sir C. P. Ramaswamy Aiyer about establishing a committee of ministers from the major states to coordinate their approach to federation and serve as a counter-voice to the Standing Committee of the Chamber; and, most importantly, the government manufactured a number of juicy carrots to sustain the ardour of the faithful and bolster the waverers. In May 1933 Delhi concluded a settlement of the long-running Berar dispute with Hyderabad which gave Osman Ali the right to be consulted about the appointment of the governor of the Central Provinces, the right to fly his flag on public buildings in

---

[58] For details of the Kashmir revolt, see Ian Copland, 'Islam and Political Mobilisation in Kashmir, 1931–34', *Pacific Affairs*, 54, 2 (1981), 228–59. On the Alwar and Bharatpur risings, see I. S. Marwah, 'Tabligh Movement Among the Meos of Mewat', in M. S. A. Rao (ed.), *Social Movements in India*, II (Delhi, 1979); and Majid Hayat Siddiqi, 'History and Society in a Popular Rebellion: Mewat, 1920–1933', *Comparative Studies in Society and History*, 1986, 442–67.

Berar, the right, with the viceroy's permission, to hold *darbars* there, an assured annual payment of 25 lakhs as a first charge on the Berar revenues, a guarantee of 'undiminished' British military support and, for his eldest son, the title of 'Prince of Berar' – on balance, a very generous deal. The following December it retroceded to Hyderabad jurisdiction over the Secunderabad residency bazaar, and opened talks with Mysore about the disposition of the Bangalore cantonment which left Mirza with the firm understanding that if Mysore acceded, retrocession would immediately follow. In February 1934 the government legislated to make it an offence to 'overawe by . . . force or the show of . . . force, the administration of any State in India' – an initiative roundly condemned by opposition members of the Central Legislative Assembly as an attempt to appease the princes in advance of the 'coming of Federation'.[59] Later the same month, after years of stone-walling, it agreed to put its dispute with Nawanagar over the jam sahib's Bedi port development in the hands of an independent arbitrator – Lord Dunedin – and graciously went along with the umpire's verdict when Dunedin found in favour of the *darbar*.[60] In April Hoare offered Liaquat the cushy job of Indian high commissioner in London; and in December he found a knighthood for Hydari.

As intended, these inducements kept the larger states solid. Meanwhile, Delhi struck back hard at the 'ringleader' of the anti-federation campaign – Patiala himself – who was threatened with what Madhava Rao characterised as 'extreme measures' if he persisted in his covert association with the Diehards. This tactic, too, seems to have had some success, for when the *Post* correspondent called on Bhupinder Singh late in October 1934, he found him tearful, 'panicky and absolutely nervous'.[61]

Last but not least, the report of the JSC, which came out in November, proved much more benign to the states than the government and its federationist allies had feared. In language even plainer than the white

[59] Speech by Sir Hari Singh Gour, 7 Feb. 1934, NAI Home (Pol.) file 42/1/34 of 1934. The Princes' Protection Act of 1934 replaced that of 1922 which the rulers had long regarded as ineffective in preventing attacks on them from British India. It carried a penalty of seven years jail and a hefty fine. *IAR*, 1933, II, 87; *CLA Debates*, 1933, VI, 1080–4.

[60] Viceroy to sec. state 16 Feb. 1934, permanent under-sec. of state Coll., 32. The settlement restored to the *darbar* the right to impose duty at Bedi on goods bound for British India up to a maximum of five lakhs a year.

[61] This crisis was defused by Gwynne and other leading Diehards furnishing Patiala with letters in which they denied that they were engaged in any conspiracy with the maharaja to discredit Lord Willingdon personally or subvert the constitutional process. The viceroy was forced, against his better judgement, to accept their disclaimer. Afterwards Patiala showed his gratitude to Madhava Rao for his help in the matter by paying – anonymously – a sizeable sum into the latter's bank account. Madhava Rao to Gwynne 24 July 1936, Gwynne Coll., 5.

paper's, the JSC report stressed that no state could be compelled to federate against its will; that it was open to each acceding state to define exactly
the extent of its participation by negotiating a legally enforceable
Instrument of Accession (IOA) with the crown; that, outside these
defined limits, the autonomy of the state would 'not be affected in any
way'. Again, contrary to expectations, the report stuck closely in its
chapter on the franchise to the generous white paper formula as regards
the size of the legislatures, and in so many words gave the green light to
the Chamber's confederation plan, albeit on a regional level; and while it
failed to adopt the suggestion put to it by Mehta and Liaquat that the
rulers should be allowed to terminate the mandate of their nominees to
the federal legislature at any time, it did take on board their proposition
that the seats awarded to non-acceding states should be distributed
among the acceding states on a proportional basis rather than being left
vacant. Probably the report's only real shock was its recommendation that
maritime states acceding to the federation should be permitted to keep
only that proportion of the sea customs duty collected at their ports which
was 'properly attributable to dutiable goods consumed' at home.
Otherwise its financial recommendations, too, closely followed those of
the white paper.[62] To the chagrin of the Patiala camp, Hydari's new
Committee of Ministers (COMs) gave the report their guarded blessing.[63] As they caucused in preparation for the up-coming meeting of the
COP, Bikaner and his friends were still resigned to waging 'a great and
uphill fight' at the cost of 'much personal unpopularity . . . amongst our
Order';[64] but they now felt they had a reasonable chance of victory.

At home, too, the Diehards lost ground over the autumn and early
winter of 1934, in part as a result of the bad publicity which attended
Churchill's mischievous breach of privilege action against Hoare and
Lord Derby, which added two months to the JSC's already protracted
schedule. At the Conservative Party annual conference at Bristol in
October, they had failed by just seventeen votes to carry an amendment
repudiating the Cabinet's India policy; this, as Barnes and Middlemas
point out, was 'the nearest to a major defeat that any Conservative leader
has come at the hands of his followers in the present century'.[65] But

---

[62] Proceedings of the Joint Committee on Indian Constitutional Reform, *Volume I (Part I): Report* (London, 1934), paras. 154–6, 200–01, 295, 208–10, 256, 263–5, 366.
[63] Hydari to Bertrand Glancy 23 Dec. 1934, AP R/1/47/10/299. Half expecting this, Patiala and Dholpur had tried to contain the damage by reminding the princes, in advance, that the decision about federation was theirs alone to make, and urging them to speak out 'freely and frankly'. Panna and Dholpur to Patiala 21 Oct. 1934, RSA, Sirohi, Sadar Office, file 129 of 1934–5.
[64] Bikaner to Srinivasa Sastri 7 Jan. 1935, Srinivasa Sastri Papers, file G-4.
[65] Keith Middlemas and John Barnes, *Baldwin: A Biography* (London, 1969), 112–13.

thereafter it was all downhill. On 4 December they suffered a decisive defeat at the Conservative Central Council meeting at Queen's Hall, a result which reflected middle-of-the-road Tory satisfaction with the JSC proposals. Even Churchill's trump card, the letter from Patiala and his friends, which he had been holding in reserve for just this occasion, proved a 'damp squib'.[66] Then, a week later, the JSC report was endorsed in the House of Commons by a majority of two to one. Now, for the Diehards, everything depended on the princes. As the date for the COP session drew near, an anxious Gwynne cabled Madhava Rao for an update on Bhupinder Singh's attitude; while Lord Rothermere kept the wires humming with a stream of shrill telegrams to the rulers likening their inevitable fate under a federal constitution to that suffered by 'the loyalists of Southern Ireland' and by 'the French aristocrats who were so simple as to welcome the revolution of 1789 but were the first to be robbed of their estates and sent to the guillotine'.[67] Madhava Rao was reassuring; Patiala had not resiled one inch from the commitments he had given over the summer. Nevertheless, the old doubts persisted. Bhupinder Singh might have been won over – and Dholpur, and Panna and Jhalawar – but they were but 4 votes out of 109. When decision time came, would the Chamber defer to its chancellor – or would it side with his old enemy? The Diehards could only wait and hope.

Bombshell at Bombay

For a while things went according to plan. When the COP session opened in the third week of January 1935 Patiala opened proceedings by reviewing the federal experience of Canada and the USA, which he contended showed that no constitution was immutable. He then reviewed – disparagingly – the JSC report, before concluding his address with an appeal to his brother princes to consider federation on its merits and not to be swayed in their decision by governmental pressure:

it is a matter for Your Highnesses seriously to consider whether we should put ourselves in the position in which practically every important body of opinion in British India considers us unwelcome partners and looks upon our entry into Federation with suspicion. The benefits of a Federal Scheme to the Indian States are in any case not so overwhelming that, whatever the opinion of British India, it would be in our best interests to join it . . . let me say most emphatically, we are not enamoured of a Federal constitution as such; we have never approached His

---

[66] Sir Frank Brown to Hydari 7 Dec. 1934, AP R/1/47/10/306.
[67] e.g., Rothermere to Sirohi 23 Jan. and 1 Feb. 1935, RSA, Sirohi, Sadar Office, file 129 of 1934–5.

Majesty's Government and requested them to devise a federal constitution in order to safeguard our future. . .[68]

It was one of the maharaja's most effective public performances and Madhava Rao, who had helped write the speech, was well pleased with the results of his handiwork. When the inevitable counter-attack by the viceroy and Bikaner in the afternoon session failed to elicit more than a polite response from the gallery, the *Post* correspondent felt that a favourable outcome was almost assured.

His elation, however, was premature. Already, unbeknown to Madhava and Maqbool, Bhupinder Singh's faith in the power of the Diehards to protect him and his fellow rebels from official reprisals had been shaken by the Diehards' comprehensive defeat in the December parliamentary debate.[69] That evening Willingdon over dinner at Bikaner House rattled him further by informing him in an icy tone that in view of the chancellor's attitude he did not feel it would be proper for him to attend the reception which Patiala was hosting to mark the end of the COP session. Then the Standing Committee weighed in with a polite but pointed reminder that the policy of the Chamber was the policy enunciated in the Delhi Pact, not the policy of a section of the Conservative Party in England. Consequently, it was a somewhat chastened Patiala who returned to the podium the next day; he looked sheepish, and spoke haltingly. He said he now regretted some of the comments he had made in his opening address, and in particular, wished to withdraw the suggestion that the princes had been subject to governmental coercion – a charge which 'was utterly without truth'.[70] When Bikaner moved that the Chamber endorse the general thrust of the JSC report, he raised no objection. This turnabout confirmed Willingdon in his opinion that the maharaja was 'as unstable as water'.[71] As for the Diehards, Madhava Rao felt 'humiliated';[72] while Gwynne was 'hurt . . . to the quick'. 'Your Highness I am sure did not intend to let your friends and supporters here down', he wrote stiffly, 'but the effect of your speech is that we shall be regarded, in the coming controversies on the India Bill, as people who have not scrupled to put forward statements which they knew to be false.'[73]

Briefly the Diehards contemplated dropping Patiala altogether and

[68] Speech of 22 Jan. 1935, quoted in Panikkar, *Indian Princes in Council*, 118–20. Madhava Rao spent seven hours with Patiala on the 21st fine-tuning the speech. It was delivered over the strong protests of Liaquat, Patiala's prime minister.
[69] Sir Frank Brown to Sir A. Hydari 21 Dec. 1934, AP R/1/47/10/326.
[70] Gwynne to Patiala 24 Jan. 1935, Gwynne Coll., 1.
[71] Willingdon to Hoare 9 Dec. 1934, Templewood Coll., 8.
[72] Madhava Rao to Gwynne 28 Jan. and 4 Feb. 1935, Gwynne Coll., 3.
[73] Gwynne to Madhava Rao 11 Feb. 1935, Gwynne Coll., 3; and Gwynne to Patiala 24 Jan. 1935, Gwynne Coll., 1.

looking for a champion elsewhere; but in the end they decided to try to repair the damage. On the evening of 24 January, Madhava Rao confronted Patiala and Dholpur and reminded them 'about the [compromising] documents in our possession'. Bhupinder Singh replied that he expected Gwynne to honour his promise of confidentiality; but to the *Post* stringer's satisfaction, 'showed great signs of nervousness'.[74] Then, Madhava Rao approached an old friend who knew the political secretary Bertrand Glancy, and prevailed on him to tell Glancy that the Diehards had decided to publish the letter from Willingdon to Patiala containing the offer to reconsider some of the maharaja's long-standing claims in the light of his cooperation over federation. As Madhava Rao had calculated, the leak prompted an instant blast from a furious Glancy and, within the hour, an urgent telegraphic cry for help from a panicky Bhupinder Singh; but the *Post* correspondent deliberately took his time about answering it in order to draw out the tension, at first pleading incapacity due to illness, then declining the invitation on the grounds that his employer was still annoyed with him. Only after receiving a third 'bleating telegram', on the eve of the Bombay conference, did the *Post* correspondent finally oblige Patiala with his presence, and then he remained distant and coy, explaining to the maharaja that while he was keen to help his old friend he did not feel able to do so until Patiala had discharged his part of the bargain and delivered on those 'things on which I have set my heart'. Willing by this stage to promise almost anything to get himself off the hook, Bhupinder Singh readily agreed to cooperate. Gwynne at once got hold of the *Post*'s legal adviser, J. H. Morgan KC, and together the two men drafted a compliant resolution for Patiala to put to the conference; thereafter, the Diehards were in 'almost hourly' communication with Bombay.[75]

Nevertheless, for all of Madhava Rao's intriguing, things would probably not have gone nearly as well as they did for the Diehards at Bombay had not Whitehall unwittingly come to their rescue. In late January a draft of the India Bill was shown to Hyderabad's legal counsel in London, Walter Monckton and Charles Brunyate; and on the 31st copies were telegraphed to India, where they were examined by the Hydari COMs. It reawakened all their old fears. Monckton and Brunyate found the 'whole approach' of the bill alarming. Brunyate thought it bristled with difficulties and anticipated that the Hyderabad *darbar* would 'like us, regard it as forbidding'.[76] Monckton went further, telling the India Office that he could not, consistent with the instructions he had been given, 'advise the

[74] Madhava Rao to Gwynne 28 Jan. 1935, Gwynne Coll., 3.
[75] Hoare to Lord Brabourne 4 Mar. 1935, Gilbert, *Churchill*, V, 1099–100.
[76] Brunyate to Hydari 25 Jan. 1935, AP R/1/47/10/406.

State to accede on the basis of the Bill as it stands'.[77] And the Hydari Committee was equally unimpressed. It had great trouble with the proposition in clause 6 that a federating ruler should accept the entire act as applicable to his state; it saw in the proposal for a federal railway authority a stalking horse for the centralisation of state lines; it did not like the suggestion that federal laws would apply to the states *proprio vigore*, ruling out parallel legislation by the *darbars*. However, the ministers' problems with the draft bill went beyond these substantive defects. When Hydari's team checked their records, they were outraged to discover that in several important respects the bill departed from the position which had been agreed upon during meetings between the states' legal representatives and the India Office and conflicted with assurances given during the JSC hearings by the secretary of state.[78] Feeling betrayed, Hydari immediately took steps to bury the hatchet with Patiala and Bhopal. For the first time in years the government found itself facing a unitedly hostile princely order.

As things turned out, the resolution put and carried at Bombay stopped short, thanks to Akbar Hydari's reasoned advocacy,[79] of outright rejection of the federal scheme. Nevertheless both the tone of the resolution, and the speeches made in support of it, were highly critical. Bhupinder Singh pronounced it a 'counterfeit' scheme which had 'nothing in common, except in name, to the general outline we accepted at the first Round Table Conference'. Bhopal agreed that the draft constitution fell 'far short of many of our vital demands'. Sir C. P., representing Travancore, predicted 'calamitous results' if the bill were passed in its current form.[80] All this was unambiguous enough; but to ensure that London got the message, Patiala, Bikaner and Bhopal sent a summary of the proceedings to the political secretary along with a curt covering letter which ended with the observation that unless the draft bill was drastically revised, it would 'be difficult for a very large number of Princes to accept [the] Federation scheme'.[81]

To say they succeeded is to put it mildly. The resolution, and still more

---

[77] Monckton to Patrick 28 Jan. 1935, IOR L/P&S/13/665.
[78] Hydari to Glancy 21 Feb. 1935, IOR L/P&S/13/607. The committee comprised Hydari, K. A. H. Abbasi (Bhopal), Sir C. P. Ramaswamy Aiyer (Travancore), Armanath Atal (Jaipur), S. M. Bapna (Indore), Col. Colvin (Kashmir), Liaquat, Mehta, Panikkar, Sir P. Pattani, S. R. Rajagopalachari (Mysore), S. A. Ranadive (Baroda), D. K. Sen (Mandi), P. K. Sen (Mayurbhanj), and Y. A. Thambore (Sangli).
[79] Sir Frank Brown to Hydari 15 Mar. 1935, AP, R/1/47/10/348. Hydari argued convincingly that an 'attitude of mere negation' would expose the states to a charge of bad faith.
[80] Verbatim record of speeches at Bombay conference, 25 Feb. 1935, IOR L/P&S/13/682.
[81] Patiala, Bhopal and Bikaner to the pol. sec. 27 Feb. 1935, Sever, *Documents and Speeches*, II, 504–7.

the verbatim record of the princes' and ministers' speeches, which were splashed across the pages of the next day's *Morning Post*, burst like a bombshell in the corridors of British power. 'Ye Gods! These reforms and these Princes', exploded Willingdon. 'Pon my word after all the work we have done it seems too d—ble that they sh[oul]d try and run out at this moment.' 'Really, the more one hears of that gathering . . . at Bombay, the more one almost despairs of the moral sense of any of them.'[82] Samuel Hoare, caught entirely off guard, and forced to defend himself in parliament against a Diehard opposition evidently better informed than the government, was equally furious. The situation as a consequence of the Bombay meeting was 'fraught with danger', he informed the viceroy. Even his colleagues in the cabinet were 'asking whether it was worth going on with the Bill at all', while in the party at large the general impression seemed to be that the government had been badly let down 'from your end'.[83]

The Diehards shared this perception; however, what was for the government a source of anguish was for them a matter for celebration. 'The Bill will now have either to be completely recast or to be dropped', crowed Rothermere.[84] 'It has been as good as killed', echoed Gwynne.[85] Churchill was no less sanguine. 'This is a political fact of capital importance', he wrote to his wife. 'It wrecks the federal scheme against which I have been fighting [for] so long.'[86]

Gwynne calls it quits

However, as in so many matters during the interwar years, Churchill's judgement proved astray. The Bombay resolution of the states temporarily rocked the federation bandwagon but it did not, surprisingly, derail it. In the end, the bill went through. Much maligned but still very much on the agenda, the goal of all-India federation survived the crisis of 1935 to haunt and mesmerise the princes and their ministers for a further four years. How did the tables get turned so quickly and – in the short term at any rate – so comprehensively?

To put it in a nutshell, the Diehards badly miscalculated. While the motivations of the *darbaris* are not altogether clear (and may not in every case have been clear to themselves) it is fairly certain that the majority of rulers and ministers who voted for the resolution did so not out of

---

[82] Willingdon to Butler 16 Mar. 1935, Butler Coll., 54; and Willingdon to Hoare 24 Mar. 1935, Templewood Coll., 8.

[83] Sec. state to viceroy 7 Mar. 1935, IOR L/PO/92; and Hoare to Willingdon 1 Mar. 1935, Templewood Coll., 4.   [84] Gwynne to Madhava Rao 1 Mar. 1935, Gwynne Coll., 3.

[85] Ibid.   [86] Churchill to Clementine Churchill 2 Mar. 1935, Gilbert, *Churchill*, V, 1097.

disenchantment with federation as such, but in the hope of extracting better terms. 'Bombay resolution was never intended to mean anything more than what it clearly stated and was deliberately worded so as to imply that with necessary amendments Federal scheme emanating from Reform Bill would be acceptable to States', Hydari assured Hyderabad's solicitors.[87] The same point was also pressed upon the viceroy by Patiala, Bhopal and Bikaner in their joint letter of 27 February, though with typical disingenuousness Bhupinder Singh omitted to mention this balancing act to his Diehard mentors. Alternatively, some delegates could well have supported the resolution with the intention of making an ambit claim on the largesse of the government. After talking to some of the rulers at a post-conference party at the Aga Khan's palace in Bombay, M. R. Jayakar came away with the impression that they had 'astutely discovered that . . . Hoare . . . will yield to pressure if any is exerted', and were determined to put this insight to the test.[88] Not long after this encounter, Hamidullah pointedly reminded the secretary of state that the question of paramountcy remained unresolved. The India Office was quite right in thinking that this approach constituted a blatant attempt at blackmail.[89]

Mistaking the import of the Bombay resolution, the Diehards also did not reckon with the vigour of the government's reaction to it. As we have seen, London's first instinct after the Bombay debacle was to withdraw or significantly amend the India Bill to make it more enticing to the states; but this timorous mood soon evaporated, to be replaced by one of icy determination. The party whips had made it plain to him, Hoare informed Willingdon, that they were not 'prepared to be blackmailed over paramountcy questions' that had nothing to do, strictly speaking, with the reform scheme before parliament. The cabinet too was keen 'to call the Princes' bluff', even if this gave rise to a 'situation that would enable Winston to torpedo . . . the Bill',[90] and was prepared to sanction strong measures to 'deflate' the rulers' pretensions so that meaningful negotiations could resume.[91] Already resolved that Patiala, for one, should 'get it in the neck', Willingdon needed no second bidding.[92] The next week he summoned the three self-proclaimed organisers of the Bombay conference to Delhi and gave them a blistering dressing-down; afterwards, in a separate interview, he warned Bhupinder Singh that charges of

---

[87] Hydari to Coward, Chance and Co. 11 Mar. 1935, IOR L/PO/92.
[88] Jayakar to Sapru 12 Apr. 1935, Jayakar Papers, 408.
[89] Croft to Lord Brabourne 8 Mar. 1935, IOR L/PO/92.
[90] Hoare to Willingdon 8 Mar. 1935, Templewood Coll., 4.
[91] Croft to Clive Wigram 7 Mar. 1935, IOR L/PO/92.
[92] Willingdon to his son 12 Apr. 1935, Willingdon Private Coll. Hoping to get a second vice-regal term, Willingdon suspected that the Bombay debacle may have queered his chances; he blamed Patiala for this threat to his career.

maladministration could follow if he maintained his intransigent posture.[93] But the most telling blows, perhaps, were delivered from London. Hoare briefed the palace and persuaded the king-emperor to tell the Standing Committee through Willingdon that, in view of the princes' behaviour at Bombay, they would not be welcome at his silver jubilee celebrations. To drive the point home he clapped a blanket ban on the India Office receiving states' ministers with Diehard links. Later in the year the chairman of the JSC, Lord Linlithgow, gave Hamidullah a 'very unpleasant ten minutes' over his letter on paramountcy.[94]

Inevitably, this campaign left its mark. Linlithgow noted that at the end of his interview with Bhopal, the nawab appeared 'shaken and distracted'; and during a session with Hoare's successor Lord Zetland, Patiala broke down and wept, promising to mend his ways. More significantly, perhaps, observers on the British side noticed a slow but constant change in Bhupinder Singh's demeanour over the spring and summer. No longer the jaunty, ebullient personality who had captured the COP in 1926, he appeared ill and tired, the epitome of a man broken in spirit.[95] Naturally the government counted this as an 'improvement',[96] and by May London felt sufficiently confident that they had broken the back of the Chamber's resistance to suggest to the king that he might wish to rescind his ban on the rulers attending his silver jubilee.

In fact, there was still a good deal of resistance to federation in the princes' ranks (as we shall see in chapter 5), but for the time being it had been driven underground, and that sufficed for the government's immediate needs with respect to the Tory back-bench. Moreover, it allowed the pro-federation forces among the princely leadership, whose voices had been temporarily drowned in the universal outcry over the draft bill, to reassert themselves, and, in so doing, to begin the task of rebuilding bridges with the authorities. Panikkar, in particular, played an important role in this process, both as a member of Hydari's COMs and as Patiala's new foreign minister, in which latter capacity he made a successful trip to London in October 1935 to argue his master's case before the secretary of state Zetland.

But reconciliation was helped, too, by some timely concessions from the government side. In late March the secretary of state announced that

[93] Madhava Rao to Gwynne 25 Mar. 1935, Gwynne Coll., 3; and Hoare to Willingdon 9 May 1935, Templewood Coll., 4.
[94] Note by Sir R. Glancy dated 25 Nov. 1935, IOR L/P&S/13/809; Zetland to Willingdon 19 July 1935, Zetland Coll., 8; 'Interview between the Marquess of Linlithgow and the Nawab of Bhopal', 22 July 1936, L/PO/91; and Harold Nicholson, *King George V: His Life and Reign* (London, 1952), 509.
[95] Gwynne to Madhava Rao 6 and 9 May 1935, Gwynne Coll., 3.
[96] Hoare to Willingdon 9 May 1935, Templewood Coll., 4.

he was proposing to amend the bill in ways that would accord the rulers greater freedom to impose reservations on the power of the federal legislature to make laws for their states and would clarify the crown's continuing obligations to the states in the non-federal sphere. This, in itself, greatly mollified *darbari* opinion. Moreover, by enlisting the cooperation of the princes' London lawyers, Hoare was able to dress up these relatively small amendments as hard-won concessions: 'the most that the [rulers'] Counsel had been able, with very great difficulty, to extract from a reluctant India Office'.[97] This gave the pro-federation ministers a hook on which to argue that the India bill was now reasonably acceptable. Hence, by the time the decisive third reading debate opened on 4 June, most of the hue and cry from the states' side had died down, leaving the Diehards bereft of new ammunition with which to assail the government. In the event, not even 'a masterly performance . . . of parliamentary oratory'[98] from Churchill was enough to save the day, and the bill passed into law with a handsome majority in the Commons of 264. It received the royal assent on 2 August 1935.

The enactment of the India Bill paved the way for an all-India federation; but it did not bring the federation into being. Under the terms of the act, the federal part of the new constitution could not be inaugurated until a majority of states had signified their adherence to it by completing IOAs. Thus, as Madhava Rao pointed out to Jinnah, the possibility still existed for the Diehards to 'hold up the Federation' by persuading 'the Princes to say no to it'.[99] Nevertheless, with the passage of the act, much of the Diehards' will to fight dissolved. For one thing, they were not eager to resume relations with the princes who had let them down so badly over the bill. For another, they felt morally obliged, now that the reform bill was an accomplished fact, to give the legislation a chance to work, unimpeded by outside interference. Quizzed by Madhava Rao about his next move, Gwynne replied: 'We have fought the policy that was enumerated in the White Paper . . . to the last ditch. But, like a cricketer who has been given "out" by the umpire, we must walk to the Pavilion accepting the verdict with all the loyalty of a good sportsman.'[100] This conviction was strengthened, if anything, after August when it became known that Lord Linlithgow, a man respected and admired on all sides 'for his sincerity of purpose . . . sympathy' and integrity (and incidentally an old friend of Gwynne's) was soon to replace Willingdon as viceroy. It seemed to the

[97] W. D. Croft to Wigram, 26 Mar. 1935, IOR L/PO/92. The India Office was rather pleased at the success of this 'Oriental mode of proceeding'.
[98] Christopher Addison to Churchill [?] June 1935, quoted in Gilbert, *Churchill*, VI, 616.
[99] Madhava Rao to Gwynne 27 Apr. 1936, Gwynne Coll., 4.
[100] Gwynne to Madhava Rao 25 Oct. 1935, Gwynne Coll., 3.

Diehards that, regardless of anything else, Linlithgow deserved a chance to repair the damage wrought to the Anglo-Indian relationship by his ill-starred predecessor.[101]

Of course, on an individual level, Conservative MPs continued to meet and correspond with Indian princes and, for a time, some of the Diehards sought to exploit these links for political purposes. However Winston Churchill was not among them. By the time parliament resumed after the general election of November 1935, he had put India on the back burner in favour of other issues and causes: German rearmament; Singapore; appeasement. In the absence of his unrivalled energy and charisma, the movement never recovered its former momentum; and when, in 1937, the group's mouthpiece, the *Morning Post*, whose circulation had dropped from a peak of half a million in the 1920s to a paltry 117,000, went into receivership,[102] Dichardism as a public phenomenon effectively expired with it.

It is not surprising that the Diehards failed to achieve their primary goal of scuttling the India Bill. For one thing, there had always been too few of them where it really counted – in the House of Commons. For another, they made some grave miscalculations. Badly advised by Madhava Rao, they vastly overrated Patiala's dominance over the princely order. They did not reckon with the power of the government's coercive apparatus, or with its determination to force the bill through almost at any cost. Taking their cue from Churchill, who still saw India through a nine-teenth-century lens, they failed to appreciate how far some of the *darbars* had moved towards an accommodation with the principle of Indian self-rule. Nevertheless it would be wrong to suggest, as historians are wont to do,[103] that they made no lasting impact. Through their scare propaganda, and indirectly through the legal advice dispensed by sympathetic lawyers such as Leslie Scott, they planted a deep suspicion about federation in the minds of many of the princes which, being at heart emotive and irrational, the latter's advisers found difficult to dispel. One might say, looking ahead, that the fatal delay which occurred between the passage of the bill and the finalisation of the terms of accession owed much to this sub-versive handiwork. Secondly, the Diehards' intrigues further undermined the solidarity of the princely order; while their success in subborning successive chancellors of the COP gravely compromised the authority of that office (already weakened by Willingdon's mischief-making). Again, both

---

[101] Gwynne to Dewas Junior 28 May 1936, Gwynne Coll., 1; and Gwynne to Madhava Rao 18 Sept. 1936, Gwynne Coll., 5.

[102] Subsequently to be taken over by its more mainstream Tory competitor, the *Telegraph*.

[103] See, e.g., Robert Rhodes James, *Churchill: A Study In Failure, 1900–1939* (London, 1970).

these achievements had arguably fatal long-term consequences for the states. Lastly, the Diehards managed to fan what till then had been a diffuse sense of uneasiness among the princes about federation into something like an organised resistance movement; implicitly, if not intentionally, an anti-government movement. Even after things were patched up in 1935, the British remembered. Bent on 'saving' the raj, the Diehards' most enduring contribution may have been to sew nagging doubts about the reliability of its most conspicuous allies.

5   On the edge of the abyss

It is a matter of supreme thankfulness that they have been warned in time; that their eyes have been opened to the deadly abyss that yawns before them.

Anonymous pamphlet, 1939

Federation becalmed

When six years of intense and often acrimonious political debate finally bore fruit, in mid-1935, with the passage of the Government of India Act, it seemed to many observers of the Indian scene that the hard work of constitution making was over, such tasks as still remained being merely matters of detail – of fine tuning an already completed machine. Of course those closer to the action – particularly the India Office officials responsible for drawing up the standard IOA which would specify what sections of the act would apply to states acceding to the federation – knew differently. Conscious of the technical complexity of the matters covered by the IOA, they were also keenly aware of the opportunities these presented for legalistic procrastination if (as seemed, on the basis of previous experience, highly likely) the princes, through their lawyers, decided to argue the toss. Nevertheless, even in official circles there was an air of cautious optimism, a sense that the biggest hurdles in the way of all-India federation had been surmounted. And this confidence was both mirrored and reinforced by the appointment in 1936 of the towering,[1] 49-year-old marquess of Linlithgow to fill Willingdon's shoes as viceroy. Although he was already more familiar than most with the intricacies of the new Indian constitution as a result of his capable chairmanship of the JSC, Linlithgow was a devout believer in federation and, legalistic difficulties notwithstanding, he was confident that he could sell the package to the princes quickly – and with a minimum of fuss. Soon after his arrival, he

[1] Linlithgow was six foot-five, a giant of a man at a time when very few male caucasians topped six feet.

told the political department's Francis Wylie that his aim was to see federation up and running by 1 April 1938.[2] Such was Linlithgow's energy and exuberance, and so contagious was his missionary spirit, that neither Wylie nor any other officials in the department initially questioned the practicality of this timetable.

However, during the interval between the passage of the act and Linlithgow's arrival a major difference of opinion had already developed between Delhi and London about the timing of the next approach to the princes. Notwithstanding persistent reminders from the viceroy that precious time was slipping by, the new secretary of state, Lord Zetland, gave no indication that he was in a hurry to consummate the federal scheme. On the contrary, his correspondence was full of plausible excuses for delay: the lawyers had not yet produced an acceptable IOA; a premature approach to the rulers might 'frighten them off';[3] alternatively, it could embroil the government in unwanted horse-trading and entrap Delhi into 'giving away valuable counters' even before serious negotiations had commenced;[4] 'the market' for federation was at present 'against' the government but could, in future, improve, permitting a 'better bargain';[5] concessions given to particular states would almost certainly be claimed by others; a policy of appeasement would be construed by the states as a gesture of weakness, and an invitation to further lobbying; it was important for the government to get the provincial parts of the act working smoothly before taking the next step. 'To tell the truth, I think some people here are inclined to feel that we shall do better not to press matters too much just now', wrote Paul Patrick with ironic understatement.[6]

The omens were grim; but Linlithgow was a fighter and he believed he had a better sense of what was needed to get federation operative than the politicians in England. After consulting his advisers and several dewans he adjudged to be sympathetic, including Hydari and Krishnamachari of Baroda,[7] the viceroy revived Arthur Lothian's plan of the previous winter for an exploratory tour of the states by two or three senior political officers. The idea was to entice the *darbars* to 'show their hand', and, thereby,

---

[2] Linlithgow to Wylie 18 Aug. 1936, IOR L/P&S/13/613.
[3] Zetland to Linlithgow 28 June 1936, Zetland Coll., 7.
[4] Patrick to Lothian 27 Apr. 1937, Lothian Coll., 1
[5] Zetland to Linlithgow 30 May 1937, IOR L/P&S/13/613.
[6] Patrick to Lothian 27 Apr. 1937, Lothian Coll., 1.
[7] Linlithgow's initial inclination was to hold a 'formal durbar of all the Princes', but Krishnamachari pointed out that a big meeting could well allow 'a few vocal malcontents to spead doubt and despondency among their more timid brethren', and recommended that the viceroy approach the states separately. Linlithgow to Hoare 6 June 1936, Linlithgow Coll., 152.

to make it difficult for them subsequently to raise the ante.[8] Again, reaction from Whitehall was conspicuously cool. However Linlithgow refused to be put off, and eventually Zetland gave in to his eloquence and persistence. On 17 August 1936 it was announced that Sir Courtney Latimer, Lothian and Wylie would visit western, southern and northern India respectively over the winter months to ascertain the attitude of the Indian princes to the scheme of federation embodied in the 1935 Act.

Divided counsels

It is true that Zetland was in no hurry to get federation up and running. His party had never been enthusiastic about central responsibility and but for the pressure of public opinion in India – and the fortuitous offer from the princes – would have stuck with Simon's recipe for a limited devolution of power to the provinces. So long as the Conservatives could not be held accountable, they were quite content, from an imperial viewpoint, to see the *status quo* continue indefinitely. Nevertheless, the main problem lay with the team responsible for drafting the IOA. Again, this was due less to procrastination from the India Office members than to internecine quarrels among the lawyers hired by the states – quarrels inspired both by professional jealousies and by the continuing factional struggle within the monarchical order.

The India Office had not expected the going to be so tough. They had assumed they would be dealing with eminent English lawyers, men well known to them personally or through the 'old boy' network; and indeed the original princely legal team assembled early in 1935 – Sir Walter Monckton and Alexander Fachiri (acting for Hyderabad, Cutch and Bhavnagar) and Sir Wilfred Greene and C. J. Colombos (acting for the Chamber) – exactly fitted the stereotype. Monckton had been attorney-general to the prince of Wales before his ill-starred elevation to the throne as Edward VIII; he and Zetland were fellow members of the board of governors of Harrow School; and Greene was 'held in the highest regard in . . . Government circles'.[9] But in late 1935 something of a turnover occurred in the COP legal camp. First, Bhupinder Singh, angered by reports that Greene had spoken about him irreverently in conversation with senior officials at the India Office, insisted on hiring his own counsel and gave the job to an American lawyer he'd met in Paris, the semi-retired New Yorker, Judge W. H. Wadhams. To their surprise, the British officials found Wadhams quite civilised and knowledgeable about international

---

[8] Note by V. Narahari Rao dated 29 Aug. 1936, NAI Home (Pol.) file 155/38.
[9] Brunyate to Hydari 1 Feb. 1935, AP R/1/47/10/411.

law. As Wylie, who met him subsequently in India, noted: 'if we had to have an American lawyer in this business we could have done worse than [the] Judge'.[10] Nevertheless Wadhams' arrival broke up the cosy circle, and his initial unfamiliarity with the act slowed the drafting process.

Then, learning that the Standing Committee wanted him in India over the winter months for consultations, Greene asked to be relieved of his brief on the grounds that the journey was too risky for a man of his age. This created the need for a replacement, which opened the way for Patiala as chancellor to press the considerable claims of Judge Wadhams; but while Bhupinder Singh was still trying to persuade the Standing Committee of Wadhams' suitability, Dholpur, in concert with Madhava Rao, unearthed an alternative candidate in the person of the *Morning Post*'s legal adviser John Hartman Morgan KC, who had helped to draft the resolution carried with such fateful consequences at Bombay in February 1935. Suspicious of Wadhams' American background, and confident that, as a member of 'the extreme right', Morgan could be relied upon not to turn into a government stooge, the Standing Committee initially voted, in January 1936, to hire the Englishman.[11] However the astute Panikkar, horrified by the idea of a Diehard lawyer being let loose on the IOA, put it to the Committee that Morgan and Wadhams, coming as they did from such differing backgrounds, possessed complementary skills which should be harnessed jointly in the Chamber's cause. This argument was accepted; moreover Panikkar saw to it that in the telegram sent to the Chamber's solicitors in London informing them of the decision Wadhams was described as chief counsel and Morgan as his junior – an arrangement he was confident would reduce, if not eliminate, Morgan's capacity for mischief.[12]

And so it might have: but for a grave miscalculation on the part of Patiala and Bikaner. As we have seen, a number of major rulers had severed their ties with the Chamber, diminishing both its prestige and resources, and, with their departure, others began to lose interest. In 1934, for the first time ever, a majority of members defaulted on their dues, leaving the Chamber technically bankrupt. The next year only thirty-three princes attended the annual session, barely enough for a quorum. Meanwhile rampant factionalism, fanned by Diehard intrigues, had become the order of the day in the Standing Committee, bringing effective decision-making, in Panikkar's words, 'practically . . . to a standstill'.[13] Although reelected comfortably in a postal ballot in February

[10] Wylie to Glancy 4 Jan. 1937, Zetland Coll., 14.
[11] Proceedings of meeting at Motibagh Palace, Patiala, 27 Jan. 1936, PSA, COP, file 31 (29) of 1936.   [12] Note by Patrick dated 5 June 1936, IOR L/P&S/13/608.
[13] Panikkar to Desmond Young 8 Feb. 1934, NAI Home (Pol.) 33/4/35.

1936, Bhupinder Singh knew that the organisation he commanded faced certain extinction unless it was reformed in ways that made it more palatable to the bigger states; but he also knew from bitter past experience that it would take some extraordinary crisis to shake the membership up sufficiently to get them to vote for a programme of radical change.

Accordingly, after talking matters over with his newly acquired allies Bhopal and Bikaner, the chancellor on 26 February told the Committee that he and Ganga Singh had decided that they could no longer serve the COP as presently constituted,[14] and would be asking the viceroy to issue a writ for fresh elections. (Both, it goes without saying, expected to be reelected.) Willingdon, however, saw here the opportunity he had been waiting for to get even with Bhupinder Singh; while accepting the tendered resignations, he blithely ignored the chancellor's request for a general spill and authorised Dholpur, as pro-chancellor, to carry on until the next annual session which was not due until February 1937. Madhava Rao was jubilant, for he reckoned that Dholpur owed him some favours and as a relatively novice princely politician would be 'leaning very heavily' on his 'assistance and support'.[15] And Udaibhan Singh did not disappoint. At its first meeting on 16 April the new Standing Committee, with the pro-chancellor in the chair, terminated Wadhams' appointment, recalled Panikkar from London whence he had been dispatched by Patiala and debited Wadhams' fees – an amount estimated at over £5,000 – to the Patiala state. Shortly afterwards, Dholpur instructed Herbert Smith and Company, a firm of solicitors who had acted for Churchill's India Defence League, to take over the Chamber's case and to brief Morgan as sole counsel. Publicly Dholpur defended the choice of Morgan by pointing to the latter's credentials as an expert in constitutional law. However new Chamber secretary M. C. Sharma was more forthcoming in a private chat with Hydari: Morgan had been recommended to the Chamber 'by friends of the British Conservative group who were of the view that, apart from being an eminent lawyer, Mr. Morgan's own leanings would induce him to take a personal interest in the Princes' case'.[16]

Morgan did, indeed, throw himself into the work with a will; and from a purely professional point of view gave the princes pretty good value for their money. On the other hand, his advent caused havoc at the negotiating table. Where Judge Wadhams was charming and urbane, Morgan was brash and acerbic. Coupled with his extremist political connections,

---

[14] Patiala to Standing Committee 26 Feb. 1935, encl. in Dholpur to Gwynne 6 May 1936, Gwynne Coll., 1.   [15] Madhava Rao to Gwynne 7 Sept 1936, Gwynne Coll., 5.
[16] Record of conversation between Sharma and Hydari encl. in Sharma to chancellor 30 May 1936, PSA, COP, file 118 (15) of 1937.

this made him so unwelcome at the India Office that the government's legal adviser, Maurice Gwyer, seriously considered quitting his post.[17] But if the officials were discomforted by Morgan's presence, Wadhams was still more so. Although the two lawyers had not met before, both knew of the other by reputation and the disrespect was mutual. As well, Wadhams was deeply incensed by the fact that Morgan had come intending to displace him as Chamber counsel. Meanwhile, Morgan was put out by Wadham's condescension and by Zetland's refusal to recognise Morgan in any other capacity than as junior to Wadhams, which, amongst other things, meant a smaller fee. Hence, while nominally members of the same team, the two Chamber lawyers spent much of their time at the India Office feuding. Later Wadhams likened the experience to 'taking part in [an] Olympic games – legal section', with himself wearing the Patiala colours 'in the lists'.[18] Yet the officials' hopes that this rivalry might permit them to divide and rule at the negotiating table were quickly dashed. On the contrary, the tense relationship that obtained between them served to keep both lawyers on their toes and prompted them to try to out-do one another in protecting their clients' interests – as when Wadhams pronounced a Morgan revise of the draft IOA inadequate because it failed to spell out in exhaustive detail 'all the safeguards requisite to protect the Indian Rulers in a Federation'.[19] Seeing no prospect of an early agreement, Zetland in August suspended the negotiations indefinitely – to the bitter disappointment of the pro-federationists and the secret satisfaction of the Dholpur faction of the COP.

However, Dholpur's growing complacency on this score was dented by the viceroy's announcement a few days later about the political officers' tour which, though advertised as exploratory, was correctly interpreted by the pro-chancellor as a tactic to bring pressure to bear on the states. Belatedly stung into action – for he had done nothing thus far to organise his constituents – Udaibhan Singh got the secretariat to send out a questionnaire inviting member states to list the reservations they intended to claim in their IOAs and asked Hydari's COMs to report back to a general meeting of princes and ministers at Bombay in October on the effectiveness of the constitutional safeguards contained in the India Act and on the number and type of reservations they considered essential to the states' needs. Through these means, he hoped to manoeuvre them into adopting a common stand when the time came for them to declare their hand to the viceroy's representatives. At the same time, Udaibhan lobbied

[17] Gwyer to Patrick 4 Apr. 1936, IOR L/P&S/13/608.
[18] Wadhams to Patiala 10 Aug. 1936, PSA, COP, file 35 (76) of 1935–8.
[19] Memo. by Wadhams dated 30 Sept. 1936, encl. in Wadhams to Glancy 11 Nov. 1936, IOR R/1/1/4703.

strenuously through private channels to ensure a large turnout at Bombay of the smaller states which he knew were more likely to run shy of federation if it came to a vote. Finally, Dholpur begged Linlithgow to give the *darbars* more time to prepare; he did not get the respite he was hoping for, but he did manage to have the starting date for the tour put back to November, a gain of several weeks.

Armed with a couple of aces in his pocket – a summary of the responses to the questionnaire, which showed that most of the rulers were prepared to federate only with extensive reservations, and the report of the COMs, which found that the safeguards contained in the act were not watertight enough to warrant the states' full participation – Dholpur arrived in Bombay in a confident frame of mind; and for the most part he got the result he wanted. Yet the pro-chancellor's victory was not quite as complete as Udaibhan himself claimed afterwards to Linlithgow's private secretary Laithwaite.[20] Although the meeting overwhelmingly endorsed the gloomy recommendations of the COMs (thus implicitly proclaiming its dissatisfaction with the federal scheme expounded in the Act) it baulked at passing, as in February 1935, a firm resolution to that effect, instead resolving to appoint two subcommittees to consider the matter – one, under Patiala's chairmanship, to investigate the constitutional issues, the other, under Bhopal's, to look into the financial aspects. This arrangement was in itself a mild rebuff; but the outcome was made worse by the election to the Patiala committee of Panikkar, Liaquat, Mehta and Haksar – all ardent federationists.[21] Secondly, despite Dholpur's entreaties, the dissidents insisted on going public. At the end of the conference Mehta and Panikkar, together with the dewans of Mandi, Sangli and Bahawalpur, issued a statement attacking Hydari for having given a 'substantially incorrect appreciation of the provisions of the Government of India Act'.[22] Recognising that he was in for a hard fight, the pro-chancellor sought to bolster his armoury by persuading the COP to bring Morgan out from England.

However, securing Morgan for the Chamber proved harder than Udaibhan and his conservative friends had anticipated. Morgan himself,

[20] Laithwaite to Stewart 22 Nov. 1936, Linlithgow Coll., 131.
[21] The members were: Patiala (Chairman), Dewas Junior, Panna, Rampur, the Yuvaraj of Limbdi, Hydari, K. A. H. Abbasi of Bhopal, Amar Nath Atal of Jaipur, Sir S. M. Bapna of Indore, K. C. Neogy of Mayurbhanj, Panikkar, Pattani, D. A. Surve of Kolhapur, Y. A. Thombare of Sangli, Mehta, Mirza Ismail, Col. Colvin of Kashmir, Krishnamachari of Baroda, Sir C. P. Ramaswamy Aiyer of Travancore, Sir Shanmukhan Chetty of Cochin, Haksar, Liaquat, Sen of Mandi, B. N. Zutshi of Rewa, B. H. Zaidi of Rampur, V. M. Pawar of Dewas Junior, Kanwar Singh of Jodhpur, Dharam Narain of Udaipur, Mohammad Hussain of Bahawalpur, Maqbool Mahmud, now representing Sachin, and Chamber Secretary Sharma.   [22] *The Times of India*, 2 Nov. 1936.

conscious of the fragility of Dholpur's position and still bristling from his 'demotion' at the hands of Udaibhan's predecessor, was reluctant to accept the brief and held out for a higher fee – £16,000 up front and £100 for every day he was required to spend in India.[23] A gloomy Madhava Rao reckoned that it would take the pro-chancellor at least three months to raise the money;[24] in fact it took him six, although most states were asked to contribute only Rs 3,500. Likewise, whilst the smaller states were generally happy to 'shelter under Mr. Morgan's capability in telling [us] how to avoid it [accession]',[25] many of the more substantial Chamber members, led by Patiala and Bikaner, voiced strong opposition. Thanks to their dogged rearguard action, Morgan's appointment was not formalised by the Standing Committee until 5 November 1936, only two weeks before he was due to leave for India.

Shrouded in controversy from the beginning, Morgan's initiation into the inner circle of princely advisers over the winter of 1936–7 proved as lively, acrimonious and divisive as his advent at the India Office had been the previous spring. When the Patiala committee got down to business on 25 January, Morgan found himself once again staring across the table at the ample face of Judge Wadhams, who had come out to India as counsel to Patiala and had been coopted at the discretion of the chairman, Bhupinder Singh. What is more, he discovered that the subcommittee had been furnished with a 34–page memorandum (unsigned, but in fact authored by Wadhams) which, while purporting to be merely 'explanatory', nevertheless concluded with the partisan proposition that 'both the essential and the negotiable proposals of the Chamber' had been 'substantially incorporated in the Act'.[26] Yet, far from fazing the Englishman, this demonstration of the subcommittee's bias only spurred him on. He began by launching a withering attack on the memorandum, accusing its anonymous author of misreading the Act, misunderstanding the common law and, above all, of ignoring overseas precedents. 'I do not quite know who is the "counsel" responsible for this highly original opinion', he declared icily, looking all the while at Wadhams, 'but I find it impossible to believe that he was an English counsel.' But he saved his heaviest salvos for the statute itself. Over several days Morgan dissected the 1935 Act with ruthless efficiency. He pointed to loopholes which made the Act's 'safeguards' illusory. He argued that the provision which

[23] Madhava Rao to Gwynne 13 July 1936, Gwynne Coll., 5.
[24] Madhava Rao to Gwynne 1 May 1936, Gwynne Coll., 4.
[25] Dewan of Bijawar to Gwynne 16 Nov. 1936, Gwynne Coll., 5.
[26] Report by Panikkar and Judge Wadhams, n.d., PSA, COP, file 31 (29) of 1936. See also 'Notes on their Government of India Act, 1935', by Panikkar dated Feb. 1937, NMML, Federal Papers, II.

allowed the centre to legislate for any federated state would diminish the authority of the princes over their subjects, whose loyalty would 'henceforth be divided between the Ruler and the Federation'. He rejected as a nonsense the notion that the states would be allowed to federate for 'policy and legislation' only, reserving to themselves the administrative function. Lastly, he used the Australian and Canadian cases to demonstrate convincingly that states which entered the federation could expect to suffer a progressive loss of power to the centre.[27] Morgan has tried 'to frighten the States clean out of Federation', wrote an irate official in the Reforms Office.[28] Watching proceedings from the wings, Dholpur congratulated himself on having made a gilt-edged investment.

Morgan's attack was forceful, cogent and erudite; but to the surprise and dismay of the Diehards it failed to impress the subcommittee. In part this was a tribute to the vigorous defence put up, in tandem, by Wadhams and Panikkar, which won over even some of those hitherto lukewarm or hostile towards federation, such as Pattani of Bhavnagar and B. H. Zaidi of Rampur. Panikkar, in particular, won plaudits for his skilful behind-the-scenes diplomacy: 'You turned the Morgan bombshell into a mere damp squib', Frank Brown of *The Times* wrote admiringly.[29] But Morgan did a lot to prejudice his own case – on the one hand by consistently overstating it, and on the other by playing the man. Almost every one of his speeches contained a sneering swipe at Wadhams. The judge was portrayed as 'a foreign lawyer imported for the occasion', a man 'hopelessly at a loss' in an unfamiliar field.[30] The London lawyer Brunyate found this hyperbole laughable. 'One can only think', he wrote to the Hyderabad foreign minister, 'that Mr. Morgan lost his head.'[31] But the ministerial members of the subcommittee, who had grown to like Wadhams and respect his legal grasp, were not in the least amused. 'I have not . . . met anyone who had a good word to say for him', confided Haksar, 'He was positively abusive.'[32] In spite of, and perhaps to some extent because of Morgan's efforts, the constitutional committee found in its report of

[27] 'Opinion of J. H. Morgan, K.C.' dated 17 Feb. 1937, NMML, Federal Papers, II. Excerpts from the Opinion can be read in *The Times of India*, 22 Feb. 1937, and *IAR*, 1937, 1, 343–6.
[28] Note by Reforms Office, n.d., NAI, Reforms Office, Federation Branch, 7/37.
[29] F. H. Brown to Panikkar 19 Mar. 1937, NMML, Federal Papers, 2.
[30] Opinion by Morgan dated 17 Feb. 1937, NMML, Federal Papers, II.
[31] Brunyate to Mirza Ali Yar Khan 12 Mar. 1937, NMML, Federal Papers, 2.
[32] Haksar to Panikkar 23 Mar. 1937, NMML, Federal Papers, 2. After it had turned in its interim report, the subcommittee met again to consider Morgan's published Opinion. The first item on the agenda was a motion of censure 'for the manner in which the Patiala counsel has been personally attacked'. It was carried unanimously. 'Proceedings of [the] Subcommittee Appointed by the Chamber of Princes to Assess J. H. Morgan's Opinion', 22 Feb. 1937, PSA, COP, file 34 (65) of 1937.

February 1937 that the princes' *sine qua nons* had been 'substantially met' by the amended Act[33] – which was about as good a result as the federationists could have hoped for. When Bhopal's subcommittee also turned in a report affirming the inevitability of a federal compact, Dholpur resigned himself to an almost certain defeat at the hands of Patiala and Bikaner at the forthcoming COP session.

Despite this, Udaibhan Singh fought hard, with a passion and determination born of genuine fear for what the federal future held for his beloved order. Against the advice of some of his friends, who didn't want to see him humiliated, he nominated for the chancellorship against his more powerful cousin Bhupinder Singh. Secondly, he stood on a defiantly anti-federation platform. As *The Times of India* editorialised, Dholpur was 'widely associated [in the minds of the rulers] with the attitude expressed ... by Mr. J. H. Morgan'.[34] Thirdly, he freely engaged with what Reginald Glancy called a 'trial of strength' against his rivals.[35] With the help of his friend Panna, who put out circulars warning the rulers against the blandishments of 'opposing forces', and more surreptitiously, of Madhava Rao, he campaigned as vigorously and as effectively as any previous aspirant, including Patiala himself, had ever done. Indeed, by the time the session opened, Udaibhan was half convinced that he was still in with a chance – particularly since a record fifty-two rulers (the majority of them from small states) had seen fit to make the trip to Delhi.

But in the end it was no contest. On 22 February the general meeting of rulers and ministers resolved, with scarcely a murmur of dissent, to adopt the reports of the two subcommittees. The vote sent a clear signal to Whitehall that the states remained, collectively, committed to federation. Two days later the Chamber elections were held, and again the pro-federation party won by a substantial margin. In the ballot for chancellor, Patiala defeated Dholpur by 30 votes to 13; and in elections for the Standing Committee, Bahawalpur, Bikaner, Dungapur, Jodhpur, Bilaspur, Wankaner, Mandi, Sachin and Sangli – all rulers associated with the Patiala ticket – prevailed after Dholpur and his four main henchmen wisely decided not to stand.[36] Within the week, Wadhams had been reinstated as sole Chamber counsel.

Hailed by the pro-federationist dewans, the defeat of Dholpur was also

[33] Report dated 6 Feb. 1937, NMML, Federal Papers, 2. Excerpts may be read in *IAR*, 1937, I, 351–4. An Amending Act of March 1936 amplified the section (285) which dealt with the crown representative's 'special responsibility' to protect the states, and added a new section (286) which expressly empowered him to draw on the military forces of the government of India to enforce this obligation.   [34] *The Times of India*, 25 Feb. 1937.

[35] Note by Sir Reginald Glancy dated 29 Jan. 1937, IOR L/P&S/13/637.

[36] *Proceedings of the Chamber of Princes*, 24–25 Feb. 1937, 18. The rulers who stood aside with Dholpur were Rampur, Cutch, Jhalawar and Dewas Junior.

welcomed in Delhi, for while the government remained unhappy about Bhupinder Singh's domestic administration, they now saw him, incongruously, as their strongest ally within the COP. Besides, they still needed him enthroned at Patiala to offset the extremists within the Sikh community. Yet their relief at Dholpur's overthrow was tempered by the news which was coming in from Latimer, Lothian and Wylie, which suggested that the rank and file of the rulers still had much to learn about the realities of a federal system. To the extent that the rulers participated in the discussions – and most did not, preferring to leave the talking to their dewans – they revealed, on the whole, little understanding of the Act and even less interest in finding out more. As for the ministers, such knowledge as they displayed seemed curiously out of date, as if they had not kept up with developments since the RTCs. 'One feature of the discussions that surprised us here and in Baroda', reported Lothian, 'was the distance travelled since the early days of the RTC . . . the conception which they still retain of Federation resembles much more closely the scheme put forward in the earlier constitutional discussions and not embodied in the Act'.[37] Again, few states visited were willing to give an unequivocal reply when asked about their likely response to the federal scheme – a tendency which Lothian, for one, had no hesitation in ascribing to the pernicious advice of 'imported eminent lawyers'.[38] Disappointingly, one of the main offenders in this regard was Ganga Singh.[39] Nevertheless, what the three agents did learn suggested that the rulers looked on federation as an evil to be kept at bay, rather than as an opportunity for them to carve out new fields of activity. Everywhere, but especially in the coastal states, a recurring question was: what could prevent a hostile ministry at the centre from squeezing a state dry by surrounding it with a land customs barrier, or by slapping a discriminatory tax on its nascent industries?[40] Last but not least, several *darbars* hinted that their attitude could be influenced by Delhi coming to the party on long-standing claims unrelated to federation, Cutch, for instance, indicating that it would become much more receptive to the idea of federation if the government resolved in its favour in its dispute with Morvi over the Adhoi Mahal.[41] The position was not hopeless, the emissaries thought, in that at least some of the states appeared to have decided that they were likely to be 'better off inside the

---

[37] Lothian to Glancy 21 Nov. 1936, IOR L/P&S/13/667. See also E. Conran-Smith to W. H. Lewis, sec. Reforms Office, 22 Nov. 1936, NAI Reforms Office, Fed. Branch, 10/37.

[38] Lothian, *Kingdoms*, 148.

[39] Wylie to Glancy 9 Jan. 1937, Zetland Coll., 14. Wylie reported encountering more 'determined opposition to the Federal ideal' in Bikaner than in any other state he visited.

[40] See Sitamau 'Memorandum Prepared for Discussions with Viceroy's Special Representative, 17–18 Dec. 1936', and Pattani to Hydari 14 Oct. 1936, NMML, Federal Papers, I.   [41] Rao of Cutch to Linlithgow 27 Dec. 1937, Linlithgow Coll., 128.

house out of the rain, than outside, under their own umbrellas'; yet, reading their joint report, Linlithgow was left with the overall impression that the states' conception of federation and that of the government remained poles apart.

Nor was this growing anxiety about the prospects of consummating the federal scheme confined to the corridors of imperial power. During the 1937 COP session, Panikkar did a discreet head count and found to his consternation that while federation still enjoyed 'preponderant support' among the rulers, covert resistance was escalating. Like the British emissaries, the Patiala minister detected a definite hardening of the stance of the maharaja of Bikaner; and he saw a similar trend developing at Hyderabad.[42] Significantly, this latter assessment was echoed by Brunyate, who found Hydari harder to read with every passing day. The 'whole summer and half the winter have been wasted', he complained to Monckton. Why 'does he not have the courage to say just where he, personally, stands?'[43]

Why *had* things gone awry? In the case of Bikaner and Hyderabad personal factors appear to have played a major part. Over the previous few years the maharaja had visibly aged; although at 57 he was still vigorous and outwardly in good health, he no longer commanded all and sundry just with his regal presence. Indeed to many of his peers he had become something of a joke.[44] Sensing that his greatest days as a princely politician were behind him, this proud, vain man wanted no part of a federation in which his would not be a dominant voice. And the same was true, up to a point, of Hydari. Never an ardent federalist by conviction, the Hyderabad minister had stayed with the federation bandwagon because, for a time, his master the nizam had found the politics of the round table beneficial to his designs over Berar, and because it had brought him international fame and British favour, ingredients which had helped to shore up his always shaky domestic position as a nationalist Muslim and nonmulki. But Hydari's need of British patronage diminished once he attained, in 1936, his long-sought career goal of the presidency of the Hyderabad council. Moreover, with his leadership of the nascent COMs under challenge from Krishnamachari and Ramaswamy Aiyer,[45] he was no longer as confident as he had been of playing a starring role in the new government as a powerbroker on behalf of the princely faction. Last but

---

[42] Panikkar to Haksar 9 Apr. 1937, Sapru Papers, 8/9.
[43] Brunyate to Monckton 4 Dec. 1937, Monckton Papers, 25.
[44] Wylie's description of him as an 'out-of-date windbag' was cruel, but summed up what many rulers were saying behind Ganga Singh's back. Quoted in Zetland to Linlithgow 15 Feb. 1937, Zetland Coll., 8; and see Linlithgow to Zetland 28 Feb. 1937, Zetland Coll., 14.   [45] Note by resdt. Hyderabad dated [?] Mar. 1936, IOR R/1/1/3222.

not least, in the context of Hyderabad politics, federation had become by 1937 something of a liability: for the Berar question had been settled; and mulki opposition to the scheme was hardening.[46] Portrayed by the government as a craven 'sellout', Hydari's new line was simply the considered response of an astute politician who saw, very clearly, where his own best interests lay.

In other quarters, though, hesitancy towards federation had more to do with all-India political developments – in particular the sudden and stunning rise to power of the INC. As we have seen, the Congress had traditionally ignored the states as a field of activity, implicitly recognising the rulers' right to make unfettered decisions about the welfare of their subjects. But this *laissez-faire* stance began to be modified in the 1930s as the party faced up to the threat – as they saw it – of a federal scheme designed explicitly to 'hold India to the Empire'. Failing to stop the RTC process by direct action, the Congress decided, after 1936, to accept the provincial parts of the Act and subsequently to contest the elections under the new constitution as a means of highlighting their popularity in the country. However the majority of party members, especially on the Left, remained steadfast in their opposition to the proposed federation and continued to look for ways to avert it. Recognising, as the Diehards had done, that the scheme's Achilles' heel was the provision that made the inauguration of federation conditional on the accession of a minimum number of states, Congressmen like Jawaharlal Nehru started putting out press statements designed to warn off the princes. In May 1937, for example, Nehru declared:

There is a great deal of talk of independence of the States and of their special treaties and the like. But the thing that is going to count in the future is the treaty that the people of India make with others. The Act will go inevitably with all its hundreds of sections and its special powers and its federation. So I would ask the Princes to consider this matter from this point of view and not to rush in where wiser people fear to tread.[47]

A number of rulers appear to have taken these warnings seriously.[48]

Nevertheless the majority of the *darbars*, sensing that Nehru's rhetoric was intended as much for his fellow socialists as for the princes, and aware that his thinking on public issues tended to run ahead of that of the Congress high command at large, were not unduly perturbed by what he and other Leftists said the Congress *might* do if they joined the

---

[46] Note by Sir T. Tasker dated [?] Dec. 1937, IOR R/1/1/3222.

[47] Quoted in *Dawn*, 4 May 1937.

[48] M. R. Jayakar attributed the 'wavering' of several of his princely clients in the Deccan specifically to Nehru's statement. Jayakar to Shadi Lal 5 May 1937, Jayakar Papers, 417. See also Sir P. Pattani to Anantrai Pattani 22/25 Oct. 1937, Monckton Papers, 25.

federation. What *did* unsettle them was Congress' spectacular showing at the elections of February 1937 – which netted it 716 'general' seats out of 1,161 – and its subsequent decision (despite strenuous opposition from Nehru!) to assume office in the six provinces where it had secured a working majority. Following the Congress victory, the reforms department of the government of India calculated, on the basis of the parties' existing strengths in the CLA and their share of the vote in the February polls, that if the Congress performed similarly in a federal election it would be likely to secure about 100/341 seats in the all-Indian assembly; Zetland thought this expectation 'not unduly alarming'.[49] However, looking at the same figures, the Chamber's Maqbool Mahmud drew a rather different moral. Maqbool reckoned that at the very least 94 'thoroughly reliable members' would need to be recruited from British India to ensure a stable majority for what he termed the constitutional party. Adding together the votes obtained by the Hindu Mahasabha and the Scheduled Caste Federation, by Anglo-Indians and Indian Christians, by the Unionist Sikhs and non-League Muslims and by the landholders and representatives of commerce and industry, labour and women, he thought he could see about 100 such winning federal lower house seats, leaving a slim but adequate safety margin. But he was far from certain that this majority would hold. If Congress, 'now in power and thus able to exercise patronage, succeeds in weaning away members of other groups (as they have already started [doing]) or a substantial flock of Muslim MLAs come under the auspices of the all-India Muslim League', or if a considerable minority of states stayed out, or if the states did not vote as a solid block under the direction of the Chamber, the 'constitutionist' majority could easily become a minority, he concluded morosely.[50] More immediate, though, was the implicit threat which the Congress' elevation to power in the provinces posed to the security of the states' borders. Shortly after the new provincial ministries were sworn in, the Congress Parliamentary Board announced that it would insist on being consulted in advance by provincial governors intending to use their discretionary powers. Such a convention, Panikkar wrote anxiously, would 'render many of the safeguards of the

---

[49] Zetland to Linlithgow 21 June 1937, quoted in Nicolas Mansergh, *The Commonwealth Experience* (London, 1969), 267. The figure of 341 was based on the cautious assumption that only the bare minimum number of states would in the first instance accede to the federation.

[50] Note by Maqbool Mahmud dated [?] Aug. 1937, PSA, COP, file 35 (71) of 1937; and see also note by Patiala (cribbed from the above) in his letter to Linlithgow of 7 Sept. 1937, Linlithgow Coll., 128. Significantly, Akbar Hydari for one was suspicious of any plan which called for alliances between the states' representatives and those from the provinces. Hydari to S. Pattabhirum 29 Nov. 1936, AP R/1/47/10/432.

States nugatory'.[51] It looked as if the enemy had arrived on the doorstep, waiting for a chance to slip inside.

Towards a 'Final Offer'

In the light of their discussions with the *darbars*, Linlithgow's emissaries had recommended 'some advance on the present position of the Secretary of State and the Government of India' as a way of making the federation scheme 'acceptable to a sufficient number of States to make federation a reality'.[52] Shocked by their revelations and by the palpable ebbing of princely support for federation following the Congress election triumph, Linlithgow reluctantly came to the same conclusion, and asked London to make further amendments to the India Act which would collectively guarantee participating states at least as much revenue as they presently enjoyed. He did not expect to win his point easily. He did not dream that it would take over two-and-a-half years of intense bureaucratic wrangling!

Why did the resolution of this matter take so long? There were basically three reasons. Firstly, the ramified bureaucratic organisation of Indian government mitigated against quick decision-making. Although outwardly a monolithic despotism, the raj at the centre was really a loose oligarchy of departments in more or less permanent competition with one another. Accordingly, policy proposals originating in one department which could conceivably affect the responsibilities of others had, as a matter of protocol, to be referred to these neighbouring departments for comment, with the result that it could take weeks even for a routine file to gather the necessary endorsements from departmental heads, much more if the file dealt with matters of moment. This was particularly the case with files emanating from the political department, which were always viewed suspiciously because of the latter's special access to the viceroy and its reputation for sometimes putting the welfare of its princely clients ahead of New Delhi's. But that was not all. Important initiatives also required the stamp of the India Office, which added another layer to the policy-making process and thereby greatly increased the risk of disagreement, to say nothing of bureaucratic delay. It might have been a thorough

---

[51] Report dated 17 July 1937, PSA, COP, file 110 of 1937. See also Sir P. Pattani to Anantrai Pattani 22/25 Oct. 1937, Monckton Papers, 25. In the event, no undertaking by the governors was given; however in practice most saw the value of taking the ministers into their confidence and did so.

[52] 'Joint Opinion of the Special Representatives Regarding Attitude of the States to Federation as Revealed on Their Recent Tour', encl. in pol. sec., GOI, to pol. sec., India Office, 25 Feb. 1937, IOR L/P&S/13/613.

system, but it was not geared to get things done in a hurry. Secondly, Linlithgow's proposals touched on matters of high principle; in calling for a quite significant scaling down of the powers and resources of the federal government *vis-à-vis* those of its constituent units, they challenged the very essence of the federal compact devised in London. 'As I see it', minuted Sir A. Parsons, 'the Viceroy's plan involves almost complete surrender to the demands of the States on almost all matters of importance . . . it very nearly amounts to federation at any price.' Construed – perhaps rightly – as a recipe for 'a sham and not a real federation',[53] Linlithgow's scheme for a radical amendment of the Act was hotly opposed by those large sections of the imperial bureacracy (notably the reforms and finance departments) which were committed to the principle of a strong centre. As a result, it initially made little headway. Last but not least, while the broad issue of principle – the balance of power in the federation – was clear enough, the specific points in the Act and the IOA which Linlithgow wanted addressed were technically complex and fraught with legal pitfalls. Again, there was no short cut or easy path through this administrative minefield.

To be sure, some vital ground was gained. For instance, on the vexed question of whether the states' public services should be permitted, under section 125, to administer federal laws, Linlithgow prised from Zetland an undertaking that the states would be allowed to opt for '125' agreements in all areas in which the centre did not already possess a cadre of officers – regardless of whether federal legislation would be 'inefficiently administered' as a result;[54] while Glancy and Latimer prevailed on the reforms office to agree to a formula under which states exercising section 125 powers would have the right to retain fees charged (for example, for arms licences). Likewise, several important concessions were made in respect of the princes' extra-territorial rights[55] – in part because of an unwelcome and potentially embarrassing ruling by the government's law officers that the federal court was probably competent after all, under section 204 (1) of the Act, to rule on them.[56] While Zetland remained adamant on the subject of an excluding clause in the IOA itself, he agreed to consider offering the states a separate agreement on the protection of

---

[53] Note by Sir A. Parsons dated 17 Sept. 1937, IOR L/P&S/13/613.
[54] Note by Latimer dated 1 Jan. 1938, NAI, Reforms Office, Fed. Branch, 20/125/37, Part I.
[55] The most important of these were immunity from legal proceedings originating in British India, limited immunity from payment of municipal tax on properties in British India, exemption from the payment of motor vehicle licences, the right to carry arms, exemption from imperial customs duty on goods imported for personal or family use and protection from subversion and slander by parties or newspapers in British India.
[56] Note in Reforms Office, GOI, dated [?] Aug. 1938, NAI, Reforms Office, Fed. Branch, 25/38, Part I.

their rights in conjunction with it; took on board most of Delhi's suggestions for sharpening up the somewhat ambiguous language of section 12 (1) (g); and, most importantly of all, promised to 'bring in [an amending] Bill in early spring' 1938 with the object of eliminating all possibility of federal court intervention in the relationship between the states and the crown.[57] And limited progress was made, too, on the fiscal front, Whitehall accepting Delhi's suggestion that the maritime and other previously exempt states should be allowed the option of not acceding for federal salt tax, and agreeing to grant the states partial exemption from paying federal corporation tax and match and sugar excise for up to ten years after the inauguration of the federation.

But the home government dug its heels in at the viceroy's suggestion that the princes should be allowed to limit the extent of their accession for financial items in their IOAs. Although the crown law officers conceded that the limitation idea was feasible, they felt it infringed the 'spirit' of the Act; while Zetland's political advisers felt the whole procedure reeked of petty horse-trading. The time has come, averred Paul Patrick, to 'bring home to the Rulers forcibly the risks they are running by this attempting to hold Government to ransom'.[58] Only after Linlithgow threatened early in 1938 to resign, declaring bluntly that an offer to the states on the financial terms favoured by the India Office would be a waste of time, did the secretary of state reluctantly agree to entertain a proposal under this head; and even then the government of India had to wear a substantial pruning of its list of 'essential' limitations – from thirty-two down to twenty-seven.[59] Thus, the constitutional package finally approved by the cabinet in the autumn of 1938, while more generous than what London had originally contemplated, still fell some way short of what the political department considered necessary to guarantee a 'yes' verdict from the *darbars*.

Moreover, these bureaucratic wars absorbed valuable time. It will be recalled that when Linlithgow took up the reins in 1936 he had hoped to have federation up and running by the beginning of 1938. This target had long been abandoned; yet the viceroy continued to hope that the offer to the states might be finalised in time for the scheme to start by the end of the year, and when he tried out this timetable on Zetland in March 1938 the secretary of state was encouraging: he intended to take the plan to

---

[57] Sec. state to crown representative 1 Nov. 1937, IOR L/P&S/13/613. Zetland had to struggle hard to get his way over this in cabinet as the prime minister, Baldwin, was initially totally opposed, holding that an amending bill ran the risk of 'reviving the divisions in our own party'. Zetland to Linlithgow 8 Oct. 1937, Zetland Coll., 8.

[58] Minutes dated 18 Dec. 1937 and 3 Jan. 1938, Zetland Coll., 9.

[59] Note by Baxter dated 22 Nov. 1938, IOR L/P&S/13/618.

cabinet 'no later than early June' and barring last minute hitches, he could see no reason why the offer could not be in the hands of the major states by the end of the summer.[60] Once again, however, these forecasts proved overly optimistic. First, international events – the Austrian *anschluss* of March 1938 and the Czechoslovak crisis of September – intervened to distract the cabinet from Indian problems.[61] Then the issue of the 'final' offer was delayed by further inter-government wrangling over tactics: which, if any, states should be excluded from the offer on grounds of size; how long the rulers should be given to respond; whether a sample of draft IOAs should be published at the same time as the offer was sent to the states in order to limit the 'opportunity for further bargaining and counter-claims' by the *darbars* and preempt any suggestion in parliament or in the British Indian press that the government 'had something to hide';[62] or whether, alternatively, it would be better to sound out 'a care-fully selected few of the major states' at a Simla summit as a prelude to the communication of the offer through regular political channels.[63] Accordingly, it was not until October that full cabinet approval was obtained, November before the procedure for communicating the offer to the princes was finalised, and (thanks in part to the Christmas holidays), late January 1939 before the offer was actually mailed out. By then, three-and-a-half years had elapsed since the passage of the enabling Act of 1935. In the interim much water had flowed under the bridge. Had the government waited too long?

It is possible to argue (and we shall return to this point later) that if the offer that went out with the viceroy's covering letter on 27 January 1939 had been good enough, it would have been accepted with alacrity by the *darbars* no matter what the circumstances. Yet it is also true to say that cir-cumstances did matter, and that the federal offer would have stood a much better chance of acceptance if it had been made one or two years earlier.

For one thing, the long delay between the passage of the Act and the communication of the offer killed the momentum which had been built up in favour of federation since 1930 and gave the more nervous elements among the rulers extra time to get cold feet. For another thing, the delay encouraged the perception that the government itself had lost interest in

---

[60] Sec. state to crown representative, 13 Apr. 1938, NAI, Reforms Office, Fed. Branch, 49/38.
[61] In May 1938 Paul Patrick admitted to Arthur Lothian that 'federal negotiations are not going with a rush'. Patrick to Lothian 17 May 1938, Lothian Coll., 9.
[62] Sec. state to crown representative, 21 Feb. and 26 Mar. 1938, NAI, Reforms Office, Fed. Branch, 49/38.
[63] Crown representative to sec. state 7 Apr. 1938, NAI, Reforms Office, Fed. Branch, 49/38.

the scheme, that they were simply going through the motions and did not really care if a sufficiency of states joined or not. All of this strengthened the hand of the Dholpurites and other opponents of the federation movement; whereas the effluxions of time were anything but kind to its leading supporters. On 23 March 1938 Maharaja Bhupinder Singh, the colossus of the COP, finally succumbed to the manifest disorders that had plagued him for most of his adult life and had kept him bed-ridden since January. Less than a year later Sayaji Rao Gaekwar, doyen of the princely order, one of the originators of the federal idea and mover of the historic motion at the RTC, died at the ripe age of 76, leaving the *gaddi* to his mediocre and self-indulgent son, Pratap Singh. What is more, the same period saw the retirement or eclipse of several of the ministers who had played a key role in devising and selling the federal strategy to the princes. After a distinguished career at Gwalior, Kailash Haksar was replaced in 1938 by his deputy Sardar Angre, who had never made any secret of his belief that Haksar had not taken a strong enough line with Linlithgow's emissaries in 1936. Likewise Panikkar, who had been an influential foreign minister at Patiala, became a much less effective voice when he moved across to Bikaner after April 1939, and fell under the spell of Ganga Singh's increasing hostility to anything which appeared to threaten his patrimony, federation included. And V. T. Krishnamachari suffered a similar fate at Baroda, as the new gaekwar moved to entrench himself in power and strengthen the Marathi element in the administration.[64] Last but not least, both Ramaswamy Aiyer at Travancore and Akbar Hydari at Hyderabad came under renewed attack during 1938–9 from powerful local interest groups, the former from the monied Syrian Christian community, angry at the Dewan's patronage of the Nayar caste at their expense,[65] the latter from *mulki* Muslims linked to the newly formed Ittihad-ul-Muslimeen of Bahadur Yar Jang.[66] Both survived; but only at

[64] Krishnamachari was closely identified with the opposing Gujarati faction. M. T. Vidyalankar to M. R. Jayakar 1 Feb. 1939, Jayakar Papers, 631.

[65] So unpopular had Sir C. P. become by the latter part of 1938, that Delhi were sceptical of him 'remaining in office long enough to negotiate the proposed terms of accession'. Note drafted in Pol. Dept., India Office, dated 19 Oct. 1938, IOR, Pol. (Intl.) Colls, 13/14 (2). Sir C. P.'s long-running vendetta with the monied Syrian Christian community, which had placed itself at the head of the demand for constitutional reforms in the state, came to a head in June 1938 when the Quilon Bank, which housed most of the community's funds, was forced into liquidation by the *darbar* on the pretext that the bank was guilty of fraudulent practice. That he survived this crisis was solely due to the power of his patron at court, the dowager maharani. For a more detailed analysis see Robin Jeffrey, 'A Sanctified Label – "Congress" in Travancore Politics, 1938–48', in D. A. Low (ed.), *Congress and the Raj: Facets of the Indian Struggle 1917–47* (London, 1977), 435–72.

[66] See above, p. 208. For more on the local backlash against Hydari see T. J. Tasker to Sir Duncan Mackenzie, resdt. Hyderabad, 13 Jan. 1938, IOR R/1/1/3039; note by Patrick on interview with Tasker dated 14 Feb. 1939, IOR L/P&S/13/667; and Gibney to Glancy 3

the price of moderating their support for the federal scheme. As it was, Hydari came within an ace of being fired in July 1939 and probably would have been had the residency not put in a good word on his behalf.[67]

However, the part of the mix which changed most during these years was the political environment. At the time of the first RTC in 1930, the *darbari* world had been a relatively isolated one; political life had run along well-worn grooves; things had seemed, on the surface at least, orderly and stable. Even at the height of the civil disobedience movement, the states had been little affected by the upheavals going on in British India. This sense of stability, of permanence, had given the rulers the confidence to reach out to the politicians in the provinces with their historic offer. In 1938, with the outbreak of Congress-inspired mass agitations across the length and breadth of princely India, this cosy world vanished, never to return; and so too did the complacent, easy-going cosmopolitanism of the princes.

Satyagraha

The *satyagraha* campaign was all the more shocking to the rulers for being sudden and unexpected. As we have seen, the formal policy of the INC during the 1920s and 1930s was to avoid entanglements in the states, both by prohibiting the setting up of local branches there and by making it clear to its supporters that it believed that the internal governance of the states was a matter for discussion and resolution between the rulers and their subjects.[68] Of course, the policy had its critics – not least from among the Congress Left wing, which acquired a sharper definition

June 1940, IOR R/1/1/3262. There are still, surprisingly, few secondary sources on Hyderabad during the 1940s. Perhaps the best coverage is to be found in Lucien D. Benichou, 'From Autocracy to Integration: Political Developments in Hyderabad State, 1938–1948', Ph.D. Thesis, University of Western Australia, 1985.

[67] The nizam's 'outburst' against Hydari that triggered rumours of his imminent dismissal is recounted in Gibney to Glancy 3 Aug. 1939, IOR R/1/1/3258; the role of the residency is touched on in Gibney to Glancy 29 July 1940, IOR R/1/1/3262.

[68] For a more detailed exposition of the evolution and subsequent amendment of this policy after 1938, see the aforementioned articles by Copland, 'Congress Paternalism', esp. 121–7, and Ramusack, 'Congress and the People's Movement'. Regional developments are explored in K. L. Kamal and Robert Stern, 'Jaipur's Freedom Struggle and the Bourgeois Revolution', *Journal of Commonwealth Political Studies*, 11 (1973), 231–50; James Manor, *Political Change in an Indian State: Mysore 1917–1955* (New Delhi, 1977), chapters 6–7; Mridula Mukherjee, 'Peasant Movement in Patiala State, 1937–48', *Studies in History*, 1, 2 (July–Dec. 1979), 215–83; Janaki Nair, 'The Emergence of Labor Politics in South India: Bangalore, 1900–1947', Ph.D. Thesis, Syracuse University, 1991; Rangaswamy, *The Story of Integration*, chapter 6; Richard Sisson, *The Congress Party in Rajasthan: Political Integration and Institution-Building in an Indian State* (Berkeley, 1972); and John R. Wood, 'Indian Nationalism in the Princely Context: The Rajkot Satyagraha of 1938–9', in Jeffrey, *People, Princes and Paramount Power*, 240–74.

after 1934 with the formation of the ginger group known as the Congress Socialist Party. One socialist, A. V. Patwardhan, went so far as to describe Gandhi's 1934 revision of the policy (which offered the people of the states 'sympathy' but nothing more) as 'a blank cheque to the Princes'.[69] And Jawaharlal Nehru, too, threw his considerable weight against it – although out of loyalty to Gandhi he kept his distance from the CSP and confined himself, in his public statements, to swipes at 'feudal and autocratic monarchies'.[70] But the high command stuck to its guns: 'Although there is a growing party among Congressmen who seek the total abolition of [the] States as a relic of [the] Middle Ages', acknowledged a Working Committee press release, 'the policy of the Congress as a whole remains one of friendliness to the States.'[71] As late as 1937 the party's preferred stance was still one of non-interference.

Then, very quickly, the emphasis changed. At the Haripura session in February 1938, Congressmen were given the right, as individuals, to participate in political struggles in the states; and a subcommittee of the CWC was established to oversee and direct the activities of existing (clandestine) branches in princely India. In December, Gandhi admitted in *Harijan* that he had been mistaken about the political potential of the states' peoples, and pronounced the policy of non-interference inappropriate 'in the face of [the] injustice[s] perpetrated in the States' by autocratic *darbars*. The following February Nehru accepted the presidency of the AISPC, asserting in his inaugural address that the time had come for the local states' struggles to be integrated 'with the major struggle against British imperialism'.[72] A month later, at Tripura, Congress leaders endorsed this united front strategy and offered to meet with the Standing Committee of the AISPC to devise a common programme of agitation.

What inspired this about-face? To some extent, the decision was forced on the high command by a build-up of pressure from below. Over the previous few years, Congress workers sympathetic to the plight of the states' people had begun openly to flout the non-intervention decree, rendering it increasingly academic; moreover, the influx of these outsiders boosted the morale of the locals and raised the tempo of political life generally, which added to the nervousness of the *darbars* and prompted confrontations on the streets between citizens and authorities attempting to enforce bans and curfews. Sooner or later, matters were bound to get out of hand, and in April 1938, at Viduraswatha in Mysore, at least twenty people were

---

[69] *The Servant of India*, 15 Nov. 1934.
[70] e.g. his presidential speech to the Lucknow Congress, 12 Apr. 1936, *IAR*, 1936, I, 18–19.
[71] Statement issued after CWC meetings of 15/19 May 1938 at Bombay, *IAR*, 1938, I, 324.
[72] Speech at Ludhiana, 15 Feb. 1939, *IAR*, 1939, I, 438.

killed and another forty injured[73] when police *lathi*-charged a peaceful demonstration – an incident quickly likened to the Jallianwallah Bagh massacre of 1919. True, Mirza managed to repair some of the damage by feting the Congress high command's emissaries, Patel and Acharya Kripalani, and compromising on the main issue which had given rise to the agitation, namely the right of the State Congress to fly the national flag. Nevertheless, a precedent for Congress involvement had been created. Moreover, the very success of the Mysore coup raised aspirations. Now even some Congress leaders began seriously to consider the possibility that the monarchical order might be overthrown in advance of the British departure. And there was also, besides, the expectation in some quarters of short-term gains. At the very least, ran one argument, a short, vigorous campaign in the states would give Congress the chance to reaffirm its credentials as an agitational, revolutionary party after several compromising years in the legislatures and in government.

Another push for revision came, ironically, from the British side. Facing in Travancore a situation similar to that in Mysore, dewan Sir C. P. Ramaswamy Aiyer sought to stifle demands for constitutional reform by suggesting that it was legally 'not possible' for the ruler to grant responsible government 'without the concurrence of the British Government'.[74] The idea, characteristically both clever and sly, was to shift the onus for his repressive domestic policy on to other shoulders, thereby earning himself a greatly needed respite. However it backfired. Determined that a 'myth' of imperial authority in the constitutional field should not gain currency, Linlithgow asked Zetland to arrange for a question to be asked in the House of Commons so that the government could clarify the position. Zetland agreed; but the response given by the parliamentary undersecretary, Winterton, on 21 February 1938 went much further than Linlithgow's advisers had contemplated: according to Winterton, 'the Paramount Power would certainly not obstruct proposals for constitutional advance' in the states. This was taken to mean that London and New Delhi were all in favour of such change.[75] Meanwhile, the former Labour minister and RTC stalwart Lord Lothian arrived in India and at once began to canvass the idea of democratic reform in the states in a series of well-publicised speeches. The theme of reform was in turn taken up by *The Times* in an editorial of 15 March. Since *The Times* was known to be an unofficial mouthpiece of government, this was construed as

---

[73] Official estimates put the casualties at ten killed and eight injured, but this is almost certainly a gross underestimate. See Rangaswami, *The Story of Integration*, 169.

[74] Statement to the Travancore Assembly 7 Feb. 1938, *The Statesman*, 8 Feb. 1938.

[75] Note by Linlithgow dated 9 Feb. 1938, and crown representative to sec. state 11 Feb. 1938, IOR R/1/1/3060; and memo. by sec. state dated 9 Feb. 1939, IOR L/PO/89.

further evidence of a significant shift in policy.[76] In January, Bhulabhai Desai's assertion, at a rally in Ajmer, that the government was unlikely to 'go to the length of assisting Indian Rulers by force of arms' to resist political reforms,[77] had been greeted with disbelief; two months later the idea did not seem so bizarre. Naturally, the idea of a campaign in the states became much easier to sell to the party rank and file once it appeared likely to end in success.

Thirdly, as Ramusack has pointed out, the Haripura policy was shaped by the internal dynamics at work within the Congress Party. The stridently anti-imperialist party president Subhas Chandra Bose supported the campaign, in part, as a way of embarrassing the Gandhian old guard who were trying to prevent him obtaining a second term. Vallabhbhai Patel, who hailed from Ahmedabad, saw a drive into the states as an effective way of broadening his Gujarati power-base and thus strengthening his claims to succeed Gandhi as Congress supremo. Nehru, likewise, wanted to keep faith with his own backers in the CSP. Even Gandhi was not unmindful of the populist value of direct action, particularly in a sphere where he could insist on maintaining a tight personal direction over any agitation that Congress decided to undertake.

Last but not least, the high command was drawn towards a more interventionist policy in the states by the lure of power at the federal centre. By 1938 Congress had to a great extent become a prisoner of its electoral success: having swept the polls, it felt, quite understandably, that it owed something to the people who had voted for it on the assumption that it would become the raj. But the fruits of victory did not stop at the boundaries of the six provinces in which Congress had obtained a majority; thanks to the system of indirect election to the federal assembly built into the Government of India Act, the party was also assured of a healthy representation at the federal centre. By the government's calculations it could anticipate holding at least 75 per cent of the General, Scheduled Caste, Labour and Women's seats in the lower house and perhaps 80 per cent in the upper house.[78] This was not enough, however, to give it an absolute majority. If it wanted to govern in its own right, Congress would have to capture, by one means or another, some of the princely seats.[79] Here, then, I would argue, was the crux of its new strategy in the states: to

---

[76] In fact, the leader caught the India Office unawares. Sec. state to crown representative 16 Mar. 1938, NAI, Reforms Office, Fed. Branch, 48/38.   [77] *The Hindu*, 26 Jan. 1938.

[78] Note by Pol. Dept., India Office dated [?] July 1938, IOR Pol. (Intl.) Colls. 13/14 (1).

[79] The India Office calculated that Congress would require 63 per cent of the states' seats in the Council and 76 percent in the Assembly, If so, it made the states' strategy extremely problematic as it meant persuading or coercing the majority of rulers – including such hard-liners as the nizam and the maharaja of Kashmir.

pressure the princes into returning only popularly elected representatives, or nominees acceptable to the *praja mandal* leaders, to the federal legislature.

Of course this still begs the big question of whether, if the opportunity had presented itself, Congress would actually have taken the plunge, since its rhetoric towards the federal provisions of the 1935 Act remained hostile. Could it possibly have bent its principles that much? Even now, most historians would probably say 'no'. Nevertheless I think a plausible argument can be advanced for the affirmative case. For one thing, a number of well-informed observers were certain that Congress intended to play ball. In a memorandum prepared for cabinet, Zetland hazarded that the Right wing of Congress (which, rather conveniently, equated with the dominant faction) 'would be willing to enter the Federation if they were satisfied that they could secure a [working] majority in the Federal Legislature'.[80] The viceroy's guess was the same. 'I too', he wrote, 'feel pretty clear that Congress, or at any rate the Right Wing of Congress, are anxious to join the Federation.'[81] Similar opinions were held by most senior political officers, by the percipient vice-chancellor of Andhra University, C. R. Reddy, by Gandhian offsider Sarvepalli Radhakrishnan and by Sapru, whose political contacts assured him that the Congress high command had already begun 'to think of their Cabinet'.[82] For another thing, we have evidence that several important (though not necessarily representative) figures in Congress were pushing their colleagues to come to an arrangement with the government that would permit them to take office with dignity: K. M. Munshi was one, Bhulabhai Desai another.[83] Thirdly, there is the undeniable fact that Congress had already significantly altered its stance on the provincial part of the new constitution. If the organisation could bend principle once, it could do so again. Indeed, in so far as the provincial experiment had been a happy one (there had been none of the expected showdowns with British imperial authority) the argument for flexibility had strengthened. By 1938 the British veto was no longer the stumbling point it had once been. Fourthly, it

---

[80] Memo by sec. state dated 9 Feb. 1939, IOR L/PO/89.
[81] Linlithgow to Zetland 2 June 1939, IOR L/P&S/13/621.
[82] Dr C. R. Reddy's views are contained in a speech to law students at Nagpur College, 17 Dec. 1938, C.R. Reddy Papers, file 20. For the political officers' impressions see Sir Francis Wylie, 'Federal Negotiations in India 1935–9 and After', in C. H. Philips and M. D. Wainright, *The Partition of India: Policies and Perspectives, 1935–1947* (London, 1970), 518. For Radhakrishnan's opinion see Zetland to Linlithgow 5 Feb. 1939, IOR R/1/1/3414. For Sapru's, see Sapru to Jayakar 29 Sept. 1938, Jayakar Papers 726. Interestingly Sapru's claim about the 'cabinet' was echoed by Subhas Bose, much to Nehru's chagrin. See Nehru to Bose 4 Feb. 1939, Jawaharlal Nehru Papers, 9/679.
[83] Sir Roger Lumley, gov. of Bombay to Linlithgow 13 Mar. 1939, IOR R/1/1/3145; and Jayakar to Sapru 21 July 1938, Jayakar Papers, 726.

would be a denial of human nature to assume that the Congress leaders, who had for years (decades in some cases) laboured with honour, but little material reward, in the political wilderness, were not drawn by the perquisites of power. Finally, we can be sure that Congress would never have embarked on such a radical and risky venture as a *satyagraha* campaign in the states if it had not felt that substantial benefits would flow to the party and to the nationalist cause as a result. But in a sense, the issue of what Congress might have done under certain circumstances is academic for our purposes. What is far more important is what the rulers and ministers *thought* was on the minds of the nationalist leaders. And almost unanimously, they came to the conclusion that the change of policy at Haripura was the first move in a Congressite bid for power at the centre. Needless to say, they saw this as a very dangerous omen for the future of the all-India federation.

However, if the princes were shocked and dismayed by the sudden turnaround in the attitude of the Congress, they were even more traumatised by the agitation which erupted in the wake of the Haripura decision. Especially in the smaller states, where there was little tradition of organised protest, mass demonstrations and peaceful *hartals* quickly escalated into open defiance of authority and acts of indiscriminate violence. In Limdi, 6,000 people out of a population of 40,000 took flight to British India to escape the depredations of roving gangs (allegedly with links to the *darbar*); as many as 30,000 inhabitants of the Orissa states did likewise. In Ramdurg and other southern Deccan states, anti-*darbar* demonstrations were followed by violent clashes between Kanarese-speaking Lingayats and Marathas. In Ranpur, in the Eastern States Agency, a British political agent, Major Bazalgette, was hacked to death. 'When I toured the State during the last winter', expostulated a bewildered raja of Sarila, 'every thing was normal and no grievances were brought to my notice.' Now 'the towns are filled with mobs, parading and taunting officials'.[84] Suddenly confronted with a world turned upsidedown, Sarila and his brother princes had to decide whether to embrace it, and share power, or fight it and risk inflaming an already volatile situation.

Many, predictably, chose to fight in the expectation that, Winterton's statement notwithstanding, the government could always be relied on to pull their irons out of the fire. But many others – frightened for the safety of their thrones and their families, and overwhelmed by the pace of events – initially chose to conciliate. The dewan of Jind started sporting a Gandhi cap and fraternising with the leaders of the Punjab Riasti Praja

[84] Sarila to Nehru 23 May 1939, Jawaharlal Nehru Papers, 91/5319.

Mandal; Gulab Singh of Rewa, not hitherto known for his love of democracy, sent elephants to the Tripura Congress and allowed the national flag
to be displayed during a visit by the viceroy; on Christmas Day 1938, the
thakore sahib of Rajkot signed an agreement with Vallabhbhai Patel by
which he undertook to initiate constitutional reforms; on 21 January
1939, Aundh, in the Bombay Deccan, became the first place in India to
enjoy full responsible government; and in September the chief of
Narsinghgarh submitted to the arbitration of Gandhi's envoy Amrit
Kaur; while Hydari, Mirza Ismail, Ramaswamy Aiyer and Hari Singh of
Kashmir all sought advice about dealing with the popular unrest from the
Congress high command. Reading these signs at their face value, a
worried Bertrand Glancy concluded that 'a general collapse among the
States' was imminent.[85] Actually things were not as desperate as they
looked, for the larger states either stood firm or made only token conces-
sions. As Patiala explained to his resident, his gift of two lakhs to the
Khalsa National College in Lahore might have looked like a cave-in to the
Akalis, but in fact it was money well spent. 'I believe', he wrote, [that] 'by
serving their mouth[s] with a morsel, I have . . . provided against an active
participation by this party in any subversive movement against my
State.'[86] Nevertheless Glancy was not altogether wrong, especially as
regards the smaller states. Had the British not responded to their urgent
pleas for protection with military aid, some, if not all, of these *darbars*
would certainly have fallen.[87]

In the event, the states were reprieved by the Mahatma. As we have
seen, the political struggle in the southern Deccan was from the start
tinged with communalism. It was the same story in Hyderabad, where the
State Congress campaign for responsible government was increasingly
overshadowed by an Arya Samaj-Mahasabha led agitation for jobs and
religious rights for Hindus;[88] and especially in Travancore, where the
'national struggle' was corrupted by the sectarian ambitions of Syrian
Christians and Ezhavas, out to break the Nayar dominance of the bureaucracy. It took time, in some cases, for the Congress high command to
come to grips with these nuances; but once they did, they moved quickly

---

[85] Linlithgow to Zetland 31 Jan. 1939, paraphrasing Sir Bertrand Glancy, Zetland Coll., 17.
See also Lothian to Glancy 28 Nov. 1938, Lothian Coll., 2, and Sapru to Jayakar 31 Jan.
1939, Jayakar Papers, 726.
[86] Yadavindra Singh, maharaja of Patiala, to resdt. Punjab States 16 Feb. 1939, IOR
R/1/1/3349.
[87] Later, Zetland recalled 'dozens of instances over the past year where the Paramount
Power has been forced to intervene to prevent the Ruler's authority from collapse in the
face of serious agitation'. Zetland to Linlithgow 26 Jan. 1940, IOR L/P&S/13/551.
[88] See Ian Copland, 'Communalism in Princely India: The Case of Hyderabad,
1930–1940', *Modern Asian Studies*, 22 (1988), 783–814.

to distance themselves from the activities of their self-styled affiliates. Again, Right-wingers in the high command, such as the industrialist G. D. Birla, remained uneasy about the prominent role being played in the campaign by 'socialists' from British India – for example in the Telengana region of Hyderabad where it appeared that they were encouraging share-croppers to rise up against their Reddy landlords. Lastly, Gandhi in particular was distressed by the burgeoning violence. Following Bazalgette's murder the CWC passed a resolution pointing out that violence did 'great injury to the cause of freedom in the States'.[89] When this hint went unheeded, Gandhi decided (as he had done before in similar cases) to pull the plug. In April 1939 he 'advised' that the agitations should cease. By the end of the autumn things were apparently back to normal.

Yet the psychological scars remained. The rulers might have emerged, thanks to the British, with their thrones intact, but they could not forget what had happened, how close they had come to catastrophe. Some felt bitterly hurt, believing that they had been betrayed by their subjects; others remembered the anger of the mobs, and wondered how long it would be before they faced a repeat performance; others again feared that Congress would use its ministerial muscle to exact 'retaliation' on the states for the sufferings undergone by its supporters.[90] Attempting to avert the predictable backlash, Linlithgow put it to the rulers that the nationalists were 'likely to be less rather than more vindictive if a State was inside rather than outside Federation';[91] but few were persuaded. The impression in most princely capitals was that Congress had at last shown its true face. Circumstances 'have so completely changed', wrote one traumatised *darbari*, 'as to make what might have been thought safe, or even desirable, at one time, positively dangerous'.[92]

However, what really spooked the rulers was not so much the *satya-graha* itself but the government's ambiguous response to it. Although the campaign was for the most part fought by the local *praja mandals*, literally tens of thousands of outsiders also took part, sometimes, as in the case of Hyderabad during 1939, in the form of organised *jathas* trucked in from far off places like the Punjab. Why, the *darbars* asked pointedly, had they

[89] Resolution of the CWC meeting at Bardoli, 11–14 Jan. 1939, *IAR*, 1939, I, 309.
[90] Evans-Gordon, resdt., Deccan States, to Glancy 10 Oct. 1938, reporting conversation with Southern Maratha Country chiefs at Kolhapur, IOR Pol. (Intl.) Colls., 19/99. At Delhi during the Chamber session, Glancy found the rulers in a 'very apprehensive state of mind' about the Congress' intentions. Memo. dated 8 Apr. 1939, IOR R/1/1/3415.
[91] Linlithgow to Zetland 8 Nov. 1938, reporting on an interview with Bhopal, IOR L/PO/91.
[92] 'Reflections Regarding Federation', RSA, Sirohi, Sadar Office, file 167 of 1939. And see also Sapru's comment to Jayakar: 'this hostility is . . . affecting the minds of, at any rate, some of the Indian Princes who think it inexpedient to join the Federation in the midst of all this bitterness'. Sapru to Jayakar 1 Mar. 1939, Jayakar Papers, 726.

been allowed to cross the border? Why had the provincial governors not used the extensive powers available under the 1934 Princes' Protection Act and discharged the special responsibility bestowed on them by the 1935 Act to safeguard the states' rights and interests? In the case of the Princes' Protection Act the imputation was rather unfair, because the penal provisions of that statute were contingent on a notification being issued by a provincial government which, after 1937, generally meant a Congress government. But there is no doubt that, if they had desired, the governors could have used their reserve powers under the 1935 Act to direct the Congress ministries to take steps against the *jathas*. That they did not do so, for what were manifestly political reasons,[93] emphasised J. H. Morgan's dire warnings two years before about the feebleness of constitutional safeguards. Krishnamachari, for one, feared that many rulers would take the lesson to heart.[94]

Secondly, there was much unhappiness on the princely side about the political department's response to the crisis. To be sure, the government had finally stepped in with troops; but some rulers felt that the help they had received from their overlords had been niggardly and too long in coming. Conversely, many *darbars* were offended by governmental threats to disallow constitutional changes which impaired in any way their capacity to discharge their obligations to the paramount power;[95] while others were shocked by Linlithgow's public humiliation of the raja of Aundh and the thakore sahib of Rajkot for having ignored warnings against seeking the mediation of Congress.[96]

Last but not least, the *satyagraha* brought about significant changes in British policy towards the states – changes which, in turn, would impact upon the *darbars*' reception of the federal offer. As we have seen, the political department felt obliged to take a hard line with states while it felt had 'let down the side' by giving in too easily to nationalist demands for radical constitutional reform.[97] One of these was Mysore. Like Aundh

[93] Note by Wylie dated 28 Aug. 1944, IOR R/1/1/4207.
[94] Krishnamachari to Sir Frank Brown 7 Dec. 1938, IOR Pol. (Intl.) Colls., 13/14 (2). See also note by Bhopal State Council dated 30 Oct. 1939, BRO, Bhopal, Chamber Section, 31, 258 of 1939.
[95] Linlithgow to Zetland 5 Apr. 1939, IOR L/P&S/13/551. This advice was consequent on an assurance given the House of Commons by Zetland on 13 March.
[96] The thakore sahib was warned that he would be deposed if he did not 'pull himself together'. Linlithgow to Zetland 16 Nov. 1938, Zetland Coll., 15.
[97] Many *darbars*, incidentally, took a similar view. Aundh, despite having a superior claim, was in 1942 passed over for membership of the COP in favour of neighbouring Phaltan because no member of the Standing Committee wanted to sit next to a man who had embraced Gandhism; while Cochin's role in allegedly providing a safe haven for agitators active in Travancore clouded relations between the two states for years. Kenneth Fitze to Lt.-Col. P. Gainsford, resdt. Deccan States 15 Oct. 1942, IOR R/1/1/4750; and Sir C. P. Ramaswamy Aiyer to Glancy 23 Mar. 1940, IOR R/1/1/3606.

and Rajkot, Mysore sinned by negotiating with the Congress high command over the flag issue; then, it compounded the crime by appearing to cave in to the Congress demand that the states' representatives in the federal legislature be chosen by popular election. Correctly, the political secretary identified Mirza Ismail as the architect of these policies. 'He wanted to convince me', noted Glancy after an interview some months later, 'that now he does not believe in Congress, but perhaps he does not know that [intelligence] material with us in this connection is much more than he can possibly imagine.'[98] Mirza was ordered to retract the offer on elections. He did so. But the political department did not stop there. They announced that in view of the state's recalcitrance they were reconsidering their position on the vexed question of the Mysore subsidy (the cancellation of which had always been one of the *darbar*'s indispensable preconditions for joining the federation). At the same time, Glancy worked assiduously through the resident to undermine Mirza's position at court, a strategy that eventually bore fruit with his dismissal in 1941. Meanwhile, though, other officials such as Francis Wylie were starting to draw a somewhat different moral from the tumultuous events of the previous year. For Wylie the problem was not rapid change but its absence. He believed that the princely order was doomed unless the states, as a body, enacted rapid and sweeping administrative reforms and made 'some reasonable concessions in the way of representative institutions'. The time was ripe, he wrote in October 1938, for an ultimatum to the princes 'on the above lines' from the viceroy.[99]

A few years earlier such a suggestion would have earned Wylie a stiff rebuke – as it had joint political secretary R. E. L. Wingate in 1934.[100] And even in the changed conditions of 1939, resistance to it was fierce, Glancy warning that the government would 'get the blame' if the experiment failed.[101] But Wylie's arguments struck a chord with Linlithgow:

I cannot help feeling [he told Zetland] that we have ourselves to thank in no small degree for the pitch which matters . . . have reached. . . . The great mistake, I am now disposed to think, lay in the change of policy after Curzon's retirement which

---

[98] Note [not signed, but evidently by Glancy] on interview with Mirza, [?] 1939, Mirza Ismail Papers, Subject File 1. It is not clear how a copy of this note got into Mirza's files. It is possible, though, that it was leaked by a friendly official at Delhi.

[99] Wylie to Lord Brabourne, acting viceroy 11 Oct. 1938, IOR Pol. (Intl.) Colls., 13/14 (2).

[100] In a 'secret' note of August 1934, Wingate proposed a revision of the non-intervention policy in the light of the revelations which had recently surfaced about Jey Singh's Alwar. It was condescendingly brushed aside by Glancy as the product of emotional strain brought about by 'pressure of work'. Note by Wingate dated 18 Aug. 1934, and note by Glancy dated 3 Dec. 1934, IOR L/P&S/13/550.

[101] Memo by Glancy dated 8 Apr. 1939, IOR R/1/1/3415.

led us to relax our control over individual Princes and over happenings inside the States . . . we and the States have now . . . to pay for 30 years of laissez-faire.[102]

In March 1939 Linlithgow used his annual address to the COP to announce a new policy of constructive engagement. Afterwards he briefed the Standing Committee: 'the fact is', he told them, 'the old order has gone for ever'.[103] Early the following year the political department's J. S. H. Shattock was posted on special duty in western India with a brief to suggest how the chaotic political map of Kathiawar might be rationalised and the lives of its people improved by the absorption, or extinction, of its petty *talukas*.

Restricted as it was, this departure from the Butler doctrine came as a rude shock to the princes. For one thing, it was quite unexpected; for another, it seemed, to many of them, unfair and unjustified. A number of states, heeding the demands of their subjects, the exhortations of the COP, and the warnings of Congress, had already started to implement piecemeal reforms: some had made concessions in the area of civil rights; others again had established or added to representative bodies; a few had even gone as far as allocating ministerial portfolios to elected members of legislative councils in imitation of the dyarchy system used in the provinces before 1937.[104] Certainly, most of these reforms would not have taken place if the *darbars* had not come under pressure from Congress and the AISPC; and it was also true, as the nationalists repeatedly pointed out, that they fell a long way short of democracy. Still, they marked a major step forward, and the rulers felt that the government had not given them the recognition they deserved. However, it was not just the apparent unfairness of the new dispensation which upset the princes, but its potential impact on their internal autonomy. For over two decades the rulers had fought to have paramountcy circumscribed and their independence in matters of internal administration recognised. Bit by bit they had persuaded, threatened and cajoled the British into putting, if not legal, then at least conventional checks on the exercise of their rights of intervention. Now, Linlithgow was threatening to turn back the clock to the days of Lord Curzon. Having beaten off their enemies, the rulers felt they were about to be mugged by their friends. Sapru, who was visiting the capital at the time of the Chamber session, found the princes 'very dissatisfied'.[105] The government's spies formed the same impression. 'My

---

[102] Linlithgow to Zetland 21 Feb. 1939, Zetland Coll., 17.
[103] Quoted in John Glendevon, *The Viceroy at Bay: Lord Linlithgow in India, 1936–1943* (London, 1971), 118.
[104] Mysore, Cochin, Gwalior and Sangli all introduced varients of this system during 1939–40. Aundh, of course, had already introduced full responsible government.
[105] Sapru to Jayakar 20 Mar. 1939, Jayakar Papers, 726.

informant [at Bahawalpur]', noted Intelligence chief J. M. Ewart, 'reports what I have now heard from a number of sources . . . that the [current] feeling of Rulers and their Ministers . . . towards the Political Department is one of resentment and hostility.'[106]

It was in this far from tranquil atmosphere that representatives of the major states gathered in Simla at the invitation of the viceroy heard, for the first time, the terms of the government's 'final offer' on accession to the federation.

Federation aborted

To be sure, the initial reaction was promising. Some twenty ministers took part in the briefing – a pretty representative sample – and the only really jarring note was struck by Hydari, who after listening patiently to what Linlithgow had to say, replied brusquely that he would not be advising the nizam to federate on terms which fell short of the state's essential requirements. Afterwards Glancy wrote: 'His attitude towards Federation appeared to have undergone a change not only since the . . . Round Table Conference, but since we had last discussed matters together.'[107] Yet even Hyderabad's stance, while disappointing, did not strike the government as immovable. Consequently, Glancy and Linlithgow returned to Delhi in October 1938 in high spirits. This new-found optimism persisted over Christmas, but it did not long survive the new year as an orchestrated backlash against federation, led by Hydari and Bikaner, rapidly built up momentum.

As noted above, Bikaner and Hydari were moved to take an anti-federation stance by personal and dynastic influences. But now, in the aftermath of the *satyagraha* movement and with the terms of the 'final offer' on the table, the two men found additional reasons to attack the scheme. When he examined the draft IOA, Hydari came to the conclusion that there was nothing in it which effectively protected treaty rights outside the federal field; and he was disturbed by the absence in the draft of any limitation on the deployment of the Indian Army in the states, which to his mind cast grave doubts on the crown's ability, in a crunch, to defend them. Likewise, Hydari found the standard administrative agreement included with the offer defective in that it did not, as expected, give the states a general right to administer federal laws under Section 125, but left the matter of delegation to the discretion of the centre. And he was also critical of the government's stance on permissable limitations,

---

[106] Note by director, Intelligence Bureau, dated 12 Jan. 1939, IOR R/1/1/3322.
[107] Note by Glancy dated 14 Sept. 1938, IOR L/P&S/13/617.

unaware, perhaps, of how far Linlithgow and Glancy had gone out on a limb with London to have the original formula relaxed in the states' interests. However, the Hyderabad minister's gripe with the offer was not merely that it fell significantly short of what the states regarded as necessary to ensure their survival, but that it marked, in many ways, a step backwards. During the JSC, Hydari noted, the ISD had been assured by Hoare that there would be no objection to the rulers protecting their treaty rights by means of a specific clause in the IOA; this promise had not been honoured. Likewise, the Administrative Agreement flew in the face of understandings reached during the earlier discussions.[108] The 'Home Gov[ernmen]t . . . has let us down', he opined bitterly.[109] Bikaner shared these reservations. As well, both he and Hydari seem to have been badly shaken by the 1938–9 agitation, and by what it demonstrated about the capacity of the British to act against the wishes of Congressite governments backed by electoral majorities. As Ganga Singh put it, with characteristic bluntness, in a letter to Linlithgow: 'I trust I shall not be misunderstood . . . when I say that some of us feel . . . that we have been – I will not use the term let down but – not supported by the Authorities in England and left to fend for ourselves.'[110] No less on political than on personal grounds, both princely statesmen were now thoroughly convinced that federation was an evil that had to be resisted and, if possible, prevented. With this end in view they launched, early in 1939, a concerted campaign to persuade the *darbars* to say 'no' to the viceroy's offer – Bikaner working on his allies among the north Indian Rajputs and Jats, and Hydari lobbying the key power-brokers in the COMs.

Bikaner's first important convert was Udaibhan Singh of Dholpur, who, as we have seen, had never come to terms with a federal compact which threatened to disturb the special relationship of the princes with the king-emperor. The next was Dholpur's close friend Yeshwant Rao Puar, the young ruler of Dewas Junior, who, as a graduate in constitutional law, needed little convincing that the 'safeguards' contained in the Act were phoney.[111] And soon after him Ganga Singh snared a really big fish in the person of the newly elected chancellor, Digvijaysinhji of Nawanagar, son of the most outspoken and loyal of the English Diehards' princely allies; he in turn brought in a number of dependent princes in Kathiawar and Gujarat. Meanwhile, Hydari's efforts bore fruit when the COMs, which had been asked by the chancellor to advise on the pros and

---

[108] Report of the [Hydari] Committee of Ministers dated 14 Apr. 1939, RSA, Bundi, English Records, Serial No. 1201, file 448.
[109] Marginal note on Sir F. Brown to Hydari 7 July 1939, n.d., AP R/1/47/10/831.
[110] Bikaner to Linlithgow 17 June 1939, IOR L/P&S/13/621.
[111] Note by Patrick on interview with Dewas Junior dated 29 June 1938, IOR L/PO/91.

cons of the government's offer, met at Bombay early in April and, following the lead of its chairman and of another recent convert Sir C. P. Ramaswamy Aiyer, gave a decisive thumbs down to the package on technical grounds while conceding that federation remained, on balance, probably the princes' best long-term prospect.[112] By the end of the month, with a crucial general conference in Bombay looming, the flight from federation had become so widespread that Indore's S. M. Bapna – who had resisted the trend – seriously wondered whether it would be worth his while attending.[113]

Rumours of what was afoot started to trickle into Delhi in February, and were confirmed by impressions gained during the annual 'Princes Week' in March. Fearing a bad result, Linlithgow asked Courtney Latimer to coordinate a crash counter-propaganda campaign in the lead-up to the Bombay meeting. However, as the India Office anticipated, Latimer's key selling point, that federation offered the princes 'the most efficacious, if not the only, means of defending themselves' in the face of the developing 'threat' from Congress,[114] did not find many buyers, particularly in the ranks of the Standing Committee. Thus the Bombay conference opened on 8 June with the rebels seemingly in firm control.

In the event, it was not a total disaster for the government. Ganga Singh in particular came in for much not-altogether good natured banter on the theme of his sudden conversion, and one minister, from Jhalawar, actually had the temerity to heckle him;[115] while Panikkar, Krishnamachari and Gopalaswamy Aiyengar of Kashmir, working quietly behind the scenes, managed to persuade the drafting committee to add a clause to the resolution to be put to the plenary session committing the princes to further negotiation – a small but crucial victory. But the debate at the conference was from the start dominated by the anti-federationists – in part because the jam sahib saw to it that the early speakers (Bikaner, Panna and Dewas Junior) were all from that camp, and in part because in the absence of the rana of Jhalawar, the opposition camp boasted no speakers of equivalent calibre. Moreover, thanks again to Digvijaysinhji's partiality, the verdict of the conference was made to appear even more

[112] Report of the Committee of Ministers, 14 Apr. 1939, Bundi, English Records, Serial No. 1201, file 448. Meanwhile Hydari continued to project, in letters to Monckton, the image of honest broker: 'we have tried our best', he wrote, 'even at this stage, not to wreck Federation'. Hydari to Monckton 14 Apr. 1939, AP R/1/47/10/812.

[113] Bapna told Glancy that 'some 95 per cent of the States' were now opposed to joining the federation, but this was a deliberate over-estimate for governmental consumption. Bapna to Glancy 23 Apr. 1939, IOR L/P&S/13/621.

[114] Note by Lothian dated 20 Mar. 1939, IOR L/P&S/13/618; and circular letter from Latimer to residents, 8 Apr. 1939, IOR L/P&S/13/621.

[115] Bikaner to Linlithgow 17 June 1939, IOR L/P&S/13/621.

negative than was actually the case. When the draft resolution was put, on 14 June, at least one ruler raised his hand in dissent, while others conspicuously abstained; yet the motion was recorded as having been carried *nem con*. Then, in his closing speech, the chancellor totally ignored the open door clause and characterised the decision as a decisive rejection of the federal offer, adding, to outraged shouts of 'no', 'no' from Krishnamachari, that members of the COP were 'morally' bound by it. Finally, just before the proceedings closed, Digvijaysinhji sought and obtained approval from the meeting to 'draw up a model reply' to the viceroy's letter for the 'assistance' of his members.[116] Angry at this blatant display of partisanship and 'sorely disappointed at the failure of ten years work', Panikkar immediately tendered his resignation from the COMs; and Bapna followed suit shortly afterwards.[117] However these rather Quixotic protests only reinforced the impression that Bikaner and company had won the day. Certainly this was the view of the press and of most senior officials.[118]

However, on more mature reflection, New Delhi decided that the situation was redeemable. For a start, the political department gathered from leaked information that the conference had been much more evenly divided on the merits of the offer than initial reports and the chancellor's claim of a unanimous vote had implied. Secondly, there were signs during the following weeks that a number of states – some of which had not been represented at Bombay – were unhappy with the outcome and believed that the wrong signals had been sent to Delhi. The raja of Sirmur, whose dewan had voted with the majority in Bombay, intimated that he was now thinking of federating. Meetings of rulers from the Punjab and Eastern States agencies publicly dissociated themselves from the Bombay

---

[116] The above discussion is based on note by N. Madhava Rau [Rao?], n.d., L/P&S/13/621; 'Appreciation of the Position Resulting From the Princes' Decision in Regard to Federation', n.d., Reforms Office, Fed. Branch, 18/39; Ganpat Rai to Jayakar 16 June 1939, Ganpat Rai Papers; circular letter from chancellor dated 18 June 1939, Jayakar Papers, 742; Sir F. Brown to Hydari 24 Aug. 1939, AP R/1/47/10/831; Linlithgow to Zetland 30 June 1939, Zetland Coll., 17; ; and Panikkar, *Autobiography*, 119. The model reply read, in part: 'In view of the aforementioned considerations I have reluctantly come to the conclusion that I am unable to accede to the Federation on the terms indicated in . . . Your Excellency's letter under reply. In coming to this decision I assure Your Excellency that I have been moved solely by the dictates of the sacred duty I owe to my State, my Dynasty and my people and of my solemn obligation to the Crown. In conclusion, I find it difficult to believe that it could be the intention of His Majesty's Government to close the door on an all-India Federation.'

[117] Panikkar, *Autobiography*, 119; and Ganpat Rai to Jayakar 16 June 1939, Ganpat Rai Papers.

[118] For a summary of press comment on the Bombay resolution see note, n.d., in Reforms Office, Fed. Branch, 18/39; and for official reaction see Fitze to Glancy 26 June 1939, IOR R/1/1/3238.

decision. Karauli changed its tack after discussions with its resident.[119] Even Hyderabad showed a welcome desire to keep talking. In truth, some of these counter-rebels were probably motivated less by an affection for federation than by a desire to get back at Ganga Singh, who had made many enemies during his long reign as a Chamber power broker. The maharaja of Bundi, for example, was still smarting over his kinsman's failure to deliver on a promise in 1938 to get Bundi added to the list of states eligible for election to the Standing Committee.[120] And others, like Porbandar, appear to have been swayed mainly by the sensible advice of legal counsel.[121] From the government's viewpoint, however, the important thing was that the rank and file princes had started to speak up. 'Rulers are tending more and more to realise the difficulty of evolving any practical alternative . . . to the federal offer', Linlithgow informed London. 'I am already receiving one or two favourable replies.'[122] This groundswell of opinion inclined Linlithgow to think that the Bombay verdict might yet be reversed.

He considered his options. One was simply to do nothing and 'play for time for a couple of months' in the hope that, aided by strident criticism from British India, the anti-Bikaner backlash would gather momentum. Another was to broaden the 'net' to include the small states which had hitherto been ignored on the grounds that their populations and revenues were inadequate to warrant their inclusion as separate units of the federation. Latimer calculated there were at least thirty states in this category which could be relied on to return a favourable reply. Yet a third was to juggle the odds by asking parliament to reduce 'by a few per cent' the quantum of acceding states needed to bring the federal part of the Act into operation.[123]

However, the plan which Linlithgow and his advisers increasingly favoured was to try to meet some of the princes' objections to the offer. All along the viceroy had been reconciled to the inevitability of further concessions. In the wake of the Bombay decision, the need to move on this front seemed to him a matter of urgency. Moreover, after reading the Hydari report he was not convinced he was in a strong position either morally or in law to refuse the princes' demands. Many of the government's arguments, he explained to Zetland, had been shown by the

[119] J. P. Thompson, resdt. Eastern Rajputana, to maharaja of Karauli 28 July 1939, RSA, Karauli, State Council, file 19 of 1939.
[120] Bikaner to Bundi 22 July 1938, RSA, Bundi, English Records, Serial No. 1182, file 365.
[121] Jayakar to maharana of Porbandar 13 June 1939, Jayakar Papers, 742.
[122] Crown representative to sec. state 18 July 1939, IOR L/P&S/13.621.
[123] Crown representative to sec. state, 21 Mar. 1939, IOR R/1/1/3415; crown representative to sec. state 30 May 1939, IOR L/P&S/13/614; and crown representative to sec. state 1 Aug. 1939, IOR L/P&S/13/621.

COMs to be 'shaky, legalistic and apparently inconsistent'. If the states' legitimate claims were refused, despite them having a good case, they would be able 'to shift the onus of their refusal [to federate] on to His Majesty's Government'.[124] In Linlithgow's mind morality and expediency alike pointed to the need for compromise; and it was also clear to him where the government needed to bend: on the sugar excise, which Kenneth Fitze had identified as the major breaking-point with the rulers of Central India, and on the issue of extra-territorial treaty rights. Confident that London would agree, the viceroy in mid-July asked Zetland to extend the deadline for replies to his letter to 1 September to enable him to make one last pitch to the rulers on the basis of an improved offer.

The home government declined to take the bait. It remained wedded to the view that further appeasement of the princes was neither proper nor likely to be productive. 'I am strongly of opinion', concluded Zetland, 'that at this stage we shall be wise to stand on the terms of the offer already made.'[125] He did, however, consent to extend the time-limit for replies until September.

Linlithgow was bitterly disappointed at London's reaction, especially by the home government's cavalier dismissal of his plea on treaty rights; but he did not allow the setback to deter him. Through Glancy he instructed his residents to keep up as much pressure on uncommitted rulers as was consistent with the government's past pledges that they would be left free to make up their own minds; and he continued to push for another summit meeting with the Chamber, which, once the idea had been approved, enabled him to go back to Zetland with another request for 'a peg, however slender', on which the jam sahib and his friends could hang a face-saving recommendation overturning the Bombay resolution.[126] By this devious route, he obtained Whitehall's leave to make several small but meaningful changes in the wording of the IOA, to vary the conditions of the standard Section 124 administrative agreement to allow the *darbars* to charge any extra costs incurred in administering federal laws to the central budget, to amend the reference to land customs in the governor-general's Instrument of Instructions to permit the states to keep the proceeds of any new transit duties imposed down to the date of the establishment of the federation, and to widen further the range of

---

[124] Crown representative to sec. state 18 July 1939, IOR L/P&S/13/621.
[125] Sec. state to crown representative, 31 May 1939, IOR L/P&S/13/621. This ruling was delivered before the Bombay meeting of the princes, but Zetland continued to resist the government of India's requests for amendments well into July. See sec. state to crown representative, 22 July 1939, *ibid.*
[126] Crown representative to sec. state 16 Aug. 1939, IOR L/P&S/13/621.

permissable limitations. Linlithgow also talked Zetland into letting him publicise these concessions at his planned meeting with the Standing Committee at Simla on 21 August. But Whitehall doggedly refused to budge on the one issue which the viceroy knew could be relied on to turn the tide – treaty rights. Privately, Linlithgow doubted whether he had gained enough to sway the hardliners, but he hoped the gesture might make a difference to the attitude of some of the princes who appeared torn between going against the chancellor and Bikaner and alienating the British.[127]

Nor was this just wishful thinking. Private correspondence in the Conrad Corfield Collection in the British Library suggests that in Rajputana, at least, the pendulum was beginning to swing the government's way. According to William Edgerton, the resident in western Rajputana, Dharam Narain, dewan of the very influential state of Udaipur, had become a firm ally, and Edgerton was confident that it was only a matter of time before Narain's arguments, spiced with the assurance (which the Englishman, improperly, did nothing to refute) that taking a lead on federation would earn the maharana a GCIE and possibly a 21–gun salute, bore dividends.[128] And similar hopes were entertained for the big states of eastern Rajputana by the resident there, Joseph Thompson. Thompson's information was that Alwar would reply 'yes' without the need for additional outside encouragement; that Prime Minister Donald Field had the maharaja of Jodhpur firmly in his pocket; that Tonk was so upset by the jam sahib's politicking that he had decided to federate out of sheer spite; and that the maharaja of Jaipur, the debonair Jai Singh, while 'truculent', was likely to accede if he was sat on firmly enough by Corfield. Ironically, part of the problem in Jaipur's case was the reluctance of the dewan, Todd, a political officer on loan to the state, to pitch in on the government's side for fear that this would be construed by other members of the State Council as bad form.[129]

Was Rajputana, though, an exception? The short answer is that we simply do not know, since most of the states never got a chance to reply to the government's revised offer. However, the outward reaction of the thirteen princes and twelve ministers who comprised the states' delegation which waited on the viceroy at Simla in August 1939 was uniformly hostile. Having armed itself in advance with a bulky *aide-mémoire* prepared by Chamber secretary Maqbool Mahmud on the basis of the Hydari report, the delegation for the most part refused to depart from the

[127] Glancy to Corfield 18 July 1939, Corfield Coll., 1.
[128] Edgerton to Corfield, 19 and 29 July 1939, Corfield Coll., 1.
[129] Thompson to Corfield 8, 20 and 21 July and 2, 6, 18 and 28 Aug. 1939, Corfield Coll., 1.

position laid down in that document. What is more, the princely delegates stayed unusually solid, only the nawab of Bahawalpur venturing to challenge Ganga Singh's trenchant summary of the states' position. Writing privately to Corfield, Glancy summarised the proceedings thus:

Our talks with the Princes here were, I think a waste of time – this was bound to happen when Z[et]L[and] ran out of rope and wouldn't let us have our way about States' rights protection and a few other things. [The] Ministers present were very sensible but Bik[aner] and the Jambo [Nawanagar] were not out to see reason themselves and apparently thought it was treason for anyone else to do so.[130]

The viceroy's reaction was similar. Linlithgow came away from the summit convinced of the futility of further negotiations and keen to wrap up the federal saga as quickly as possible. On 27 August he informed the chancellor that the government stood by its revised offer, and that no further amendments could be expected. Simultaneously, reminders were sent to the rulers who had still not replied. The plan was to publish the terms of the offer and a summary of the rulers' replies in the form of a white paper to be laid before parliament when it resumed after the summer recess.

All this, however, was based on the assumption that there would be no radical change in the international situation. That was not to be. On 1 September Hitler's forces crossed into Poland; two days later Britain was at war with Germany. When the viceroy's letter of 24 August relating his reactions to the Simla conference reached the India Office, it was already out of date. 'The federal offer', wrote Zetland in the margin, 'is now in cold storage.'[131]

We shall be arguing below that, contrary to the popular impression, federation was not comprehensively rejected by the Indian states in 1939; that in fact the government came tantalisingly close to achieving its goal. Nevertheless, in spite (and perhaps because) of this, the dominant reaction in the India Office – and to some extent also in Delhi – to the news that the federal scheme had been aborted was one of bitter disappointment. While some officials shared the viceroy's view that federation had simply been deferred for a few years, the majority felt, instinctively, that a watershed had been crossed and that if all-India unity was ever going to be attained it would be on a quite different basis to that enshrined in the Government of India Act. As Zetland, more prescient in this matter than Linlithgow, put it in a submission to Cabinet:

---

[130] Glancy to Lothian 25 Aug. 1939, Lothian Coll., 1. For the princes' reaction to the talks see chancellor to Glancy 23 Aug. 1939 and circular from chancellor dated 24 Aug. 1939, PSA, COP, file 123 of 1939.
[131] Note by Zetland, n.d., on Linlithgow to Zetland 24 Aug. 1939, IOR L/P&S/13/621.

it seems to me self-evident that when the time comes to resume work in that connection, it will be impossible, in view of the hostility with which the Federal provisions of the Act have been met, though for different reasons, by the Princes, the Moslems and the Hindus of India, to . . . put into operation Part II of the Act as it stands.[132]

Moreover, the general feeling was that any new initiative on the federal front was likely to be tougher than that embodied in the 1939 offer. 'It is very difficult to see', noted Paul Patrick in reference to the additional concessions announced at Simla, 'how the ground gained in this matter can be preserved.' Sir Reginald Glancy concurred: 'The next deal', he minuted, 'will no doubt be less favourable to the Princes.'[133]

In part these prognostications were founded on the reasonable assumption that the forces for political change unleashed on the states in 1938 were likely to increase, rather than diminish, over the course of time, and that these forces would be even less inclined in future than they had been in the 1930s to tolerate a constitutional set-up in which autocrats personally controlled the disposition of two-fifths of the seats in the legislature. But they also embodied a tinge of wishful thinking. In the aftermath of the Bombay conference bombshell of 1935, Hyderabad's solicitor and London agent Charles Brunyate had tried to warn Hydari against the consequences of playing the Diehards' game: 'if sufficient States do not accede', he had written, 'the word will go out that the Indian Princes have let His Majesty's Government down'.[134] That is exactly what happened in 1939. To British officialdom, the virtual abandonment of federation after ten years intensive effort – an effort which had left some, like Courtney Latimer, 'near breaking point'[135] – represented more than just a grave political setback to their plans, shared with the politicians, to underwrite the raj by building an effective counterpoise to Congressite democracy. It represented a personal defeat, the end of something to which they had devoted, in many cases, a substantial part of their working lives. Frustrated and bitter, they looked for scapegoats, and – being understandably reluctant to put the blame on themselves, and curiously unwilling to blame the Muslim League – they seized on the princes. 'I regard them', Linlithgow told Zetland, 'as having themselves to a considerable extent to thank for any difficulties which now confront us.'[136] Rightly or wrongly, the British believed they had been betrayed.

---

[132] Memo by sec. state dated 25 Sept. 1939, NMML, Cabinet Papers, WP (G) (39) 21.
[133] Notes by Patrick dated 29 Sept. 1939 and Glancy dated 2 Oct. 1939, IOR L/P&S/13/626.   [134] Brunyate to Hydari 18 Feb. 1935, AP R/1/47/10/361.
[135] Note by Patrick dated 29 Sept. 1939 on letter from Latimer to Laithwaite 8 Sept. 1939, IOR L/P&S/13/626.
[136] Viceroy to sec. state 24 Oct. 1939, NMML, Cabinet Papers, WP (G) (39) 54.

6   Indian summer

We have got to deal with facts as they are. . . The Indian States are governed by treaties . . . The Indian States, if they do not join this Union, will remain in exactly the same situation as they are today.

Sir Stafford Cripps, 1942

Reprieve

The convulsions wrought by the Pacific War are rightly considered by historians to have been instrumental in the collapse of European colonialism in Asia; but in the short term the outbreak of war, in India at least, had the effect of reinforcing the imperial presence, strengthening the colonial government's control over public life and temporarily halting moves to devolve power through constitutional change. In turn, this paradoxical outcome made life much tougher for the Congress, which after three comfortable years in ministerial office found itself again on the receiving end of police repression. Yet there were winners as well as losers from this new dispensation. While Congress languished in opposition, other groups and parties flourished in the political vacuum opened up by its withdrawal from the legislatures. One was the Muslim League; another, the princes.

The war was kind to the rulers in several ways. Firstly, it generated a martial, authoritarian culture in India which was on the whole congenial to their talents and traditions as blue-blooded *kshatriyas*. Several younger rulers distinguished themselves on active service, the maharaja of Bundi, for example, earning the Military Cross for valour in Burma; while older members of the order such as Ganga Singh and Hamidullah took a prominent part in the planning and promotion of the war effort. Likewise, the resignation of the Congress governments, the introduction of authoritarian wartime measures such as the Defence of India Rules and the jailing in August 1942 of the greater part of the Congress leadership made life that much easier, on the domestic front, for the princes who remained at home.

Table 6.1 *Index of industrial growth in selected states, 1931–1951 (1931=100)*

State	1931	1936	1941	1946	1951
Baroda	100	114	218	472	505
Bhavnagar	100	107	131	162	187
Cochin	100	103	107	125	145
Gwalior	100	109	129	290	349
Hyderabad	100	119	151	230	234
Mysore	100	171	187	246	282
Travancore	100	112	121	197	269

Source: State Administration Reports; *Census of India*, 1931, 1941, 1951; *Statistical Abstract For British India . . . 1931/2 to 1939/40* (Delhi, 1942). The index is a composite of several variables: number of 'factory' units; number of 'factory' operatives; percentage of the workforce in non-agricultural jobs.

Secondly, by cutting off the supply of imported manufactured goods, and generating additional demand at home, the war gave a hefty stimulus to the states' economic development. Traditionally they had lagged well behind the provinces in manufacturing and mining. In 1921, the states accounted for just 6.0 per cent of the Indian output of of cotton yarn, 7.7 per cent of that of piece-goods and 11.0 per cent of that of woollens. Their share of coal production was 5.0 per cent, that of other minerals 6.0 per cent.[1] Even in 1939, the picture was not broadly very different.[2] But over the next four years it changed dramatically. In one year alone, 1943–4, over 5 crores of new industrial capital flowed into the states, attracted by tax breaks (few states levied income or corporate taxes), lax labour laws and handsome government subsidies.[3] Some of this was absorbed in mining: nickle in Gwalior, gold in Mysore, iron in Bastar, mineral sands in Travancore; but the greater part went into factories and infrastructure. Mysore invested heavily in woollens, aircraft construction and car-making, Rampur in the small-scale production of *dhotis*, Porbandar in cement, Baroda in cotton piece-goods, Tonk in carpet-weaving, Hyderabad in cement, chemicals and fertilizers. Indore by war's end had

[1] *The British Crown and the Indian States*, 184–5.
[2] Except perhaps in Mysore, where development slackened after a boom period in the 1930s. Economic developments in Mysore are addressed in Bjorn Hettne, *The Political Economy of Indirect Rule: Mysore 1881–1947* (New Delhi, 1978); and Janaki Nair, 'The Emergence of Labor Politics', chapter 2.
[3] The US consul in Madras, Louise Schaffner, gathered that the state would welcome American technical assistance and investment 'on almost any terms'. Report by Schaffner dated 16 Aug. 1945, US State Dept decimal file 845.00/7–1645.

become the third biggest silk-weaving centre in the country. Table 6.1 above summarises the picture for several major states statistically. But visitors to the princely capitals did not need to look up the statistics to realise that a boom was in progress. In cities like Jaipur, Bangalore, Rampur and Hyderabad-Secunderabad, the signs of prosperity were unmistakeable. As Lord Wavell remarked dryly after paying a call on the nizam in 1944, 'Hyderabad has made a lot of money out of the war.'[4]

Thirdly, and perhaps most importantly, the outbreak of war allowed the princes to dramatise their loyalty to the crown and thereby partially to redeem themselves with the British for their failure to deliver the goods on federation. Travancore built at its own expense a patrol boat for the Indian navy; Bhopal spent its entire stock of US securities on the purchase of American fighter planes; Jodhpur contributed money for a Halifax bomber; Kashmir donated eighteen field ambulances; Hyderabad, determined that in this as in all things it should be the premier performer, paid for no less than three squadrons of war-planes. Altogether, the cost of war materials provided by the states down to 1945 exceeded £5 million. In addition, the states made numerous direct grants of cash and gave generously of their land, buildings and workforces for war purposes, Mysore handing over all state-owned buildings in Bangalore for the use of the army, Nawanagar starting a torpedo training school, Gwalior converting its Hattersley Mills in Bombay to the production of webbing for parachutes and Bikaner building a military hospital. By 1945 Hyderabad had spent Rs 5.27 crores on war-related projects, Bhopal over 2 crores. Again, the *darbars* made an important indirect contribution to the war effort by actively promoting it among their subjects.[5] By the end of 1944 over 300,000 men from 59 states had signed up for military service and 15,000 more for war-related jobs in industry – a higher *per-capita* response than that of any of the provinces except for the Punjab – while some Rs 180 million had been contributed by the states' people in subscriptions to government war bonds and securities and through donations to the viceroy's War Purposes Fund – again, a result that put British India to shame.[6] Last but not least, the princes aided the

---

[4] Wavell to Amery 20 Dec. 1944, *TOP*, V, 316.

[5] For details of government propaganda in Indore see subhadar, Rampura-Bhampura-Garoth to assist. foreign sec. 9 Jan. 1941, MSPA, Indore, Foreign Dept., file 36 of 1940. A close reading of the Indore files suggests that considerable official pressure – up to and including threats of reprisals – was applied to induce subjects to part with cash.

[6] Information compiled from: 'Indian States Information Bulletin', Oct. 1941, MPSA, Indore, Huzur Office, file 109 of 1941; 'Bhopal and its War Efforts', BRO, Bhopal, Pol. Dept., Chamber section, 45, 4/31, 1941–2; Amery to Linlithgow 24 Aug. 1942, *TOP*, II, 817; statement by chancellor at SC meeting in Bombay, 15–18 July 1944, BRO, Bhopal, Pol. Dept., Chamber section, 6, 1/6, 1944; notes, n.d., in BRO, Bhopal, Pol. Dept., War, files 257 and 344 of 1946; F. Pearson, DSP, to private sec. to C-in-C, 28 Dec. 1944, IOR

British by keeping the lid on internal unrest during the Quit India campaign of 1942–3, thereby freeing up thousands of police and troops for deployment in the troublespots of Bengal, Bombay and the NWFP.[7]

In truth, not all the princes were quite as solidly behind the war effort as they made out. For one thing it would seem that during 1942 several rulers made secret plans for survival in the eventuality of a British collapse. Both Bhopal and Patiala, for example, spent heavily in this period on armaments, Hamidullah attempting to augment his army with Pathan mercenaries from the NWFP, and rumours abounded that this rearmament drive had less to do with fighting the Japanese than with domestic political agendas, in Yadavindra Singh's case an ambitious scheme to rebuild the kingdom of Lahore by annexing large parts of the Punjab. Likewise, controversy surrounded Yeshwant Rao Holkar's declaration that, rather than have his state subjected to 'scorched earth' treatment in the event of a Japanese advance, he would declare Indore 'an open city' to avoid 'trouble coming there' – which many people took to mean that he intended to collaborate with the enemy.[8] Again, it is fair to say that the aid rendered by the states, while freely given, carried with it firm expectations of political rewards when and if the imperial cause prevailed.

R/1/1/4133; note by pol. adviser, n.d., for meeting with the chancellor in Mar. 1946, IOR R/3/1/110; and *Asiatic Review*, 36, 726–30.

[7] There was some trouble in Indore, the Deccan states, Mysore and the Eastern States Agency of Orissa, but only in the last two places did it reach serious proportions. On the Deccan see resdt. Kolhapur to Fitze 15 Aug. 1942, IOR R/1/1/3806; on Indore see memo by I-G Police dated 5 Oct. 1942, MSPA, Indore, Foreign Dept., file 28 of 1942; on Mysore see Manor, *Political Change*, 139–45; on Orissa, see Biswamoy Pati, 'The Climax Of Popular Protest: The Quit India Movement in Orissa', *IESHR*, 29, 1 (1992), 1–36. Although the *darbars* got the credit for this 'good' result, factional problems in the AISPC also contributed to it. In 1940, following Gandhi's call for individual civil disobedience, the AISPC handed over its affairs to an emergency committee in the expectation that the elected Standing Committee would be offering *satyagraha*. This did not eventuate; nevertheless the emergency committee refused to disband. This caused the party's financial backers in Bombay to withhold vitally needed funds. See S. G. Vaze, Servants of India Society to Gandhi 8 May 1941, Kanhailal Vaidya, sec., C.I. SPC to Jai Narain Vyas 7 May 1941, Vaze to Gandhi 6 May 1941, and Vyas to [?] Upadhaya 23 June 1941, Jai Narain Vyas Papers, file 3/2. On the other hand, some *praja mandals* managed to reach an accommodation with their *darbars*, usually on the basis of a qualified support for the war. This occurred, for example, in Jodhpur, where Prime Minister Donald Field agreed to release all detainees and allow members of the Lok Parishad to contest elections to the Representative Assembly in an individual capacity after Narain Vyas, the Parishad's general secretary gave his word that it would not engage in any activities 'that would embarras[s] His Highness'. Field to Vyas 16 May 1940 and Vyas to Field 27 May 1940, Vyas Papers, files 2 and 3/3. In Jaipur negotiations fell through, but Gandhi advised the Rajya Praja Mandal leaders there to do 'constructive work' in view of the 'tense international situation'. Karpoochandra Patru, general sec. Jaipur RPM to [?] 23 Dec. 1941, AISPC, 78, Part I of 1940–2.

[8] Memo by Kanji Dwarkadas dated 28 Jan. 1945, encl. in US consul-general, Bombay, to sec. state Washington 10 Apr. 1947, US State Dept. decimal file 845.00/4–1047.

However, any reservations which the British might have had about the princes' loyalty were overshadowed by their gratitude for the states' lavish material contribution to the war-effort. Linlithgow praised the *darbars'* response as 'astoundingly helpful and reassuring'.[9] Comment in London, where former Conservative Party rebel Winston Churchill had taken over the prime ministership from Neville Chamberlain and the romantically minded Leo Amery had replaced Zetland at the India Office,[10] was just as laudatory. By the end of Lord Linlithgow's six-year reign in 1943, the goodwill generated in London and New Delhi by virtue of the states' war services had gone a very long way to repairing the damage done to the special relationship between the rulers and the crown by the federation debacle.

This wartime *rapprochement* was symbolised publicly by the appointment of representatives from the states to various government agencies connected with the running of the war. Following discussions with the chancellor over the winter, Linlithgow in August 1940 nominated three princes, plus Akbar Hydari, to the newly established War Advisory Council. Later, several more rulers and dewans were appointed to its successor, the National Defence Council, and other ministers to the Eastern Group Supply Council, the Export Advisory Committee, the Petrol Rationing Conference, the Central Price Control Conference and the several provincial Transport Boards. Last but not least, in June 1942, Ramaswamy Aiyer of Travancore and Jogendra Singh of Patiala were added to an expanded executive council, the former as minister for information and the latter as minister for civil aviation.

However, the most important repercussions of the princes' return to favour were felt in the political arena. A year before, residents had been instructed to push reform remorselessly; they were now instructed to caution the *darbars* against making hasty changes, indeed to discourage constitutional changes of any kind 'for the period of the war, and probably for some time afterwards'.[11] This about-face was highlighted by the Rewa case of 1942, when, confronted by iron-clad evidence of criminal misconduct on the part of Gulab Singh, the government let the maharaja

[9] Linlithgow to Amery 24 Aug. 1942, *TOP*, II, 814
[10] For a recent reassessment of Amery's term at the India Office see William Roger Louis, *In the Name of God, Go! Leo Amery and the British Empire in the Age of Churchill* (New York, 1992).
[11] Amery to Wavell 21 Jan. 1944, *TOP*, IV, 662. See also note on interview between the PM, Indore, and the resdt., C.I. 15 Feb. 1940, MSPA, Indore, Foreign Dept., file 65 of 1940; and Linlithgow to Amery 30 June 1942, *TOP*, II, 295. About this time Corfield, the resident in Rajputana, sent up to headquarters a 'model' constitution act for states in his jurisdiction. It was treated, he recalled later, 'as an improper suggestion'. Note by Corfield dated [Mar. 1968], Corfield Coll., 4.

plead his case before an independent commission of enquiry under the seldom used regulation of 1920, to grant him full legal representation, to forego some of the less serious charges relating to fraud, and not to introduce into evidence references to the homosexual adventures which, in part, had led to his troubles.[12] Last but not least, the exigencies of war and rebellion triggered a spate of reassurances from highly placed British officials about the future of the monarchical order. In his 'August Offer' of 1940, which carried the imprimatur of the cabinet, Linlithgow emphasised the right of the states to stand aside from any Indian union formed as a result of post-war constitutional discussions. Early in 1942 this 'pledge' was quietly reaffirmed by Amery in an exchange of letters with Churchill and more publicly by the lord privy seal, Sir Stafford Cripps, who, in the course of his March mission to India to try to persuade the Congress to drop its opposition to the war, told the Standing Committee:

So far as the undertaking of our obligations of defence of the States was concerned, ... there was no insuperable difficulty from the naval point of view so long as we held Ceylon, or from the air point of view so long as we had the aerodromes that were necessary in one or other of the States . . . that, summing it all up, we should stand by our treaties with the States unless they asked us to revoke them.[13]

Moreover, when Cripps, subsequently repenting this rash assurance, tried to set the record straight by declaring in parliament that it was his understanding that states which elected not to join the Indian union would cease to have relations with the crown,[14] he was unceremoniously disavowed by the cabinet, and political secretary Fitze was authorised to inform the chancellor that scrupulous fulfilment of treaty obligations

[12] The charges included fraud, bribery, the obstruction of justice and being an accessory to murder. Resdt., C.I. to Rewa (delivered verbally) 11 Feb. 1942, note by Rewa dated 15 Feb. 1942, Rewa to Resdt. 24 Feb. 1942 and 12 Apr. 1942, and Rewa to viceroy 30 May 1942, IOR R/1/1/3811(1); Pol. Dept. notification dated 4 June 1942, IOR R/1/1/3811(2); note by J. M. Thompson dated 22 Dec. 1941, Fisher to Fitze 9 Jan. 1942 and note by Fitze dated 13 Jan. 1942, IOR R/1/1/3812; and PSV to gov. of UP 29 Dec. 1941, IOR R/1/1/3816. The political department's reservations about the procedure were vindicated when, in 1942, the five-member commission found the maharaja 'not guilty'.

[13] Amery to Churchill 25 Feb. 1942, *TOP*, I, 240; note by Cripps on meeting with Chamber delegation 28 Mar. 1942, *TOP*, I, 510; and unofficial summary of the above meeting by Maqbool Mahmud, encl. in Maqbool to Turnbull 29 Mar. 1942, *ibid.*, 534. (A longer version of the same document may be cited in BRO, Bhopal, Chamber Section, 18, 3/1–A, 1942.) The unreservedness of Cripp's formulation shocked the Congress and seems to have played a significant part (though one curiously neglected by historians) in the CWC's rejection of the Cripps 'offer' a week or so later. See notes by Cripps on interview with Nehru 29 Mar. 1942, and Pattabhi Sitaramayya, 31 Mar. 1942, *TOP*, I, 528, 579; and resolution of the CWC 11 Apr. 1942, *TOP*, I, 746.

[14] Speech of 29 Apr. 1942, quoted in sec. to crown rep. to pol. sec., India Office, 25 June 1942, *TOP*, II, 268. Cripps had originally intended to say 'democracy' but was talked out of doing so at the last minute by Amery. See Amery to Linlithgow 24 Apr. 1942, *TOP*, I, 843.

remained 'an integral part of His Majesty's Government's policy', that there would be 'no unilateral denunciation' of the treaties, and that London had no objection to the states forming subsidiary unions among themselves.[15] The message coming from London was that the British government had every intention of 'protecting the interests of those who have proved themselves our friends and loyal supporters'.[16]

On the face of it the early years of the war, at least, were good ones for the Indian princes – with hindsight, their Indian summer. But Indian summers are notoriously fickle. They do not last. Given that the wartime *rapprochement* between the princes and the crown rested on shaky foundations – on the very special circumstances created by the Japanese advance into Southeast Asia and the Congress rebellion of 1942, and by the presence of friendly statesmen in London and New Delhi – how well did the *darbars*, individually and through the agency of the Chamber, use the respite purchased by their sacrifices for the imperial cause?

The reconstruction of the Chamber

The early war years did bring one very substantial gain: the reconstruction of the COP. When in 1938 Digvijaysinhji of Nawanagar took over the chancellorship from Bhupinder Singh of Patiala on the latter's decease, he was considered by many inadequate for the job. He had been on the throne of Nawanagar for only five years, and on the Standing Committee for barely two, and clearly lacked political experience. But the 42-year-old tyro proved a surprise packet. He showed himself to be not only, like his late father, a person of warmth and decency, but also (unlike Ranjitsinhji) one endowed with a gift for politics. He had energy; he was a pretty good public speaker; and he had a healthy streak of political realism or, as Amery put it, 'practical commonsense'.[17] Perceiving clearly that the monarchical order would need to organise itself better than it had hitherto if it intended to survive into the post-war era, Nawanagar dedicated his first term in office to rescuing the COP from the oblivion it had seemed destined for since the mid-1930s.

The first goal which Digvijaysinhji set himself was to make the Chamber more attractive to the rulers of the larger states which, since

---

[15] Draft of letter from pol. sec. to chancellor, encl. in Linlithgow to Amery 14 Dec. 1942, *TOP*, III, 370. The war cabinet's debate on the constitutional position of the states followed a formal protest from the chancellor to Linlithgow over Cripps' remarks in parliament. The arguments can be read in memo by the lord privy seal dated 21 Sept. 1942, *TOP*, III, 4–5, memo. by the minister for economic warfare dated 25 Sept. 1942, *TOP*, III, 26–7, and minutes of war cabinet meeting, 24 Sept. 1942, *TOP*, III, 32.

[16] Linlithgow to Amery 13 Sept. 1943, *TOP*, IV, 244.

[17] Amery to Linlithgow 13 Nov. 1942, *TOP*, III, 251.

1933, had been deserting it in droves; in February 1938 he set up a working party under the maharaja of Bikaner to advise him on ways and means. It recommended a quadrupling of the standing committee, the introduction of postal voting and a two-year term for the chancellor, the reservation of seats for the major states, the creation of geographically based electoral colleges and the formalisation of the Chamber's relationship with the COM.[18] Predictably, these proposals received a cool reception from the smaller states when they were put to a meeting at Bombay in November. Nevertheless, all got through, and the Bikaner scheme was implemented with viceregal assent in July 1939. As Nawanagar had hoped, the new arrangements resulted in an immediate boost to the Chamber's credibility, with Baroda, Kashmir, Gwalior, Indore, Jaipur, Jodhpur, Bhopal and Rampur all returning to the fold at the annual session of March 1940.[19] Meanwhile, steps were taken to expand the representativeness of the Chamber by granting full membership to some of the lesser states which had been overlooked in 1921 because they were not technically 'full-powered'. By July 1941 the chancellor had won approval for the admission of twenty-six new members, bringing the total to 135.[20] Thanks to these Nawanagar-sponsored reforms, the turnout at the following annual sessions of March 1942 and October 1943 was around seventy, almost twice the interwar average.

Digvijaysinhji next turned his attention to the Chamber's finances, which had been much depleted by the legal expenditures of the 1930s. In 1939, with the aid of an informal task-force consisting of Bhopal, Bikaner, Dholpur and Patiala, he launched a vigorous campaign for the recovery of membership dues and other promised contributions which had not been forthcoming; by 1942, this had netted almost Rs 50,000, reducing the arrears to something over two lakhs. At the same time, he came up with a clever, if rather shabby scheme, to profit from the growth in Chamber membership. From October 1939, all aspiring members were 'invited' to

---

[18] Attachment to circular from the chancellor dated 24 Oct. 1938, Bundi, English Records, Serial No. 1181, File No. 364.

[19] There were still hiccups, however. After rejoining in 1940, Hamidullah of Bhopal chose to 'temporarily abstain' again in March 1942 in protest at the decision of the Standing Committee to give Nawanagar a second term, which he believed infringed the new rules. With hindsight we can see that this was really about Bhopal distancing himself from the incumbent administration preparatory to making a bid for power himself. Bhopal to Linlithgow 11 Mar. 1942, BRO, Pol. Dept., Chamber Section, 57, 4/56, 1942. Likewise both Travancore and Kolhapur rebuffed overtures from the chancellor to renew their association with the COP.

[20] The states admitted were: Bhor, Akalkot, Jath, Miraj Senior, Jamkhandi, Bashahr, Patna, Kalahandi, Sonepur, Bamra, Baud, Gangpur, Keonjhar, Dhenkenal, Nayagarh, Bastar, Seraikela, Kanker, Surguja, Jashpur, Raigarh, Surangar, Khairagarh, Korea, Nandgaon and Nagod. Another – Shahpura – was added in 1942.

pay Rs 5000 each towards the Chamber fund. The tacit understanding was that if they didn't pay, their membership application would not go forward. A British resident with a sense of humour likened it to 'purchasing a season-ticket to the Opera'.[21] The scam – if that is what it was – brought in another lakh. With these extra funds, Digvijaysinhji was able both to enlarge his secretariat and increase the remuneration of the secretary, a post now filled full-time by the resourceful Maqbool Mahmud.[22]

By 1940 Digvijaysinhji had rescued the COP from extinction; thereafter his energies were concentrated on making it a more effective vehicle for the defence of princely interests, particularly *vis-à-vis* British India. Early in 1941 he proposed to the viceroy that formal arrangements should be devised to give the states a say in the framing of central or provincial bills which stood to affect them economically. Linlithgow demurred, citing wartime difficulties; but a further approach to the political adviser in March 1941 elicited a promise that the government would, in the future, 'carefully consider' any representations the states might bring forward. Acting on this assurance, the jam sahib persuaded the Chamber to authorise an additional expenditure of Rs 12,000 per annum to fund two expert committees to review, respectively, central and provincial legislation and the annual budget. These committees met for the first time in March 1942.[23] Next, in September 1941, the chancellor established two ministerial 'study circles' to conduct 'exploratory spadework on questions [with] which the States are likely to be confronted, after the war, in connection with the proposed constitutional arrangements for all-India'. One 'circle', under the chairmanship of Baroda's Sir V. T. Krishnamachari, was briefed to look into the fiscal and financial aspects, the other, chaired by the nawab of Chhattari, Hydari's successor at Hyderabad, into the constitutional ones. Chhattari's group met for the first time at Delhi on 5 December, Krishnamachari's two weeks later in Bombay. Significantly, both took as their starting point the assumption that the 1935 federal scheme had 'failed' and would need to be substantially 'rewritten' or, perhaps, replaced with a different form of association.[24] This initiative was followed by the establishment, in May

[21] Lt.-Col. P. Gaisford, resdt. Deccan States to Kenneth Fitze 23 Mar. 1941, IOR R/1/1/4750.

[22] See secretariat budget for 1941, BRO, Pol. Dept., Chamber Section, 13, 1/13, 1941.

[23] Memo on 'Matters of Common Concern With British India', encl. in circular letter from sec. to chancellor dated 28 July 1941; K. A. H. Abbasi, pol. member, Bhopal to Maqbool Mahmud 2 Aug. 1941; and minutes of Standing Committee meetings, Bombay, 4 Aug. 1941 and [?] Apr. 1942, BRO, Bhopal, Chamber Section, 30, 4/16, 1941–2.

[24] Maqbool Mahmud to Sir Joseph Bhore, pol. adviser, Bhopal 5 Sept. 1941; and minutes of meeting of the Constitutional Study Circle, Delhi, 5 Dec. 1941, BRO, Bhopal, Pol. Dept., Chamber Section, 6, 1/6/1, 1941.

1943, of a working party on post-war planning and reconstruction. Third, Digvijaysinhji attempted to improve the princes' somewhat tarnished image with the politicians. Yet another effort was made to utilise newspapers for propaganda, focussing this time on the *Daily Herald* of Lahore whose proprietor, Bishendas Mehta, was eager to move his paper to Delhi.[25] Rulers visiting England were utilised to bring before the British public and parliament 'the importance of the Princely cause'.[26] And non-Congress provincial political leaders such as Punjab Premier Sir Sikander Hyat Khan – brother of the *dewan* of Patiala and brother-in-law of Maqbool Mahmud – were sounded out on the idea of a common approach to post-war constitutional advance.[27] Not all these initiatives would bear fruit. Nevertheless, it is fair to say that under Digvijasinhji leadership the COP came of age as a political organisation.

Yet Nawanagar's timely administrative reforms were not matched by commensurate progress on the political and constitutional fronts. Few new initiatives were undertaken, and those that were frequently foundered – like Indore's bold scheme for a regional pooling of police and judicial services – on the rock of entrenched sectional interest. Indeed, the dominant political trend in the states during 1939–45 was more reactionary than progressive, with most states retaining bans on *praja mandal* activity and many reversing, or (like Hyderabad) deferring promised advances.[28] Why, on balance, was so little accomplished? To judge from their public statements, it was because most *darbars* felt they had already liberalised enough during 1938–9; but behind this rationalisation lay a major shakeup in the leadership of the order. Hydari, whose career at

[25] Statement by chancellor at Standing Committee meeting, New Delhi, 9 Mar. 1940, and note on propaganda compiled by COMs, June 1940, BRO, Bhopal, Pol. Dept., Chamber Section, 1, 1/1, 1940–1. The COMs took the view that it was essential for the Chamber to extend its patronage 'to such friendly papers as may permit the hospitality of their columns to news items and articles concerning the healthy activities of the States', and suggested that ministers seized every opportunity to 'cultivate personal relations' with the editors of important papers.

[26] Note by Latimer on meeting between viceroy and Standing Committee, Delhi, 25 Jan. 1940, IOR L/P&S/13/626.

[27] B. Shiva Rao to Sapru 16 July 1941, Shiva Rao Papers; and Nawanagar to Sir Henry Craik 10 July 1942, *TOP*, II, 358.

[28] Constitutional reform in Hyderabad was in the wind from 1938, when the Aiyyengar Committee was appointed to frame a scheme. But the Committee's report was shelved until 1941 under the impetus of attacks on its proposals by the fundamentalist Ittihad-ul-Muslimeen, and then only partially implemented (at the municipal level). What was to be done about the legislature had still not been resolved as late as 1946. If Hyderabad is a prime instance of the princes' failure to follow through on promises, Mysore exemplifies the hard line which most *darbars* took after 1939. Having introduced a fairly liberal constitution, which produced a State Congress majority after the first elections in 1941, the *dewan* backtracked on his undertaking to observe the conventions of responsible government by selecting the executive from members of the majority party.

Hyderabad had been built, and sustained, on the British government's determination that the nizam's state should be part of an all-India federation, retired gracefully in August 1941 before his master, who was already in correspondence with a couple of potential successors,[29] could dismiss him. Appointed to the executive council by Linlithgow in gratitude for his past services, he died at New Delhi in January 1942. About the same time Mirza Ismail departed Mysore, although in 1942 he found a new perch at Jaipur. Shortly after, it was the turn of Kailash Haksar, who took early retirement from Bikaner, handing over the dewanship to his old friend and partner, K. M. Panikkar. However the event which most truly defined the passing of the old regime was the death, in February 1943, of Maharaja Ganga Singh. He might have been disliked, and, towards the end, mocked for his pretensions, but the 62-year-old ruler embodied the ideals and aspirations of the Chamber like no other. He was a living legend; a fount of experience and accumulated wisdom; with Bhupinder Singh already five years in his grave, the last of the princely titans. The political department's Charles Herbert spoke from the heart, but accurately, when he declared: 'we shall not see his like again'.[30]

Of course, there were still some good men left: Digvijaysinhji for one, Hamidullah for another. And the early 1940s saw the emergence of some capable younger princes, such as the England returned Mayurdhwaj Sinhji of Dhrangadra and the 'lawyerish looking' Anand Chand of Bilaspur, who impressed the usually unimpressable Francis Wylie with his alertness and sincerity.[31] But others of this younger generation were made of much poorer stuff. 'The Maharaja himself, unlike his father, is not noted for his intelligence, initiative, or administrative qualities', observed the American consul in Madras of Mysore's Jaya Chamaraja Wadiyar.[32] Of Yadavindra Singh, successor to Bhupinder Singh, Francis Wylie noted caustically: 'The Maharaja . . . is magnificent to look at but is conceited and not very intelligent.'[33] Likewise, Baroda's Pratap Singh, lackadaisical except in matters of the turf, and Bikaner's Sadul Singh, vain and dictatorial, also compared unfavourably with their illustrious predecessors.

However, the ruler who perhaps best epitomised the 1940s era, both in his vices and virtues, was Yeshwant Rao Holkar of Indore. Yeshwant Rao

---

[29] One of these was Sir Mirza Ismail, at that time still at Mysore; but the negotiations fell through – partly because Mirza was *persona non grata* with the British, partly because of staunch domestic opposition among Mulkis who saw Mirza as yet another outsider, and partly because of the intervention of Jinnah, to whom Mirza was that most treasonous of animals – a Congressite Muslim.   [30] Herbert to Lothian 12 Feb. 1943, Lothian Coll., 9.
[31] Note by Wylie dated 12 June 1943, IOR R/1/1/4258.
[32] Consul, Madras to sec. state, Washington 11 Jan. 1947, US State Dept. decimal file 845.00/1–1147.   [33] Note by Wylie dated 9 Aug. 1944, IOR R/1/1/4152.

was older than the others, having been born in 1908, and technically he had ruled Indore since 1926. However, for several years after his accession, restrictions imposed by the British on his powers on account of his youth and the excesses of his predecessor made him him virtually a palace cipher; and when these were lifted indifferent health and a shyness born of a weedy, unprepossessing physique kept him out of the limelight. Then, in 1935 occurred the first of several familial disasters for the young prince when his only child, 19-year-old Usha, died in a road accident. Soon after, angered by her husband's flirtation with a visiting American lady, Margaret Lawler, the girl's mother walked out and went back to her family. Ignoring the scandal, Yeshwant Rao took the American as his bride and persuaded the viceroy to recognise her as the senior maharani; but after a few years she, too, left, taking with her a small fortune in jewels. Angry, 'heart-broken and desperate', the maharaja pursued her through the American law courts and eventually gained a divorce, though at the cost of most of his parcel of US securities. But by then it was 1942 and he had been away over seven years – an absence that led the resident, Fitze, to propose at an Indore garden party that the current hit song, 'Some Day My Prince Will Come', be adopted as the state's new anthem. Nevertheless when Yeshwant Rao did, at length, set foot in his capital (with another American beauty on his arm!) he threw himself vigorously into the business of domestic administration and into the affairs of the Chamber, becoming an active and, as we shall see, controversial member of the Standing Committee. Yet for all his keenness, idealism and firm political grasp, Yeshwant Rao never lived up to his promise. He remained an impulsive, erratic performer, working sometimes till three in the morning and other days not at all; and the refusal of the government to recognise his new American wife (the couple were married in July 1943) gradually took its toll of his highly strung temperament. Contrary to rumour, Yeshwant Rao was no 'blackguard', and, with proper handling by the British, and if time had allowed, he might eventually have matured into a fairly decent ruler. Instead he floundered, a pathetic figure out of luck and increasingly out of his depth.[34]

Again, while the calibre of the ministers remained high, the retirement of Hydari and Haksar and the decision of Panikkar and Mirza, after the federation debacle, to hold aloof from all-India affairs and concentrate on internal administration[35] left something of a vacuum at the top level of princely leadership at a time when not only talent, but vision was needed

---

[34] Amery to Wavell 2 Dec. 1943, *TOP*, IV, 514; memo by Kanji Dwarkadas dated 28 Jan. 1945, encl. in consul Bombay to sec. state Washington 10 Apr. 1947, US State Dept. decimal file 845.00/4–1047.   [35] Panikkar, *Autobiography*, 120.

there. After Hydari's departure, the chairmanship of the COMs devolved to the nawab of Chhattari, a man of intelligence, charm and tact – but, in comparison with Hydari, a political light-weight. He in turn was followed by Sir Gopalaswamy Aiyengar of Kashmir, who, for all his industry and integrity, did not possess the commitment to princely India that had driven the careers of men like Haksar, Liaquat and Manubhai Mehta.

To sum up, then, one can say that while the Chamber as a bureaucratic organisation went from strength to strength during the 1940s, there was a general decline in the quality of the princely leadership. As the external challenges to the monarchical order mounted steadily in the latter years of the war, this dearth of inspiration and commitment became a serious liability.

The breach with Wavell

The first of these challenges was a traditional one, though no less threatening for that: a reassertion by the political department of the crown's paramountcy power to oversee the internal governance of the states. In part, the return to a policy of intervention was rooted in imperial frustration at the evident incapacity of the Chamber to devise and carry through, as promised, a voluntarist programme of administrative reform – an incapacity epitomised by its refusal, in 1943, to endorse the Standing Committee's very moderate proposals for a standard princely civil list.[36] Also, there was a growing feeling in the political department that the princes were getting above themselves. As noted above, the COP under Digvijaysinhji's leadership had grown more assertive, and while the British were happy to see the organisation taking on a more educative role vis-à-vis its own members, they did not feel comfortable with the idea of it as a political party or lobby group making demands on the government.[37] This view was reinforced, during 1942, when the heir-apparent to the gaddi of Dhrangadhra, Mayurdhwaj Singhji, made his acceptance of the traditional KCIE conditional on the king accepting a reciprocal honour from the state, and turned up to his installation in plain clothes;[38] and when Yeshwant Rao of Indore addressed an open letter to the American president suggesting that Roosevelt arbitrate, perhaps in concert with

---

[36] Draft report of Special Committee on the Question of the Civil List and Privy Purse, encl. in circular letter from chancellor dated 3 Feb. 1942, BRO, Bhopal, Pol. Dept. Chamber Section, file 70, 4/59, 1942; report of the Finance Committee of the COMs, encl. in circular letter from chancellor dated 20 May 1942, *ibid.*, 48, 4/4, 1943; and Bikaner to chancellor 30 Oct. 1943, *ibid.*

[37] Secret memo by pol. dept., India Office dated 26 Oct. 1943, IOR L/P&S/13/552. For an example of these demands see Bikaner to Churchill 9 Nov. 1941, IOR L/P&S/13/789.

[38] Allen and Dwivedi, *Lives*, 249.

Chiang Kai-shek, between 'the various groups in India'.[39] Thirdly, global events lent a sense of urgency to the government's agenda. Following Allied victories at Midway, El Alamein and Stalingrad it was clear that the tide of war was turning. Hitherto the future of the new, post-war India – and the place in it of the princely states – had seemed distant and somewhat academic. Now, with peace in prospect, a sense of urgency took hold, and, with it, the conviction that the future of the princely states – indeed their very survival – hinged on their rapid modernisation. 'While we must bear in mind the risk of antagonising the one undeniably loyal element in India', mused Leo Amery in 1942, 'I feel we must squarely face the probability that without more strenuous and unremitting effort on our part, the smaller States at any rate will in a not distant future . . . go under.'[40]

Thus, by the end of 1942, there was a disposition both in New Delhi and in London to halt the slide back into *laissez-faire* and to return to the offensive programme which Linlithgow and Glancy had mapped out in the aftermath of the 1938–9 *satyagraha*. Yet it is unlikely that this renewed offensive would have gone so far, or as quickly, had Francis Wylie not been chosen by Linlithgow to replace Glancy on the latter's appointment as governor of the Punjab in 1941. As we have seen, Wylie had long been recognised in Delhi as a man of exceptional administrative grasp and intelligence. Indeed, many of his colleagues thought him rather too smart for the needs of the political department and better suited to a senior civil job – a prediction fulfilled when in 1937 Wylie became a very successful governor of the CP. But Wylie was more than just able; he was a man of 'almost subversively' liberal political views,[41] and from the departmental perspective somewhat of an outsider who, as Linlithgow noted when he appointed him, could be counted on to 'bring in [an] experience of British India and possibly a rather broader point of view'.[42] What is more, Wylie had something of an intimidating personality. Toweringly tall, he

[39] Linlithgow to Indore 3 June 1942, and Indore to Linlithgow 28 June 1942, *TOP*, II, 174. Holkar was summoned to Delhi to explain himself. He found the viceroy, as he recalled later, 'bursting with rage'. There were rumours that he would be forced to abdicate. In the end, though, the government settled for a stiff warning against any repetition of the indiscretion. Indore to Bhopal 30 Jan. 1945, encl. in US consul, Bombay, to sec. state, Washington 11 Feb. 1945, US State Dept. decimal file 845.00/2–1145.

[40] Amery to Linlithgow 27 May 1942, *TOP*, II, 137. See also Amery to Linlithgow 16 Aug. 1942, *ibid.*, 714.

[41] Clayton Lane, office of the President's personal rep. to India, to the sec. state. Washington 11 Jan. 1945, US State Dept. decimal file 845.00/1–1145.

[42] Linlithgow to Zetland 9 June 1939, Zetland Coll., 17. Glancy, who did not get on with the bookish Fitze and thought Lothian too wooden, plumped for Corfield, but Linlithgow ruled him out as too young. He had only been in the Political Service twenty years!

exuded energy and impatience, had a sharp tongue, and like many clever men found it hard to stomach the company of fools. In short, he lacked tact. Contemporaries were divided about whether Wylie's coming would make or break the department but none doubted that it would stir things up.

They were right. Almost from his first day in the job, Wylie started ringing the changes. Convinced that many of the senior residents had become too partial toward the princes,[43] he accelerated the promotion of younger men and brought in others personally known to him from the CP, including – to the dismay of the secretariat – a handful of Indians. One of the latter, a man named Ramadhyani, almost at once clashed with his superior, Colonel Hancock, over the issue of land reform in Kathiawar, but Wylie unhesitatingly took his protégé's side in the dispute, declaring that he had much more confidence in the 'alive and daring approach of the modern I.C.S. offficer of the Provinces, an expert in his own line and whole-heartedly opposed . . . to outworn privilege', than in the 'crusted attitude of the [career] P.O'.[44] Then, in August 1941, the political adviser broke with tradition by undertaking a personal tour of the southern states, which Lothian, speaking for the Service, angrily interpreted as signalling a desire to cut out the men on the spot 'alto-gether'.[45] All this, though, was by way of preparation for what Wylie saw as his historic mission to lick the states into shape before the British handed over to the Congress. Back in Delhi, Wylie began mapping out a strategy for 'relegating the . . . States to their rightful place in the Indian scheme of things',[46] and assembling arguments to persuade his superiors to let him get tough.

However, before he could do very much in this way, he was called away on special war duty in Afghanistan which kept him occupied for nearly a year, and when he returned to Delhi he found that Linlithgow had again softened his line on the princes in the light of the Quit India rebellion and with the intention of ending his seven-year term as viceroy (the longest term since Curzon's) on a note of reconciliation. Hence it was not until after Linlithgow's retirement in October 1943, and the arrival at viceregal lodge of Lord Wavell, a good-hearted but blunt military man whose knowledge of the states was so slight that he coined for himself the

---

[43] Note dated 6 Feb. 1941 on report by Col. Fisher, resdt. Rajputana, IOR R/1/1/3594. On another occasion Wylie as good as accused Corfield of having been taken in by the plausi-ble but slippery Yadavindra Singh on the matter of debt reduction in Patiala. See note dated 13 Sept. 1943, IOR R/1/1/4007.
[44] Wylie to Patrick 18 Nov. 1943, IOR Pol. (Intl.) Colls., 13/99A.
[45] Lothian to Wylie 26 Oct. 1943, Lothian Coll., 19.
[46] Wylie to Mountbatten 12 Aug. 1947, TOP, XII, 681.

mnemonic, 'Hot Kippers Make Good Breakfasts', to help him fix the names of the five most important ones,[47] that Wylie was able to obtain the *carte blanche* he needed to fully implement his plans. But thereafter he quickly made up for lost time.

With regard to the larger states, Wylie began by ordering his residents to be more assertive in offering advice to the *darbars*, and although not all conformed with this instruction, the overall result was a more confrontationist style of diplomatic management, typified by the observation of the resident, Madras States, to the dewan of Pudukkotai, that in his book 'friendly advice', 'moral pressure' and 'command' meant much the same thing.[48] Next, he introduced what became known within departmental circles, somewhat pointedly, as the 'Wylie scheme', which essentially required rulers gaining their majority to enact a constitution, to establish a civil list (not exceeding, in the case of large states, 10 per cent of the gross revenue), to appoint an executive council staffed by competent officials, and for five years to submit to the arbitration of the resident any disagreements between the council and the palace. Third, he reversed the earlier decision on Rewa, compelling the maharaja to step down from the *gaddi* and, when Gulab Singh refused to observe the conditions of his externment, formally deposing him in 1945 as an object lesson to other recalcitrants. Even in New Delhi it was acknowledged – somewhat nervously – that these initiatives represented 'a fundamental change of policy'.[49] To the consumers of paramountcy on the other side of the political fence they signalled that 'Lord Wavell and Sir Francis Wylie were [out to] put . . . the screw on the Indian Princes.'[50]

However Wylie reserved his sternest measures for the small states of Kathiawar and central India, which had long been recognised as the weak link in the system. During his absence in Afghanistan, Fitze and others had encouraged 'voluntary combination[s]' of resources and services as a step towards political union, which was the remedy officially favoured by the COP. But to Wylie the 'cooperative grouping business' was a sham and a waste of time. That grouping 'can provide a solution for the evil of the small Indian State is in my opinion', he wrote, 'contrary to all

[47] Moon, *Wavell*, 463.
[48] Sir Alexander Tottenham, dewan of Pudukkotai, to Lt.-Col. G. G. N. Edwards, resdt. Madras States 11 May 1945, Edwards to Tottenham 17 May 1945, and same to same 1 June 1945, IOR R/1/1/4244.   [49] Note by Fitze dated 10 Aug. 1942, IOR R/1/1/3859.
[50] Memo by Kanji Dwarkadas, dated 28 Jan. 1945, reporting a conversation with Yeshwant Rao Holkar in Dec. 1944, encl. in US consul-gen. Bombay to sec. state Washington 10 Apr. 1947, US State Dept. decimal file 845.00/4–1047. The maharana of Porbandar expressed himself similarly to the American consul. See US consul Bombay to sec. state Washington 23 Feb. 1945, US State Dept. decimal file 845.00/2–2345.

administrative experience'.[51] Wylie's preferred option was 'to redraw the map' to eliminate the unviable states once and for all,[52] and this meant merger. Accordingly, between August and December 1943, 482 fourth and fifth-class Kathiawar principalities (up to and including 300 square mile Jasdan), inhabited by nearly 1.2 million people, were 'attached' by executive order to larger neighbours. It was a major coup, aside from the rendition of Mysore the biggest territorial transfer[53] since the revolt of 1857.

Anxious about other aspects of Wylie's policy, the Chamber princes were divided about the merits of the attachment scheme. Certainly, the implication inherent in the scheme that the rights of rulers could be removed simply at the whim of the Paramount Power – in this case by a mere viceregal notification – bothered them deeply,[54] and Wavell was not all that wide of the mark in his surmise that 'they suspect us of plain dishonesty in the whole business'.[55] Yet the large majority of the Chamber rulers and their advisers, sensitive to the harm that the continuing saga of poverty and corruption in the very small states was doing to the image of the monarchical order, privately welcomed their passing. 'To be frank', wrote the organisation's newly appointed economic adviser Sir Joseph Bhore, 'I do not feel that there is any case for the continuance of these [pigmy states] . . . as independent entities.'[56] Besides, some states – the attaching states – stood to benefit considerably from the carve-up, a point not missed by Holkar when he tried to dissuade the political department from acting on the grouping proposal put forward by some small Malwa states and to endorse one of his own for associating them administratively with Indore.[57] Thus, left to itself, it is unlikely that the COP would have raised the hue and cry over the matter that it eventually did. But it was not given the chance to back away. In December 1943 the talukdar of Bhadwa, one of the rulers caught up in the first throw of Wylie's net, challenged the lawfulness of the scheme in the court of the judicial commissioner, Kathiawar. To the surprise of all concerned, the suit was upheld on the grounds that the viceroy's notification infringed Section 2(1) of the

---

[51] Note by Wylie dated 28 Aug. 1944, Wavell Coll., 12. In this minute the political adviser makes reference to his note of 21 Aug. 1943 which put the case for a shift of policy, and to the viceroy's rejoinder dated 10 Sept. 1943.

[52] Wylie to Lothian, 5 Aug. 1941, Lothian Coll., 9. In this he was at odds with J. H. Shattock who, as we have seen, had been commissioned in 1940 to report on the future of the small Gujarat states. Shattock's preferred solution was also grouping.

[53] I am speaking here of transfers of territory between British and princely India.

[54] See memo by COMs dated 15 Jan. 1944, BRO, Bhopal, Pol. Dept., Chamber Section, 13, 1/4–A of 1943.   [55] Wavell to Amery 22 Dec. 1943, *TOP*, IV, 563.

[56] Bhore to pol. member, Bhopal 4 Dec. 1943, BRO, Bhopal, Pol. Dept., Chamber Section, 52, 4/9 of 1943.

[57] Indore to Wylie 17 Mar. 1944, MPSA, Indore, Huzur Office, file 40 of 1942.

India Act of 1935. Already, isolated acts of resistance had broken out in the affected region; but with the handing down of the Bhadwa decision, these multiplied and strengthened. In some talukas, rulers ordered their subjects not to comply with orders given by minions of the attaching *darbars*. Elsewhere, the attaching states were threatened with legal action unless they withdrew. In Sitapur district, Bhavnagar officials were jostled and abused.[58] Initially spontaneous, these gestures gradually coalesced under the joint leadership of Bhadwa and the talukdar of Ghodesar into a coordinated and quite sophisticated campaign of defiance in which measures of passive resistance, such as 'lying on the ground' and forming human cordons around state property, were combined with political initiatives such as the lobbying of senior members of the Chamber and the hiring of M. R. Jayakar to assist in the pursuance of their claims in the courts.[59] Meanwhile, Delhi and London pondered how best to deal with the judicial setback to their plans. Wavell urged caution; but Amery, anxious to protect the gains that had been made, insisted on retrospective legislation. In February 1944 the India (Attachment of States) Bill was rushed through parliament. Besieged by appeals for aid from the Gujarat talukdars, the Standing Committee now found itself confronted with a *fait accompli* of the most dangerous kind – one which flew in the face of the generally accepted notion that British legislation did not apply to the persons and territories of Indian rulers.[60]

Much as it might have wished that the attachment issue had never arisen, the COP could hardly remain deaf to the appeals of its own constituents; still less could it turn a blind eye to Amery's legislation. Therefore the chancellor asked London to stay proclaiming the bill 'for at least three months' pending discussions,[61] and for an 'authoritative and unequivocal' statement that there would be no extension of the scheme to other regions of India.[62] However, while the viceroy was in a mind to be accommodating, his advisers and, more importantly, the secretary of state, were not.[63] So the transformation of the political map of Gujarat proceeded, despite continuing local resistance. Indeed, with the elevation

---

[58] Crown rep. to sec. state 26 Jan. 1944, Cabinet Papers, NMML, WP (44) 57.
[59] Source report received by CIO Bombay, n.d., and note by CIO Bombay dated 22 June 1944, IOR R/1/1/4140; and Thakore-saheb Fatesinghj of Ghosdesar to Dewas Junior 17 Feb. 1944, BRO, Bhopal, Pol. Dept., Chamber Section, 18, 3/5 of 1944.
[60] Wavell to Amery 22 Feb. 1944, encl. telegram from chancellor Nawanagar, *TOP*, IV, 722.
[61] Bhopal to Wavell 23 Feb. 1944, *TOP*, IV, 755.
[62] Final Report of the Porbandar subcommittee [of the Standing Committee] on attachment dated 18 June 1944, BRO, Bhopal, Pol. Dept., Chamber Section, 7, 1/7 of 1944.
[63] Pol. sec. to chancellor 4 Nov. 1944, encl. minutes of meeting with Standing Committee on 15/16 Sept. 1944, *TOP*, V, 203; and Amery to Wavell 3 Oct. 1944, IOR L/PO/21. The political secretary, Lepel Griffin, had earlier gone on record as saying that the desired assurance could not 'possibly be given'. Griffin to PSV 22 July 1944, Wavell Coll., 11.

of Sir Cyril Hancock to the post of resident, Western India, the tempo of change was accelerated, the chiefs still holding out being given four days to comply on pain of having their administrative powers suspended.[64] Meanwhile, ignoring Wavell's reservations, Wylie pressed ahead with plans to expand the scheme to states of the third class and to widen its geographical scope.

The second storm to interrupt the princes' Indian summer also had its source in the capital, but this time principally in the financial and post-war planning divisions of the government. As remarked earlier in the chapter, industrialisation in the princely states proceeded apace during the late 1930s and early 1940s. But this vigorous growth failed to win any plaudits from the government of India, first, because it threatened to divert scarce domestic and foreign capital away from the provinces, where it was sorely needed, and second, because it seemed to New Delhi to rest on *darbari* policies which were unfair if not downright fraudulent. 'The existence of taxation vacua or low pressure taxation areas within the geographical limits of India not only tends to suck . . . [new] industries out of British India into the States but creates conditions of unequal competition between [established] industries in the two areas,' complained the political department's Lepel Griffin.[65] Another bone of contention was excise. When in 1934 the government went over to a system of protection for developing industries such as sugar, it sought to compensate for the expected loss of customs revenue by levying an excise duty on domestic production. Ordinarily, this would have given producers in the states an edge; but Delhi persuaded the *darbars* to impose a reciprocal levy in return for their produce being allowed into British India free of customs duty pending the establishment of the federation. Exports from the states boomed accordingly; and with the indefinite deferment of federation looked set to make further inroads into the provincial market. Meanwhile, a number of states continued to levy land customs duties at their borders, enriching themselves while making it hard for British Indian merchants to compete with local producers. Thirdly, Delhi had a shrewd idea that some of the maritime states, including Nawanagar, were

[64] Statement by Darbar Sahib of Vadia dated 13 July 1945, encl. in Bhopal to Wavell 16 July 1945, Wavell Coll., 14. See also US consul Bombay to sec. state Washington 7 July 1945, US State Dept. decimal file 845.00/7–745; same to same 14 July 1945, decimal file 845.00/7–1445; *TOI* 14 July 1945; and Hancock to Ivor Jehu, editor *Times of India*, 28 July 1945, IOR R/1/1/4331. When one talukdar, Vadia, threatened to put himself 'in the hands' of the chancellor, Hancock allegedly replied: 'Who is the Chamber to oppose the will of the Crown Representative? The Chamber is dead.'

[65] Griffin to chancellor 28 June 1944, Wavell Coll., 11. In fact, average tax levels in the states were marginally higher overall than in the provinces because of the heavier incidence in the former of land tax.

evading its export controls, and sending piece-goods overseas at considerable profit. Finally, there was much (legitimate) criticism of the laxity of the *darbars'* labour laws and the absence in all but a handful of the states of workers' compensation schemes, which allowed factories located there to operate more cheaply for longer and with less union interference.[66] For a while New Delhi limited itself to protesting these 'rorts' through diplomatic channels; but in 1944 it got tough. A new uniform labour code was drafted and plans made to implement it in the states by what Wylie called 'the firm use of paramountcy'.[67] After July businesses in the states supplying goods to the government under wartime contracts were forced to accept payment through their head offices or affiliate companies in British India, which made such payments liable to provincial taxation.[68] Import and foreign exchange controls were tightened. And the raising of new venture capital in British India by the *darbars* was made conditional on their agreeing to subject the profits of these ventures to corporation tax at British Indian rates.[69]

It is easy to see why the princes might have felt threatened by these measures. At the very least, they promised financial hardship; at worst, economic ruin. However the states' fight with Delhi over industrial policy was not just about revenue. It was also about status and power. At a time when important decisions were being taken about India's post-war economic development, the *darbars* found themselves shut out of strategic planning and fact-finding bodies, such as the central roads board and the post-war mission of Indian industrialists to Britain and the USA. When they applied to Delhi for import licences for much needed plant and equipment, they were fobbed off (or so it seemed) with elaborate diatribes about bottlenecks and low foreign exchange reserves. In 1944, a plan for the development of air transport in India was released; states like Bhopal, centrally situated and boasting modern airfields and ancillary facilities, were dismayed to find themselves excluded from the projected network of trunk passenger routes.[70] *Darbari* pride took these machinations as

---

[66] Wavell to Amery 12 Sept. 1944, IOR L/PO/10/21; note by V. Narahari Rao, Finance Dept., GOI dated 22 Oct. 1944, IOR R/1/1/4120 (1); and memo by Kanji Dwarkadas dated 28 Jan. 1945 encl. in consul-gen. Bombay to sec. state Washington 10 Apr. 1947, US State Dept. decimal file 845.00/4–1047.

[67] Quoted in Wavell to Amery 10 Apr. 1945, IOR L/PO/10/22.

[68] 'Record of Main Points Urged by the Chancellor and the Delegation of Princes . . . ', encl. in Bhopal to PSV 13 Oct. 1944, Wavell Coll., 12.

[69] Consul Bombay to sec. state Washington 13 Feb. 1945, US State Dept. decimal file 845.00/2–1345.

[70] Recommendations of Aviation Sub-Committee of COMs, 16 Apr. 1944, BRO, Bhopal, Pol. Dept., Chamber Section, 7, 1/7 of 1944; Griffin to PSV 22 July 1944, Wavell Coll., 11; aide-mémoire encl. in chancellor to PSV 26 Aug. 1944, Wavell Coll., 12; note by Wylie dated 8 Sept. 1944, IOR R/1/1/4161; and *IAR* 1944, II, 264.

deliberate snubs, intended to hurt and humiliate; *darbari* paranoia saw in them a hidden agenda, namely the use of governmental licensing and planning powers to keep the states industrially weak and thus politically dependant.[71] Indeed, several states harboured bitter memories of political department interference designed to achieve exactly this result. Mysore, for example, had been warned, in the early days of the war, against undertaking a joint venture with the Walchand Hirachand group to produce motor cars; while Dewas Junior's attempt, in 1941, to set up a rural development bank had foundered on the resident's aversion to Gujarati 'banias'.[72]

Deeply suspicious of the government's motives, the states welcomed the summoning in October 1944 of an all-India conference on post-war industrial development as an opportunity to put their case and extract some assurances from the finance ministry in regard to their access to capital. However, though the states' representatives, Sir Manubhai Mehta and Sir Joseph Bhore, argued their case loudly and eloquently and forced the finance member Sir Jeremy Raisman to retract his accusation that the *darbars'* price controls were ineffective, not one of their substantive demands were conceded. Mehta and Bhore came away from the meeting gripped 'with a feeling of dismay'. Forecasting a 'dark future' for the states, if the policies of the finance department under Raisman were not changed, the two ministers urged the princes to take their case directly to the viceroy.[73] But Wavell was no more forthcoming than his departmental head had been.

By the mid-1940s, therefore, the princes found themselves besieged on two broad fronts – politically and economically – a development which both puzzled and angered them, since it seemed alarmingly at odds with the approbation they had received earlier from Linlithgow and Amery, and a poor reward for their wartime sacrifices. They might, nonetheless, have swallowed this humiliation had it not been for two things: Wavell's ingrained honesty; and the election of a new chancellor.

As we have seen, the Chamber's leaders had not particularly relished

---

[71] The states could not see how measures of subsidy and tax-relief which had been used by dozens of countries around the world to nurture nascent industries – and were employed by India itself, in the shape of tariff protection – could be construed as illegitimate. One can see their point.

[72] Unsigned note, n.d., Mirza Ismail Papers, subject file 1; and Fisher to Fitze 8 November 1941, IOR R/1/1/3818. Janaki Nair argues that one reason for the veto on the automobile project may have been that it sought to link up with an American firm, Chrysler, rather than a British one.

[73] Report of States' representatives at the all-India Industrial Conference, Delhi, 23 Oct. 1944, encl. in US consul Bombay to sec. state Washington 13 Feb. 1945, US State Dept. decimal file 845.00/2–1345.

getting caught up in the attachment issue, and had pursued a restrained line with the government in trying to find a face-saving way out of the tangle. Nevertheless, the experience left them with an bitter aftertaste, for it showed that their patron, the British crown, was capable of legislating 'sovereign' states out of existence where they appeared to stand in the way of India's advancement. To be sure, the victims of this expedient policy so far had all been tiny *talukas* not subject to express imperial guarantees. But the princes could not help thinking that Gujarat was merely the thin end of the wedge; that sooner or later Delhi would try something similar with the larger states – states with treaties – treaties which, if read literally, embodied guarantees of imperial support in perpetuity. Now they began to wonder, like Dholpur, about the status of 'those promises once held with such [conviction as to the] value of their inviolability'. Would it not be better, they reasoned, if the government for once came clean and told them what 'their real position' was?[74] After much anguished introspection along these lines, the Standing Committee resolved to call the government's bluff at the Chamber session scheduled for December 1944, and to this end drafted a resolution for inclusion in the address in reply urging the viceroy to lay to rest 'the[ir] grave misgivings and apprehensions'.[75]

Wavell, however, was in no mind to comply. Since 1939 official opinion on the future of the princes and their treaties had been slowly but inexorably changing. The government was not yet mentally prepared to sever its historic ties root and branch. For one thing, the states were still useful, immediately for what they were contributing to the war effort, potentially as counterweights to the hard-line nationalists when serious talks on independence got going at war's end. For another, Delhi could see no simple way to extricate itself from the relationship; the legal bonds were apparently indissoluble. But it was now prepared to admit – to itself if not openly to the rulers – that its ties with the states were probably incompatible with a smooth devolution of power. Moreover, whereas Amery favoured a policy of sweeping the whole messy business under the mat for the duration of the war, Wavell was not prepared to say publicly what he did not believe in conscience to be true.[76] Accordingly, the viceroy informed the Standing Committee that while he could tell them authoritatively that there had been 'no change in the policy of His Majesty's Government towards the Indian Princes', he was not prepared to make any public statement in the Chamber relating to the princes' links with

---

[74] Dholpur to Bhopal 1 July 1944, encl. in Bhopal to PSV 26 Aug. 1944, Wavell Coll., 12.
[75] *IAR*, 1944, Part I, p. 268.
[76] Wavell to Amery 20 Apr. 1944, *TOP*, IV, 901; Amery to Wavell 26 Oct. 1944, *TOP* V, 150; and Wavell to Amery 29 Dec. 1943, *TOP*, IV, 578.

the crown and urged the chancellor to delete the section on treaties from the address in reply.[77] This more or less brought the princes' simmering discontent to the boil.

Again, though, this upwelling of princely outrage might not have taken the form that it did had Digvijaysinhji still been at the helm. But by 1944 the fortunes of the COP were in the hands of an altogether stronger and more passionate man, Hamidullah of Bhopal. In a sense this was unexpected, because Bhopal had not enjoyed his first tilt at the chancellorship in the early 1930s and thereafter had played only a marginal role in the life of the Chamber. Indeed, by 1942 he was privately questioning whether the organisation had a future at all:

Is the Chamber, with its present unwieldy Standing Committee which is not fully representative of the Major States and its cumbersome procedure for dealing with day to day questions of great importance, best suited to deal with the future problems of the [Bhopal] State through a most difficult period . . . ?
. . . Would it be feasible [instead] to create a separate body of Princes of Major States to work out their own plans and policy for the future, say, the first 12 or 15 States [in order of precedence]?[78]

On further reflection, however, Hamidullah came around to the view that the Chamber was too firmly entrenched, too much part of princely tradition, to be casually swept aside, and that a public schism between the big and small states would be fatally damaging to the monarchical cause. Accordingly, he shelved his plans for a separate organisation of princes and limited himself to inviting representatives of Hyderabad, Baroda, Mysore, Gwalior, Travancore and Indore to join him in setting up a Major States Committee [MSC].[79] Besides, he was sick of semi-retirement. He itched to again exercise his considerable talents on the all-India stage, to realise the great destiny which he believed had been carved out for him. And the passage of time had eliminated almost all of his potential rivals. Bhupinder Singh and Ganga Singh were both dead, and Rewa remained under a cloud of suspicion despite being technically cleared by the 1942 enquiry. Aside from Digvijaysinhji himself, the only announced candidate for the chancellorial poll set for January 1944 was Udaibhan Singh, and the nawab's self-appointed campaign manager, Maqbool Mahmud, assured him after taking soundings that in a straight run-off against Dholpur he could be assured of at least twenty-two votes

---

[77] Griffin to chancellor 2 Dec. 1944, Wavell Coll., 12.
[78] Draft memo by Sir Joseph Bhore, constitutional adviser, Bhopal, dated [?] Jan. 1942, as amended by Hamidullah in his own hand, BRO, Bhopal, Pol. Dept., Chamber Section, 55, 4/44 of 1941.
[79] e.g. Bhopal to Indore 4 Feb. 1942, MPSA, Indore, Foreign Dept., file 18 of 1942. The MSC gradually superseded the COMs, which was already dominated by the larger states.

compared to the maharaj-rana's twelve.[80] This was a contest Bhopal felt certain he could win.

Perhaps the crucial factor, though, was Bhopal's desire to strike a blow for the Muslim cause. As we have seen, Hamidullah had grown up a staunch nationalist, and for a long while he remained a true believer in Hindu–Muslim unity. However, during the late 1920s his communal orientation began to change. Bound by ties of sentiment and patronage to the British crown, he found himself increasingly at odds with a Congress that had become openly republican.[81] Likewise, he was offended by the failure of the nationalists at the All-Parties convention and later to concede the Muslim claim for one-third of the seats in the central legislature, which seemed to him eminently fair. Then, around 1930, his search for developmental capital drew him into the orbit of the nizam who was himself moving closer to the Muslim Leaguc.[82] Finally, as his own outlook grew more communal, he became more sensitive of the communal orientations of others, particularly of some of the Hindu rulers of north and central India, who by the 1940s were making no secret of their financial backing for the Mahasabha.[83] By 1944 he was ready to be turned. Sensing this, Chamber secretary Maqbool consulted Liaquat Hyat Khan and Liaquat's brother, the Punjab premier Sikander, and on their urging put it to Bhopal that his leadership of the princely order was 'vital to the [Muslim] cause' in the current climate of 'crisis'. The very next day he formally announced his candidacy.[84] Prudently (for he

---

[80] Note in Pol. Dept., Bhopal, dated [?] 1944, BRO, Bhopal, Pol. Dept., Chamber Section, 94, 10/1 of 1943.

[81] These views hardened during the war, and especially after the August 1942 Quit India resolution. In 1941 he described Gandhi's individual civil disobedience campaign as 'tantamount . . . to collaborating with the enemy'. Bhopal to Linlithgow 18 June 1941, IOR R/1/1/3751.

[82] By the late 1930s Bhopal owed something over 1 crore to Hyderabad. The nizam never actually used the debt to extract reciprocal favours from Hamidullah, but both men were conscious of the obligations that attached to the latter's client status.

[83] For details of donations by Hindu rulers to the Hindu Mahasabha see, e.g., note by Bikaner dated 7 Nov. 1931, RSA, Bikaner, PM's Office, A 984–7 of 1931, and correspondence from Bikaner and others in the B. S. Moonje Papers, NMML. When, during the 1944 chancellorial election campaign, Yadavindra Singh urged Indore not to vote for Bhopal on the grounds that that would be a vote for an outside political party – the League – Indore retorted that the precedent had already been established since he, Baroda and Gwalior already supported the Mahasabha! Memo. by Kanji Dwarkadas dated 28 Jan. 1945 encl. in consul-gen. Bombay to sec. state Washington 10 Apr. 1947, US State Dept. decimal file 845.00/4–1047.

[84] Maqbool to Liaquat 26 June 1943, BRO, Bhopal, Pol. Dept., Chamber Section, 94, 10/1, 1943. The fact that Maqbool and Liaquat had in the past both worked for non-Muslim rulers (Jhalawar and Patiala respectively) suggests that something quite fundamental was happening to the once proudly eclectic *darbari* polity. The roots of this sea-change have yet to be adequately explored.

needed the votes of some of the Hindu princes to get elected) Hamidullah played down the communal angle during the campaign.[85] But once elected, he moved quickly to consolidate the Chamber's links with the League, manoeuvring the nawab of Chhattari into the chairmanship of the COMs, selecting Sir Sultan Ahmad (over Krishnamachari and Ramaswamy Aiyer) for the new post of constitutional adviser to the Chamber, and jobbing at least a dozen of his co-religionists into senior positions in the secretariat.

Yet it would be misleading to suggest – as Panikkar does in his auto-biography – that Bhopal was just an imperialist stooge. He remained during the 1940s, as he had been throughout the 1930s, a trenchant critic of unfettered paramountcy; regarding himself, rightly, as the intellectual equal of most of the British officials he came in contact with, he dealt with them politely but never obsequiously; as an experienced politician (with a longer memory of Indian politics than many people in Delhi) he felt no inhibitions about offering gratuitous advice to the government at the highest level – as when, several days after taking office, he suggested to Lord Wavell's private secretary that he be made ambassador at large to the Middle East.[86] In short, while Hamidullah was a true loyalist he was not an uncompromising one. Even at 50, something of the youthful rebel still clung to him. Briefing Wavell, Linlithgow described him, patronis-ingly but not inaptly, as 'a mischievous boy with a catapult'.[87] When sec-retary Griffin's letter conveying Wavell's response to the Standing Committee's request for a statement on the treaty position reached him at his Delhi residence at 8 p.m. on 2 December 1944, it had the effect of a red rag waved before a raging bull.

As it happened, the Standing Committee was due to meet the next day to fix the agenda for the 1944 annual session, so a number of princes were already, like Hamidullah, in Delhi. He spoke to several by phone and all agreed with him that the government's letter represented a 'sad and severe blow' which could not be allowed to pass without protest.[88] The most eager for action, Holkar, later explained to Sir Homi Mody that the princes were fed up with being seen as abject collaborators who lacked

[85] His opponents were not so reticent, labelling him (unjustly) as an 'out and out Pakistani'. Liaquat to Palanpur 20 Jan. 1944, relating the contents of a memo authored by Haksar which was doing the rounds in New Delhi. BRO, Bhopal, Pol. Dept., Chamber Section, 94, 10/1, 1943. Panikkar, a vehement opponent, saw him as 'a Muslim partisan and enemy of the Hindus', *Autobiography*, 138. For an insight into why, nonetheless, Hamidullah prevailed in the polls (by a big majority) see Palanpur to Bhopal 13 Jan. 1944, BRO, Bhopal, Pol. Dept., Chamber Section, 94, 10/1 of 1943.
[86] Interview between Bhopal and PSV 5 Mar. 1944, Wavell Coll., 17.
[87] Moon, *Wavell*, 32 (entry dated 19 Oct. 1943).
[88] Bhopal to Wavell 14 Mar. 1945, *TOP*, V, 693.

'the guts or the brains to oppose the Viceroy'.[89] Nevertheless, Bhopal decided to give Wavell one more chance to reconsider. He sought an audience. According to the Wavell papers, Bhopal ranted a lot while he himself was conciliatory; Hamidullah's recounting, however, had the viceroy threatening 'to throw [the rulers] . . . to the wolves' unless they backed down. Accepting Bhopal's version, the Standing Committee elected unanimously to resign.[90]

Again, though, Hamidullah equivocated. When he returned to Viceregal Lodge on 4 December to brief Wavell about what had transpired, he reported merely that the Standing Committee *intended* to resign. Moreover, he endeavoured to distance himself from the previous day's proceedings. The princes, he said, had been giving him trouble; they were angry and 'out of control'; but he 'was going back to try to persuade them into a more reasonable attitude'.[91] In part Hamidullah's duplicity may have been designed to cushion the blow. More likely it was predicated on the assumption that the mere threat of resignation would suffice, allowing him to play the historic role he had always coveted – namely that of honest broker between the rulers and the government. Either way, Bhopal badly miscalculated. The viceroy was angry that the Standing Committee was prepared even to contemplate resignation, calling it a 'grave discourtesy to the Crown'.[92] He was angrier still when he learned later that the Committee had already resigned and that the chancellor had chosen to keep that information to himself. Bhopal, he decided, had succumbed to 'megalomania'.[93] Thus, to his consternation, Hamidullah was forced to match bluster with bluff. Drawing on all the dignity he could muster, he submitted his and his colleagues' resignations to Wavell that evening, adding, in a covering letter, that their action should be construed as an 'emphatic protest' against the harsh treatment meted out to the princes since 1943.[94] Next day the Standing Committee reconstituted itself as a 'Committee of Action', hired Bhulabhai Desai as legal counsel, and put out feelers to moderate nationalist politicians seeking moral support.

[89] Indore to Bhopal 30 Jan. 1945, encl. in US consul Bombay to sec. state Washington 11 Feb. 1945, US State Dept. decimal file 845.00/2–1145. The other 'ringleaders', as Wavell later described them, were Porbandar, Gwalior and Rampur.

[90] Bhopal to Wavell 3 Dec. 1944, encl. letters of resignation from himself, Nawanagar, Patiala, Indore, Gwalior, Rampur, Bikaner, Jaipur, Kota, Dholpur, Dungapur, Dewas Senior, Kurwai, Faridkot, Bilaspur, Tehri-Garhwal, Vadia, Maihar, Korea, Akalkot and Seraikela. *TOP*, V, 262. The other members of the Committee, less enthusiastic perhaps about the proposed course of action, sent in their resignations one by one between 6 December and 29 January 1945. See also Wavell to Amery 4 Dec. 1944, *TOP*, V, 265–6.

[91] Note by Wavell dated 6 Dec. 1944, Wavell Coll., 12; and Wavell to Amery 7 Dec. 1944, *TOP*, V, 283.   [92] Moon, *Wavell*, 104 (diary entry for 6 Dec. 1944).

[93] Wavell to Amery 7 Dec. 1944, *TOP*, V, 283.

[94] Bhopal to Wavell 26 Feb. 1945, *TOP*, V, 618.

Having been manoeuvred into this confrontational position Hamidullah felt obliged to maintain the charade. When Wylie discreetly suggested to him that the Standing Committee should withdraw, he replied defiantly that they were determined to prevail or perish. But his public bravado masked a growing sense of desperation, as he realised that Wavell proposed to make him suffer for his temerity.[95] Moreover, as the months went by, support for the 'strike' within the princely leadership began to dwindle. Pronouncing it a 'childish stratagem', Panikkar urged his master Bikaner to retract his resignation.[96] In May the raja of Faridkot dissociated himself from the new Committee. In June Anand Chand of Bilaspur announced that he was withholding all further financial contributions to the Chamber until such time as the chancellor agreed to 'break the present deadlock'.[97] Nor did the rebel princes gain much support from the nationalists or the English-language press, which declined to take their action seriously. So, from spring 1945 the Committee of Action searched for a face-saving exit. Prompted by Amery, who had had to fend off a barrage of awkward parliamentary questions, the viceroy provided one with a letter in June offering Bhopal a veiled apology for his earlier 'insensitivity' and the hope of a better deal from the Department of Post-War Reconstruction as regards allocations of capital equipment. Further mollified by an announcement that Wylie was to be replaced by Conrad Corfield, a career political officer known for his unfailing courtesy,[98] the Committee of Action met on 10 July and resolved 'to restore the normal working of the Chamber of Princes'.[99] When Wavell next met the Standing Committee, in early October, he was gratified to find them in a much 'better frame of mind'.[100]

However, even as the Standing Committee was congratulating itself on having made its point to the government, forces were gathering that would subject the alliance between the princes and the crown to unprecedented stresses and strains. May 1945 brought an end to the war in Europe, and within weeks the last of the Congress leaders still held in detention had been released and all remaining bans on political activity lifted. And July

[95] Wavell thought it 'essential to make clear to [the] Princes that [the] technique of resignation does not pay and must not be repeated'. Amery concurred: the rulers must be deterred from further 'Trades Union methods'. Wavell to Amery 21 Jan. 1945 and Amery to Wavell 31 Jan. 1945, *TOP*, V, 435 and 497.   [96] Panikkar, *Autobiography*, 139.

[97] Bilaspur to chancellor 2 June 1945, BRO, Bhopal, Pol. Dept., Chamber Section, 70, 4/40 of 1945–6.

[98] There is no suggestion that Wylie was sacked. His next appointment was to a plum governorship – that of the UP. However Wavell could have kept him on if he had wanted to. He chose to let him go with public plaudits and a private sigh of relief.

[99] Bhopal to Wavell 15 July 1945, *TOP*, V, 1256.

[100] Wavell to Lord Pethick-Lawrence 1 Oct. 1945, IOR L/PO/10/22.

saw the election in Britain of a socialist Labour government, committed, at least on paper, to the speedy decolonisation of the subcontinent. At first, so immersed were they in their own local worlds, many princes failed to grasp that big constitutional changes were in the offing – changes that would inevitably impinge on their relationship with the British. The general assumption seemed to be that any devolution of power would be confined to the provinces, and that the imperial links with the states would continue. Indeed it was Ramaswamy Aiyer's firm opinion that the majority of rulers remained, at heart, unconvinced that the British really intended to vacate India.[101] However, not all the princely leadership was so myopic. Ministers like Ramaswamy Aiyer, Panikkar, Mirza and Sir Sultan Ahmad were well aware that time was running short. 'The moment Congress assumes power in the Provinces and at the Centre, and the Constitution-making body is formed', Mirza warned the nizam, 'the cause of the Indian States might suffer incalculable harm at the hands of Indian Ministers, if . . . a fight is not put up in their defence.'[102] And similarly sober sentiments characterised the report of an *ad hoc* committee of ministers set up early in 1945 to advise the Chamber on post-war planning:

we will be failing in our duty if we do not submit that [the] 'march of time' is ranged heavily against autocratic forms of government, no matter howsoever tempered by benevolence . . . There are talks even now among responsible critics that the days of Indian Kingship are over. We do not share this outlook of defeatism; at the same time there is no denying that the Rulers stand on a perilous precipice.[103]

Not all rulers heard or heeded; but Bhopal did. As peace descended on Southeast Asia and the Pacific, Hamidullah, in concert with his Chamber advisers, put the final touches to a grand strategy designed to insulate the princes and their states from the impact of an early British departure from the subcontinent.

Challenge and response

Bhopal's rearguard strategy comprised five discrete but interlocking elements: the further rebuilding of the COP; accelerated internal reforms; the maintenance of the imperial connection; a tactical alliance with the Muslim League; and a negotiated settlement with the Congress. Not all these elements, however, evolved simultaneously. The third and fourth

[101] US consul-gen. Bombay to sec. state Washington 8 Nov. 1946 reporting interview with Sir C. P. Ramaswamy Aiyer on 3 Nov., US State Dept. decimal file 845.00/11–846.4
[102] Mirza to the Nizam 8 Dec. 1945, Mirza Ismail Papers.
[103] Interim report of *ad hoc* COMs dated 1 Feb. 1935, BRO, Bhopal, Pol. Dept., Chamber Section, 58, 4/36 of 1944. The report was commissioned by a special committee of rulers headed by Sardul Singh of Bikaner.

came into play later, in response to developments we shall address in the next section. In 1945 Hamidullah's priority was reform: reforming the Chamber, and promoting the idea of reform – especially constitutional reform – among his members.

Bhopal inherited an organisation that had been brought back to life, yet remained somewhat amateurish and grossly under-resourced, and as the tasks which fell to the Chamber grew heavier and more complex as the pace of decolonisation and nation-building picked up, the two-man executive team of the chancellor and his secretary found themselves increasingly overwhelmed. As Hamidullah minuted angrily, after an embarrassing session spent discussing industrial development and air navigation with a delegation of Indian officials on the basis of an inadequate brief:

Because . . . Maqbool Mahmud was in England . . . and because there is no-one else in the secretariat who can conduct the day to day business of the Chamber our case was poorly presented . . . If something is not done soon I am afraid we are faced with the prospect of complete failures in all the negotiations with the Central Government and with His Majesty's Government in regard to the most vital questions of life and death affecting the States . . . if the present state of affairs continues, I am totally helpless . . . I must be equipped with the most modern and up-to-date weapons to combat all [the] onslaughts on me.[104]

Accordingly, in November 1945, Bhopal obtained the Standing Committee's permission to upgrade the secretariat. A new post of personal advisor to the chancellor, carrying a salary of Rs4,000 a month, was created for Maqbool; five new assistant-secretaryships were added to the senior establishment; a new public relations bureau was set up; and the general office staff was expanded from twenty to sixty. The costs were heavy. The old secretariat had cost about a lakh to run; the budgetary projection for the new one was six-and-a-half lakhs, which translated into an additional contribution from member states of between Rs5,000 and Rs25,000 a year. However, once the new scheme started operating its obvious benefits dampened criticism. After 1945 the Chamber performed markedly better – not always, it must be said, wisely – but with consistent professionalism; while the publicity (in effect propaganda) bureau did useful work pushing the states' case, raising their collective image abroad and – though this was of course never publicly acknowledged – buying off leaders of the states subjects' organisations, the *praja mandals*.[105]

---

[104] Bhopal circular to Standing Committee 27 May 1945, BRO, Bhopal, Pol. Dept., Chamber Section, 43, 4/9 of 1945–6.

[105] For examples of successful press liaison by the bureau, see 'Press Reactions to Events in Indian States', 30 Nov. 1946, IOR R/1/1/4512; and for a candid statement of its aims, see note by its director encl. in consul-general Bombay to sec. state Washington 14 Feb. 1945, US State Dept. decimal file 845.00/2–1445.

It was the issue of internal reform, however, that mainly exercised the minds of the chancellor and his advisers in those early post-war months: first, because it was the keystone of their strategic plan to be able to front up to the post-war bargaining table with the backing of a solid core of 'loyal subjects'; secondly, because a large number of rulers – perhaps the majority of the membership – found it hard to accept the ministers' view that they had an 'impending crisis' on their hands which required 'a courageous stroke of bold statesmanship'.[106] When Holkar – whose consuming passion for all things American made him rather better disposed than most towards the notion of democracy – offered to host an informal meeting 'to . . . consider the Princes' future', he was told by the maharani of Baroda that her husband, the gaekwar, would not be able to attend since on the weekend nominated he had planned to go to Bombay for the races which 'were far more important than any [political] meeting'. In the event, the only invitee who actually turned up was Hamidullah, Holkar's closest friend.[107] Likewise Panikkar, who came back from a Commonwealth conference in London in February 1945 convinced that the princes' 'political standing was deteriorating day by day', spent a frustrating five weeks trying to persuade his master, Sadul Singh, that something ought to be done about it. Nevertheless, bit by bit, the message hit home, and by May Hamidullah had sufficient backing to call a general 'crisis' meeting at Bombay's Taj Mahal Hotel.

Subsequently Panikkar described this four-day talk-fest as a 'landmark in recent Indian history'. It was only a minor exaggeration. Thanks largely to an hour-long harangue from Ramaswamy Aiyer, the rulers gathered at Bombay committed themselves, almost without demur, to recasting their administrations 'along democratic lines in preparation for the part which the Indian States expect to play in the event of a national government in India'. What is more, they agreed to do so within a defined time-period and with reference to externally developed criteria – a task entrusted to a new high-powered advisory committee headed by the chancellor.[108] The following January, echoing the recommendations of this committee, Bhopal called on all Chamber states to adopt 'forthwith' written constitutions providing for popular institutions with

---

[106] Circular by chancellor 30 Sept. 1944, MPSA, Indore, Huzur Office, 28–II of 1944; and interim report of *ad hoc* COMs, 1 Feb. 1945, BRO, Bhopal, Pol. Dept., Chamber Section, 58, 4/36 of 1944.

[107] Memo by Kanji Dwarkadas dated 28 Jan. 1945, encl. in US consul-gen. Bombay to sec. state Washington 10 Apr. 1947, US State Dept. decimal file 845.00/4–1847.

[108] Panikkar, *Autobiography*, 142–6; consul Bombay to sec. state Washington 12 May 1945, US State Dept. decimal file 845.00/5–1245; and circular from chancellor dated 18 July 1945, BRO, Bhopal, Pol. Dept., Chamber Section, 54, 4/24 of 1945–6. The first meeting of the Constitutional Advisory Committee took place on 11 July.

elected majorities.[109] And in June 1946 the Standing Committee fixed a twelve-month time-limit for the commencement of this process.[110] Meanwhile, the Chamber hierarchy pushed ahead with plans, initially conceived in the early 1940s, to bring up to scratch the administration of backward member states. By early 1946 a 'model budget' for the smaller states had been drawn up and a 'large measure of agreement' reached on the content of a uniform civil list. Collectively, these initiatives promised to transform the political culture of the states, to turn them, by degrees, into Western-type constitutional monarchies.

Moreover, they produced results. Compared to the glacial pace of constitutional change before 1945, developments in the twenty-seven months from the end of the war until the demission of power in August 1947 were positively frenetic. In June 1945 the Bikaner legislature was enlarged to provide for an effective majority of elected members; in September the Jaipur Representative Assembly held its inaugural session; in July 1946 Kolhapur converted to a dyarchical system, similar to that which had prevailed in the provinces in the 1920s; and Bikaner and Cochin followed suit one month later, both advertising the changes as interim measures pending a transition to full responsible government; in January 1947, the maharaja of Mysore ordered his dewan to draw up proposals for a sweeping expansion of the franchise; in April, the twin states of Miraj Senior and Junior transferred all ministerial portfolios except those dealing with external and palace affairs to elected members of their legislatures; and in May 1947, Jawhar and Manipur, states populated mainly by tribals, held their first-ever elections. In sum, between 1945 and 1947, the proportion of Chamber states endowed with representative institutions went up from three-quarters to seven-eighths, while the number boasting partly responsible executives rose from 5 to nearly 25 per cent.[111]

Likewise, the Standing Committee achieved considerable success in

---

[109] Speech to COP 18 Jan. 1946, *IAR*, 1946, I, 349.

[110] Press statement by Standing Committee 11 June 1946 encl. in Bhopal to Wavell 19 June 1946, *TOP*, VII, 980–1. The *Bombay Chronicle*, 11 June 1946, headed its coverage of the SC meeting: 'INDIAN PRINCES PLUMP FOR DEMOCRACY.'

[111] Information derived from: commissioner New Delhi to sec. state Washington 26 June 1945, US State Dept. decimal file 845.00/6–2545; 'Constitutional Reforms in Indian States', issued by the director of Public Relations, COP [?] July 1945; commissioner New Delhi to sec. state Washington 14 Sept. 1945, US State Dept. decimal file 845.00/9–1445; *The Times of India*, 6 July 1946; *Bombay Sentinel*, 21 Aug. 1946; *Indian India*, 1, No.12 (31 Aug. 1946), 23; consul Madras to sec. state Washington 11 Jan. 1947, US State Dept. decimal file 845.00/1–1147; Pethick-Lawrence to Wavell 7 Mar. 1947, IOR L/PO/10/23; *The Times of India*, 11 Apr. 1947; consul-gen. Bombay to sec. state Washington 25 Apr. 1947, US State Dept. decimal file 845.00/4–2547; *The Times of India*, 19 May 1947; and the *National Herald*, 2 Aug. 1947.

pushing the concept of regional confederation as a way of strengthening the bargaining position of the states with the centre. Late in 1945 the annual conference of the rulers of the Eastern (Orissa) States appointed a special committee to draw up a scheme of federation; early in the new year Mirza Ismail, who at this stage was still dewan of Jaipur, initiated discussions among the Rajasthan states with the aim of setting up joint services; in May, ten Deccan states (Aundh, Jath, Ramdurg, Jamkhandi, Phaltan, Sangli, Kurunwad Senior and Junior and Miraj Senior and Junior) agreed at a meeting at Kolhapur to pool their revenues and administrative resources, establish a common legislature and, as far as possible, obliterate their frontiers; in July, the major Kathiawar states, meeting at the instigation of Mayurdhwaj Sinhji of Dhrangadhra, appointed a subcommittee under the chairmanship of the jam sahib to draft a constitution for a Kathiawari union; in September, a broader proposal embracing not only Gujarat but southern Rajasthan was floated by the ruler of Kota; in November, discussions were held at Patiala about the possibility of forming a union of Sikh states; and early in the new year the report of the Nawanagar committee, which had drawn heavily on the drafting talents of M. R. Jayakar, was enthusiastically adopted by representatives of over fifty states from Gujarat, Rajasthan and central India assembled in Bombay.[112]

Nevertheless, Bhopal knew that these initiatives would be useless in the absence of a commitment by the principal players to the survival of the states as constitutional monarchies within the framework of the new India. Therefore he continued to press the British (though less importunately than in 1944) on the treaties. Did Cripps' assurance of 1942 that the states would not be dragooned into the Indian union still hold good? What would be the precise constitutional position of states which opted to stay out? Would there be any obstacles to the maintenance of the ties between the princes and the crown – and the development of new commercial and diplomatic links between the states and the United Kingdom government – after the transfer of power? In his own mind the nawab was confident that the British would do the right thing by their allies; but he

---

[112] Resdt. Deccan States to pol. sec., 24 May 1946, IOR PSV R/3/1/111; consul-gen. Bombay to sec. state Washington 27 May 1946, US State Dept. decimal file 845.00/5–2746; same to same 13 July 1946, US State Dept. decimal file 845.00/7–1346; note by Corfield dated 22 July 1946, IOR R/1/1/4474; *The Times of India*, 24 Sept. 1946; consul-gen. Bombay to sec. state Washington 15 Nov. 1946, US State Dept. decimal file 845.00/11–1546; Proc.'s of Chamber Committee on Grouping, Delhi, 7 Dec. 1946, BRO, Bhopal, Pol. Dept., Special Branch, 78, 30/S.B./46; Minutes of 7th Eastern States Rulers Conf., Raipur, 21/22 Dec. 1946, IOR R/1/1/4611; consul Bombay to sec. state Washington 24 Jan. 1947, US State Dept. decimal file 845.00/1–2447; note by Wavell on interview with Sir C. P. Ramaswamy Aiyer dated 3 Mar. 1947, *TOP*, IX, 835.

wanted them to state their intentions publicly, in order to put an end to the uncertainty. Not knowing was sapping the princes' morale and beginning to undermine his personal stock in the Chamber.

Again, Hamidullah faced an uphill battle. Wavell remained, as he had been in 1944, opposed to governmental declarations that raised false princely hopes; and the Labour cabinet headed by Clement Attlee was ideologically opposed to making the military and political commitments that the chancellor sought. Political events, however, came to Bhopal's assistance. As the months went by, opinion in Delhi (if not in London) warmed towards the princes in exact measure as it cooled towards the politicians following the collapse of the Simla talks and the resurgence of Congress militancy. The viceroy began to carp about the Congress' ideological rigidity, accusing it of harbouring 'fascist' tendencies.[113] He complained that its 'sapping' tactics were frightening the Muslims.[114] Following the mass demonstrations that greeted the INA trials in November 1945, he warned London to 'be prepared for a serious attempt by the Congress, probably next spring . . . to subvert by force the present administration in India';[115] eleven months later he was forecasting famine, the breakup of the Indian Army and even civil war unless the ambitions of the Congress were contained.[116] Facing what, to him and others in the government, looked like impending 'chaos', Wavell found reassurance in the assessment by the chiefs of staff that the states could be relied on to render military as well as moral assistance.[117] But he also came, in this hour of desperation, to see the states themselves in a better light: as islands of political 'stability' run by 'practical', 'lucid' men with a 'businesslike' and 'sensible' outlook on public affairs – men, in short, rather like himself.[118] As Wavell's attitude to the states softened, so he became more solicitous of the welfare of their rulers.

However, this transformation in Wavell was not wholly a product of changing circumstances; it also reflected the strengthening influence of

---

[113] Wavell to Gov. C. P. 17 Aug. 1946, IOR, PSV R/3/1/112.

[114] Note by Wavell dated 2 Dec. 1946, *TOP*, IX, 241.

[115] Memo, n.d., encl. in Wavell to Pethick-Lawrence 6 Nov. 1945, *TOP*, VI, 452.

[116] Wavell to Pethick-Lawrence 23 Oct. 1946, *TOP*, VIII, 796.

[117] Memo for Cabinet on 'Implications of a Prepared Course of Action if There is a Breach Over the Cabinet Mission Plan', dated 12 June 1946, *TOP*, VII, 891. See also memo. by Wavell dated 30 May 1946, *TOP*, VII, 732. He also saw the states as potential safe harbours for British civil personnel in the event that the political situation deteriorated to the point where a strategic withdrawal from the subcontinent became necessary. See record of meeting between the Cabinet Delegation and Wavell, 22 May 1946, *TOP*, VII, 657–8; and record of meeting at 10 Downing Street between Wavell and the I&B Committee of Cabinet, 5 Dec. 1946, *TOP*, IX, 278.

[118] Moon, *Wavell*, 245 (diary entry for 15 Apr. 1946); and Wavell to Nehru 6 Feb. 1947, *TOP*, IX, 625.

the viceroy's new political adviser, Conrad Corfield. Now, Corfield generally has had a bad press from historians, but much of what has been said about him is inaccurate. For instance, he was not just a plodding 'reactionary'.[119] Underneath a somewhat stodgy exterior lurked a sharp intelligence. Wylie, whose ideological outlook was quite different, described him as 'a Resident of real quality who misses very little and on whose percipience and judgement His Excellency can I think rely absolutely'.[120] Moreover, while old-fashioned and conservative, Corfield was never a defender of princely oppression or an apologist for naked autocracy. He supported fully his predecessor's tough stand against Rewa.[121] Yet there is substance in the claim that Corfield was a princes' man. From the moment in 1921 when he first encountered the states as a junior member of Reading's viceregal touring party, he became an ardent believer in the myth of 'the real India' and a lifelong admirer of *darbari* culture. Realising his term would be a transitional one, and suspecting that his superiors in Whitehall had plans for India that did not include the *darbars*, he devoted the final and culminating phase of his career to seeing that the princes were given a fighting chance to retain their patrimony. In the circumstances of 1946 this meant convincing Wavell, and through him the Labour government, that the British had an obligation to arrange 'reasonable terms for accession to the new Federation' for those which wished to join, and to lend recognition and assistance to those which didn't.[122] By the spring of 1946 he had pretty much gained the first of these objectives and felt sufficiently encouraged by Paul Patrick's informal responses to his feelers on the second to assure Hamidullah in private conversation that London acknowledged 'the right of States, on the lapse of Paramountcy, to enter into negotiations with foreign powers'.[123] This was exactly what Bhopal had hoped to hear.

As to the other principal player, the Congress, Hamidullah, like most rulers, saw it essentially as an enemy of the monarchical order – which was not an unreasonable attitude given the party's republican and socialist manifesto. And he found it difficult, when talking to the Congress leaders, to forget or forgive their ambivalent role during the war. Nevertheless, he was enough of a pragmatist to realise that the Congress would sooner or later have to be reckoned with. Accordingly, while welcoming on behalf of the COP the viceroy's initiative in calling the Simla

---

[119] Cripps' term, but one often reiterated since. Moon, *Wavell*, 257 (diary entry dated 4 May 1946).   [120] Note by Wylie dated 9 Aug. 1944, IOR R/1/1/4097.

[121] Note by Corfield dated 29 Nov. 1945, IOR R/1/1/4236.

[122] Corfield to Sir George Abell 20 Mar. 1946, *TOP*, VI, 1229.

[123] Extract from political adviser's talk with Bhopal 5 June 1946, encl. in Abell to Turnbull 13 June 1946, *TOP*, VII, 908.

summit, and congratulating Congress on its strong showing in the December 1945 elections,[124] he authorised a resumption of Digvijay-sinhji's policy, suspended in 1942, of holding informal talks with the Congress high command about its attitude to the future of the states, he himself meeting secretly with Nehru at Chiklod in Bhopal in April 1946. If it showed how far apart the two sides still were, and if it involved, on the princes' part, a degree of dissimulation, this dialogue did result in a limited acknowledgement by the Congress of the states' right to exist as separate units in the new India – a concession formalised at the AISPC's annual session at Udaipur in January 1946.[125]

It had been a fruitful twelve months; but Hamidullah's grand design was still far from complete when, in February, Attlee announced that a cabinet delegation consisting of Cripps, Secretary of State Lord Pethick-Lawrence and First Lord of the Admiralty A.V. Alexander, would shortly arrive in India to finalise arrangements for an early British withdrawal from the subcontinent.

The Cabinet Mission

Even before the change of government in 1945, opinion in Whitehall had started to come to grips with the complicated issue of how to reconcile the crown's political obligations to the states with the promise contained in the Cripps offer of an early demission of power in the provinces. Not that the Tories, in particular, wanted to give India its freedom at any price, or abandon to the mercies of fate and the Congress allies who had for a century and more given good service to the imperial cause. For one thing, there was a possibility that the rulers might still prove useful. As we have seen, Wavell and the service chiefs had big plans for the states in the event of the resumption of widespread agitation by the Congress, and the viceroy also saw a continuing role for them during the interim period (which, in 1945–6, was expected to last for several years at least) as mediators between the two nationalist parties. Disowned, the states would lose prestige and political influence and might well prove uncooperative. For

---

[124] Congress captured nearly all the general seats, giving it control at the centre and in eight provinces. The League, conversely, won 75 per cent of the vote in the seats reserved for Muslims, but gained a majority only in Bengal.

[125] The understanding incorporated in the Udaipur resolution was that this privilege would be confined to states 'able to maintain modern standards of social and economic welfare', that is, states with a minimum population of 20 lakhs and a minimum population of 50 lakhs. The dissimulation was Bhopal's assurance to Nehru that the princes 'wanted to give up their association with the British Crown completely'. Note by Nehru on conversation with Bhopal and Shuaib Qureshi on 21 and 22 Apr. 1946, *PC*, III, 329–34.

another thing, the princes had some powerful friends at court. In 1944 when the proposal to repudiate the princely alliance was first mooted, Amery sounded out members of the Tory back-bench. The results were not encouraging. It would, he decided, 'require the presentation of a very strong case to induce my colleagues to approve action liable to be represented in certain quarters as a betrayal of our best friends in India'.[126] Although the parliamentary balance of power had shifted in the interim, the threat of another diehard revolt – particularly in the Lords where the Tories still held sway – could not be discounted. Likewise, the princes had a potentially powerful patron in the person of the king, George VI, who, though a constitutional monarch, had the capacity to cause a lot of headaches for the government if he chose to make an issue of the rulers' dynastic connection with his house. Last but not least, it threatened to be very costly. Over the years the states had paid dearly for the privilege of British protection. They had ceded vast tracts of territory, given up the right to mint coinage, levy sea customs duties and issue their own postage stamps, and abandoned local production of salt and opium. If the treaties were repudiated, the states would have a good legal case either for demanding retrocession of the ceded rights and territories or cash compensation in lieu. At best the government faced the prospect of having to shell out in the vicinity of £2,500,000; at worst of having to hand back Berar to the nizam, thereby crippling the finances of the Central Provinces.[127]

Nevertheless, London was prepared to pay the price. Unlike its predecessor, the incoming Labour ministry had few inhibiting personal ties with the Indian princes. And they were not well disposed, ideologically, to the perpetuation of monarchies – particularly monarchies that in many cases denied their citizens democratic institutions and basic civil rights. As well, Labour's attitude was influenced by what the government of India was saying about the political imperatives of economic development. The advice from New Delhi was that the states were too small, by and large, to stand on their own feet, represented barriers to trade and communications and were likely, on past performance, to present a serious impediment to rational economic planning.[128] From several points of view, it seemed clear to Attlee, Cripps, and the other members of the cabinet's India and Burma Committee, that a prolongation of the monarchical system was incompatible with the goal of a free, prosperous India. However the main thing that drove the Labour government to pull

[126] Amery to Wavell 26 Oct. 1944, *TOP*, V, 150–1.
[127] Note by Pethick-Lawrence dated 11 Mar. 1946, *TOP*, VI, 1140; and Sir Frederick Browne, gov. C. P. to Wavell 27 Dec. 1946, IOR PSV R/3/1/112.
[128] Sir John Colville, acting viceroy, to Amery 10 Apr. 1945, *TOP*, V, 863.

the plug was the knowledge that the princely partnership had become insupportable. While Whitehall saw no insurmountable obstacles to maintaining a diplomatic link with the states after independence – say, via the United Kingdom high commission in Delhi – such as would permit them to continue to regulate the personal and dynastic aspects of paramountcy (successions, honours and the like) they could see no way of fulfilling their obligation to protect them:

> The real difficulty [Pethick-Lawrence explained to the cabinet] centres on protection obligations (presently covered by Sections 286 and 52 of the Government of India Act). It must be presumed that these instruments will not be available under any constitution for a self-governing Union or Unions. The question therefore arises whether the Crown will have in India British troops under its sole command and, if so, whether any treaty provision could be made which would secure free passage for them to any non-adhering State in which their use was required . . . I fear that the answer to both questions may be in the negative.[129]

This still left the military options canvassed by Cripps in 1942, namely the use of sea- and air-power and the stationing of troops in maritime states such as Cochin and Junagadh; but by the beginning of 1946 even these dubious expedients had been firmly ruled out as likely to jeopardise relations with the Congress which, following the provincial elections, had reemerged as the dominant political force in the country. As Pethick-Lawrence wryly observed, in a memorandum for Attlee, it was not really 'a possible solution to maintain British troops in States . . . to resist infiltration from British India' when the Congress, which encouraged such action, was 'in office with our approval'.[130] Quite early on, therefore, the Attlee government came to the conclusion that Britain's pledges to the states would have to be repudiated.

Yet, implementing this decision was no easy matter. First and foremost, the government had to surmount the obstacle of the treaties. Although only about forty states possessed formal treaties with the crown, the sweeping and in some cases quite specific language of these documents more than made up for their relative rarity. Under the treaties of 1795 and 1802 with Hyderabad, for example, the Delhi government was required to furnish, when needed, a force of not less than 5,000 infantry and 2,000 cavalry and 4 battalions of artillery – all under the command of British officers – for the protection of the nizam's dominions. Moreover, while references in many of the earlier treaties, such as those of 1804 and 1818 between the East India Company and Jaipur, to bonds of 'friendship' and

---

[129] Memo by the sec. state for the India and Burma Committee of Cabinet dated 9 Oct. 1945, *TOP*, VI, 328.
[130] Memo., n.d., encl. in Pethick-Lawrence to Attlee 21 Dec. 1946, *TOP*, IX, 400.

'alliance' between 'states'[131] bespoke anachronism, even obsolescence, the inclusion of words such as 'permanent' and 'perpetual' made it hard for the British to claim that they had 'lapsed' with the effluxion of time. While opinions varied, the consensus was that the military obligation to the nizam, at any rate, was still binding.[132] Of course treaties can be – and often are – unilaterally repudiated. But as well as being legally dubious, a point we shall return to later, this course of action lays the infracting party open to a charge of betrayal and may gain it a reputation for untrustworthiness; this may in turn destabilise its relations with other states. All these considerations weighed heavily with the British who understood that their country's prospects in the post-war world depended on keeping intact its reputation for probity and fair-dealing. In addition, they were constrained by the draft declaration taken out to India by Cripps which declared that such treaty revision as was required by the changed conditions of the post-war period would be negotiated. In the secretary of state's view this 'rul[ed] out any idea of unilateral denunciation of these Treaties and engagements'.[133]

The treaties, moreover, did not exhaust the ties which bound the British crown to the Indian states. Almost as compromising were the assurances of friendship and support given the princes by successive British sovereigns, notably by Victoria in 1858 and by George V in 1911 and 1921. Such public pronouncements were not, it is true, legally binding; yet they carried considerable moral force, all the greater because they involved the honour of the crown. Much as they didn't relish the thought, many Whitehall officials in 1945–6 believed, with the Bhopal *darbar*, that the crown was locked into a relationship which could not be unilaterally revoked 'by any party so long as it exists in the world'.[134]

What was needed was a formula that would extricate the government from its legal obligations under the treaties in a way that would not leave it open to accusations of bad faith – not by any means a simple thing to

---

[131] These treaties are reproduced as Appendices I and II of H.C. Batra, *The Relations of Jaipur State with the East India Company 1803–1858* (Delhi, 1955).

[132] See for example memo. by under-sec. state dated 12 June 1946, *TOP*, VII, 902: 'the Nizam could . . . invoke the treaty obligations of the Crown to [compel it] to come to his aid in resistance to any attempt by Hindustan to liquidate his dynastic position and authority'.

[133] Appendix to memo by sec. state dated 1 Feb. 1945, *TOP*, V, 514. By 'engagements', the secretary of state meant documents issued from time to time to the states which, while specifying duties and obligations, did not have the contractual status of treaties. The most important of these were the 150–odd adoption *sanads* issued by Canning to the princes after the Mutiny, which contained an implicit pledge of dynastic perpetuation.

[134] Memo. by Mohammad Munir Ansari, assist. sec., Political Ministry, 11 Jan. 1947, BRO, Bhopal, Pol. Dept., Special, 85/37/ S.B./46

manufacture. Nevertheless, by October 1945, Pethick-Lawrence's advisers in the India Office felt they had the legal angle covered. As Cripps (who presumably had a better grasp of these matters than the secretary of state) explained to the cabinet, the official view was now that:

While we were bound by the assurances we had given, the practical point . . . was that [the] treaties which were now 80 to 100 years old were by the efflux of time and change of circumstances ceasing to be appropriate to the conditions of the modern world. Thus paramountcy itself essentially derived from the fact that we were the paramount power in British India. If . . . India acquired an independent status, certain of our obligations which we had undertaken, in quite different conditions, would clearly not admit . . . [of] being discharged.[135]

In other words, the treaties had been rendered nugatory by the passage of time and could be denounced unilaterally without fear of legal repercussions in the unlikely event that the princes tried to 'implead the sanctity of the agreements contracted with them by the Crown' in the International Court, or some other such tribunal.[136] As to the moral aspect, the Labour government was prepared, if challenged, to argue the greater good: namely that their dynastic obligations to the princes were outweighed by their obligations to the country as a whole and particularly to the peoples of British India to whom they had also made solemn promises. But quite apart from this, London felt few pangs of guilt about terminating the princely alliance, for it seemed to them that the ledger had already been balanced by Delhi's intimation that in many cases the princes were secretly just as anxious to see the end of British dominion in India as the Congress.

Still, the Labour government was concerned to do the right thing and, what is more, to be seen doing the right thing. Therefore they undertook to help the rulers obtain a position within the post-colonial polity that was at once 'secure' and 'commensurate with their historical and factual status'.[137] First, they announced that under no circumstances would they hand over the crown's paramountcy power to a third party. Second, they came up with a raft of measures designed to cushion the blow to the princes' sensibilities: these included a United Nations brokered security pact covering the entire subcontinent; a treaty with the union reserving the dynastic aspects of paramountcy, for example, successions, and containing an exit clause giving acceding states the right to secede in the event of India leaving the Commonwealth; and a 'gentlemen's agreement' confirming nizam Osman Ali in his sovereignty over Berar in return

[135] Minutes of India and Burma Committee meeting dated 11 Sept. 1945, *TOP*, VI, 253.
[136] Note by Pethick-Lawrence dated 11 Mar. 1946, *TOP*, VI, 1140.
[137] Pethick-Lawrence to Wavell 25 Sept. 1945, *TOP*, VI, 298.

for him withdrawing his claim to Rs 25 lakhs quit-rent.[138] Third, while making clear their belief that there was no future for the states outside the constitutional confines of the Indian union, and enjoining the Cabinet Mission to press the advantages of accession on the princes, the government ruled out using its paramountcy powers to compel the states to accede to the union.[139]

Thus, even before the Cabinet Mission left for India in March 1946, there was something of a schizophrenic air about Labour's policy towards the princely states; and this duality was compounded by the understandable but inexcusable reluctance of the cabinet team, in their discussions with Bhopal and the other princely leaders, and later in their published statements, to say frankly what the government had in mind for them – a tendency that led Wavell (who himself was by no means unsympathetic to the rulers' position) to complain that the Mission 'gave away much which I should certainly not have done at this stage'.[140] For example, the document issued on 16 May which summarised the Mission's findings and recommendations, made only the following brief and cryptic reference to the states:

Paramountcy can neither be retained ... nor transferred ... The representatives of the States have assured the Cabinet Delegation that they are ready and willing to cooperate in the new development of India, but the precise form which their cooperation will take must be a matter for negotiation, and the outcome of that negotiation may not prove to be identical for all the States.[141]

while the Mission's 'Memorandum on States' Treaties and Paramountcy', published on 22 May, observed merely:

When a new fully self-governing or independent Government or Governments come into being in British India ... the rights of the States which flow from their relationship to the Crown will no longer exist and ... all the rights surrendered by the States to the paramount power will return to the States ... The void will have to be filled either by the States entering into a federal relationship with the successor Government or Governments in British India, or, failing this, entering into particular political arrangements with it or them.[142]

In their studied ambiguity, these documents invited speculation and controversy – an outcome greatly assisted by Cripps' cavalier observation, at

---

[138] Appendix to memo by sec. state dated 1 Feb. 1945, *TOP*, V, 514; minute by Patrick dated 30 Mar. 1945, *TOP*, V, 789; Turnbull to Clauson 5 Feb. 1946, *TOP*, VI, 883; note by Pethick-Lawrence dated 15 Feb. 1946, *TOP*, VI, 987; and Pethick-Lawrence to Mountbatten 31 Mar. 1947, *TOP* X, 56.
[139] 'Revised Draft Directive to Cabinet Mission', App. 2 to minutes of discussions at Chequers 24 Feb. 1946, *TOP*, VI, 1063.
[140] Moon, *Wavell*, 235 (diary entry dated 2 Apr. 1946).
[141] Cabinet Mission Statement, 16 May 1947, *TOP*, VII, 585.
[142] The complete text can be read in Menon, *Story*, App. II, 475–6.

the press conference held to launch the 16 May Statement, that the logical implication of the delegation's proposals was that the states would 'become wholly independent'.[143] Subsequently, the waters were further muddied when Congress started to place reservations on its acceptance of other major features of the Cabinet Mission Plan, thereby provoking Jinnah to withdraw that of the League.

The princes, though, welcomed the scheme. While Conservative elements in Britain spoke of betrayal – Sir Walter Monckton told Churchill that the proposal to set aside the treaties stuck in his 'gizzard'[144] – a conference at Bombay on 11 June attended by over sixty rulers unanimously endorsed a Standing Committee motion accepting the broad parameters of the plan as it affected the states. After all, it gave – or seemed to give – the states something they had long craved. In their discussions with the delegation, the rulers had argued that on the transfer of power 'each State must be allowed to regain its former independence, and [be] left to itself to do what it wanted'.[145] The knowledge that their sovereign rights were indeed to be returned to them – that they were once again, in Cripps' fateful words, to be 'wholly independent' – more than compensated, in the minds of most princes, for the threatened withdrawal of imperial patronage.

Yet, while it appeared to give the princes much of what they had been hankering for, the Cabinet Mission Plan set in train a sequence of political developments which had the potential to threaten Hamidullah's grand design for the preservation of the monarchical order. One was its provision for the summoning of an all-India assembly to settle the details of the new constitution; another the recommendation that effective control over internal matters be handed over immediately to a popular interim government.

Now Bhopal was not in principle opposed to the states becoming part of a free, federal India – a cause, after all, which he had been instrumental in pushing in the early 1930s. Indeed, he still fancied himself playing a key role, possibly as the leader of a cross-communal centre party, in the government of the new India. However, Hamidullah had serious reservations about the states sending delegates to a Constituent Assembly which Congressmen were already referring to as a 'sovereign' body. Joining the Assembly at the outset would constrain the *darbars'* freedom of manoeuvre by locking them into particular constitutional arrangements.

---

[143] Verbatim record of the Cabinet Mission's press conference, 16 May 1946, *TOP*, VII, 597.   [144] Monckton to Churchill 6 May 1946, quoted in Birkenhead, *Monckton*, 221.

[145] Note on discussions between the Cabinet Delegation, Wavell and the rulers of Dungapur and Bilaspur, 4 Apr. 1946, *TOP*, VII, 128–9. The remark was made by the raja of Bilaspur.

There was a danger that, once inside, the states' delegates would fall under the sway of Congress power and the spell of nationalist rhetoric and commit their *darbars* to things not in the best princely interest. If some states entered and others did not, the solidarity so essential to the princely cause would be compromised. After the League's decision on 29 July not to participate in the Assembly – which removed the only real bulwark against Congress domination – these reservations hardened into an attitude of implacable hostility. Bhopal's strategy now focussed on trying to extricate the Chamber, without loss of credibility, from its commitment to open negotiations with the British Indian politicians.[146]

Unwittingly, Stafford Cripps supplied him with a loophole. On 18 July Cripps told parliament that it was his understanding that discussions would take place between the states negotiating committee and 'the major British Indian parties both as to the representation of the States in the Constituent Assembly and as to their ultimate position in the Union'. His use of the plural, implying League as well as Congress, allowed the rulers to claim that they were not bound to have any discussions with the still-to-be-established Assembly committee unless it contained members of both parties.[147] However, lest this did not suffice, Bhopal persuaded the Standing Committee to lay down elaborate (some might have said unrealistic) preconditions for the states' entry. In regard to the selection of delegates, the COP rejected the mechanism of popular election and resolved to limit the proportion of non-officials.[148] It announced that the states would expect weighted representation, as under the Act of 1935; and would reserve to themselves the same 'grouping' rights for legislative purposes as had been conceded to the provinces. It declared that it would oppose any attempt to saddle the new constitution with a code of fundamental rights, or provisions antagonistic to the monarchical form of government, yet gave notice that it would move to insert a clause

---

[146] Hamidullah fought hard to get Jinnah to change his mind; and in September and October 1946 he hosted talks at Bhopal and at his residence in Delhi between the Congress and the League in an effort to build a bridge between the parties. When these initiatives failed, he felt he had no option but to pull the princes out too, for the Chamber had always insisted that its participation was conditional on the Constituent Assembly being representative. See Sir Sultan Ahmad's interview with the *Daily Telegraph*, 21 Sept. 1946; and Sir J. Colville (acting viceroy) to Pethick-Lawrence 18 Dec. 1946, *TOP*, IX, 380–1.

[147] *Aide-mémoire* prepared by Corfield for the Residents' Conference, 16/17 Dec. 1946, IOR R/1/1/4602.

[148] Confidential circular from Bhopal quoted in the *Bombay Chronicle*, 19 Aug. 1946; and circular from Maqbool Mahmud dated 17 Dec. 1946, *TOP*, IX, 365. The British did not much like either arrangement, but comforted themselves with the thought that if things went wrong the princes would 'not be able to blame any one but themselves'. Note by I. B. Scott dated 26 June 1946, IOR, PSV R/3/1/111.

requiring important pieces of legislation affecting the states to be subject to the assent of a majority of delegates from the states. It insisted that acceding states be allowed to retain 'full rights of internal administration', subject only to central supervision, conclude treaties with foreign powers and appoint overseas trade agents, keep their own local forces and control over their own railways. It recommended that they should have the right, after ten years, to secede.[149] It was Hamidullah's hope that Congress would be so enraged by these *sine qua nons* that it would refuse to talk while they remained on the table, allowing the princes to retain command of the high moral ground.

In the event, however, he was not required to play this dangerous card for several months, thanks to the continued wrangling between the two major parties. Given the green light by the Cabinet Mission in May, the Constituent Assembly did not hold its first session until 9 December; and on 21st it adjourned its proceedings until 20 January. Likewise, while the interim government led by Jawaharlal Nehru started work in September, it was held on a pretty tight rein, with regard to the princes, by Corfield and Wavell, who steadfastly refused to let the importunate Nehru see political department files or raise internal states issues in the executive council.[150] And after October Nehru was distracted by having to cope with an unruly clutch of ministers from the Muslim League, which believed that New Delhi had no business poking its nose into the princes' affairs.[151] Thus, the looming confrontation between the Chamber and the

---

[149] Record of interviews between Cabinet Delegation, Wavell and Bhopal, 9 and 12 May 1946, *TOP*, VII, 473–3 and 521; note by M. N. Ansari, assist. pol. sec. Bhopal dated 24 May 1946, BRO, Bhopal, Pol. Dept., Special Branch, 76, 29/S.B./46; Bhopal to Wavell 29 July 1946, *TOP*, VIII, 134; 'Memo [by Major States Organization] on the Proposed Union Subjects', n.d., BRO, Bhopal, Pol. Dept., Special Branch, 80, 32/S.B./46; and resolution put to COMs meeting, New Delhi, 27 Jan. 1947, BRO, Bhopal, Pol. Dept., Special Branch, 102, 57/S.B./47.

[150] Moon, *Wavell*, 257 (diary entry for 4 May 1946); Wavell to Pethick-Lawrence 25 Sept. 1946, *TOP*, VIII, 586; and minutes of residents' conference 9/10 Apr. 1947, IOR PSV R/3/1/136. The standoff was mutual. Corfield tried to arrange for regular meetings between the cabinet and a Liaison Committee which had been set up by the COP, and to assert his own right, as the *de facto* 'political' member of council, to participate in cabinet discussions which impinged on his portfolio. His initiatives were received, he recalls, with 'stony silence' by the politicians. And he had no more luck when he tried to approach the prime minister directly over AISPC involvement in Datia. Nehru could not be reached. Note by Corfield on questions put to him by Prof. C. H. Philips [?] Mar. 1968, Corfield Coll., 4; and Corfield to Abell 23 Apr. 1947, *TOP*, X, 384. On the princes' hopes for better consultation, see Bhopal to Wavell [?] Apr. 1946, *TOP*, VII, 354, and circular from COP secretariat dated 2 July 1946, BRO, Bhopal, Pol. Dept., Special Branch, 66, 20/S.B./46.

[151] On the League's strategy towards the states, see Ian Copland, 'The Princely States, the Muslim League and the Partition of India In 1947', *The International History Review*, 13, 1 (1991), 38–69.

Congress was temporarily averted. A little fortuitously perhaps, Bhopal had gained valuable breathing space for the monarchical order.

But was it merely a reprieve – or something more substantial? Was there still time for the states to secure their future?

The states in 1946

If the princes were doomed in 1946, few had any premonition of the fate that awaited them just around the corner. On the contrary, the prevalent *darbari* mood was one of unvarnished optimism. 'Nobody thought that princely rule would end at that time', the maharaja of Dungapur recalled later. 'Even in 1945 I never thought it would end.'[152] Indeed, so confident was Hyderabad about its political prospects that in 1946 it made a serious overture to the Portuguese government for the lease of Goa as a free port, and set aside the considerable sum of Rs 240 million for a scheme to dam the Godavary and irrigate 800,000 acres of farmland – a project which in its scale and ambition reminded the American vice-consul in Madras, Louise Schaffner, of what her countrymen had done in the 1930s in the Tennessee Valley.[153] British observers, more prescient (or perhaps simply more jaundiced) thought the rulers' confidence misplaced. After a visit to Rampur (where, among other diversions, he was treated to a jazz recital by the nawab's private band, Rampur himself playing drums) Francis Wylie came away convinced that 'the Princes are in dreamland'.[154] And the same thought struck Philip Mason when he arrived in Hyderabad in 1946 to take up the post of tutor to the nizam's grandchildren. 'It was like the spring of 1789 at Versailles', he records in his autobiography.[155] History, of course, has confirmed their judgement.

However, while it might now seem complacent and extravagant, the princes' roseate outlook in 1946 was to some extent well founded. It is true, as a ministers' report pointedly observed in 1945, that the states no longer enjoyed the 'position of vantage which they [had] occupied during the federal negotiations when their accession was made a condition precedent to responsibility at the Centre'.[156] But they were not weak or helpless. The larger *darbars* commanded sizeable armies, quite capable of

[152] Quoted in Allen and Dwivedi, *Lives*, 316.
[153] Report by Louise Schaffner, US vice-consul Madras, dated 16 Aug. 1945, US State Dept. decimal file 845.00/8–1645. On Goa see minutes of meeting between Alexander, Wavell, Nawab Ali Yavar Jung, the Nawab of Chhatari and Walter Monckton on 17 May 1946, *TOP*, VII, 602.   [154] Wylie to Wavell 7 Feb. 1947, *TOP*, IX, 640.
[155] Philip Mason, *A Shaft of Sunlight: Memories of a Varied Life* (London, 1978), 200.
[156] Resolution of the Study Circle, Bombay [?] Apr. 1945, encl. in chancellor's circular to Standing Committee 20 May 1945, BRO, Bhopal, Pol. Dept., Chamber Section, 2, 1/3 of 1945–6.

dealing with the ordinary run of internal dissent. They were by and large extremely wealthy. Quite apart from the princes' legendary private hoards of jewels and coin, many of the bigger states had built up large portfolios of investments, Gwalior alone holding government of India securities to the value of over 16 million rupees.[157] Their economies were growing fast and, with industrialisation, becoming more diversified. Moreover, all the anecdotal evidence (which in the absence of opinion polls is all we have) points strongly to the conclusion that while, by the mid-1940s, there was growing antipathy towards princely governments (especially those headed by expatriate dewans), the princes themselves remained over-whelmingly popular figures in the eyes of their subjects.[158] Visiting Rampur in 1944, Lord Mountbatten found that the nawab was 'obviously really respected by his subjects who welcome him . . . enthusiastically everywhere'.[159] In July 1947 Hamidullah was met at the Bhopal aero-drome by a crowd of 50,000 subjects 'all in [a state of] great excitement' who refused to let him leave till he had promised them that he had no intention of abdicating.[160] Similar emotional scenes transpired at the state funeral of the maharaja of Kapurthala in 1948. And it was not just the uneducated peasantry that felt this way. In 1938 a Patiala journalist assured Gandhi that '99.9% of the subjects of the State are peaceful and loyal, sincere and faithful, to the ruler . . . of Patiala. . . . whom they love and regard as a natural master';[161] in 1940 a prominent Jodhpur national-ist, Jai Narain Vyas, claimed that 'every Marwari is loyal . . . to the person and throne of His Highness';[162] and in 1946 Congress workers in Datia went on a hunger-strike in support of the ruler's refusal to implement the residency's orders that he reinstate an unpopular dewan. As Louise Schaffner remarked with some foresight of Hyderabad: '[It] is not a polit-ical pawn. It is strong enough to choose sides effectively, and is likely to become [an] increasingly powerful . . . force on the Indian scene.'[163]

---

[157] Note by P. A. Gwalior encl. in letter to pol. sec. GOI 10 Nov. 1945, IOR R/1/1/4427.

[158] For the princes' views see Allen and Dwivedi, *Lives*, 93, 297, 300, 310; rana of Barwani to Patiala 26 Mar. 1927, BRO, Bhopal, Chamber Section, 11, 46/1 of 1927; Panna to Patiala 28 Mar. 1927, *ibid*; address by Indore read to the second session of the RTC, 28 Nov. 1931, B. S. Moonje Papers, NMML, subject file 18; and speech by Bikaner 22 Dec. 1936, RSA, Bikaner, PMO, A 442–513 of 1936–8.

[159] Philip Zeigler (ed.), *The Personal Diary of Admiral The Lord Louis Mountbatten, Supreme Allied Commander, Southeast Asia 1943–1946* (London, 1988), 71 (diary entry 26 Feb. 1944).

[160] In fact he was planning to do so; but the spontaneous demonstration at the airport caused him to change his mind. Press statement from Government of Bhopal dated 14 Aug. 1947, IOR, PSV R/3/1/143; and Bhopal to Mountbatten 14 Aug. 1947, *TOP*, XII, 731n.

[161] R. S. Azad to Gandhi 25 Sept. 1938, NMML, AICC, file G-35 (3) of 1938.

[162] Jai Narain Vyas to Sir Donald Field, chief minister of Jodhpur, May 1940, Jai Narain Vyas Papers, NMML, file 3.   [163] Report by Schaffner, 16 Aug. 1945.

Again, it would be wrong to suggest that in 1946 the states faced an inevitable and hopeless showdown with the forces of nationalism. Although, as we've seen, an established local opposition to autocratic rule in the shape of *praja mandals* affiliated to the AISPC and clandestine branches of the INC was operating by this time in most states, and had become undeniably stronger and more militant as a result of the confrontation of 1938–9, it was not yet formidable enough to challenge the *darbars* head on. The *praja mandals* remained overwhelmingly urban, middle-class bodies with limited membership and funds. The majority in central India, V. P. Menon discovered, 'existed only in name'.[164] Moreover a number were split into rival factions, which left them vulnerable to the politics of divide-and-rule. In Jodhpur, for example, the *darbar* by 1946 had won over to their side as many as seventeen prominent politicians. Again, while the *praja mandals* itched to take power, they remained chary about the path of revolution and in favour of an orderly constitutional transition to democracy.[165] Significantly, when the states were democratised in the late 1940s, the former *praja mandal* leaders generally had no trouble working under the princes as constitutional heads.

Last but not least, the *darbars* possessed, as Schaffner discerned, political choices. The rulers could still count on the sympathy of the viceroy and the assistance of Corfield's political department; Bhopal's reorganisation of the secretariat had strengthened their negotiating position with the centre; they had much to offer by way of bargaining chips; and they were well positioned to profit from the rivalry between League and Congress.

In short, the rulers still possessed a strong suit. But as any expert will tell you, success at the bridge-table depends not just on what cards you hold, but on how skilfully you play them.

---

[164] Menon, *Story*, 217.

[165] There were, to be sure, some significant exceptions to this rule, notably in the large southern states of Mysore and Travancore. On Mysore see Manor, *Indian State*, chapters 7–8; on Travancore, Robin Jeffrey, 'Status, Class and the Growth of Radical Politics, 1860–1940', in Jeffrey, *People, Princes and Paramount Power*, 136–69.

7   Fin de Siècle

It appears . . . as if this great problem of the States has been satisfactorily
solved within the last three weeks of British rule.

Earl Mountbatten, 16 August 1947

Inertia

Asked in October 1946 about the prospects for the new year, Yeshwant
Rao Holkar's personal astrologer made this prediction: 'Guru has been
the only protective planet in the Horoscope but he also becomes suddenly
weak and evil from January 1947 . . . the evil influence on health [and
prosperity] which is . . . absent now will start from the end of January
1947 and become dangerous . . . from March 1947 onwards till August
1948.'[1] When the axe came down on the rulers in August 1947, Yeshwant
Rao doubtless gained some comfort from the knowledge that his fate and
that of his brother princes was predestined and thus unavoidable; but in
reality the demise of the princes – at least, in its final form of 1948 – was a
product not of mysterious cosmic forces but of earthly ones: of power
shifts, economic imperatives and human miscalculations.

Among the latter perhaps the greatest – for it lay at the root of many
others – was the widespread belief within the ranks of the rulers that there
was no necessity for drastic change and that 'reforms' could be introduced without significant effect on their own lifestyles. As we saw in the
previous chapter, the COP had been trying for years, without success, to
formulate a common policy on the matter of the rulers' use of state funds
for private purposes. Bhopal, to his credit, made another attempt in 1945,
reviving the Bikaner civil list committee which had lapsed in 1943; but
Sadul Singh's committee again took the easy way out, plumping for a
generous sliding scale which ensured that no ruler got less than 10 per
cent of the revenue (and rulers of small states as much as 30 per cent), a

---

[1] Ramkrishna H. Pandit to V. G. Jadhav, Huzur sec. Indore, 29 Oct. 1946, MPSA, Indore,
Huzur Office, 180 of 1942.

definition of 'revenue' which did not include jagirs, shareholdings and other income-earning investments owned by the princes, and designated the education and marriage expenses of the royal family and the maintenance of palaces as items chargeable to the regular administrative budget. Moreover, while privately appalled at the committee's lack of gumption, the chancellor made little effort to strengthen its recommendations, or to pressure his members to adopt them. Instead, a bland memorandum setting out details of the sliding scale and list of exemptions was circulated to the Chamber's members with an apologetic covering letter from Bhopal explaining that the document contained only personal 'expressions of opinion'.[2] The maharaja of Baroda's response to this missive was to defiantly raise his privy purse from 23 lakhs to 50. Other princes simply ignored it. As of March 1947 some 30 per cent of states associated with the Chamber were still debating whether to set *any* constitutional limits on their personal incomes and expenditures.

It was a similar story with that other revolutionary Chamber initiative: princely union. As noted above, several schemes were mooted during late 1945 and 1946, but the process of translating desire into reality proved painfully slow, with the result that by January 1947 only the Deccan princes had actually reached the stage of forming a confederation (it was scheduled to come into operation in May). Of course, the path of union was always going to be difficult; quite apart from the vexed issue of sovereignty, there were all sorts of administrative problems that needed to be worked through – not least the problem of deciding where to situate the federal capital. But the main obstacle to progress was the complacent mentality of the princely rank and file. After learning, at the annual Orissa

---

[2] The details of the sliding scale proposed by the Bikaner Committee were as follows:

Revenue	Proportion of revenue allocated to Civil List
below 5 lakhs	30 per cent
5 to 10 lakhs	20 per cent
10 to 25 lakhs	13 per cent
25 to 75 lakhs	12 per cent
75 to 100 lakhs	10 per cent
1 *crore* and above	10 per cent plus
on amount in excess of 1 *crore*	7 per cent
on amount in excess of 2 *crores*	5 per cent
on amount in excess of 3 *crores*	3 per cent
on amount in excess of 4 *crores*	2 per cent.

Report of meeting of Finance Subcommittee, 21 Sept. 1945, BRO, Bhopal, Pol. Dept., Chamber Section, 11, 1/12 of 1945–6; circular from chancellor dated 11 Dec. 1945, *ibid.*, 97, 4/71 of 1945–6; note by Corfield dated 24 Oct. 1945, Sir Sultan Ahmad to Herbert 5 Jan. 1946, and Corfield to Bhopal 26 Jan. 1946, IOR R/1/1/4327.

and Chattisgarh chiefs' conference at Raipur in December 1946, that the push for a regional union was no further advanced than it had been a year previously, the British resident opined feelingly that 'what was urgently needed was to get something going'.[3] His nominal superior, the governor of Orissa, agreed, but added morosely: 'there has been very little sense of urgency on the part of the Rulers [of whom most] . . . still live in a . . . semi-feudal atmosphere and seem to think that they can continue more or less in this state'.[4] It was no different in central India, where only a handful of rulers bothered to congregate in Indore in April 1947 to discuss the energetic maharaja of Dewas Junior's plan for a 'Madhya Bharat Central India States Conference'.[5]

Again, the tempo of *darbari* administrative rationalization and constitutional reform which, under chancellor Hamidullah's energetic prompting, had picked up considerably since 1945, showed signs of flagging. On the administrative front, Hamidullah had challenged his members in March 1946 to lift their spending on agricultural research, health, education and other community services to match what was being done in the neighbouring province.[6] Although the target was a modest one (the most parsimonious province spent a mere 12.01 per cent of its budget on 'beneficent' undertakings), the following year saw, if anything, a widening of the gap. What is more, it seemed to many outside observers that, where spending on public works did increase, the extra funds were often wasted on extravagant and high-profile projects designed more to reflect well of the *darbar* than improve the lot of the subjects. Visiting Srinagar, Wavell was asked to open a new hospital, advertised by his hosts as a showcase of Kashmir's modernization; but on closer examination the hospital turned out to be

a very complete piece of camouflage; it was unfinished and would not take patients for many months; but a complete staff of doctors, nurses, orderlies, etc. had been assembled, the finished wards were complete with beds, blankets, flowers and every detail; instruments, X-ray apparatus, operating tables and so on had been installed in their proper places; the dispensaries had an entire stock of medicines; even the offices were full of stationery, ash-trays etc, as if in use. Next day I suppose it was all moved back to the other hospitals from which it had been taken.[7]

[3] Minutes of 7th Rulers Conference (Eastern States), Raipur, 21/22 Dec. 1946, IOR R/1/1/4611.
[4] Sir C. Trivedi, gov. Orissa, to Sir John Colville, acting viceroy, 28 May 1947, IOR R/3/1/136.
[5] Proc's of General Conf. of Rulers and Reps. at Indore, 17 Apr. 1947, BRO, Bhopal, Pol. Dept., Special Branch, 98, 51/S.B./47.
[6] Statement by chancellor at General Conference of Rulers and Ministers, 10 Mar. 1946, MPSA, Indore, Foreign Dept., 643 of 1940.
[7] Moon, *Wavell*, 177 (diary entry for 17 Oct. 1945).

Similar criticisms were made of Mirza Ismail's vaunted programme of public works in Jaipur, which had turned the capital city into a showpiece but had done little for the majority of people living in the villages.

As for constitutional reform, the period 1945–7 saw a quite unprecedented flurry of activity: but here again, a good deal of what passed for reform was really 'window-dressing', designed to appease nationalist opinion in British India, or, in the case of the reforms announced in late 1945 by the thakore of Lakhtar on behalf of the Kathiawar non-salute states group, to stave off the threat of attachment.[8] Moreover, while a few *darbars* daringly embraced dyarchy (a stage of constitutional advancement which the provinces had outgrown over a decade earlier) hardly any were prepared to go further. Indeed, as of December 1946, the Chamber was still pushing the line that constitutional change should reflect 'the composite character of the Society and the main elements in the life of each State', and that representation based on 'numbers' was to be avoided.[9] This, of course, put the *darbars* on course for a showdown with the AISPC and state branches of the Congress, which were committed to the goal of responsible government based on adult suffidge; and in several states agitation became quite violent, sparking reprisals in kind from the authorities. In the Alleppy district of Travancore, for instance, the *dewan*'s announcement in October 1946, at a time of heightened tensions due to high food prices and the return of cashiered ex-INA soldiers, that responsible government of the English type was 'not contemplated', touched off what the *Free Press Journal* of Bombay described not inaptly as an 'undeclared war' between *darbari* police and around 8,000 coir workers armed with sticks, knives and spears. In two bloody clashes, at Vayalar and Punnapra, at least 200 and possibly as many as 2,000 agitators were shot. Elsewhere, as in Faridkot, police battled organised *jathas* of demonstrators bused in from British India by the AISPC. At a time when the rulers desperately needed firm friends – particularly among their own subjects – such excesses were politically suicidal.

The story of the last days of princely India is then, at one level, a sad tale of squandered chances and lost opportunities. However in the short run it was not so much conservatism and timidity which wrecked the monarchi-

---

[8] Consul Bombay to sec. state Washington 7 Aug. 1945, US State Dept. decimal file 845.00/8–745. The Americans were even suspicious of the outwardly quite liberal reforms introduced in Travancore by Sir C. P Ramaswamy Aiyer in January 1946, likening them to 'an artfully arranged cloak to give a dictatorship the appearance of a democracy'. Consul Madras to sec. state Washington 23 Jan. 1946, US State Dept. decimal file 845.00/1–2346.

[9] Circular letter from D. R. Rutnam, sec. to chancellor 21 Dec. 1946, BRO, Bhopal, Pol. Dept., War, 362/395 of 1946; and interim report of COMs appointed to advise the Bikaner Committee on Standards of Administration dated 1 Feb. 1945, IOR R/1/1/4258.

cal cause as the failure of the rulers to stick together. As both the chancellor and his British patrons realised, group loyalty and unity of purpose was essential if the princes hoped to broker a reasonable settlement with the nationalist centre. 'It is most important', opined the political secretary in a cable to the resident in Kashmir, 'that at this critical stage the states should maintain a common front for the purpose of negotiating with British India in the Constituent Assembly. If this is not secured the communal wedge will be driven into the Princes' ranks with disastrous results.'[10] The chancellor put it more bluntly: 'we must', he told his members, 'hold together'.[11] But the message failed to register. By the spring of 1947 the princely order had to all practical purposes disintegrated, leaving all but perhaps the very biggest states exposed and vulnerable to the assaults of their opponents.

Schism

The first significant gap to emerge within the monarchical order was between the rulers of large and small states. This was of course not a new phenomenon. But it grew much more pronounced during the closing years of the colonial period as it became clear that there was going to be room for only a minority of the states in the new India. AISPC policy, which by this stage had the general support of Congress, was that membership of the Indian union should be restricted to states with populations of at least 1 million and incomes of at least Rs ½ a million; which translated into a raw total of twenty-one. On the other hand Nehru's own view, with which Conrad Corfield, interestingly, concurred, was that only about a dozen states had 'inherent survival value'.[12] Needless to say, this notion of inherent viability was a bitter pill for the small states, and they disputed it hotly. The real issue, protested Sangli, who prided himself on presiding over a state with a 'level of administration corresponding to that in the neighbouring British [Indian] districts', was 'not size but efficiency'.[13] The correct measure of the 'survival value of a state', added Bilaspur, lay not in its power but in its 'geography and history'.[14] Yet for precisely opposite reasons it went down well with the big states, who believed their future assured. In talks with the Cabinet

[10] Polindia to resdt. Kashmir 11 Dec. 1946, R/3/1/112.
[11] Circular from chancellor 31 Dec. 1946, BRO, Bhopal, Pol. Dept., Special Branch, 78, 30/SB/46.
[12] Note by Corfield on interview with Nehru dated 27 Apr. 1947, *TOP*, X, 463.
[13] Sangli to Sir P. Cadell 10 June 1944, IOR R/1/1/4136.
[14] Note on discussions between the CD, the viceroy and the rulers of Dungapur and Bilaspur, dated 4 Apr. 1946, *TOP*, VII, 128.

Mission, Sir C. P. Ramaswamy Aiyer caused raised eyebrows by suggesting, on behalf of Travancore, Cochin, Gwalior and Bikaner, that only
twenty to twenty-five states were entitled to individual membership in
the proposed Indian dominion; and Wavell got a similar serve from the
nizam. The only states which should be allowed to survive, averred
Osman Ali, were those 'capable of standing on their own legs'.[15] In the
Darwinian universe of post-war India, the more powerful princes not
only saw a political advantage in standing apart from the rest, but
worried that an uncompromising stand by the Chamber or the COMs in
support of the right of the whole order to survive might damage their
own chances.

Monarchical solidarity was also eroded by linguistic and religious
communalism. As already remarked in chapter 4, the states between the
wars had remained comparatively free of the ethnic-related violence
which by this stage was becoming endemic in British India – partly, it is
true, because the states were mostly situated in regions well away from the
major centres of Hindu–Muslim conflict, but also because the *darbars*, by
and large, were run by outsiders who had no natural ties with the local
communities. In the 1940s, however, as the barriers which had kept the
two Indias partially insulated from one another since the Mutiny finally
crumbled, this syncretic *darbari* political culture began to wane. To be
sure, in some cases the old values were given up grudgingly under pressure from unruly, extremist groups of subjects such as those belonging to
the Ittihad-ul-Muslimeen in Hyderabad, which in March 1946 hastened
the departure of the moderate and urbane nawab of Chhatari from the
premiership by burning down his house and attacking him with 'sticks
and stones'[16] and in 1947 forced the nizam to sack his successor, Mirza
Ismail, or the Rashtriya Swayamsevak Sangh (RSS), which by the mid-
forties had gained a substantial foothold in several of the states of north

---

[15] Moon, *Wavell*, 241 (diary entry for 9 Apr. 1946); note on discussions between the CD, the
viceroy and Ramaswamy Aiyer dated 9 Apr. 1946, *TOP*, VII, 185; and Hyderabad to
Wavell 13 May 1946, *TOP*, VII, 543. Sir C. P.'s views echoed those of a ministers' committee chaired by D. K. Sen, which recommended in July 1946 that 'to qualify for adherence at Union level, a unit should have revenue of about Rs.1 crore, a population
sufficient at least to warrant one seat in the Union legislature, and should have implemented all reforms suggested in the Chancellor's declaration at the last session of the
Chamber of Princes'. Report of the Special Ministers Committee On Grouping, 31 July
1946, BRO, Bhopal, Pol. Dept., Special Branch, 78, 30/S.B./46.

[16] The house belonging to the Revenue and Police Member, Grigson, was also destroyed.
The pretext for the riot of 15 March was the government's decision to issue a permit for
the demolition of a mosque. Memo. by vice-consul Louise Schaffner, encl. in consul
Madras to sec. state Washington 6 Apr. 1946, US State Dept. decimal file 845.00/4–646.
The nizam deplored the incident but accepted that Chhatari by his misjudgement had
'lost his prestige . . . inside and outside the country. . . . He will retire either in June or
September'. Nizam to Sir Sultan Ahmed 25 Mar. 1946, Mirza Ismail Papers.

India.[17] For example, we have evidence that in early 1947 the maharaja of Faridkot was subjected to strong coercion from the Akali leadership to take a more active role in the Sikh political movement;[18] and it is probable that behind-the-scenes lobbying from politicians connected with the push for a unified Kannada-speaking province was the major factor in Jamkhandi's and Ramdurg's decision to withdraw from the Deccan confederation on the eve of its establishment in July. But for the most part the *darbars* needed no prompting. The rulers and their ministers may have preferred, all things being equal, to follow tolerant policies from the standpoint of administrative convenience, but they were still, at heart, Sikhs, Muslims, Rajputs and Marathas. Like most other Indians at the time, they found it difficult to resist the primordial appeal of ethnicity at a time when masses of people were killing and dying in its name. Sir C. P. Ramaswamy Aiyer had always seemed, to the British at least, the acme of a civilised statesman; yet by 1946 he was writing to an American acquaintance: 'Personally, I prefer civil war to [the establishment of] Pakistan and hold that to prevent secession such a civil war may become unfortunately inevitable as it was in the case of the U.S.A.'[19] Similar sentiments were aired by the gaekwar and Scindia – already well known as donors to the Mahasabha.[20]

However, perhaps the single most important transformation of these formative years took place on the Muslim side, in the mind of the nawab of Bhopal. As we have seen, Hamidullah had long been close to Jinnah and the Muslim League; but after the breakdown of negotiations between the parties over the proper interpretation of the Cabinet Mission statement – a breakdown that Bhopal, like most Muslims, attributed squarely to the intransigence and desire for aggrandisement of the Congress leadership – he grew steadily more strident and public in his support for the Muslim cause, to the point where he began to talk openly of abdicating the throne and devoting the remainder of his life to saving his co-religionists from political 'annihilation'.[21] Moreover while Bhopal had once seen the Chamber, and the princely order for which it spoke, as a bulwark against Congress domination, he now began to wonder whether, in the

[17] On RSS activities in Bhopal see P. A. Bhopal to nawab of Bhopal 19 June 1943, BRO, Bhopal, Pol. Dept., 35, 2/4, 1943; and J. F. Conlon, I.-G. Police to Major T. Davy, P. S. Nawab 10 Feb. 1948, BRO, Bhopal, Pol. Dept., 126, 2/21, 1947.
[18] Sir Evan Jenkins, gov. of Punjab, to Mountbatten 9 Apr. 1947, *TOP*, X, 173.
[19] Aiyer to Mrs Marley 20 Dec. 1945, encl. in consul-gen. Bombay to sec. state Washington 20 Jan. 1946, US State Dept. decimal file 845.00/1–2046.
[20] Memo. by Kanji Dwarkadas dated 28 Jan. 1945, encl. in consul-gen. Bombay to sec. state Washington 10 Apr. 1947, US State Dept. decimal file 845.00/4–1047. See also, in this context, the raja of Aundh's passionate plea for a ban on cow-slaughter in his letter to Patel of 14 Nov. 1947, *PC*, V, 468.   [21] Bhopal to Wavell 17 Aug. 1946, IOR R/3/1/143.

light of London's continued hedging on the issue of future relations with the states and the increasingly communal orientation of many of the Hindu princes, there was much purpose to be served in trying to keep the states together. At one of his lowest moments, in late November 1946, he wrote to Corfield:

I am unhappy about everything in this country. The British seem to have abdicated power and what is worse they have handed it over . . . to the enemies of all their friends . . . I look upon it as one of the greatest, if not the greatest, tragedies that has ever befallen mankind, and I find it difficult to overcome the shock. The States, the Moslems, and the entire mass of people who relied on British justice, and their sense of fair play, suddenly find themselves totally helpless, unorganised and unsupported . . . What should a Prince, who has some life, honour and ambition left in him, do in such circumstances? . . . I am tired of leading a team who have neither the will nor the desire to survive. I am tired of intrigue, calumny and communal feelings of the worst type. I want to resign the Chancellorship . . . I want to die in the cause of the Moslems of the world . . . The Princes betrayed by the British are already a lost cause and I feel I am wasting my energies . . . in trying to protect their case. I am a Moslem in a crowd of Hindu Princes, who suspect me all round, who are blind to their own interests and who are at the moment only guided by one desire . . . namely . . . to kill, destroy . . . and wipe off the Moslems from the face of the earth. I am a complete misfit in this crowd and I am sure my place lies somewhere else.[22]

Somewhat against his better judgement, Hamidullah was persuaded by Corfield to stay on; but relations between the chancellor and his Standing Committee continued to cool to the point where the Committee felt obliged to complain about his behaviour. This, in turn, prompted Bhopal to raise – unsuccessfully – with Corfield the 'question of keeping [official] correspondence between [the] Crown Representative and himself secret' from his colleagues.[23] As late as January 1947 the monarchical order remained outwardly united, but just below the surface communal tension boiled. When he visited Rampur at the end of the month, Francis Wylie learned from the nawab's lips what he already suspected, namely that the princes were 'dividing off into communal groups'.[24] Even before the terms of the states' entry into the Constituent Assembly had been decided, knowledgeable observers were predicting that their representatives would vote along religious lines.[25]

However the wedge which eventually split the princely camp asunder was not class, nor ethnicity as such, but ideology. For decades the

---

[22] Bhopal to Corfield 23 Nov. 1946, *TOP*, IX, 156–7.
[23] Corfield to Abell 10 Feb. 1947, IOR R/3/1/112.
[24] Wylie to Wavell 7 Feb. 1947, *TOP*, IX, 640.
[25] Consul-gen. Bombay to sec. state Washington 8 Nov. 1946, reporting an interview with Sir C. P. Ramaswamy Aiyer on 3 Nov., US State Dept. decimal file 845.00/11–846.

rulers had actively opposed the spread of democracy, at least in application to their own states; they had vigorously championed the imperial
connection; and they had stood shoulder to shoulder with their British
patrons in resisting the political claims of the Congress. Now, as the
British departure drew near, some of them began to change their tune.
'We the princes', wrote Sadul Singh of Bikaner, 'should [conduct] ourselves as true, patriotic and worthy sons of India . . . Let [us] . . . rise to
the occasion, to be hailed as co-architects of the structure of India's
independence and greatness.'[26] Inaugurating his state's first-ever legislative council, the raja of Jawhar declared: 'we are all patriots inspired
and striving for the glory of a united India'.[27] What is more, these
nationalistic statements were accompanied in several cases by real dialogue. During 1946–7, Eastern States rulers had meetings with Orissan
premier Harekrishna Mahtab;[28] Mayurdhwaj Sinhji of Dhrangadhra
kept 'in close and clandestine touch and frequent consultation' with
Kathiawari leaders such as Durbar Gopaldas and U. N. Dhebar,[29]
Mirza conspired with the non-Brahmin politicians of Berar; Zaidi of
Rampur consulted regularly with ministers in the government of the
UP; and the Deccan rulers sought Gandhi's approval for their planned
merger.

There were many reasons for this *volte face* and, obviously, the imminent withdrawal of imperial protection was a major one. Although the
princely states were not exactly helpless – even a moderately small state
like Junagadh had in 1947 about 2,400 men under arms, while at the top
end of the scale Hyderabad could put a full division into the field – they
were clearly no match, even collectively, for the mechanised might of the
Indian Army. As Nehru smugly observed at a press conference in July
1946, for any 'local army' to prevail against the 'rest of India' was a 'physical impossibility'.[30] Moreover, given that virtually all the states were
completely surrounded by Indian territory and that many of them, like
Mysore and Bikaner, were dependent upon the neighbouring provinces
for food and water for irrigation, they were clearly vulnerable to economic

---

[26] Note by Bikaner dated 2 Apr. 1947, quoted in the *Free Press Journal*, 3 Apr. 1947. In
Sadul Singh's case, this was no last-minute conversion; he had been saying similar things
for the previous two years. When Mountbatten visited Bikaner as supreme commander
SEA in April 1945 he found the maharaja's 'views on the future of India as reasonable as
any ruling prince could be expected to express'. Zeigler, *Diary*, 201 (entry for 13 Apr.
1945).   [27] Speech of 18 May 1947, quoted in the *Times of India*, 19 May 1947.
[28] To the anguish of AISPC president, Pattabhi Sitaramayya, Mahtab offered several of the
leading rulers posts in his cabinet as an incentive for them to merge their states with his
province. Sitaramayya to Mahtab 21 July 1947, AISPC, file 129, Part I of 1948.
[29] Dhrangadhra to Hariprasad Shastri 28 Feb. 1983 (letter supplied to the author by H. H.
of Dhrangadhra).   [30] Press conference, Bombay, 10 July 1946, *TOP*, VIII, 30.

blockade. The Congress leaders knew this[31] – and so did the *darbars*. 'The princes are fighting a losing battle', reported the American consul in Bombay, 'and most of them realize it.'[32] With the odds stacked against them, the majority of rulers decided that appeasement was the better part of valour.

In addition, the rulers were influenced by tactical considerations. Most understood that if they were going to salvage anything from the past, they would need friends in the new administration. In the absence of the Muslim League, which looked increasingly bent on building its own empire in Pakistan, that meant making peace with the old foe the Congress Party, which, committed as it was to secularism, at least seemed to have 'the potential to extend itself beyond communities'[33] – an important selling-point for the Sikh princes and Muslim rulers like Rampur who were tied to Hindustan by the bonds of geography. And it was also clear to most princes that by remaining aloof from developments at the centre, they risked having the Congress impose a constitutional settlement on them, whereas, if they swallowed their pride and entered the Constituent Assembly on terms satisfactory to the Congress, they would get a say – perhaps a crucial say – in framing the constitution. Again, some *darbars* were swayed by the mounting tide of communal and class war which threatened to consume the states as it was already consuming the provinces. Irritated by Hamidullah's apparent procrastination, the dewan of Baroda protested to the chancellor: 'Times is pressing, and the delay in settling the constitution is strengthening the elements in the Country – Communists and others – who are determined that there should be disorder. It is high time that the constructive elements . . . came together to fight these forces.'[34] Bikaner's Sadul Singh felt the same. 'States like Travancore and Mysore, placed as they are far from the centre of communal tension, can perhaps afford to go slow', he opined in a letter to the viceroy. 'With us in Rajputana, the Punjab and Central India, the matter is immediate [because] . . . any weakening of the central authority will involve us in chaos.'[35] Compared to the prospect of mob rule, a strong Congress-dominated centre seemed much the lesser of two evils.

However not all the rulers who beat a path to the Congress door did so entirely out of self-interest. If the princely order contained its share of

---

[31] See, for example, Krishna Menon to Nehru 13 Mar. 1947, *TOP*, IX, 950.

[32] Consul Bombay to sec. state Washington 11 Feb. 1945, US State Dept. decimal file 845.00/2–1145.

[33] Note of interview between Mountbatten and Bikaner 24 Mar. 1947, *TOP*, X, 11.

[34] Krishnamachari to Bhopal, 14 Apr. 1947, *TOP*, X, 241.

[35] Bikaner to Mountbatten 3 Apr. 1947, *TOP*, X, 110. See also note of interview between Mountbatten and Panikkar 5 May 1947, *TOP*, X, 624; editorial in the *Hindustan Times*, 6 Dec. 1947; and Alan Campbell-Johnson, *Mission with Mountbatten* (London, 1951), 38.

debauched reactionaries, it also housed a sprinkling of genuine liberals such as Dhrangadhra, Apa Pant of Aundh, Harish Chandra of Jhalawar and the jazz-playing Raza Ali Khan of Rampur; these men welcomed a closer association with the new Indian dominion because they believed that that was what their subjects wanted and because they believed, with the Congress, that a unified India would be strong and prosperous. Meanwhile, other rulers, instinctively more cautious in their outlook, were gently prodded and guided in the same direction by nationalist-leaning ministers such as Panikkar at Bikaner and former Advocate-General B. L. Mitter who in January 1945 took over the helm at Baroda in succession to Sir V. T. Krishnamachari.[36]

To repeat: hoping to preserve something of the monarchical order and to secure for themselves an honourable place in the new India, a minority of rulers began to contemplate a deal with the Congress. Yet one thing held them back: their fear of Jawaharlal Nehru's rampant republicanism. If Nehru truly spoke for Congress, the princely states faced an uncertain future and their rulers no future at all. How could they bargain, if there was no readiness on the other side to compromise?

Throughout 1945 and the first half of 1946 the Congress kept up its traditional hard line and the prospects of a *rapprochement* with the *darbars* started to look bleak. But then, quite suddenly, the rhetoric changed. It may have been the restraining effect of the Congress' entry into government in September, or the prospect of an early transfer of power signalled by Attlee's statement of 20 February 1947 (of which more later), or the high command's anxiety to distance itself from the communists and socialists,[37] or just the Congress bosses' belated realisation that quiet diplomacy could serve them better than threats, but by the winter of

---

[36] In *The Basis of an Indo-British Treaty*, published in 1946, Panikkar argued for a 'strong, well-organised, industrially advanced India' which could stand up for itself in international affairs. See the *Modern Review*, Dec. 1946, 489. Interestingly, the sagacious Ganga Singh had predicted something like this outcome years before: 'the young rulers are impatient', he had warned in 1941. '[They] . . . may decide to make their own bargain with the Congress – if only to preserve their own existence.' Bikaner to Churchill 9/10 Nov. 1941, IOR L/P&S/13/789.

[37] On the CPI policy towards the states, which was basically to expunge them root and branch, see the party's memorandum for the CD dated 15 Apr. 1946, US State Dept. decimal file 845.00/4–1846. The Socialist Party, previously known as the CSP, favoured a similar policy; indeed one of the main reasons they had severed their ties with the Congress was their displeasure at its inaction on the states front. See T. B. Creagh-Coen to H. J. Todd, resdt. Eastern States, 26 Mar. 1947, IOR R/1/1/4623. Conversely the Congress right was paranoid about socialist infiltration in the states, K. M. Munshi alleging in June 1946 that 'Communists were responsible for a good deal of the trouble in Kashmir.' Consul-gen. Bombay to sec. state Washington 26 June 1946, reporting conversation with Munshi by Col. Hennesey of British Military Intelligence on 25 June, US State Dept. decimal file 845.00/6–2646.

1947–8, even Nehru was talking of the need for an amicable settlement which reflected the will of the states' subjects. Moving the objectives resolution in the Constituent Assembly he declared, rather to the consternation of some of the other delegates: 'I do not wish . . . to impose anything on the States against their will. If the people of a particular State desire to have a certain form of government, even though it might be monarchical, it is open to them to have it.'[38] A few weeks later the WC made this commitment official, adding, by way of explanation, that it seemed to them important 'in considering the problem of the States . . . to give up the abstract theoretical point of view and consider the problem from the slippery ground of practical politics'.[39]

Nevertheless, there was nothing inevitable about the crisis which overtook the princely order in February 1947; if more tact and farsightedness had been exhibited by the chancellor and his conservative friends on the Standing Committee it could easily have been averted. Instead, Hamidullah succumbed to his prejudices. Determined to keep control, he treated the dissidents as traitors to the monarchical order, and attempted to forbid their entry to the Constituent Assembly. This forced the nationalist princes into the open, and effectively pushed them into the waiting arms of the Congress.

It happened like this. As we have seen, Bhopal had a plan which he believed would secure the preservation of the princely states within the constitutional framework of independent India: but its success hinged on the states' ninety-three representatives holding the balance of power in a single Constituent Assembly; and this in turn depended on the states remaining united and agreed on a common set of demands, and on the League abandoning its dream of Pakistan and entering the Assembly. Faced with growing signs of restlessness within the Chamber, and worried that he might soon no longer be in a position to control events, Bhopal summoned a general meeting of princes and ministers at Delhi on 28 January and put to them a bold if utopian scheme for a confederation of states to be called 'Rajasthan'. The idea – which may have come from

---

[38] Speech of 13 Dec. 1946, BRO, Bhopal, Pol. Dept., Special Branch, 75, 28/SB/46. Former Kashmir Dewan Gopalaswamy Aiyengar was among those taken aback by Nehru's remarks.
[39] Press release from Shankerrao Deo, Congress gen. sec., encl. in consul-gen. Bombay to sec. state Washington, US State Dept. decimal file 845.00/1–747. The tenor of the AISPC's statements reflected this new line, striking the American ambassador as 'noticeably more moderate' than those of a year before. Ambassador New Delhi to sec. state Washington 24 Feb. 1947, US State Dept. decimal file 845.00/2–2447. Another interested observer, Corfield, was also impressed with the change. Meeting Nehru in April 1947 after an interval of many months, he found him 'much more receptive than during my last interview with him'. Note dated 27 Apr., *TOP*, X, 461.

Sir Sultan Ahmad – did not, however, find much favour among the delegates. On the opening day of the conference Panikkar accused Hamidullah of proposing a 'vivisection of Hindu power', and on the second day Ramaswamy Aiyer effectively killed further discussion by announcing that even if the confederation was formed Travancore would never agree to be a part of it.[40] With this stinging rebuff, one arch in Hamidullah's grand design collapsed in ruins. Then, barely twenty-four hours later, on 31 January, the Muslim League destroyed another span by reaffirming its earlier decision to stay out of the Constituent Assembly. As February dawned, Bhopal confronted the daunting prospect of having to lead a rebellious and bickering team in talks designed to smooth the way for the states' participation in a constitution-making forum, which, in the absence of the League, he no longer regarded as legitimate.

Yet his resolve did not break. Convinced (probably rightly) that he still spoke for the majority of the princes, Hamidullah came up with a plan to sabotage the talks with the Assembly in a way which would make it look as if the Congress was actually the intransigent party. On 29 January, the last scheduled day of the Delhi conclave, he moved that the states' entry should be subject to the prior acceptance by the Assembly negotiating committee of certain *sine qua nons*, namely the preservation of the system of monarchy, right of secession if India became a republic, and recognition of all existing state boundaries. Only the first of these had so far been tentatively accepted by the Congress, and then with much heartburning, while the Assembly had already voted in principle for a republic – a decision which Sir Sultan Ahmad had warned would 'make it difficult for the Princes to negotiate' with it.[41] Bhopal was confident that the rest would be turned down flat, thereby precipitating a deadlock for which the rulers could not be held responsible. Realising what the chancellor was up to, the opposing faction protested vehemently: 'if you adopt this resolution', fumed the dewan of Udaipur, 'it will be your own death warrant'.[42] This time, however, the rebels found themselves in a minority. Hamidullah made one of the most impassioned yet reasoned speeches of his chancellorship, and he received vigorous support from the influential Ramaswamy Aiyer, who, if he had little else in common with Bhopal, fully

---

[40] Panikkar, *Autobiography*, 149–50. Afterwards, Panikkar opined to Mountbatten's aide Alan Campbell-Johnson that the chancellor seemed to be 'trying to enunciate a new doctrine of paramountcy – namely that no action should be taken by States individually, but only in concert, with approval of the Chamber of Princes'. Campbell-Johnson, *Mission*, 38.

[41] Moon, *Wavell*, 412 (diary entry for 21 Jan. 1947). Apparently when Sir Sultan told Nehru this, the Congress leader blew up and said he 'did not care a damn for the Princes' – thereby confirming Bhopal's deepest suspicions.

[42] Quoted in Panikkar, *Autobiography*, 154.

shared his determination to keep the states out of the clutches of the Congress. The resolution was carried. Congress sources that K. M. Panikkar spoke to afterwards told him they thought the princes had thrown in their lot with the League.[43]

Staring in the face of disaster, the dissidents hastened to reassure the Congress leaders. That evening Sadul Singh of Bikaner, Yadavindra Singh of Patiala, and the dewans of Jodhpur, Jaipur, Udaipur, Gwalior, Patiala, Rewa and Bikaner met with Nehru, Congress president Maulana Azad and Nehru's main states' adviser Gopalaswamy Aiyengar over dinner at Bikaner's Delhi residence. The following day Panikkar and V. T. Krishnamachari had further informal discussions with Aiyengar and Vallabhbhai Patel. The dissidents reiterated their determination to enter the Constituent Assembly and declared that they would not be bound by Bhopal's list of *sine qua nons*; in reply, the Congress leaders affirmed their in-principle commitment to the monarchical system, Nehru adding earnestly that, whatever happened, 'he would try to adjust matters so as to avoid harming the Princes or their families'.[44] Yet motes of suspicion lingered; and when the two negotiating committees met officially on 8 February it was Bhopal who seized the initiative, insisting that before the talks could proceed, the Assembly would have to accept the terms enshrined in the princes' resolution. It now seemed certain that the talks would collapse and that the implacable Bhopal would, once again, carry the day.[45] It was at this crucial juncture that the astute Krishnamachari came up with a plan, which he unfolded over dinner that evening at Bikaner House to Bikaner, Patiala, Nehru and Patel, to outmanoeuvre the chancellor.[46]

The ruse depended on clockwork timing; it could have easily backfired. But in the event the co-conspirators all played their parts perfectly. When, the following morning, the two committees met to resume their negotiations, Bhopal sought to drive home his advantage by urging a suspension of the talks pending agreement on the 'fundamental propositions' listed in the resolution of 31 January. However, before the nawab was able to distil this proposition into a formal motion, Patiala's voice cut across the

---

[43] Panikkar to Major Woodrow Wyatt 15 Feb. 1947, *TOP*, IX, 724. 'It was clear to me', added Panikkar, 'that what was intended was to put the blame on the British Indian leaders.'

[44] Panikkar, *Autobiography*, 155; and ambassador New Delhi to sec. state Washington 24 Feb. 1947, reporting conversation between the second sec. of the embassy and Hardit Singh Malik, PM of Patiala on 20 Feb., US State Dept. decimal file 845.00/2–2447.

[45] Bikaner to Mountbatten 3 Apr. 1947, *TOP*, X, 109.

[46] Afterwards the Baroda minister Brojendralal Mitter claimed most of the credit for what transpired. Press statement, 14 Feb. 1947, quoted in *The Times*, 15 Feb. 1947. But he was, at most, a minor intermediary.

chancellor's. Would it help to clarify matters, he asked innocently, if they heard from the other committee 'a brief resume of the position as it [had] emerged the previous day'? As arranged, Nehru at once launched into a set-piece speech in which he disposed, at length and with meticulous patience, of the major objections raised by Hamidullah. When he was finished there was a short silence. The atmosphere was electric. Then Yadavindra Singh thumped the table and looking belligerently at Bhopal, exclaimed: 'What more assurances do we want?' There was a general murmur of agreement. Hamidullah glowered but said nothing. The old fox had run out of arguments. Without further ado, the meeting proceeded to the detailed business of working out arrangements for filling the ninety-three states seats in the Constituent Assembly.[47]

When Wavell received Bhopal a week or so later the nawab was still smarting from his defeat in Delhi. Patiala and the major Rajputana states, he grumbled to the viceroy, all seemed 'now definitely to have gone over to the Congress side'.[48] But Hamidullah's fit of depression did not last very long. For one thing he was too doughty and seasoned a campaigner to be thrown off his game for long by one tactical setback; for another, Maqbool soon had better news to report.

We have already made passing reference to Clement Attlee's historic announcement of 20 February 1947 setting a firm date for the transfer of power. While not meant to apply to the states, the pronouncement's studied ambiguity on the issue of how, and to whom, power was actually going to be devolved, implanted hope in the minds of princes like Bhopal that the British government was rethinking its opposition to the idea of a states dominion; and in the meantime provided the die-hard faction with what Sadul Singh angrily described as a 'handle to try to delay matters' on the plea that 'a new situation had been created'.[49] Secondly, Bhopal's position was bolstered by the deliberately distorted interpretation put on the above events by the political department. According to Corfield there was simply 'no split' among the rulers. The Delhi meetings had been notably fruitful and friendly.[50] Crude though it was, this propaganda

---

[47] Panikkar, *Autobiography*, 157; Panikkar to Major Woodrow Wyatt 15 Feb. 1947, *TOP*, IX, 725–6; 'Summary of Proceedings of the Meeting of the States NC With the NC Appointed by the Constituent Assembly', 9 Feb. 1947, BRO, Bhopal, Pol. Dept., Special Branch, 78, 30/SB/46. According to Panikkar, Patiala had with him a letter of resignation from the Chamber which he planned to produce if negotiations broke down.

[48] Note by Wavell on interview with Bhopal dated 3 Mar. 1947, *TOP*, IX, 834.

[49] Bikaner to Mountbatten 3 Apr. 1947, *TOP*, X, 109. Incidentally, the notion that a 'new situation' in regard to the states had been created by Attlee's statement was shared by Wavell. See Wavell to Pethick-Lawrence 5 Mar. 1947, *TOP*, IX, 856.

[50] Statement given to the American Embassy on 23 Feb. Ambassador New Delhi to sec. state Washington 24 Feb. 1947, US State Dept. decimal file 845.00/2–2447.

caused a number of smaller, less well-informed states, which had been conjuring with the idea of going over to the rebel camp, to reexamine their position. Thirdly, whatever damage the events at Delhi may have done to Bhopal's reputation as a leader was to a large extent offset by his success at subsequent meetings of the negotiating committees in wringing substantial concessions from the Congress side as regards the procedure for selecting the states' representatives. The Assembly team began by demanding that a minimum of two-thirds of their ninety-three delegates be directly elected; in the end they were prevailed upon to accept a minimum of half, on the understanding that the *darbars* would 'endeavour to see that not less than 50' delegates were so returned.[51] Last but not least the conservative cause was helped, unwittingly, by Nehru. Addressing an AISPC gathering at Gwalior on 19 April he accused the rulers of having a 'shop-keeper mentality' and declared that any state which refused to enter the Constituent Assembly would be treated as 'hostile'. Upbraided by the viceroy for this unstatesmanlike outburst, Nehru explained that it had been inspired by the need to conciliate a restless audience, and there seems to have been some truth in this; nevertheless, whatever its motivation, the speech did great harm to the growing but still fragile relationship between the princes and the Congress.[52] Sensing an opportunity to make up lost ground, Hamidullah called the Chamber's constitutional advisory committee together and in the face of vehement objections from Sadul Singh got its permission to draft a motion, to be put to a general conference of princes at Bombay, authorising him as chairman of the states negotiating committee to suspend discussions with the Assembly until such time as the latter accepted the *sine qua nons* listed in the resolution of 29 January.

More than ever convinced of the justice of his cause, and as always supremely confident of his power to sway a crowd, it never for a moment occurred to Bhopal that the motion might not gain overwhelming support. Yet, no sooner had the Bombay conference opened, than the first symptoms of rebellion appeared. At a preliminary Standing Committee meeting on 1 April, Bikaner sat patiently but silently as a string of rulers –

---

[51] Circular letter from Chancellor dated 10 Mar. 1947, BRO, Bhopal, Pol. Dept., Special Branch, 74, 27/SB/46.

[52] *IAR*, 1947, I, 214–16; ambassador New Delhi to sec. state Washington 24 Apr. 1947, US State Dept. decimal file 845.00/4–2447; and note of interview between Nehru and Mountbatten, 22 Apr. 1947, *TOP*, X, 361. The purpose of the conference was to pass judgement on the arrangements worked out for the states entry to the CA. As we shall shall see, these represented a significant concession towards the princes' viewpoint. Even with Nehru's rhetoric behind it, a resolution endorsing the settlement barely passed. For some princely reactions see minutes of viceroy's 19th Staff Meeting, 21 Apr. 1947, *TOP*, X, 352.

Dungapur, Dholpur, Alwar and Nawanagar – indicated their support for the chancellor's motion; then, after about fifteen minutes, he rose and 'went quietly out of the room' and back to his suite where he penned two notes: one, very short, to Bhopal asking to be excused from further meetings of the Standing Committee; the other, much longer, to the assembled delegates imploring them to 'act in the larger interests of India' and warning them of the serious consequences that could follow from an impetuous decision to hold aloof from the Assembly.[53] Many were impressed by its arguments. Thus, by the time the conference proper commenced next morning, Sadul Singh's group had already gained a number of new adherents. Yet even then Bhopal might have prevailed if he had restricted himself to moving the Standing Committee's motion about *sine qua nons*. He didn't. Determined to make Bikaner pay for his trouble-making, he tacked on a second, linked resolution to the effect that no state should enter the Assembly until it had finished its initial work of drafting constitutions for the groups and the provinces – work which was expected to consume at least a further six months. As soon as this clearly mischievous motion was read out there was an uproar; and when it had subsided Bikaner announced, to a chorus of resounding cheers, that if the resolution was passed his state would ignore it and enter anyway. This gave Gwalior, a Bikaner sympathiser but also a firm believer in the virtue of princely unity, an opportunity to move an amendment to the motion, which was carried, that the question of entry to the Constituent Assembly should be a matter for the discretion of individual states.

Afterwards Bhopal assured the press that the conference had 'ended happily' and that there was 'no rift';[54] but the truth of the situation became plain to see a few weeks later when, on 28 April, delegates from Cochin, Patiala, Baroda, Jaipur, Rewa, Jodhpur and Bikaner took their seats in the Assembly. There may not have been a formal 'split', but with the public defection of these seven important states the princely order ceased to be, in any meaningful sense, united. As that veteran of so many princely quarrels, Udaibhan Singh of Dholpur sadly remarked to the viceroy, now 'two different views conspicuously mark the division of thought and action of the Order'.[55] What is more, its leadership had been fatally compromised. While the Congress' K. M. Munshi might have had an axe to grind, his observation that the conference 'marked an end to the

[53] Consul-gen. Bombay to sec. state Washington 7 Apr. 1947, US State Dept. decimal file 845.00/4–747; Bikaner to Mountbatten 3 Apr. 1947, *TOP*, X, 107; and minutes of SC meeting 1 Apr. 1947, BRO, Bhopal, Pol. Dept., Special Branch, 106, 61/SB/47. For the full text of Bikaner's note see the *Free Press Journal*, 3 Apr. 1947.
[54] Consul-gen. Bombay to sec. state Washington 7 Apr. 1947, US State Dept. decimal file 845.00/4–747.   [55] Dholpur to Mountbatten 20 July 1947, IOR R/3/1/138.

domination of the Nawab of Bhopal'[56] was a shrewd and, with hindsight, accurate one. Although Hamidullah tried valiantly to pretend that he was still in charge, his policy statements now rang hollow. At length, persuaded by Corfield that his duty henceforward lay in looking after the vital interests of his own state,[57] he resigned the chancellorship on 3 June.

As for the Chamber itself, it lingered on under the token leadership of Yadavindra Singh until 14 August; but after April it steadily lost members and prestige, and in June the Standing Committee started to wind down its operations and dispose of its assets. Nor, with one exception, which we shall hear about shortly, did it meet again as a body.

Yet, the schism which rent the princely order in the early months of 1947 did not of itself bring down the princes or spell an end to the states as political entities. On the contrary, the outlook for the states remained, throughout the autumn, quite hopeful. Those who had chosen to make their future within the bosom of the Indian union had the consolation of Nehru's statement, not so far disavowed, that the objectives resolution of December 1946 did not imply that the new government would seek to abolish the system of monarchy or tinker with state boundaries. And those who, like Bhopal and Travancore, were looking to make good their independence, took heart, first, from Attlee's reaffirmation in his statement of 20 February of the British government's commitment to the cabinet mission memorandum of May 1946, and second, from the news that Lord Louis Mountbatten would replace Wavell as viceroy in March. A man of royal blood, cousin no less to the king-emperor, already well known to the princes from his time as supreme commander SEA and counted a close personal friend by Bikaner, Bhopal and Rampur, Mountbatten appeared tailor-made to guide the states through a period of crisis. As Sadul Singh put it in a welcoming letter of 3 April, 'in Your Excellency we [believe we] have a real friend in whose hands the interests of the Princes . . . are safe, and who will see that justice is done to us'.[58] By August, though, most of the rulers were singing a different tune.

Accession

Mountbatten's instructions from Attlee enjoined him to help the princes make 'fair and just arrangements with the leaders of British India' with

[56] Consul-gen. Bombay to sec. state Washington 14 Apr. 1947, reporting conversation with Munshi on 12 Apr., US State Dept. decimal file 845.00/4–1447. On 9 June the Deccan states announced that they had chosen former MLA M. S. Aney to represent them in the Assembly; on 24 June Mysore sent delegates. By the end of July all but a handful of states, of which Bhopal and Hyderabad were the most notable, had joined.

[57] Note by Corfield dated [?] Mar. 1968, Corfield Coll., 4.

[58] Bikaner to Mountbatten 3 Apr. 1947, *TOP*, X, 107.

the object of facilitating the merger of the states with the provinces; and he was authorised, to this end, to 'enter into negotiations with individual States'.[59] Beyond this Mountbatten himself had a personal interest in the welfare of an order which he knew well from previous visits and which included, as we've seen, some of his oldest and closest friends. Indeed, if what he told Hamidullah later was true, one of the primary goals he set himself when he took on the top Indian job was to help to 'preserve constitutional monarchy as an institution' and to see that the states got as fair a deal as it was possible for him to arrange.[60] Last but not least, the king-emperor George VI, in a private interview granted just before his departure, bade him do his best for an order which, over the decades, had served his family faithfully and well. Thus, even before Mountbatten arrived in India, where he was briefed yet again by the outgoing viceroy, he was well aware that the disposition of the states and the fate of the monarchical system constituted a ticklish problem for the British government which would need to be resolved before power was transferred to Indian hands.

Nevertheless, once in office, he appeared to lose sight of the problem. Later, he blamed his political superiors, insisting that there 'had been no indication [when he talked to Attlee and Cripps] in London . . . of a need for urgency'[61] or, indeed, any sense of the political difficulties involved. 'I had been given no inkling', he wrote defensively at the end of his term, 'that this [states problem] was going to be as hard, if not harder to solve, as that of British India.'[62] Again, Mountbatten was prevented, in the first few months of his viceroyalty, from giving his full attention to the states by the overriding need to reach a settlement with the nationalists. Once he reached India and started negotiating with the political leaders, his whole energies became focussed, first on reconciling the Congress to what he quickly saw as the inevitability of partition, and then on devising a form of partition acceptable to the Muslim League. The question of the states seemed – as it was – a lesser priority. Also, the viceroy's apprehension of the problem of the states as it developed over the spring and early summer of 1947 was curtained to some extent by his cool personal relations with Corfield. His aristocratic lineage notwithstanding, viscount Mountbatten was a liberal, and found his top political adviser stuffy and narrow in his views; while Corfield was repelled by the viceroy's penchant for showmanship and obvious partiality for Nehru. Thus while their relations

[59] Attlee to Mountbatten 18 Mar. 1947, *TOP*, IX, 972–3.
[60] Mountbatten to Bhopal 16 May 1948, Mountbatten Coll., 27.
[61] Minutes of viceroy's meeting with States Neg. Cttee 3 June 1947, *TOP*, XI, 81.
[62] 'Report on the Last Viceroyalty', Sept. 1948, cited in R. J. Moore, *Escape From Empire: the Attlee Government and the Indian Problem* (Oxford, 1983), 290.

remained at all times correct, neither man made much effort to take the other into his confidence, with the result that much of what should have gone straight to the viceroy as regards the retraction of paramountcy, passed him by.

Probably the main factor, though, was Mountbatten's ego. Experienced in tackling large problems, totally convinced of his ability to handle them, aware that he enjoyed something of a special relationship with the princes, he pushed the issue of the states to the back of his mind, believing that once the future of the provinces had been decided there would be ample time to deal with it before the deadline expired. Of course this thinking was shaped in part by Attlee's leisurely timetable for a transfer of power by June 1948, which Mountbatten himself was soon to revise; but it also says a lot for his self-assurance. Never once did it occur to the viceroy that when the moment for action arrived, he would not be able to bend the rulers to his will.

So, for several months, Mountbatten procrastinated. Indeed as late as July 1947 – three-fifths of the way into his term – he was forced to admit that he had 'not been able to grip this States problem before'.[63] Of course he could not ignore it altogether, for, if nothing else, the rulers were persistent in their demands on his time – wanting answers to the questions which had been nagging them since the Cabinet Mission published its memorandum: if a states union was formed would it be offered dominion status; and did the British government intend to enter into bilateral relations with states that declined to join the Indian union? However, while Mountbatten quickly concluded that both options were wholly untenable, being, as he informed Sir Eric Mieville, sure to 'cause the disintegration of India',[64] he hesitated to express this view openly to the rulers and their ministers. More importantly still, Mountbatten failed to make public his increasing doubts about the Cabinet Mission line on paramountcy. His revised plan for devolution, which won the approval of London on 31 May and the acceptance of the Indian leaders on 3 June, closed off the option of provincial autonomy which had been offered by the Cabinet Mission, but it conspicuously left open the question of the states' relations with the new dominions. As the statement broadcast simultaneously by Attlee in England and Mountbatten in India brusquely noted, British policy toward the princely states remained 'unchanged'.[65]

---

[63] Personal report No.12 dated 11 July 1947, *TOP*, XII, 99.

[64] Abell to Mieville 20 May 1947, *TOP*, X, 922.

[65] Govt. of India, *White Paper on the Indian States* (New Delhi, 1950), p. 31. The statement read: 'His Majesty's Government wish to make it clear that the decisions announced above relate only to British India and that their policy towards the Indian States contained in the Cabinet Mission Memorandum of 12th May 1946 remains unchanged.'

Mountbatten's decision to put the problem of the states on the back burner while he dealt with the more urgent question of British India annoyed loyalist princes like Bhopal and Nawanagar who had expected to be consulted night and day by the viceroy's staff and instead found themselves having to make appointments; yet it was not without benefit to the *darbars*, for it not only gave them time to plan their own futures, but added to the freedom of manoeuvre of their most powerful governmental ally, Corfield. Throughout the winter, Corfield had been quietly campaigning for an early retraction of paramountcy as a means of confounding the territorial ambitions of the Congressite interim government. As he explained to Paul Patrick:

> It seems clear . . . that Nehru and the Congress Party do not accept [the] position as stated by [the] Cabinet Mission . . . memorandum. . . . [Failing a change of policy by the Congress, the] only equitable alternative is for [the] Crown to begin at once restoration of States' rights . . . and to give practical effect to principles which, if British India had proved cooperative, might have remained merely theoretical, to be used as bargaining counters.[66]

By December he had won over Wavell;[67] by February, with the viceroy's help, Pethick-Lawrence. On 3 March, to Nehru's fury, cabinet authorised a scheme of staged retraction identical in its basic features to that which the political adviser had earlier outlined to his senior residents at their annual conference.[68] Shortly after this, Corfield instructed the residents to lift all restrictions on *darbars* which could be removed without danger to their stability, to bestow full powers on minor rulers close to their majority, and to cease arbitrating boundary disputes. Later he would claim this as the most significant victory of his distinguished Indian career.

However the indefatigable Corfield did not stop there. He prevailed on Wavell, before he left in March, to lift the restrictions which had been

---

Mountbatten, responding to Nehru's objections, had pressed London to make some mention of their belief that the states should join one or other constituent assembly, but the new secretary of state, Lord Listowel, rejected the formulation which he said made it look as if HMG were 'pressing the States to enter'. W. H. Morris-Jones, 'The Transfer of Power, 1947: A View From the Sidelines', *Modern Asian Studies*, 16, 1 (1982), 13. It should be noted that Mountbatten's comments at his press conference the next day were much more forthcoming, Monckton, for one, seeing in them a clear indication that 'no relations of any sort with [the] United Kingdom' would be permitted. Monckton to Mountbatten 14 June 1947, *TOP*, XI, 386.

[66] Corfield to Patrick 30 Nov. 1946, *TOP*, IX, 230–1.
[67] Minute by Abell dated 3 Dec. 1946, and minute by Wavell dated 8 Dec. 1946, *TOP*, IX, 245–6.
[68] Memo. by sec. state for the I&B Committee of Cabinet dated 3 Mar. 1947, *TOP*, IX, 837. For Nehru's reaction see Sir Eric Mieville's account of a talk with Nehru in his letter to Mountbatten 30 Apr. 1947, *TOP*, X, 489.

placed on the nizam by Irwin in 1927. He lent his support to Hyderabad's bid to lease or buy Goa from the Portuguese for use as a duty-free port. He took on the Defence Ministry when it came to light that Baldev Singh had refused to sanction supplies of arms ordered by *darbars* for their police forces, threatening, if the weapons in question were not delivered promptly, to arrange for direct arms shipments from abroad or even for the setting up of munitions factories in the states. He pressed the interim government to expedite the handing back to the states of all ceded territories not required by the Indian Army, noting pointedly in a letter to Mountbatten's private secretary that, if Nehru and the cabinet proved uncooperative, the crown representative had the right and duty 'to make independent decisions'.[69] More controversially still, he ordered his subordinates to stop including in their regular reports any matter bearing on the 'personal affairs of Rulers' or containing 'any reflections against them', and – if the rumours circulating at the time are correct – to get rid of all incriminating material in the department's files.[70] As we have seen, he gave strong support throughout the autumn to Hamidullah in his struggle to keep control of the COP and continued, even after the Chamber's implosion, to caution the rulers privately against entering the rump Constituent Assembly.[71] Lastly, with the help of the viceroy's chief-of-staff 'Pug' Ismay, who, apparently without asking leave of his boss, took the political adviser with him when he flew to London in May with the viceroy's first plan for devolution, Corfield managed to persuade the new secretary of state, Lord Listowel, to insert in the draft policy statement responding to the plan a reference to the Cabinet Mission memorandum. It was thus largely thanks to Corfield that the 3 June announcement took the cryptic form that it did with regard to the states.[72]

As for the *darbars*, they were not idle either. Appreciating, in the words of Hyderabad's minister for commerce, that they had 'been given breathing space', the states which had high hopes of making good their autonomy strove to use this time of grace 'to advantage, internally and externally'.[73] Hyderabad itself appointed a trade commissioner in

---

[69] Corfield to Lt.-Col. Erskine-Crum 14 June 1947, *TOP*, XI, 382.

[70] Afterwards Corfield denied that he authorised any systematic destruction of records, though he admitted that some routine files were culled. The allegation seems plausible, but I have seen no evidence which either confirms or refutes it.

[71] Corfield argued, as Bhopal did, that the CA without the League was 'not the fully representative Assembly' envisaged in the CM Plan. See, e.g., Corfield to Abell 21 Apr. 1947, *TOP*, X, 354.

[72] Note of discussion at the India Office, 9 May 1947, *TOP*, X, 718; and note by Corfield dated [? Mar. 1968], Corfield Coll., 4.

[73] Minister for Commerce, Industries and Local Government to PM Hyderabad 16 Aug. 1947, Mountbatten Coll., 70.

London, Mir Nawaz Jung; had discussions with the French government about establishing a Hyderabad diplomatic mission for Europe, and with the Portuguese about the use of Goa; and asked British air chief marshal Sir Christopher Courtney for advice on the creation of a modern air-force.[74] Not to be outdone, Travancore accredited a representative to Delhi and nominated another to go to Pakistan after August 15; raised the question of diplomatic recognition with the Americans; and sealed a deal with Jinnah whereby in the event of an economic blockade Travancore would have 'first call' on any surplus food supplies available in Pakistan; while Bhopal investigated the purchase of Mistri Airlines as a state carrier and explored with the Quaid-i-Azam the possibility of the north-western states forming some sort of confederation in association with Pakistan.[75] In addition to these diplomatic initiatives, efforts were made, reminiscent of those in the 1930s, to win the support of the Conservative Party. Late in April (significantly just after Nehru's Gwalior harangue about 'shop-keeper' princes) Digvijaysinhji travelled to London to reactivate his father's links with the Tory peers; and Walter Monckton left Mountbatten in no doubt that if the door to direct relations with the United Kingdom was closed, he too would be forced to operate through 'political chan-nels'.[76] Likewise, much energy and apparently money – significantly, Rs 50 lakhs in bonds is said to have been transferred about this time from the dewan of Travancore's slush fund to an account under the control of the nawab of Bhopal – was expended on propaganda and on 'influencing people in key positions in the British press'.[77]

Of course, with the benefit of hindsight it is tempting to say that the states here were clutching at straws; however, initially at least, the

[74] Note by Sir O. Sergeant on interview with Portuguese ambassador to London 27 Mar. 1947, *TOP*, X, 1009; minutes of Viceroy's 46th Staff Meeting, 23 June 1947, *TOP*, XI, 577; and Listowel to Mountbatten 19 July 1947, *TOP*, XII, 266.

[75] Note by Wavell on interview with Bhopal 3 Mar. 1947, Wavell Coll., 17; Nehru to Mountbatten 22 June 1947, *TOP*, XI, 556; interview between Sir C. P. Ramaswamy Aiyer and Mr Symon 21 July 1947, *TOP*, XII, 281; and ambassador New Delhi to sec. state Washington, 22 July 1947, reporting conversation with Ramaswamy Aiyer and Edwin Pawley on 21 July, US State Dept. decimal file 845.00/7–2247.

[76] Ambassador New Delhi to sec. state Washington 24 Apr. 1947, US State Dept. decimal file 845.00/4–2447; Monckton to Ismay 9 June 1947, *TOP*, XI, 214; and Ismay to Mountbatten 19 June 1947, *TOP*, XI, 504.

[77] Indian HC London to Nehru 1 July 1947, *TOP*, XI, 817. Key intermediaries in this cam-paign were said to be Walter Elliot and Lord Tweedsmuir. On the Travancore connection, see *Malayala Manorama*, 10 Mar., 23 Nov. and 28 Dec. 1949. Twenty-five lakhs was apparently returned to Travancore after the collapse of Bhopal's bid for independence. Money may also have been loaned to Hyderabad and Kashmir. We know from the Travancore government files that, as of 1944, Sir C. P. had at least 1 *crore* 45 lakhs in his discretionary account. Manager, Imperial Bank Trivandrum to Ramaswamy Aiyer 13 Mar. 1944, Travancore, Confidential Section, file 820 of 1944 (I am indebted to Professor Robin Jeffrey for these references.)

responses to these overtures gave them reason to hope. If the Americans reacted coolly, France and several Arab countries gave strong signals that they were willing to consider diplomatic ties with such states as did not accede to India or Pakistan; Courtney and for that matter the joint chiefs-of-staff warmly welcomed the nizam's request for assistance as affording a golden opportunity for the United Kingdom to retain a 'strong foothold' in southern India; the Tories rallied to the support of their old friends in the debate on the India Bill in July; *The Times* in particular ran a similar line in its leader columns; and even within the cabinet voices were heard to argue that Travancore's pleas for diplomatic recognition should be heeded in view of the state's importance as the United Kingdom's major source of monazite, a basic ingredient of the fissionable mineral thorium.[78] Most importantly of all, the government's anxiety over Walter Monckton's threat to make the fate of the states a party political issue drew an assurance from Secretary of State Listowel, which Mountbatten at once passed on via Ismay, that while dominionhood for non-acceding states was no longer on offer London 'would certainly not refuse to have direct relations with them'.[79] Coming after the June 3 statement, this conciliatory declaration seemed to Bhopal and the other non-acceding princes to put the issue of their future independence beyond doubt; and so, if matters had been left in the hands of the home government, it might have done. Unfortunately for their hopes and ambitions, Mountbatten chose this moment to do what he should have done months before – devote his full attention to the states and their problems.

It was Jawaharlal Nehru, Mountbatten's closest ally in the interim government, who initially drew his attention to the fact that important questions about the future of the states remained pending. We have already noted Nehru's threatening stance toward states which continued to stand out of the Constituent Assembly. Over the autumn and early summer he reiterated this line several times publicly and also to the viceroy's face, telling Mountbatten in agitated tones that he would 'encourage rebellion in all States that go against us';[80] and in May he had to be restrained from visiting Kashmir on a quixotic crusade to rescue his close friend Sheikh Abdullah who had been jailed by Hari Singh.

[78] House of Commons Debates vol. 439, 10 July 1947, columns 2465, 2470–1, and vol. 440, 15 July 1947, columns 237–8; memo by chiefs of staff Joint Planning Committee 15 July 1947, *TOP*, XII, 174–6; memo by minister of supply dated 18 July 1947, *TP*, XII, 232; Colonial Office to HC New Delhi 8 Aug. 1947, *TOP*, XII, 582; and for a representative *Times* leader see 20 June 1947. For a recent scholarly perspective on the 'nuclear' aspect of the Travancore problem see A. Martin Wainright, *Inheritance of Empire: Britain, India and the Balance of Power in Asia, 1938–55* (Westport, CT, 1994), 99–108.   [79] Ismay to Sir David Monteath 19 June 1947, *TOP*, XI, 505–6.
[80] Record of interview No. 146 dated 10 June 1947, *TOP*, XI, 232.

Although Mountbatten had always known that Nehru held rabidly republican views, these almost 'pathological'[81] outbursts caught him by surprise, and to an extent shocked him into reassessing his leisured approach to the states' problem. As well, Nehru fed the viceroy's growing sense of unease by plying him with reports of political department skullduggery. Under cover of the retraction of paramountcy, he alleged, the department was burning incriminating documents to stop them falling into the hands of the government; it was aiding and abetting a 'sly' Hyderabad scheme to exploit the rich iron resources of Bastar in Orissa; and it was encouraging the rulers to hold out against accession. This campaign climaxed at a meeting with party leaders attended by Corfield on 13 June, when Nehru levelled a formal allegation of 'misfeasance' against the political adviser.[82] Afterwards the viceroy apologised to Corfield for this slur on his record; significantly, however, he did not contradict the charge.

Meanwhile, Mountbatten's complacency was further dented by announcements from several of the largest – and potentially most self-sufficient – states that they were taking steps to assert their independence in anticipation of the withdrawal of British paramountcy. On 5 June, Hamidullah informed the viceroy that, in the light of the 3 June plan for a strong Indian centre, Bhopal intended to boycott the Constituent Assembly and to work towards the establishment of diplomatic relations jointly with India and Pakistan. Shortly after, Sir C. P. Ramaswamy Aiyer made a similar declaration in an address to the Travancore legislature. Hoping to stem the tide before it became a flood, Mountbatten asked his residents in Kashmir and Hyderabad to 'make every effort to ensure that those States did not make any public pronouncement before he had visited them'.[83] He was successful in the former case, but not in the latter. On 11 July Mirza Ismail resigned the chief ministership – clearly at odds with his colleagues. Next day the Hyderabad executive council issued a statement affirming that the state had no plans to join either India or Pakistan. The threat posed by these developments made action imperative; as, of course, did Mountbatten's own decision, in June, to bring the transfer of power forward to 15 August which left him just nine weeks to settle with the recalcitrant rulers.

The main thing which changed Mountbatten's mind about the importance of the states, however, was the realisation that they probably held the key to a negotiated settlement with the Congress. Early in May, Reforms Commissioner V. P. Menon put it to him that the accession of

[81] Personal report No. 10 dated 27 June 1947, *TOP*, XI, 687.
[82] Minutes of viceroy's 18th Miscellaneous Meeting 13 June 1947, *TOP*, XI, 321.
[83] Minutes of viceroy's 40th Staff Meeting 9 June 1947, *TOP*, XI, 199.

the states – whose combined area and population nearly matched that of the districts claimed by the League for Pakistan – might help to reconcile the still edgy Congress high command to the necessity of partition. Considerably 'touched' by this argument,[84] the viceroy at once tried it out on Nehru and Sardar Patel.[85] Likewise, Mountbatten found the Congress leaders much more amenable to his proposal for an early devolution of power on the basis of dominion status, once he made clear to them that he had set his face against any continuing relationship between the United Kingdom and the non-acceding states.[86] In this fashion the rulers became unwittingly entangled in a game played for bigger stakes: the preservation of the empire-commonwealth.

Finally realising the importance of the princely states in the Indian constitutional equation and the difficulties that lay in the path of an amicable settlement – and regretful, now, that he had dallied for so long – Mountbatten hastened to make up for lost time. From the beginning of July 1947 he made the states his 'primary consideration'.[87] And within two weeks he had reached a momentous conclusion. 'As soon as I turned my attention to the problem of the states', he wrote later, 'it became evident to me that their [aspirations to] independence . . . would not be worth a moment's purchase unless they had the support of one or other of the Dominions.'[88] With the problem redefined in this way, its solution became – at least to the viceroy – obvious. Somehow he had to devise a form of accession which was at once substantial enough to satisfy the Congress and limited enough to appeal to the *darbars*.

The solution was provided by Menon.[89] Sometime in July, the Reforms Commissioner proposed to Patel, and then, with the Sardar's blessing, to Mountbatten, that the states should be asked to accede only in respect of defence, foreign affairs and communications – areas over which they had long ceased to exercise jurisdiction – and without financial or other entanglements. Seeing the ingenuity of this plan, the viceroy at once made a formal approach to Patel.[90] The Sardar, however, seems to have had doubts about whether Mountbatten would be able to deliver. As late as 25

---

[84] Menon to Leonard Mosley, n.d., cited in Mosley, *The Last Days of the British Raj* (Bombay, 1972), 192.

[85] Mountbatten's version of the story is detailed in his letter to Listowel 8 Aug. 1947, *TOP*, XII, 584.

[86] Mountbatten rather jumped the gun here but, typically, was able to persuade the cabinet to back him up by convincing them that it was a *sine qua non* of Congress accepting the dominion status deal. Note by Listowel dated 24 May 1947, *TOP*, X, 533.

[87] Minutes of viceroy's 55th staff meeting 9 July 1947, *TOP*, XII, 36.

[88] Mountbatten to Listowel 8 Aug. 1947, *TOP*, Xii, 585.

[89] Robin Moore, however, notes that Nehru was already thinking along the same lines. Moore, *Escape From Empire*, 303.   [90] Menon, *The Story of Integration*, 93–7.

July the viceroy reported that he had 'not yet got Patel to agree to all of these terms'.[91] But at length a deal was struck. As Hodson tells it, Patel agreed to three subject accession on condition Mountbatten came up with 'a full basket of apples'.[92] This, needless to say, was a big task, and rather revealingly Mountbatten neglected to tell the India Office what he had agreed to, for fear that if Attlee or Listowel got wind of the terms of the arrangement 'before it was clear that the majority of States were going to accept them', it would be repudiated.[93] Yet the viceroy did not demur. The stakes were too important, the prize too tempting: 'if I can bring in a basket-full of States before the 15th August', he exulted, 'Congress will pay whatever price I insist on for the basket'.[94]

Nevertheless, if the details of the compact remained, for some time, a tightly guarded secret, it soon became obvious that the viceroy's policy towards the princes had changed. From June, he no longer equivocated on the issue of the states' eligibility for dominion status but told the rulers that the only way they could stay in the commonwealth was to join up with India or Pakistan; he poured cold water on their plans for the formation of states unions; despite vociferous protests from the princes, and a stinging rebuke from Corfield, which just stopped short of an accusation of 'a gross breach of faith',[95] he did nothing to expedite the return of ceded territories and turned a blind eye to the unofficial sanctions which the interim government had placed on the states in regard to the delivery of arms and ammunition;[96] most conspicuously of all, perhaps, he gave his assent at the end of the month to the establishment of a new central department under Patel's ministerial control to oversee 'matters of common concern' with the states.[97] Thus, when the three-subject accession plan was formally unveiled to the rulers and ministers at a hastily convened meeting of the COP on 25

[91] Personal report No. 4 dated 25 July 1947, *TOP*, XII, 338.
[92] H. V. Hodson, *The Great Divide: Britain-India-Pakistan* (London, 1969), 368.
[93] Note of interview with Monckton and Menon 19 Oct. 1947, Mountbatten Coll., 71.
[94] Personal report No.4 dated 25 July 1947, *TOP*, Xii, 338.
[95] Memo by Corfield dated 29 May 1947, encl. in Corfield to Mieville 29 May 1947, *TOP*, X, 1031.
[96] The backlog by July was: 9,000 muskets, 8,000 rifles, 1,600 revolvers, 62 automatic weapons and 4 million rounds of ammunition. Mountbatten to Listowel 19 July 1947, *TOP*, XII, 267. By August the situation in Hyderabad had become so critical that the resident applied on his own authorisation for an emergency issue from the Secunderabad Ordnance Depot. On the ceded territories issue, Mountbatten did go so far as to raise with Whitehall the possibility of financial compensation *in lieu*, but got no support, Listowel's legal advisers maintaining that in acceding for defence, the states had in effect waived any legal entitlement to compensation since most territory had been ceded in exchange for military guarantees. Listowel to Mountbatten 13 Aug. 1947, *TOP*, XII, 695.
[97] For the background to the formation of the States Department see *White Paper on the Indian States, 1950*, 32–3.

July, it came as no real surprise and perhaps even as something of a relief. This, in part, explains why it was so readily accepted by the majority of the rulers.

But there were other factors, too. On the face of it, the deal was a generous one, especially compared to that which the princes had bucked at in 1939. Clause 7 of the standard IOA prepared by the political department to Mountbatten's instructions[98] made it clear that acceding states were not bound, 'in any way', to the future constitution of India and clause 8 guaranteed that in all areas besides defence, foreign affairs and communications (which as Mountbatten reminded them were already exercised *de facto* on their behalf by the Delhi government), sovereignty would continue to lie with their rulers; moreover, the instrument required them to cede these three powers only for policy, legislation and administration; it said nothing about tax liability. In addition the *darbars* were given verbal assurances that their extra-territorial rights would be respected, that they would be allowed to democratise slowly, in accordance with the timetable that Hamidullah had framed for the Chamber in 1945, that 'none of the 18 major States would be called upon to merge', and that if India became a republic the IOAs would lapse, allowing any states so minded to secede.[99] A final sweetener was the cabinet's pledge, following a personal plea by Mountbatten, that the princes would not be debarred after 1947 from accepting British honours and appointment as honorary ADCs to the king.[100]

Another factor was the almost childlike trust which was reposed by the rulers in the integrity of the viceroy and his states minister. Charming, eloquent (he spoke to the Chamber on 25 July for over an hour without recourse to notes), Mountbatten had a natural gift for communication. Even his critics conceded that he was a great salesman. And of course he possessed the considerable advantage, when it came to dealing with the princes, of a royal pedigree. Although Mountbatten often made a great show of informality, the rulers were ever-mindful of the fact he was the kinsman of their liege-lord, the king-emperor. So, when he told the princes on 25 July: 'My scheme leaves you with all [the] practical independence you can possibly use', hardly any of them doubted that he spoke

---

[98] Ironically, it was modelled on the Instrument prepared by the India Office in the leadup to federation!

[99] The text of the IOAs can be read in *TOP*, XII, 468–71. For the 'asssurances' that were given see ambassador New Delhi to sec. state 11 Dec. 1947, reporting conversation with Menon on 10 Dec., US State Dept. decimal file 845.00/12–1147; note of interview with Bhopal 28 Feb. 1948, IOR R/3/1/143; and Hodson, *Great Divide*, 379.

[100] Viceroy's personal report No. 16 dated 8 Aug. 1947, *TOP*, XII, 696.

the unvarnished truth.[101] And in a very different way Patel, too, inspired confidence: for though he was gruff and taciturn, he spoke with a reassuring directness and absence of ideological fervour; and was reputed to be a man who kept his word.[102] Accordingly, when Patel in his maiden ministerial speech claimed that it was 'not the desire of Congress to interfere in any manner whatever in the domestic affairs of the States', and that the high command were 'no enemies of the Princely Order',[103] he, also, was widely believed.

Last but not least, accession was facilitated by pressure – subtle, gentlemanly but relentless pressure from the viceroy and his minister. Even as he outlined the merits of his scheme on the 25th, Mountbatten began to turn the screws. According to eye-witnesses (the text was later heavily edited) the speech was unlike any delivered before by a viceroy to the COP, indeed more of a harangue than a speech in the conventional sense. And it was heavy with menace. The rulers should not think twice, he warned, because the offer might not last. He had 'still to persuade the Government of India to accept it'. Later, when fending questions from the floor, Mountbatten resorted to pantomime, pretending to 'read' an absent prince's mind with the aid of a glass paperweight which he described mischievously as 'my crystal ball'. Later still that day, at a reception for the rulers at viceregal lodge, he employed the old auctioneer's trick of playing off the bidders: 'Those of Their Highnesses who had not already signified their intention of signing the Instrument of Accession', recalls Alan Campbell-Johnson, 'were duly shepherded by the ADCs one by one for a friendly chat with Mountbatten. He in turn passed them on in full view of the company to V. P. [Menon] who conducted them across the room to . . . Patel.'[104] By this time, the mutterings of 'bullying' were loud enough for the viceroy to ask Gwalior's M. A. Sreenivasan after the reception whether he thought the accusation warranted.[105]

Nor did Mountbatten resile from a little gentle blackmail. Whenever he talked to the rulers he traded unashamedly on his royal heritage. In

---

[101] An edited text of Mountbatten's address can be found in *TOP*, XII, 349. The dewan of Gwalior, M. A. Sreenivasan, opined to Sir C. P. Ramaswamy Aiyer about this time: 'it was on [the basis of] these solemn assurances and promises that several States . . . signed the Instruments of Accession'. M. A. Sreenivasan, *Of the Raj, Maharajas and Me* (New Delhi, 1991), 214.

[102] Even Bhopal warmly welcomed Patel's appointment as states minister. Viceroy's personal report No. 10 dated 27 June 1947, *TOP*, XI, 689.

[103] Speech of 5 July 1947, quoted in Philips, *Evolution of India and Pakistan*, 436–7.

[104] Campbell-Johnson, *Mission*, 121.

[105] Sreenivasan, *Of the Raj*, 216. Sreenivasan replied that he thought it *was* justified, but that there were extenuating circumstances.

particular, he suggested that the king would be displeased if, by standing out, they severed their connection with him.[106] However Mountbatten reserved the heaviest weapons in his armoury for the large states who showed signs of intransigence. The dewan of Indore, Horton, who 'had the nerve' to categorise the viceroy's letter to Yeshwant Rao Holkar about the merits of accession as a threat was severely rebuked for his trouble.[107] Afterwards Horton expostulated to Corfield that 'he now knew what Dolfuss felt like when he was sent for to see Hitler; he had not expected to be spoken to like that by a British officer'.[108] Holkar, too, was carpeted; while Hamidullah and Ramaswamy Aiyer were bombarded with dire warnings about what might happen if they did not place themselves under the defensive umbrella of the government of India. On Menon's advice, Mountbatten in discussions with the deeply conservative Sir C. P. also played heavily on the 'communist menace';[109] while Bhopal was reminded of the dangers his exposed state faced from Hindu communalism. Last but not least the nizam was wooed with 'hints' that if he 'behaved really well', his long-denied request for a title for his second son might be reconsidered.[110]

Only one senior person on the government side raised real objections to these draconian tactics – Conrad Corfield. But the political adviser's influence had long been on the wane, and on 23 July he took early retirement and flew home, consumed, as he says in his memoirs, 'with a feeling of nausea, as though my own honour had been [be]smirched'.[111] As for the rulers, their protests – like that of veteran loyalist Udaibhan Singh, who could not quite comprehend that a scion of the House of Windsor could allow himself to be associated with an attempt 'to hustle the Indian Princes'[112] – were generally muted. Most simply accepted their fate and signed. Ironically, one of the first to do so was the maharaja of Travancore, Rama Varma, losing all heart for the independence struggle after Ramaswamy Aiyer narrowly escaped assassination in Trivandrum at the end of July.

Commentators have generally hailed Mountbatten's coup in getting the states to accede as a personal triumph, E. W. R Lumby calling it a 'spectacular' accomplishment, his biographer Philip Ziegler rating it an 'astonishing'

---

[106] See, e.g., Mountbatten to Dholpur 29 July 1947, *TOP*, XII, 392.

[107] Personal report No. 15 dated 1 Aug. 1947, *TOP*, XII, 454.

[108] Draft copy of Corfield's memoirs in the Corfield Coll., IOL. This passage, which was excised from the published version, does not mention Horton by name, but it is fairly clear who is meant.   [109] Menon to Abell, 29 July 1947, *TOP*, XII, 274.

[110] Record of interview between Mountbatten and Monckton 8 July 1947, *TOP*, XII, 11.

[111] Conrad Corfield, *The Princely India I Knew* (Madras, 1975), 159.

[112] Dholpur to Mountbatten 20 July 1947, IOR R/3/1/138.

one.[113] But while it was indubitably a considerable feat it had limits and drawbacks which have not been sufficiently recognised. In the first place there was some resistance. Yeshwant Rao and Hamidullah, working as a team, sent telegrams and in some cases emissaries to states they felt were wavering about accession urging them to hold out for better terms, and according to sources in the states department 'very nearly succeeded in weaning away some of the ... rulers who had already agreed to sign the Instrument of Accession'.[114] Likewise Hyderabad sought to stiffen the resistance of those states such as Bahawalpur, Junagadh and Dungapur which were 'looking to ... [it] for leadership' by sending a delegation under constitutional affairs minister Ali Yavar Jung to the Chamber session on 25 July to confront the viceroy publicly about his policy. Afterwards, the Dungapur told Ali that their show of defiance had left him feeling much 'encouraged'.[115] And there was even muttering in some quarters about armed resistance. On 12 July Jinnah called on Mountbatten and warned him that if the Congress 'attempted to exert any pressure on Hyderabad', a 'hundred million Muslims ... would rise as one' to defend her;[116] and Monckton made a similar prediction in conversation with Menon a few weeks later.[117] Meanwhile, Yeshwant Rao approached Bharatpur with a request for mercenaries and was told that the men would be sent 'down in batches from this month [August]'.[118] Again, several princes, determined that whatever happened the Congress should not get its hands on their wealth, hatched complicated schemes to smuggle funds and jewellery abroad.[119]

---

[113] E. W. R Lumby, *The Transfer of Power in India, 1945–7*, London, 1954, 236; and Philip Ziegler, *Mountbatten* (London, 1985), 414.

[114] Note encl. in A. S. Pai to V. Shankar 18 Aug. 1947, *PC*, V, 342–3. Indore admitted to Mountbatten that his relations with Bhopal were 'very close' and that they had 'pledged' themselves 'to unity of action in regard to all matters relating to ... future constitutional developments'. Indore to Mountbatten 31 July 1947, *TOP*, XII, 435.

[115] Note by Ali Yavar Jung dated 26 July 1947, *TOP*, XII, 356–8.

[116] Viceroy's interview No. 162, 12 July 1947, Mountbatten Coll., file 194.

[117] Minutes of meeting between Mountbatten, Menon, the nawab of Chhatari and Monckton (Monckton's draft), 3 Aug. 1947, *TOP*, XII, 497. Monckton added, for Menon's benefit, that he 'was not betting that Congress would last that long'.

[118] Bharatpur to Indore 12 Aug. 1947, quoted in ambassador New Delhi to sec. state Washington 17 Feb. 1948, US State Dept. decimal file 845.00/2–1748.

[119] States involved in these transactions included Baroda, Gondal, Cutch, Jaipur, Faridkot and Indore. Predictably, the most bizarre was Holkar's attempt to send jewellery to America via Srinigar and Pakistan in the personal aeroplane of his ADC Colonel Nedou. The gaekwar did things a little differently, converting the several *crores* of state assets already lodged abroad into jewels and motor cars from the USA. Resdt. C.I. to Pol. Dept. 22 Jan 1947, IOR R/1/1/4612; Sir Terence Shone to Patrick 2 Sept. 1947, IOR L/P&S/13/1848; note by Erskine-Crum, sec. to gov.-gen., dated 31 May 1948, Mountbatten Coll., 55; UN Dhebar, chief minister Saurashtra, to Gondal 8 Mar. 1949, *PC*, VIII, 475; External Affairs Ministry New Delhi to regional commr. Madhya Bharat, [?] Oct. 1949, *PC*, VIII, 513; Sir F. Brown to Mirza Ismail 10 Aug. 1956, Mirza Ismail Papers; and Menon, *Story*, 402.

Secondly, contrary to popular belief, the viceroy did not achieve any-thing approaching the 'full basket' of accessions he had promised Patel by 14 August 1947. The two largest states, Hyderabad and Kashmir, exer-cised their legal right under the Indian Independence Act and opted for autonomy; two Kathiawar states, Junagadh and its tiny neighbour Manavadar, ignored Mountbatten's 'rule' of contiguity and signed IOAs with Pakistan;[120] and at least a dozen other major states including Indore, Jodhpur and Radhanpur – plus a host of smaller principalities – failed to return signed instruments by the agreed date, one – Piploda in central India – holding out defiantly until March 1948.[121] Moreover, there were several close shaves with respect to 'border' states claimed jointly by India and Pakistan. In May, Bhavnagar dissociated itself from the scheme for a Kathiawar Confederation and said that it would 'give consideration to the desirability of combining with other states in the area headed by Muslim princes and of joining a Pakistan Government'.[122] In June, Bilaspur pointedly asked the viceroy how a state or group of states might join a Dominion government with whose territory they were not contiguous, adding that the 'Punjab States were proposing to act together in the manner that would best safeguard their future'.[123] In July League agents put out feelers to Patiala and Jaisalmer, offering them, rumour had it, 'all manner of inducements'.[124] And in August Bikaner informed Mountbatten that if the deliberations of the Radcliffe boundary commis-sion put the neighbouring district of Ferozepur, the source of much of his state's irrigation water, into Pakistan, he would have no choice but to follow suit. Finally, on the eve of independence, Hanwant Singh of Jodhpur came within an ace of signing with Pakistan after he was given a blank sheet of paper and invited by the League president to 'fill in all your conditions'.[125]

Thirdly and most importantly, the scheme of three-subject accession

---

[120] Again, they were theoretically quite free to do so. But the viceroy held that there were 'certain geographical compulsions which cannot be evaded'. Essentially his position was that only states within or which had borders with Pakistan were free to associate them-selves with the Karachi regime.

[121] 'Accession of State to the Dominion of India', and C. C. Desai, Jt, sec., States Ministry to Capt. R. V. Brockman, priv. sec. to the gov.-gen. 1 Nov. and 24 Dec. 1947 and 15 Jan. 1948, IOR, R/3/1/140; and consul-gen. Bombay to sec. state Washington 6 Feb. 1948, US State Dept. decimal file 845.00/2–648.

[122] Consul-gen., Bombay to sec. state Washington May 1947, US State Dept. decimal file 845.00/5–1347.   [123] Mountbatten to Corfield 30 June 1947, TOP, XI, 764.

[124] The Tribune (Ambala), 19 July 1959.

[125] Memo. by Mountbatten on conversation with Bhopal dated 11 Aug. 1947, TOP, XII, 659–661; viceroy's personal report No. 17 dated 16 Aug. 1947, TOP, XII, 767; Menon, Story of the Integration, 88; Panikkar, Autobiography, 161. According to Panikkar, Jodhpur was attracted by the prospect of making himself a sort of suzerain over 'Pakistani' Rajputana.

was inherently flawed: for while it met what was then the government's most urgent need – namely, to prevent the Balkanisation of the sub-continent – it failed to address the on-going concerns of Congress and others about the viability of the states and the future of the monarchical system. In this respect the real architects of the 'final solution' to the 'problem' of the states – the infelicitous phrase was V. P. Menon's[126] – were not Mountbatten and Attlee but V. P. himself and his boss at the states department, Vallabhbhai Patel.

The passing of the maharajas

Even as they signed on the dotted line, many princes harboured a sense of unease. For one thing, they found it hard to trust the Congress, the old enemy; for another, the settlement seemed too good to be true. Of Menon, Bhopal remarked enigmatically that only time would tell 'to what extent [he] . . . was . . . a man who did not keep his word'.[127] Another ruler told the United States consul in Bombay that he 'did not expect the Government of India to live up to the agreement [for] more than 3 years' – a view with which the American reluctantly concurred.[128] The tide of events over the following forty-eight months went a long way to confirm-ing the essential accuracy of these cynical forecasts.

The first thing the new government did, in defiance of the settlement of August 1947, was to occupy the vacuum left by the departing British. They sent regional commissioners – residents in all but name – to Rajkot and Sambalpur; 'advised' Holkar to sack his dewan, Horton, and other rulers to give way to demands for constitutional change; detained the raja of Faridkot when he tried to decamp to Australia; told Jodhpur to cut down on his consumption of whisky and to stop playing around with women; and forced Alwar to step down pending inquiries into allegations that he had abetted Gandhi's assassin. They took control of the border states of Cutch, Tripura and Manipur (on grounds of security) and took charge of the administration in Nilgiri and Bharatpur (on the pretext of an impending breakdown in law and order). They clapped a blockade on

---

[126] Speech to the rulers of Kathiawar, 17 Jan. 1948, Menon, *Story of the Integration*, 174. Menon afterwards stoutly defended himself and Sardar Patel against allegations of duplicity. 'There was no question at the time that we would extinguish the States at all', he wrote in a letter of 1957. It is hard, however, to imagine that someone as intelligent and politically sagacious as Menon would not have seen that the three-subject accession formula was unlikely to last. See Menon to Mirza Ismail, 2 Mar. 1957, Mirza Ismail Papers, NMML.

[127] Note of interview with Bhopal 28 Feb. 1948, IOR R/3/1/143.

[128] Consul-gen. Bombay to sec. state 24 Feb. 1948, US State Dept. decimal file 845.00/2-2448.

intransigent Junagadh, forcing the nawab to flee to Pakistan. Last but not least, in September 1948 they invaded Hyderabad, shattering nizam Osman Ali's dream of reigning over a third Indian dominion. As Hodson remarks (and the British High Commissioner noted at the time) these proceedings amounted to a 'virtual recreation' of the paramountcy system.[129]

However, if there was continuity there was also dramatic change. No sooner had the ink dried on the princes' IOAs, than Patel and Menon began to plot their downfall. This project, which took about two years, involved, in more or less chronological order (although the processes overlapped), the amalgamation of the states into larger administrative units and/or merger with the erstwhile provinces, their rapid democratisation, and their total subordination to the federal centre.

Given that the merger of even the smaller states necessitated a repudiation of guarantees made by the viceroy, Patel – and certainly Nehru – would have preferred to postpone taking action until Mountbatten's term as governor-general had expired; but events, particularly in the Orissa states, where *adivasi* revolt threatened life and property, forced their hand. In mid-December 1947 princes belonging to the erstwhile Eastern and Chhatisgarh political agencies were called to a meeting in Cuttack and there persuaded by Menon, in the course of an all-night sitting, to sign new covenants integrating their states into Orissa. In January 1948 a similar scenario was enacted at Rajkot, where the Kathiawar princes finally put their differences behind them and voted to establish, within the month, a unitary state to be known as Saurashtra. After that it was the turn of the smaller Deccan and Gujarat states, which were merged with Bombay, and in March, of the so-called Punjab 'hill states', which were absorbed into a new centrally administered unit called Himachal Pradesh.[130] Alarmed by the rapidity of these developments, a number of prominent rulers sought an interview with the states minister in January 1948. Menon assured them, on his boss's behalf, 'that the principle of

---

[129] Consul-gen. Bombay to sec. state Washington, 25 Aug. 1947, US State Dept. decimal file 845.00/8–2547; note by Mountbatten dated 6 Feb. 1948, Mountbatten Coll., 2; note by GG's private sec. dated 4 May 1948, Mountbatten Coll., 86; note by Erskine-Crum dated 31 May 1948, and note of interview between GG, GG-designate and Gwalior, Jaipur, Patiala and Bikaner dated 5 June 1948, Mountbatten Coll., 55; and Sir Terence Shone to Paul Patrick, CRO, 2 Sept. 1947, quoted in memo. by Commonwealth Relations minister for the India and Burma Committee of Cabinet dated 12 Sept. 1947, IOR L/P&S/13/1848; Hodson, *Great Divide*, 502.

[130] One of the more curious aspects of the integration story is the extent to which Patel – and even more Menon – made and executed the policy. Apparently the original decision to merge the Orissa states was taken after a mere two-minute discussion in cabinet. And Menon seems to have negotiated the Kathiawar settlement without prior reference to Delhi. All this sits oddly with what we know of Nehru's passionate interest in the subject.

merger would not be applied to those States which had individual representation in the Constituent Assembly and which obviously had a future'.[131] Nevertheless it was. Buoyed by their initial success, which had come about much more easily than either Patel or Menon had expected, concerned about the strategic implications of an agglomeration of weak, independent states strung along what would become, in the event of an all-out war with Pakistan, 'the front line defence of the Indo-Gangetic Plains', eager to clean up the administrative map of central India as they had done that of neighbouring Kathiawar, and convinced that a unified Malwa had the potential to become 'a veritable granary' such as might, in time, compensate for the loss of West Punjab,[132] and mindful, perhaps, of the role that Yeshwant Rao Holkar had played in the princely resistance movement against accession, Patel and Menon orchestrated the merger, in April 1948, of Indore and Gwalior (and some twenty small states) into the Union of Madhya Bharat. This precedent was then extended to cover the incorporation of Udaipur (and later Jaipur, Jodhpur, Jaisalmer and Bikaner) in Rajasthan, of Patiala in PEPSU,[133] and of Baroda in Bombay. By November 1949 only 6 of the 552 states that had acceded to India – namely Hyderabad, Mysore, Bhopal, Tripura, Manipur and Cooch-Behar – remained as separate entities within their old boundaries.[134]

The next stage – which we have labelled 'democratisation' – had, of course, already begun; nevertheless the transition to popular rule was given a big impetus by the devolution of power itself, which raised expectations of a similar transformation in the states, and by the leverage which Congress now exercised on developments therein through the states department. On 15 August 1947, independence day, Gwalior announced the appointment of a committee to draw up a democratic constitution; two weeks later, an elected cabinet took office in Cochin; in November, after negotiations with leaders of the local *praja mandal*, an

---

Did the responsibilities of the premiership and the overriding problems of Kashmir and Hyderabad leave him no time for the other states, or was he skilfully kept at a distance by the states minister? Hints in the Nehru papers point to the latter, as when, in March 1948, he suggested to the Sardar that the time may have come for 'some kind of review of the work by Cabinet' – but more research is needed. See Hodson, *Great Divide*, 494–5; and Nehru to Patel 2 Mar. 1948, Jawaharlal Nehru Papers, 1st instalment, file 7.

[131] Menon, *Story*, 164.

[132] Proposal for the formation of the United State of Gwalior, Indore and Malwa as summarised for cabinet by Menon, 25 Apr. 1948, Mountbatten Coll., 147. See also note by Menon for cabinet on the merger of the Gujarat states dated 22 Mar. 1948, Mountbatten Coll., 146.   [133] Patiala and East Punjab States Union.

[134] Jammu and Kashmir still existed as a separate entity but after the tribal invasion of October 1947 and the consequent border war between India and Pakistan it became effectively a partitioned state. Sikkim and Bhutan likewise remained nominally independent but these border states had always been treated separately from the rest.

interim government of popular ministers was set up in Kolhapur; in early December, Sadul Singh gave his assent to a reforms package which went a long way towards turning Bikaner into a constitutional monarchy; after taking advice from Gandhi the ruler of Bhavnagar in January 1948 followed Cochin's lead and introduced full responsible government; in April a popular ministry was set up in Bhopal; and in June the gaekwar reluctantly bowed to popular pressure and conceded a substantial measure of responsible government in Baroda.

Yet, swift though it had been by pre-independence standards, this constitutional transformation increasingly fell short of the expectations of the union government; and as early as December 1947 Menon began to consider the feasibility of *requiring* the rulers of states that had acceded to 'take practical steps towards the establishment of popular government'.[135] In turn, this line of thought fed speculation about integration as a way of reducing the number of intransigent *darbars*, and after a while the states department saw how it could achieve these two objects simultaneously by the simple expedient of getting the heads of the merged states to sign special covenants binding them to act as constitutional monarchs. As a result, most people in what was left of princely India came to enjoy, by the middle of 1948, a large measure of responsible government – although, like their fellow citizens in the former provinces, they had to wait until 1951 to experience the full fruits of democracy.

Merger and democratisation together brought the states into line with the rest of the country as regards the manner of their governance; but one anomaly still remained. In their relations with the centre, the 'princely' unions continued to be cocooned by the IOAs signed by the rulers in August 1947, which restricted the extent of their accession to the Indian union to only three subjects. Of course, the IOAs were meant to be permanent. However, in private the Congress leaders had always assumed that the settlement of 1947 would have to be renegotiated eventually in the interests of national development and social justice, and by April 1948 it seemed to Menon, at least, that the time for action had arrived. In a submission to cabinet he outlined the case for a further transfer of powers.[136] This initiative led to a summit meeting in Delhi in the first week of May, at the end of which the governors of Rajasthan, Madhya Bharat, Saurashtra, Vindhya Pradesh and Matsya jointly, and with surprising alacrity, signed new IOAs ceding to the union the power to pass

---

[135] In conversation with the American ambassador. See ambassador New Delhi to sec. state Washington 10 Dec. 1947, US State Dept. decimal file 845.00/12–1047.

[136] Summary for Cabinet by V. P. Menon on the formation of the United State of Gwalior, Indore and Malwa dated 25 Apr. 1948, Mountbatten Collection, 147.

laws in respect of all matters falling within the federal and concurrent legislative lists included the seventh schedule of the Government of India Act of 1935.[137] At this point princely India, and its age-old monarchical system, effectively disappeared down the trapdoor of history. Patel could claim, with some justice, that he had engineered a great and relatively peaceful political revolution.[138]

How did our protagonists, the princes, cope with this sudden reversal in their fortunes? Thanks to the sagacity of Patel and Menon, who recognised that the ex-rulers had the potential to be either a useful resource for the Indian state or, if alienated and marginalised, a dangerous thorn in its side, the immediate blow was cushioned by outwardly generous personal concessions. All the merging rulers were given handsome tax-free pensions linked to the revenues of their states (the basic formula, worked out in the course of Menon's negotiations with the Orissa princes in December 1947, was 15 per cent of the first lakh, 10 per cent of the next four lakhs and 7.5 per cent of all revenue over 5 lakhs),[139] free lifetime medical care for themselves and their families, free electricity, exemption from customs duty, the right to go about with armed escorts, a state funeral with military honours and qualified immunity from civil prosecution.[140] In addition, most of the old 21–gunners were neatly assimilated into the new constitutional order as *rajpramukhs* and *uprajpramukhs* (governors and lieutenant-governors) – posts which, though mainly ceremonial, were not devoid of discretionary power until they, too, were swept away in the states reorganisation of

---

[137] *The Sunday Statesman*, 9 May 1948; and UK High Commissioner New Delhi to Commonwealth Relations Office 17 May 1948, IOR L/P&S/13/1848. The rajpramukhs – led by Saurashtra's elder statesman, and former chancellor of the Chamber of Princes, Digvijaysinhji of Nawanagar, did score one win. They persuaded Menon that the princely unions should not have to pay federal tax for up to fifteen years. However, this concession was later revoked on the recommendation of the Krishnamachari Committee of 1950–1.

[138] Speech to the Constituent Assembly, [?] 1948, quoted in Menon, *Story*, 466. For Nehru's impressions, see his letter to his sister, Vijaylakshmi Pandit, 25 Mar. 1948, Jawaharlal Nehru Papers, 1st instalment, file 7.

[139] Note for cabinet by Menon dated 15 Dec. 1947, Mountbatten Coll., 146. It was eventually agreed that payment should be guaranteed by the insertion of special clauses in the constitution. This was done in the summer of 1950 while Nehru was away in Indonesia. As to their 'generosity', Sreenivasan argues with some force that the 'privy purse' settlements – whose total cost to the union was R.580 lakhs – should be measured against the 'value of the assets inherited from the States by the Government of India' – which amounted to Rs.77 *crores*! Sreenivasan, *Of The Raj*, 233.

[140] Francine Frankel, *India's Political Economy: The Gradual Revolution* (Princeton, N.J., 1978), 80 and 80n. Again, the Americans were sceptical of this arrangement holding for very long, giving it 'perhaps five years'. Consul-gen. Bombay to sec. state Washington 24 Feb. 1948, US State Dept. decimal file 845.00/2–2448. But in this case they were wrong. The privy purses survived until 1971, when they were legislated out of existence, along with the maharajas' other privileges, by the government of Mrs Indira Gandhi.

1956;[141] while others were bought off with offers of prestigious but essentially decorative embassy jobs: Yadavindra Singh in Italy, Madansinhji of Cutch in London, Norway and Chile, Jai Mansingh of Jaipur in Spain, Digvijaysinhji at the United Nations.

Nevertheless, most ruling princes found the transition to the new democratic order difficult and traumatic. Acutely conscious of his dynastic heritage, Udaibhan Singh of Dholpur could not rid himself of a nagging sense of guilt that by merging his state he had let down his 'revered' ancestors.[142] He was by no means alone. Other princes, who had signed willingly in August 1947 on the assumption that the IOAs were binding documents, felt that they themselves had been betrayed by Delhi. Admonished by Patel for failing to attend the opening in 1949 of the new Rajasthan legislature, Bikaner retorted bluntly: 'ties of blood extending over the last five centuries have been severed by a stroke'.[143] He died soon after, a morose and embittered man.[144] Others again, remembering with nostalgic exaggeration how well things had worked under the old regime, retired into their shells in silent protest at what they saw as a general decline in the quality of governance.[145] Nearly all experienced, with Cutch, a sense of 'strain and tension' as they tried to 'adapt . . . to the changed circumstances' of being private citizens in their former kingdoms.[146]

Perhaps the hardest hit by integration were the rulers who, still nursing political ambitions, found that avenue blocked to them. Hamidullah of Bhopal, having fought harder than anyone to keep the states out of the clutches of New Delhi, did not expect any favours from that quarter; but he hoped his friendship with Jinnah might help him 'take office in Pakistan', either as a member of the government or as a provincial governor. Indeed, his long-term ambition was to succeed to the governor-generalship of Pakistan after Jinnah's death. However these plans foundered on the rock-like opposition of Liaquat Ali Khan (which Hamidullah attributed to the prime minister's fear that he might 'outdo him in popularity'), and he eventually had to settle for a secluded and, by his standards, inglorious retirement in the Middle East.[147] Nawanagar's

---

[141] For instance in the early period, before the establishment of full democratic government in the states, the *rajpramukhs* were responsible for appointing and removing ministers, and seem to have been often asked by their ministers for advice.

[142] Dholpur to Mountbatten 5 Mar. 1948, IOR R/3/1/140.

[143] Bikaner to Patel 29 Mar. 1949, *PC*, 8, 501.

[144] Dr Karni Singh, Sadul Singh's son, in Allen and Dwivedi, *Lives*, 332. In Jaipur for a princely wedding, Hamidullah found the mood there one of 'frustration and even desperation'. Bhopal to Mountbatten 28 May 1948, Mountbatten Coll., 27.

[145] e.g, Dungapur to Lothian 1 Feb. 1950, Lothian Coll., 1.

[146] Cutch to Patel 7 Sept. 1950, *PC*, X, 62.

[147] For a while the government of India refused to let Hamidullah go abroad. In the end they agreed on condition that the nawab used his good offices to help bring about a

experience after 1948, too, did not match his high hopes; nor did Holkar's, although the latter's disappointment was to some extent assuaged by New Delhi's recognition, in 1950, of the child of his American wife. Conversely, the transition was much easier for princes who had never taken much interest in administration and wished merely to be left alone to enjoy their pensions. For example, integration freed Hanwant Singh of Jodhpur to marry his Scottish mistress, Sandie McBride, a step he had long contemplated but could not take while he sat on the throne. Still, it would be fair to say that most former rulers entered private life in the new India reluctantly, with many a backward glance at what they had lost and no clear plan for the future.[148]

Yet if the last generation of ruling princes found it hard to carve out new roles for themselves, the same cannot be said of their descendants. The princely families may no longer rule, in the old autocratic sense, but they still wield considerable power – as local magnates, company directors, patrons, and especially as politicians. At first, innured to a universe of inherited authority in which the only substantial competition came from rival dynasties, the princes were reluctant to put their reputations on the line by engaging in open, public combat; and rather ironically, the first rulers who ventured into the electoral domain did so at the behest of their former adversaries, the party leaders, who grasped, more quickly than the princes did themselves, what formidable political assets (wealth, charisma, contacts, political experience) they actually possessed.[149] However, once the ice had been broken, this shyness quickly vanished; according to William Richter's calculations, forty-three members of

settlement with the nizam. Before leaving Bhopal Hamidullah abdicated in favour of his eldest daughter, Princess Abida. Abida herself later moved to Pakistan. Note by G.-G'.s private sec. on interview with Bhopal 22 Aug. 1947, IOR R/3/1/140; G.-G'.s private sec. to the prime minister's private sec. 10 Feb. 1948, IOR R/3/1/143; Bhopal to Mountbatten 21 May 1948, and Mountbatten to Bhopal 3 June 1948, Mountbatten Coll., 27;

[148] This was reflected in the princes' indecision about whether they should continue to pursue a collective political role. In January 1948 a meeting was called to discuss the formation of an organisation to replace the COP. It was well-attended, but took no action. It was twenty years before the Consultation of Rulers of Indian States was set up, primarily to fight moves to abolish the rulers' privy purses. See William L. Richter and Barbara Ramusack, 'The Chamber and the Consultation: Changing Forms of Princely Association In India', *Journal of Asian Studies*, 34 (1975), 755–66.

[149] For example, after Chhatisgarh was merged with Madhya Pradesh in 1948, its rulers were encouraged to enter politics and 'help make this democratic system a success' by the Congress chief minister, R. S. Shukla. William L. Richter, 'Traditional Rulers in Post-Traditional Societies: The Princes of India and Pakistan', in Jeffrey, *People, Princes and Paramount Power*, 336. Two recent studies of princely adaptation to a post-monarchical world are: Christiane Hurtig, *Les Maharajas et la politique dans l'Inde contemporaine* (Paris, 1988); and Barbara N. Ramusack, 'Tourism and Icons: The Packaging of the Princely States of Rajasthan', in Catherine B. Asher and Thomas R. Metcalf (eds.), *Perceptions of South Asia's Visual Past* (New Delhi, 1994), 235–55.

princely families contested state and national seats in the period 1957–60, fifty-one in the period 1961–6, and seventy-five in the period 1967–70. What is more, the princes have proved consistent winners, with a success rate at the polls, according to Richter, of around 85 per cent.[150] Indeed, the maharani of Jaipur still holds the world record for an electoral majority, 175,000 votes, a feat achieved at the 1962 Lok Sabha polls![151] And this popularity with the voters has in turn given the ex-princes great leverage within the legislatures; a number have gone on to serve as party leaders, as ministers, even as heads of state governments. One, Mahavrao Scindia, may yet become prime minister of India.

For the most part, the rulers whose careers we have charted did not live to see this renaissance. Gulab Singh died in 1950, Udaibhan Singh in 1954, Hamidullah in 1960, Hari Singh and Yeshwant Rao in 1961, Digvijaysinhji in 1966, Osman Ali in 1967. But their legacy survives. Fifty years after the integration of the states, against all predictions and in defiance of the presumed logic of history, scions of the Indian old ruling class in the guise of MPs and MLAs continue to play a dominant role in the regions their families once ruled as monarchs.

[150] Richter, 'Princes in Indian Politics', 537.
[151] Andrew Robinson and Sumio Uchiyama, *Maharaja: The Spectacular Heritage of Princely India* (London, 1988), 58.

Conclusion

I fear that nothing could have saved them.

Paul Patrick, 1956

During the nineteenth and early twentieth centuries, huge tracts of territory in Asia and Africa inhabited by hundreds of millions of people came
under the control of governments led and directed by tiny handfuls of
white men – some, mere boys in uniform. The whites held sway, against
the odds, in part because they enjoyed a decisive military edge over the
locals and were ruthless in their coercion of those who dared to resist
them, but mostly because their rule was actively supported by significant
sections of the local landed, religious and intellectual elites.

In the context of the Indian Empire, the most conspicuous example of
such collaboration was the alliance that was forged between the British
and the 600–odd surviving descendants of the subcontinent's former
ruling dynasties – the 'native princes'. Time and again, at critical junc-
tures, the princes showed themselves loyal and useful friends. In the revolt
of 1857–8, during the anti-partition agitation of 1905, in the war crises of
1914 and 1939, during the Quit India movement of 1942, princely
money, princely forces and princely charismatic authority lent vital
material and moral support to the imperial cause. Conversely, no other
group of Indians was so consistently and fulsomely feted by the British. In
1858 and 1918, their services were recognised with land grants. A special
royal order – the Star of India – was created especially to honour them.
They had privileged access to viceroys and secretaries of state. Ganga
Singh of Bikaner was the first Indian added to Lloyd George's war
cabinet, Hamidullah of Bhopal the first Indian raised to the rank of air
vice-marshal. Indeed, so close had the relationship between the crown
and the princes become by the 1920s, that a retired senior official could
unblushingly describe them in a speech to the East Indian Association in
1929 as 'our sheet anchor in India'.[1] However, if the princely alliance was

---

[1] Sir Louis Dane, foreign sec., GOI, 1902–8. Speech of 21 Jan. 1929, *The Asiatic Review*
(1929), 295.

paradigmatic it was also unique, for while other systems of collaboration in India were sustained by the spoils of patronage, it alone was underwritten by legal contract. The solemnly worded treaties and *sanads*, and the hardly less solemn pledges of successive British monarchs, gave the compact between the raj and the rulers an appearance of rock-like solidity and permanence.

But the appearance was deceptive. In its mature form the alliance lasted barely three decades, from about 1917 to 1947 – a period more or less coincident with the institutional life of the COP. When the British quit India in August 1947 they severed all but a couple of purely ceremonial ties with the princes, leaving their erstwhile allies to make the best bargain they could with the new Congress government in New Delhi. Within twenty-one months the princes had been toppled from their thrones and the states integrated into the bosom of the Indian union.

Commenting on these changes in a letter to the nawab of Bhopal, Jawaharlal Nehru advanced the convenient and comforting hypothesis that the states were irrevocably doomed, by the twentieth century, by virtue of their monarchical polities. The destruction of the princes was 'bound to happen', he mused, 'whether we wanted it or not. All we could do was to see that the changes that were inevitable took place in as reasonable and amicable way as possible.'[2] The view that the states were a twentieth century anachronism, out of place in the modern world, has since been restated by many scholars. Likewise, a number have echoed Nehru's attribution of agency to metahistorical forces. In Steve Ashton's words, 'Irrespective of British policy, this [the disppearance of the states] had become an inevitable development.'[3] Indeed, by now even some of the princes' descendants have come round to the view that their extinction as rulers was something that 'had to happen'.[4]

However I have seen no empirical evidence that suggests that the states were about to self-destruct. On the contrary, as chapter 6 explains, the indicators for the larger states, at least, in 1945–6, were quite positive.

---

[2] Nehru to Bhopal 9 July 1948, Nehru Papers, 1st instalment, file 11.

[3] Ashton, *British policy*, 193. See also Ramusack, *The Princes of India*, 242. This approach is reminiscent of what has been called the 'declinology' school of writing about the twentieth century British Empire which, drawing on organic theories of growth and decay, holds that the end of empire was unavoidable. For a critique of the 'declinologists' see D. Cameron Watt, 'Between Great Britain and Little England', *The Times Literary Supplement*, 11 Feb. 1994. Significantly Morris-Jones, who was there, puts much more stress on the *ad hoc* nature of the 'solution' that was devised by Mountbatten. Morris-Jones, 'The Transfer of Power', esp. 12–20.

[4] Bhawani Singh of Jaipur in conversation with British journalist Derek Brown, *The Sunday Age* (Melbourne), 29 Nov. 1992.

Their economies were booming, in some cases growing at a rate which exceeded that of the British provinces; they possessed ample financial reserves, and a wealth of administrative expertise; opposition in the form of the *praja mandals* was for the most part weak, factionalised, moderate and parochial; and their rulers remained, in defiance of the historical tide, overwhelmingly popular figures with the masses of their subjects. Likewise, there is little evidence to support the view that the princes were victims of the revolutionary class struggle – that the states were destroyed by irresistible popular pressure from below. To repeat: there was opposition; and certainly it was more general and more militant in 1947–8 than it had been ten years earlier. Yet large-scale, violent, and potentially revolutionary as some of these popular movements were, almost nowhere did they carry the day. Only in a handful of the tiny Orissan and Punjab 'hill' states were the *darbari* regimes actually toppled at the point of a gun. Elsewhere the *darbars* remained in control.[5] In the states, as in British India, power was transferred, not seized.

Nevertheless, while the revolution of 1947–9 was mainly a 'bloodless' one (to use Patel's term), it cannot be said that the princes went willingly, out of a patriotic concern for the larger national benefit (as Menon's *Story of Integration* would have us believe). They succumbed because, once the Muslim League decided in January 1947 not to enter the Constituent Assembly and to hold out, instead, for Pakistan, they had no way of resisting diplomatically, in the absence of their imperial patrons, the implacable demands of the Congress-dominated Union government – demands backed by implicit threats of public exposure, licenced rebellion and the use, if need be, of military force. As the American ambassador commented dryly after Menon's Orissa coup in December 1947, 'the Embassy feels that the proposals of the Government of India were placed before the Princes in such a manner that they had no alternative [but] to accept them'.[6] In short, the princes were brought down by the opportunistic use of paramountcy – a power that the Cabinet Mission had assured them would never be transferred to a successor government in

[5] In the last few months of the princely era, as it became clear that change was imminent and that bureaucratic heads would roll, the quality of government in the states did fall away somewhat. For example, Princess Abida, Hamidullah's daughter and designated heir, recalls that in June and July 1947 a number of state servants deserted their posts, believing that they had no future in Bhopal. But there was no general collapse.

[6] Ambassador New Delhi to sec. state Washington, 31 Dec. 1947, US State Dept. decimal file 845.00/12–3147. A couple of months later, after the Deccan rulers surrendered their powers, the American consul-general in Bombay wrote: 'The attitude of the Princes . . . was undoubtedly that . . . [they were facing] an inevitable defeat which it was better to accept on present terms rather than hold out and eventually be forced to unconditional surrender.' Consul-gen. Bombay to sec. state Washington 24 Feb. 1948, US State Dept. decimal file 845.00/2–2448.

New Delhi.[7] Yet, while this much is self-evident, it does not in itself provide a sufficient explanation for their demise. In particular, it begs the question of why these loyal allies were abandoned by their British patrons, the Cabinet Mission notwithstanding, to the tender mercies of the nationalists, or, to put it another way, why the rulers' 'best card', namely the fact that 'the faith of the British Crown [was] . . . involved in honouring the treaties',[8] proved, in the end, worthless.

For the British Labour government and its viceroy in India, Lord Mountbatten, the abrogation of the treaty-alliance with the princes was a regrettable but unavoidable eventuality, since the treaties contained military guarantees that London had no hope of honouring without offending the new dominion government in Delhi, whose friendship was crucial to the salvation of wider British economic and strategic interests east of Suez. As Mountbatten put it pithily: 'The Indian Dominion, consisting of nearly 3/4ths of India, and with its immense resources and important strategic position in the Indian Ocean, is a Dominion which we cannot afford to estrange for the sake of the so-called independence of the States.'[9] However, to explain is not necessarily to excuse, and many aspects of the British government's policy, particularly as interpreted and executed by Mountbatten in his capacity as viceroy-plenipotentiary, remain open to question. For instance, could the British have done more for their former clients? Did Mountbatten sell three-subject accession to the rulers in July–August 1947 as a 'solution' to the constitutional problem knowing that the settlement was unlikely to stick?

It is impossible to prove conclusively that the viceroy knew, or guessed that Menon and Patel intended to repudiate the IOAs once they got into power;[10] probably he did not. But this does not, of itself, render him guiltless. Mountbatten seems to have taken the Orissa coup in his stride. There is no sign, in the documents I have seen, of the 'distress and indig-

---

[7] Nehru's term: see Nehru to Rajagopalachari 6 May 1948, JN Papers, 1st Instalment, file 9. The prime minister occasionally gave voice, as in the above letter, to his unease about the way his ministers – including Patel – were descending to *Realpolitik*, but he never intervened in the running of the States Department, preferring in the end to judge by results. Menon freely admits that promises to the princes were broken, but insists that the government of India acted legally. As he told Pratap Singh Gaekwar, 'Quite independently . . . of the terms of any agreement, the Constitution framed by this sovereign body [the CA], stands supreme and is binding on every citizen of India.' Menon to Baroda 27 Dec. 1950, Menon, *Story of the Integration*, 409.

[8] Wavell, diary entry 21 Oct. 1943, Moon, *Wavell*, 35.

[9] Mountbatten to Listowel 8 Aug. 1947, *TOP*, XII, 587.

[10] Even before the transfer of power Menon gave a pretty clear indication of his intentions when he announced at a meeting with Mountbatten, the nawab of Chhatari and Walter Monckton, *apropos* the viceroy's assurances, that 'Congress did not regard themselves as bound by these pledges and statements.' Minutes of meeting 3 Aug. 1947, *TOP*, XII, 496. But Mountbatten seems not to have taken this remark amiss.

nation' referred to by Ziegler.[11] Indeed, when a posse of anxious rulers came to see him to ascertain his views, Mountbatten heartily commended the Indian government's action, which he compared to Napoleon's mediatisation of the German states at the beginning of the nineteenth century.[12] Even when it became obvious that the policy of full integration was not going to be restricted, as he first assumed, to the smaller states, Mountbatten made no effort, as head of state, to call Patel to account. Moreover, while we may take at face value Menon's testimony that when he put the three-subject scheme to Mountbatten in July he and Patel were still open-minded about the ultimate fate of the states,[13] the viceroy – as an accomplished, experienced politician – should have known better. Corfield, indeed, warned him that the deal was not likely to last. But he refused to listen. On the contrary, he went out of his way to assure the rulers that the scheme *would* hold and put considerable pressure on them to accept it – not least in his notoriously partisan speech of 25 July to the COP.[14] Since many rulers, on their own admission, would never have signed if the king's trusted representative hadn't told them that it was the right thing to do,[15] Mountbatten must bear at least some personal responsibility for the fate that befell them.

As to the larger policy decision which Mountbatten inherited and carried out so efficiently – the decision to terminate paramountcy by repudiating the treaties – most historians have followed E. W. R. Lumby in concluding that Whitehall acted with perfect correctness:

The case for holding that when Britain relinquished her power in British India she could consider herself released from her engagements to the Princes rested on stronger grounds than these [the treaties] for the real basis of Paramountcy was not treaties, grants, pledges or promises, but the fact of British supremacy throughout India. When the British authorities had entered into these engagements they had done so on the assumption that they would continue to hold the

---

[11] Ziegler, *Mountbatten*, 418.
[12] Minutes of meeting at Government House, New Delhi, 7 Jan. 1948, Mountbatten Coll., 145.
[13] See, for example, Menon to Sir Mirza Ismail, 2 Mar. 1957, Mirza Ismail Papers.
[14] Mountbatten's willingness to use 'bullying' tactics in 1947 – the word is his own, though he did not entirely accept the charge – contrasts with the position he took up in 1944 when as supreme commander SEA, he opined that a Colonial Office scheme to mediatise the Malay sultans after the war 'lay [the British government] . . . open to a charge of hypocrisy'. Mountbatten to Lord Stanley 29 July 1944, quoted in Steven Ashton, 'The India Office and the Malayan Union: the Problem of the Indian Princes and its Possible Relevance For Policy Towards the Malay Rulers, 1943–1946', in R. B. Smith and A. J. Stockwell (eds.), *British Policy and the Transfer of power in Asia: Documentary Perspectives* (London, 1988), 136.
[15] See Travancore to Mountbatten 30 July 1947 and Kolhapur to Mountbatten 11 Aug. 1947, *TOP*, XII, 414 and 654, and comments by Kurunwad Senior's lawyer to reporter Tim McGirk, quoted in *The Age* (Melbourne), 5 Jan. 1993.

sovereign power in the country . . . That she could give up British India and yet continue to afford military protection to the States . . . was not practical politics . . . Hence, in so far as *rebus sic stantibus* is a condition of all human arrangements, it could hardly be maintained that Britain must still contrive by some other means to honour her engagements to the Indian Rulers. . . .[16]

However, even from a legal perspective (putting aside the awkward issue of the morality of the decision) Lumby's reading is seriously flawed. In international law there are only three possible grounds for the unilateral termination of a treaty. The first is that the terms of the treaty have been breached by the other party. The second is that the terms of the treaty have become impossible of fulfilment. And the third is that the terms of the treaty have become obsolete, owing to what Oppenheim defines as a 'vital change of circumstances' from those contemplated by the parties at the time the treaty was signed (the doctrine of *rebus sic stantibus* – 'so long as conditions remain the same' – referred to by Lumby).[17] Now, since there had been no overt breach of the treaties by the states, the Labour government took its stand, deferring to a submission by Cripps, on the principles of impossibility of fulfilment and obsolescence. But what Cripps failed to grasp, or more likely chose to overlook, was that these principles were (and are) highly contentious. For instance, the doctrine of 'impossibility' is usually held to apply only to changes of a physical nature (such as the silting up of a harbour which one of the parties has con-tracted to protect from seaborne assault); it is not generally applied to political cases; while *rebus sic stantibus* is regarded by many authorities, particularly in Britain and America, as incompatible with the first princi-ple of international law, namely the 'binding nature of treaty obliga-tions'.[18] In the words of the eminent Scottish jurist Lord McNair, the 'normal basis of approach in the United Kingdom towards a treaty is that it is intended to be of perpetual duration and incapable of unilateral termination unless, expressly or by implication, the treaty contains a right of unilateral termination or some other provisions for its coming to an end'.[19] None of the Indian treaties contained such a provision. What is more, by resting its case on *rebus sic stantibus* the Labour government put itself at odds with British political tradition. To quote McNair again, the

[16] Lumby, *The Transfer of Power*, 217.
[17] Ingrid Detter, *Essays in the Law of Treaties* (London, 1967), 88–94; Gyorgy Haraszti, *Some Fundamental Problems of the Law of Treaties* (Budapest, 1973), 231–423; C. Hill, 'The Doctrine of *Rebus Sic Stantibus* in International Law', *The University of Missouri Studies in Law*, 9, (1934), 1–36; Arnold Duncan McNair, *The Law of Treaties: British Practice and Opinions* (Oxford, 1938, revised 1961), 351–76; and Opinion by J. H. Morgan K. C. 11 Feb. 1948, Douglas Yates Fell Coll., 2.
[18] B. Sen, *A Diplomats' Handbook of International Law and Practice* (The Hague, 1965), 442.
[19] McNair, *The Law of Treaties*, 351.

'general conclusion which can be drawn from the practice of successive British Governments is that they do not recognize . . . that changes in the balance of power, or in the relative strength and influence of the contracting parties . . . can be advanced . . . as a ground . . . entitling one party to terminate a treaty without the consent of the other'.[20] The legally correct view was that expressed by Paul Patrick to the American ambassador in April 1945, namely that 'Britain could not legally break these ties without being released by the other parties to the treaties.'[21] And, as we saw above, consent was never sought. It was simply assumed.

Moreover, whatever may be said in mitigation of the decision itself, as one based on the harsh but practical imperatives of *Realpolitik*, there is little excuse for the way it was implemented – unilaterally, and with scant warning. Although the decision to sever ties with the princes was not taken until February 1946, the India Office had been reconciled to the inevitable for several years. In fact, the notion of disengagement seems to have first entered the official mind in 1940, in the aftermath of the rulers' snub of federation. Yet no hint of this speculation was made public. Almost to the end of the war, the line emanating from London and Delhi was that the princes were valued clients who could continue to rely on British military support, regardless of what happened in the provinces. Even Cripps said as much in an unguarded moment. Again, whilst London never warmed to the idea of the states forming separate Pakistan-style unions within the British commonwealth, nothing was done, until quite late, to discourage *darbari* aspirations along these lines. When the jam sahib visited Amery at the India Office in January 1943, he pointed to a map of India on the wall and observed: 'it is almost easier geographically for the States to form an effective working union than it is for the provinces of British India'.[22] Amery's response is unrecorded, but since Digvijaysinhji left in high spirits we can assume that it was not one of demur. Likewise, when Arthur Lothian was briefed by the nawab of Chhatari in 1942 on the nizam's plans for a Hyderabadi dominion, with

---

[20] *ibid.*, 376. Incidentally, contrary to the impression give by Cripps, the age of a treaty in itself makes no difference to its validity. The more modern approach to *rebus sic stantibus*, as reflected in the Vienna Convention on the Law of Treaties of 23 May 1969, is to admit its validity subject to severe qualifications; but we are concerned here with the legal position in the 1940s. See Shabtai Rosenne, *The Law of Treaties: A Guide to the Legislative History of the Vienna Convention* (Doon Ferry, NY, 1969), 300, 320, 324. Ironically, at the very moment that Mountbatten was bringing paramountcy to an end in India, the British representative on the UN Security Council, Lord Cadogan, was stoutly defending the sanctity of treaties in the debate over Egypt's announced intention to terminate the Anglo-Egyptian Accord of 1936 – on the ground of *rebus sic stantibus*! *Security Council Official Records*, No. 70 (1947), 1173.

[21] US Ambassador London to sec. state 21 Apr. 1945, US State Dept. decimal file 845.00/4–2145.   [22] Amery to Linlithgow 12 Jan. 1943, *TOP*, III, 495.

'an access to the sea' and its defence underwritten by the crown, the resident was warmly supportive, opining that an autonomous Hyderabad would make 'a distinct imperial asset'.[23] In short, from 1940 to 1946 the Indian princes were exposed to a cynical charade, kept in the dark to ensure that they remained pliable instruments of imperialism during the final, transitional phase of British rule.

Again, it can be argued that the British did not do nearly enough to ready their clients for the time when they would have to stand on their own feet, without the support of imperial patronage. For thirty years, from about 1909 to 1939, the guiding philosophy of the political department was *laissez-faire* which, while it helped to keep the princes on side, and thus paid significant political dividends, reinforced the backwardness and stagnation endemic among the smaller states and allowed blatant corruption to flourish in some of the larger ones, such as Alwar and Rewa. And though that policy was sharply condemned by Glancy and Linlithgow in 1939, and outwardly reversed, the department remained chary about forcing really drastic changes on the *darbars*, particularly in the area of constitutional reform. As late as 1946, the official line was cautionary, Corfield advising his residents that 'constitutional integration in any *final* form' was 'still premature'.[24] The British wanted the states to reform – but in ways they approved and to a timetable they controlled.

Nevertheless, we should be careful about portraying the princes merely as pathetic victims of perfidious Albion. If they were let down badly in the end, they could still look back on thirty pretty comfortable years under the umbrella of paramountcy. Moreover, they were complicit partners in the project. They readily, even enthusiastically, played along with the orientalist myths that the Europeans constructed about them. They swallowed wholesale the myth of the 'two Indias'. They laid on the pomp and the pageantry. At a time when personal traditions of governance were fast disappearing, they reinvented them. All this 'make-believe',[25] of course, made it that much harder for the *darbars* to face up to the threatening reality of a fast-changing political order in the other India.

More importantly, the princes individually and collectively made a number of serious strategic blunders which materially contributed to their demise. Firstly, despite sharing essentially common values as members of a monarchical order, and being linked organically after 1921 through the COP, the princes conspicuously failed to stick together.

[23] Chhatari to Lothian 20 Dec. 1942, and Lothian to Fitze 25 Jan 1943, *TOP*, III, 400 and 537–8.
[24] *Aide-mémoire* prepared for Residents' Conference 16/17 Dec. 1946, IOR R/1/1/4602.
[25] A suggestive term which I owe to Sir Walter Lawrence, *The India We Served* (London, 1928), 42–3.

When, in 1916–17, Bikaner, Baroda, Alwar and Nawanagar began to push under cover of wartime exigency for an extension of princely control over their internal affairs, this initiative was actively sabotaged by some of the larger states such as Hyderabad. And later attempts by Bikaner, Patiala and others to achieve the same ends indirectly by harnessing the states to the chariot of Indian constitutional reform after 1929 met with an equally mixed response. Likewise, despite the strenuous efforts of Hamidullah of Bhopal (efforts which were compromised from the outset by Hamidullah's known links with the Muslim League) the *darbars* never managed to forge and maintain a united front against the nationalist forces threatening them from outside, partly because they could not agree about how serious this threat was, but mainly because they were more intent on looking out for themselves.

Secondly, it can be argued that the princes did not do nearly enough to shore up their domestic power-bases in advance of the British departure. As we have seen, the larger states, at any rate, possessed a variety of bankable political assets. They had powerful patrons; they were generally wealthy; they had some very able administrators on their payrolls; above all, their rulers commanded an immense reservoir of parochial loyalty. With so much going for them politically, the states had a marvellous opportunity, in the early twentieth century, to consolidate themselves and their dynasties by building diplomatic bridges with the nationalists in the provinces while formally incorporating elite sections of their own peoples, particularly the growing commercial and professional middle class, into the local *darbari* system. Indeed, this was precisely the vision of the future which captivated the more liberal dewans, like Kailash Haksar, Prabhashankar Pattani and Manubhai Mehta in the 1920s.[26]

Now, it would be wrong to say that this good advice fell entirely on deaf ears. Some princes listened. Hamidullah came to see speedy reform as imperative to the states' survival.[27] Even Ganga Singh, temperamentally the most authoritarian of rulers, realised that responsible government in the states could not be delayed indefinitely and saw sense in a preemptive strategy that might ensure 'that the nobler element of the hostile camp survive and remain strong enough to dominate the political arena after we

---

[26] See, for example, memo, n.d., submitted by Mehta to the Bikaner conference of 14 July 1924, in which the Baroda minister argued that states subjects, 'actuated by feelings of local patriotism, could be safely trusted to represent the true interests of their States with a proper feeling of responsibility'. GSAB, Baroda, Pol. Dept., Section 341, file 48.

[27] Significantly, Bhopal sold reform to his members not as part of a last-ditch 'delaying action', but as a strategy for the long term. Circular letter from chancellor 18 July 1945, BRO, Bhopal, Pol. Dept., Chamber Section, 54, 4/24 of 1945–6.

retire'.[28] More to the point, under the aegis of the COP, which from the late 1920s coupled a push for domestic reform with a covert campaign to cultivate moderate sections of the British Indian political elite, the princely order did take some concrete steps to implement what we might call the Mehta programme – notably in 1930 when the ISD to the first RTC offered to support the nationalist demand for dominion status.

Still, much more ought to have been achieved. Progress was patchy, hardly touching many parts of central India, Chhatisgarh and Orissa; and it was far too slow. By August 1947 only a handful of states had introduced even partially elected ministries, and none adult franchise. In their defence it can be said that some rulers, like Dholpur, harboured sincere ideological doubts about the appropriateness of democratic government to 'Indian conditions'; that others were deterred by the uncompromising views on monarchy articulated by Congressmen like Nehru, which appeared to render all solutions short of abdication pointless; that others again were constrained by a lack of money and trained staff and by what they saw as a dynastic obligation to hand over their patrimony intact to their successors.[29] Likewise, it should be noted that *darbari* post-war planning was predicated on the reasonable assumption 'that the settlement of the States situation, *vis-à-vis* the new India, would be a long process' lasting up to ten years.[30] Who can say what spectacular transformations might have been accomplished if this transitional period had actually run its full course? In the event, though, the consequences of delay were fatal. Denied a constructive *darbari* role, nationalists like Jodhpur's Jai Narain Vyas – who, given a chance, would certainly have rallied around the throne – were converted into disgruntled critics and agitators. Likewise, the princes' campaign to woo the British Indian politicians did not, in the end, do them much good because the COP's leaders consistently chose the wrong allies. Almost to the end, they forsook the Congress in preference for unaligned moderates such as Sapru

---

[28] Bikaner to Sir Donald Field, PM of Jodhpur, 21 Feb. 1937, Jai Narain Vyas Papers, file 3/1. For more evidence of state particularism in Rajasthan, see note by C. L. Agrawal, gen. sec., Jaipur Praja Mandal Progressive Party, dated [1942?], AISPC, file 78, Part I, of 1940–2.

[29] See, for example, speech by Maharaja of Patna, 16 Oct. 1946, *Indian India*, 1 (2), 18; record of discussions between the CD, the viceroy and Sir C. P. Ramaswamy Aiyer, 9 Apr. 1946, *TOP*, VII, 186; note by Kanji Dwarkadas giving details of a conversation with Nawanagar, dated 14 Jan. 1946, encl. in consul-gen. Bombay to sec. state Washington 17 Jan 1946, US State Dept. decimal file 845.00/1–1746; note by Corfield dated 30 Apr. 1946, IOR R/3/1/111; Moon, *Wavell*, 261 (diary entry for 8 May 1946); and note by pol. sec., Bhopal dated 9 Jan. 1947, BRO, Bhopal, Pol. Dept., Special Branch, 50, 9/SB/46/I.

[30] Cripps, at a meeting of the Cabinet Mission with the viceroy, 28 May 1946, *TOP*, VII, 25. And see also memo. by Corfield dated 29 May 1947 in *TOP*, X, 1029. Corfield's understanding too, in 1946, was that the windup of paramountcy would take 'years'.

and Jayakar, whose influence had long waned, or communal parties such as the Muslim League. Had they shown more foresight, events may well have unfolded differently, possibly more along the Malayan pattern where British plans to extinguish the sovereignty of the sultans were stymied by a campaign of mass agitation masterminded by the United Malays National Organisation.[31] But the Indian princes could not bring themselves to ditch the British. The habit of dependence had penetrated too deeply. In Linlithgow's morose but accurate summation, 'we have . . . emasculated them'.[32] They stayed loyal – and paid the price.

Thirdly, and perhaps crucially, the princes missed a golden opportunity to entrench themselves constitutionally by accepting the offer made to them in 1939 to join an all-India federation. Now, some historians will say that the federal scheme embodied in the India Act had no hope of succeeding; indeed, may even have been intended to fail by its machiavellian British sponsors. But I dispute this. Not only is this negative line of argument at variance with almost everything that was written and said in the late 1930s, which took the coming of federation pretty much for granted, but, more importantly, it overlooks the fact that in 1939 the states came tantalisingly near to closing on the deal. By the end of September, when the scheme was shelved for the duration of the war, 101 states had responded to the viceroy's offer. Of these 101 replies, 51 were generally in the affirmative.[33] This translated into 35 upper house seats out of the 52 needed to bring the federation into being – which, as Linlithgow pointed out to Zetland, put the government 'within measurable distance of our goal'.[34] Moreover, the viceroy remained sanguine that the gap could be closed. 'I have very little doubt', wrote Linlithgow, 'that . . . we shall have a quorum by the day peace is declared'[35] – and at that stage no-one was predicting a long war. In sum, then, federation was not by any means a hopeless cause. It was workable; the British were

---

[31] See Ashton, 'India Office and the Malayan Union', in Smith and Stockwell, *British Policy and the Transfer of Power in Asia*,' 140. Mirza Ismail believed that, as late as early 1947, Congress was prepared to concede some sort of quasi-independence for Hyderabad in return for a grant of responsible government and the nizam's accession to the union in respect of a limited number of central subjects. Mason, *Shaft of Sunlight*, 206.

[32] Linlithgow to Amery 3 Oct. 1942, *TOP*, III, 85.

[33] Some states attached conditions to their acceptance, but in almost all cases these were not major and could easily have been met by the government.

[34] Linlithgow to Zetland 7 Sept. 1939, IOR L/P&S/13/626. The princes' replies can be read in IOR L/P&S/13/625. The figures on seats include Baroda, whose affirmative reply was hedged with conditions.

[35] Linlithgow to Zetland 14 Sept. 1939, IOR L/P&S/13/626. There were certainly some grounds for optimism in the case of Mysore and Travancore (whose accession would in itself have been enough to carry the British over the line), and even Hyderabad was not altogether a lost cause.

committed to it; and they came in 1939 within an ace of bringing the scheme off. Yet, when all is said and done, the fact remains that Whitehall ran out of time. If the goal was achievable, what prevented the British from capturing the prize?

The conventional view is that the princes were 'frightened off' by the Congress-led *satyagraha* of 1938–9[36] and there is, indeed, some evidence for this hypothesis: not only the obvious element of coincidence, but also the testimony of key players such as Ganga Singh, who couched his rejection of the federal offer very much in these terms.[37] However there are some serious problems with it too. For one thing, the political situation had greatly improved by the time the princes were required to come to a decision; for another, many *darbars*, influenced, perhaps, by the sober and sensible advice of the COMs, seem to have drawn quite the opposite moral from the agitation than Bikaner, namely, that it demonstrated how much safer the states would be *inside* the federation, where they would 'have opportunities [in the legislature] of counteracting the political pressure' to which the governor-general would otherwise be subject.[38] In the words of the maharaja of Tehri-Garhwal: 'Some of the unfortunate happenings in the Indian States during the last year, which have been regarded by some as a reason for holding up the Federal Scheme . . . to my mind, on the contrary . . . [constitute a good] reason for its inauguration with all expedition.'[39] Clearly, political considerations played a part in the outcome of 1939 but when it came to the crunch, other factors, two in particular, counted for more.

One was the way the federation package was marketed by the government. There was not nearly enough hard sell. Corfield, Lothian and other senior politicals were convinced that the rulers were open to persuasion, indeed, were anxious for their residents to give them a lead on the response they should make to the viceroy's offer. But they were expressly prohibited by Zetland from canvassing for 'yes' votes on the dubious and hypocritical ground that the government did not want to defend itself in parliament against allegations of pressure. That this was a costly prohibition is borne out by the fact that in Rajputana, where Corfield, with Glancy's blessing, effectively turned a blind eye to the secretary of state's instructions, a better than 50 per cent affirmative return was received –

[36] e.g., Ashton, *British Policy*, p. 197.
[37] Bikaner to Linlithgow 17 July 1939, IOR L/P&S/13/624.
[38] Report of the COMs dated 14 Apr. 1939, RSA, Bundi, English Records, Serial No. 1201, file No. 448. The report concluded on this point: 'It will therefore be a grave error to be so unduly alarmed at recent events . . . as to omit entirely from [your] consideration the main issues which originally guided the States in their resolve to accept the ideal of Federation.'
[39] Tehri-Garhwal to Linlithgow 30 July 1939, IOR L/P&S/13/625.

the only large agency where this happened.[40] But then, Corfield, Lothian (and at an earlier stage, Keyes) were rather exceptional within the political department in being sincere believers in the advantages of federation both for the raj and for the princely states. Others were lukewarm or fiercely opposed to the scheme, and, according to Krishnamachari, advice along these lines was widely disseminated during the spring and summer of 1939[41] (as, of course, it had been earlier in the aftermath of the first RTC). And others again, who may have approved of the scheme in principle, lacked the intellectual nous and the personal charm and flair to interpret it to the rulers in ways which might have convinced them of its essential merits.[42] However, if a measure of blame belongs with the men on the spot, still more rests with their superiors. Apart from, perhaps, Ramsay MacDonald, the British architects of federation all embraced the scheme dutifully rather than enthusiastically; they did what was necessary, but they did it without flair, and without much ideological commitment. They allowed things to drift. On the pretext of thoroughness and attention to detail, they allowed the drafting of the standard IOA to become bogged down in petty bureaucratic wrangling between rival departmental interests. As a result precious time – and momentum – was dissipated.

Federation, then, was not pushed, even by its sponsors, with the vigour that one might have expected. But that doesn't by any means exhaust the indictment. As we saw in chapter 3, there is much evidence to substantiate the accusation that the government of India under Willingdon did its best, covertly, to subvert the RTC scheme; and the same may have been true of elements in the India Office after 1935, although the latter charge is harder to prove. And while talking of London, let us not forget the contribution of the Tory Diehards, who, though they failed to stop the passage of the government's reform legislation, nevertheless succeeded in planting enough suspicion about

[40] Linlithgow to Amery 13 Sept. 1943, *TOP*, IV, 243; and Lothian to Mirza Ismail 13 Sept. [1955], Mirza Ismail Papers. Some corroborative evidence for this thesis can be found in the following admission by the dewan of Idar: 'we cannot afford to offend the authorities; we can indirectly avoid or possibly indefinitely postpone compliance with their wishes but cannot directly or immediately go against them'. Dewan of Idar to Walter Monckton 30 Dec. 1936, Jayakar Papers, 650.

[41] Minute by Patrick on conversation with Krishnamachari dated 5 Apr. 1945, *TOP*, V, 843.

[42] Sir Edward Wakefield, who was in the secretariat in 1939, believed that many politicals were incapable 'of understanding the implications of accession'. Note encl. in letter to Corfield 13 Mar. 1968, Corfield Coll., 4. For a colourful portrait of the deficiencies of several senior residents by a disillusioned junior political, see Arthur Hopkinson to his wife 29 Feb. 1940, Hopkinson Coll., 14. On the general intellectual calibre of the political service see Ian Copland, 'The Other Guardians: Ideology and Performance in the Indian Political Service', in Jeffrey, *People, Princes and Paramount Power*, 275–305.

federation in the minds of the princes to seriously jeopardise the implementation of the crucial part of the Act relating to all-India. Finally, a crucial subversive role was played by the princes' English legal advisers who, even where they were not personally opposed to the 1935 reforms (as was clearly the case with Scott and Morgan), nevertheless took the view that they had a professional obligation to their clients to point out every adverse consequence to the states that could conceivably flow from the legislation or the IOA. As Jayakar, himself a seasoned lawyer, perceptively observed: 'If a State chooses to pay its Counsel by the lakh, it must not complain if Counsel proposes bulky modifications [to the standard IOA] . . . The Counsel has to justify the high fees, and few people would have the courage to pocket a big fee and be honest in their brevity.'[43]

The other important factor was princely pragmatism. If the federal scheme is to be judged by what was contained in the viceroy's 'final' offer of 1939, one has to say that the decision to reject federation was in some ways both rational and responsible. First, the final offer failed to honour undertakings given to the ISD in the JSC hearings of 1934 and various private promises made to individual states such as Hyderabad as late as 1938.[44] 'It is plain', wrote Courtney Latimer in a post-mortem of 1940, 'that even if the States can not succeed in establishing the violation of any clear and definite promises, they can show that certain distinct expectations were held out to them by very high authority and that these expectations have not been fulfilled.'[45] Second, the terms of the final offer departed in significant respects from the original RTC conception to which the princes had adhered in November 1930. Where the 1930 version had been administratively loose, the 1939 one was tight; where the former had been fiscally neutral, the latter made substantial financial demands on the states in the form of new taxes. Of course, the British had a ready reply to *darbari* complaints about these changes, which was that the original scheme would not have worked. And they may well have been right. Nevertheless, it was manifestly unfair of the press to accuse the princes in 1939 of 'reneging' on their pledge to federate when what was offered differed so fundamentally from the arrangements foreshadowed in

[43] Jayakar to Sapru 3 Oct. 1938, Jayakar Papers, 408. Unlike the English federalist lawyers such as Monckton, Jayakar did not shrink from giving broader, political advice. Significantly, almost all of Jayakar's clients (he advised several Deccan states as well as Porbandar in Kathiawar) returned affirmative replies in 1939.

[44] According to Hyderabadi sources, Glancy told Hydari, during the viceroy's visit in the spring of 1938, that 'almost 95 per cent' of Hyderabad's demands would be met. They were not. Ali Yavar Jang to Monckton 5 May 1938, Monckton Papers, 25.

[45] Note encl. in Latimer to Patrick 20 Mar. 1940, IOR L/P&S/13/626.

London.[46] Thirdly, despite British assurances that the states under federation would not have to part with any powers additional to those which were already exercised on their behalf by the political department, the truth was that they stood to lose a significant quantum of their sovereignty and autonomy, particularly in the field of taxation. Informal intervention under paramountcy was one thing, but binding legislation quite another. Likewise, the princes' lawyers were correct in pronouncing the constitutional 'safeguards' against federal encroachment embodied in the Act and the standard IOA as essentially worthless. Even the British admitted privately to having doubts on that score.[47] And of course no amount of guarantees could protect the states against the effect of future political changes at the centre. Last but not least, for many states, entering federation on the terms contained in the 1939 offer was simply not a sound fiscal proposition. Collectively the *darbars* faced continuing outlays of up to 8 *crores* in respect of interest payments on India's public debt, pensions, currency department losses on silver coinage returned from circulation, and shortfalls on pre-federation central revenue on account of subventions to the provinces, the loss to provincial revenues of jute duty and half of the income tax, and the separation of Burma. As well, they faced a significant net loss of revenue as the proceeds of growth taxes such as excises on sugar, salt and tobacco, corporation tax, and in the case of the maritime states customs receipts, were progressively transferred to the federal fisc. Against this, the states stood to gain perhaps 50 lakhs in respect of remissions of tribute, payments for ceded territories, and compensation for the surrender of existing fiscal immunities, spread over a period of between ten and twenty years – in the circumstances, hardly a great incentive. But these aggregate figures do not tell the whole story. Some states were due for much bigger payouts than others. Udaipur, Kota, Bhopal, Baroda, Gwalior and Indore, for instance, all stood to benefit handsomely by Davidson's calculations. Conversely, most of the Kathiawar states, Travancore, Cochin, Rampur and Jodhpur stood to lose heavily – Bhavnagar and Nawanagar by as much as 36 lakhs a year. Not surprisingly most of the former returned

---

[46] This was the burden of Hamidullah's negative response. Bhopal to Linlithgow 20 July 1939, BRO, Bhopal, Pol. Dept. A, file 7, 1/27 of 1936. The consistency of the states' position was reluctantly admitted by the British. See E. Conran-Smith to W. H. Lewis 30 Nov. 1936, NAI, Reforms Office, Fed. Branch, 10/37; and note by Sir Vernon Dawson dated 3 Aug. 1939, IOR L/P&S/13/621.

[47] e.g., Zetland to Linlithgow 17 July 1939, Zetland Coll., 11. In an unguarded moment Hoare once opined that he doubted whether the states would 'last' longer than ten years as separate entities inside the federation! Memo. by Robert Stopford on the second RTC dated 28 July 1976, Stopford Coll., 3.

unambiguously affirmative replies to the viceroy's letter, most of the latter firm 'no's'.[48]

Of course, most rulers did not make their decision purely on a calculation of material benefit. Political fears and ambitions also played a part, as suggested earlier, and so too, oddly enough, did altruism. Sangli, for example, voted 'yes' in the 'profound conviction that my response . . . should be determined not on the basis of the comparative advantages and disadvantages of the alternative courses open to me but [on the basis] of the higher interests of the country'.[49] But in almost all cases, there was a measured weighing up of the pros and cons, material and otherwise. On this basis a large minority of rulers decided that the potential returns from an investment in federation were too small or too uncertain to make up for the immediate sacrifices to purse and privilege that all-India union entailed.

It was, nevertheless, a myopic decision. Had federation got up (which it might well have, if the *darbars* had been more cooperative with Whitehall in the mid-1930s) the princes would have secured, for the life of the India Act, both the integrity of their states and their position as hereditary rulers. Moreover, the weightage built into the franchise provisions of the Act would have given the states a substantial amount of influence in the federal legislature, which could have been used to ameliorate any immediate Congressite or other centrist pressures on their internal autonomy. Of course the British would still have pulled out; federation would not have changed the metropolitan and international factors making for decolonisation. But being part of an established Indian government at the centre would have given them a much better chance of pressing their claims for dominionhood within the commonwealth; at the very least they would not have been left in the cold by a sudden British departure. In short, if the states had grasped the nettle in 1936 or 1937, and really pushed the federal cause instead of retarding it, the history of the subcontinent in the late twentieth century might easily have taken a different, and perhaps less traumatic turn.[50]

---

[48] A summary of what the states stood to get under the Davidson scheme can be read in IOR L/P&S/13/604. On the Kathiawar states see A. H. Lloyd, joint sec. Finance Dept. to under-sec. state 10 Feb. 1933, IOR L/P&S/13/590. On Rampur see note by E. Conran-Smith dated 26 Nov. 1936, NAI Reforms Office, Fed. Branch, 10/37. On Mysore see Linlithgow to Zetland 19 Aug.1939, IOR L/P&S/13/613. Mysore was a complicated case. On the one hand it stood to gain substantially from the remission of its tribute; on the other hand it was looking at a yearly shortfall of nearly 20 lakhs on account of the loss of its match and sugar excises. All up, the state faced a nett loss of about 6 lakhs annually.
[49] Sangli to Linlithgow 30 Aug. 1939, IOR L/P&S/13/624.
[50] For example it can be argued that if the states had entered a federation of the sort proposed in 1939 (that is, one with a fairly weak centre), the Muslims might not have turned their backs on a united India, sparing the country the holocaust of partition. Against this, however, it has to be admitted that down to 1939 the AIML was very critical of the federal

In one of his last public speeches as chancellor of the COP, nawab Hamidullah of Bhopal declared:

I am clear in my mind that the most progressive among Rulers have done more to advance the sum total of the happiness of the people entrusted to their care than has been secured in many places by following the mere outward forms and machinery of democratic governance . . . In the vast majority of cases the tenor of peoples' lives [in the states] has been peaceful, contented and unruffled, and their loyalty to the Ruler has generally been unquestioned . . . Such loyalty and affection cannot be bought or coerced. I think I can assert without fear of contradiction that there is not one among us who does not regard the interests of his people, their welfare and prosperity, as the touch-stone on which our administrations should be tested.[51]

Most people, reading this text now, fifty years on, would be tempted to dismiss its roseate view of princely rule as the fevered propaganda of a beleaguered leader. And it is true that Bhopal does seek to gild the lily. For instance, he conveniently passes over the sins of the recently deposed maharaja of Rewa, or the earlier excesses of Ripudaman Singh of Nabha and Jey Singh of Alwar, or, for that matter, the backward condition of most of the smaller states of western, central and eastern India (a problem which had plagued his chancellorship). Yet Hamidullah's central claim – that the best of the rulers took the administrative responsibilities bestowed on them seriously and tried hard to improve the lot of their subjects – has a good deal of merit. Since E. M. Forster,[52] the Indian princes have been pictured in literature – and to a large extent, too, in history – as Gilbertian buffoons who frittered away their lives in self-indulgence. In reality, though there were of course some significant exceptions, such as Jey Singh and the gross Bhupinder Singh of Patiala, the majority of twentieth-century rulers were fairly upright, cultured and hard-working. More importantly, a number of them (including, ironically, Alwar and Patiala) were also considerable political thinkers and strategists – men quite capable of holding their own with the British officials and Indian politicians who crossed their paths.

---

scheme on other grounds. Whether it – and the Congress – would have buried their objections rather than risk being excluded from the political process, is something we shall never know. For an optimistic assessment, see memo by K. Ishwara Butt, publicity officer Indore, in sec., Office of the Presidential Rep. to sec. state Washington 19 Jan. 1945, US State Dept. decimal file 845.00/1–1945. The India Office, too, thought that the princes had shot themselves in the foot. Some of this, no doubt, was sour grapes, but Zetland's summation was nonetheless prophetic: 'in the long run, he [Bikaner] and his fellow Princes are likely to have cause to bitterly repent their folly'. Zetland to Linlithgow 19 Aug. 1939, IOR L/P&S/13/621.

[51] Speech by chancellor to General Conference of Rulers, Bombay, 2 Apr. 1947, BRO, Bhopal, Pol. Dept., Special Branch, 75, 28/S.B./46.

[52] Forster, *Hill of Devi*; and Shirley Chew, 'Fictions of Princely States and Empire', *Ariel*, 17 (July 1986), 103–17.

However the argument for taking the Indian princes and their *darbars* more seriously than they have been hitherto, does not rest exclusively or even primarily on the calibre of the rulers' performances as imperial or all-Indian politicians (for, as we've seen, they committed many crucial tactical mistakes along the way to their eventual demise in 1948–9, not least over federation). Rather, it rests on the fact that in the twentieth century the princes and their states played a vital and central role in what has been called the end-game of empire. At the end of the First World War, and again during the 1930s, they contributed directly and with some effect to the debate about constitutional reform and administrative devolution. By their offer in November 1930 to federate with the provinces, they made themselves the keystone of the India Act of 1935, and, in consequence, gained enormous leverage both with the British and the moderate nationalists, for whom federation represented a short-cut to the promised land of dominion status. Indeed, for a decade, the princes virtually held 'the future of India . . . in the hollow of their hands'.[53] Conversely, the states' back-peddling over the federal scheme from 1931, and especially after 1935, destroyed what was London's best and effectively last chance to 'hold India to the empire' within a single, sub-continental constitutional framework.

Through, and despite all of this, the princes proved loyal allies of the crown and more generally active supporters of the raj in its fight to contain the forces of Indian nationalism. Nevertheless, the question must be asked: did the princely alliance, like other collaborative systems in South Asia based on the patronage of landed magnates,[54] ultimately 'fail'; and if so, did this 'failure' contribute – as collaboration theory would suggest – to the British decision to pull out in 1947? The superficial answer is 'no'. Unlike the UP *taluqdars*, whose hegemony crumbled at the ballot box in 1937, or the Punjab *zamindars*, whose influence over the peasantry was eroded during the Second World War, the princes remained powerful intermediaries within their states; moreover they did not, for the most part, desert the imperial cause as the Punjab Unionists did after 1945 when it became apparent that there was a popular groundswell for the establishment of Pakistan, which the British at that point opposed. Nevertheless, if the alliance did not collapse, it certainly

---

[53] 'Policy Pursued by Indian States Delegation at the Round Table Conference', by K. N. Haksar, Confdl. Memo No. 2, n.d., RSA, Sirohi, Sadar Office, file 127 of 1931.

[54] On the failure of the pro-*taluqdari* policy in the United Provinces, see Peter Reeves, *Landlords and Governments in Uttar Pradesh: A Study of Their Relations Until Zamindari Abolition* (Bombay, 1991); on the collapse of similar arrangements with the Punjab land-lords, see I. A. Talbot, 'Deserted Collaborators: The Political Background to the Rise and Fall of the Punjab Unionist Party, 1923–1947', *Journal of Imperial and Commonwealth History*, 11, 1 (1982), 73–92.

became, over time, less useful to the British as a pillar of their imperial rule. When the alliance was forged, around the turn of the century, the princes were almost god-figures to their subjects, and objects of respect and veneration to many other Indians besides; by the 1940s, while still quite popular at home, they no longer commanded anything like the same influence abroad. Conversely, whereas domestic and provincial opposition to *darbari* rule was virtually non-existent in 1917, it was widespread by 1946–7. After 1938, the states could no longer be counted on as political safe havens. This made them much less attractive to imperial strategists engaged in a battle for the hearts and minds of the population. Last but not least, the very development which the British had encouraged with an eye to offsetting the growing power of Congress, namely the princes' movement into the all-India political arena, gradually undermined their value as collaborators, because it made them more independent and less willing to fall in with the plans of their British patrons – a trend which of course reached its apogee with the rulers' embarrassing about-face over federation in 1939.

Whether the British government's reappraisal of the alliance with the princes after 1940 was a cause of its withdrawal from the subcontinent in 1947, or simply a by-product of it, is a question that cannot be answered definitively except as part of a larger re-examination of the whole problem of decolonisation after the Second World War. The likelihood, though, is that further research will reveal the princes and their states to have been a crucial factor in the British decision to relinquish power in India – just as they had been, for a hundred years, a vital element in its maintenance.

Bibliography

A UNPUBLISHED SOURCES

1 Private papers

British Library, London
Atholl Collection (Papers, 1928–39, of Katherine Stewart-Murray, 8th Duchess of Atholl) Mss. Eur D 903
Bailey Collection (Papers of Lt.-Col. Sir F. M. Bailey, 1905–35) Mss. Eur F 157
Brown Collection (Correspondence, 1930–52, of Sir Frank Brown) Mss. Eur E 253
Butler Collection (Papers of Sir Spencer Harcourt Butler, 1880–1938) Mss. Eur F 116
Corfield Collection (Papers, 1939–72, of Sir Conrad Corfield) Mss. Eur D 850
Creagh-Coen Collection (Papers of Sir Terence Creagh-Coen) Mss. Eur D 845
Douglas Yates Fell Collection Mss. Eur D 971
Gwynne Collection (Papers of Howell Arthur Gwynne, 1865–1950) Mss. Eur D 1101
Halifax Collection (Correspondence and Papers of Edward Frederick Linley Wood [Lord Irwin], 1926–31) Mss. Eur C 152
Hopkinson Collection (Papers of Arthur John Hopkinson, IPS, 1934–53) Mss. Eur D 998
Keyes Collection (Papers of Sir Terence Keyes) Mss. Eur F 131
Linlithgow Collection (Correspondence and Papers of Victor Alexander John Hope, 2nd marquess, 1936–43) Mss. Eur F 125
Lothian Collection (Papers of Sir A. C. Lothian) Mss. Eur F 144
Mountbatten Collection (Copies of papers in the Broadland Archives of Earl Mountbatten of Burma, 1900–79) Mss. Eur F 200
Reading Collection (Correspondence and papers of Rufus Isaacs, 1st Marquess Reading) Part I, Mss. E 238, and Part II, Mss. Eur F 118
Findlater Stewart Collection (Papers of Sir Findlater Stewart, 1920–40) Mss. Eur D 890
Stopford Collection (Papers of Robert J. Stopford) Mss. Eur E 346
Tasker Collection (Papers of Sir Theodore Tasker) Mss. Eur D 798
Templewood Collection (India papers of Samuel John Gurney Hoare, 1931–35), Mss. Eur E 240
Thompson Collection (Papers of Sir J. P. Thompson) Mss. Eur F 137

Wavell Collection (Papers of Field-Marshal Viscount Wavell, 1883–1950) Mss.
    Eur D 977
Willingdon (Private) Collection (Papers of Freeman Freeman-Thomas, 1st
    Marquess Willingdon, 1866–1941) Mss. Eur F 237
Zetland Collection (Correspondence and papers of Lawrence John Lumley
    Dundas, 2nd marquess, 1935–40) Mss. Eur D 609

Public Record Office, London
Cripps Collection (Correspondence and papers of Sir Stafford Cripps) CAB
    127/57–154

Bodleian Library, Oxford
Sir Walter Monckton Papers (Correspondence and papers of Viscount Monckton
    of Brenchley), vols. 25–34

Nehru Memorial Museum and Library, New Delhi
Seth Jamnalal Bajaj Papers, Mss. Serial No.124
Nawab of Chhatari Papers, Mss. Serial No.65
Dr Harikrishna Mahtab Papers, Mss. Serial No.105
Correspondence and papers of Dr B. S. Moonje, Mss. Serial No. 45
Padmaja Naidu Papers, Mss. Serial No. 139
Jawaharlal Nehru Papers, Mss. Serial No. 2, and Jawaharlal Nehru Papers, 1947–
    (first instalment)
Correspondence and papers of V. Srinivasa Sastri, Mss. Serial No.100
Jai Narain Vyas Papers, Mss. Serial No.57A

National Archives of India, New Delhi
Jayakar Papers (Correspondence and papers of M. R. Jayakar)

Quaid-i-Azam Academy, Karachi
Quaid-i-Azam Papers (Correspondence and papers of Muhammad Ali Jinnah)
Shamsul Hasan Collection

National Library of Australia, Canberra
Copies of the Sir Tej Bahadur Sapru Papers (microfilm G 2139–49)

2 Official Records

India Office Library, London
Crown Representative Records (R/1) (Records of the Foreign and Political
    Department of the Government of India, transferred to London after
    1947)
Private [India] Office Papers (L/PO)
Records of the Political and Secret Department of the India Office (L/P&S)
Residency Records (R/2)

National Archives of India, New Delhi
Foreign and Political Department Records

Home Department (Political Section) Records
Reforms Office (Federation Branch) Records

Nehru Memorial Museum and Library, New Delhi
All-India Congress Committee Files
All-India States Peoples' Conference Papers
Cabinet Papers 1939–44 (CAB 66/10, 66/21, 66/22, 66/26, 66/27, 66/28, 66/29,
     66/31, 66/37, 66/41, 66/46, 66/49, 67/1, 67/2, 67/8, 68/1, 68/2, 68/5, 68/7, 68/8)
Federal Papers, 1937
Indore Rajya Praja Mandal Papers

Andhra Pradesh Archives, Tarnaka, Hyderabad
Records of the Constitutional Affairs Secretariat, Hyderabad

Bhopal Record Office
Records of the Political Department, Bhopal

Gujarat State Archives, Baroda
Records of the Political Department, Baroda

Madhya Pradesh State Archives, Bhopal
Records of the Huzur Office, Indore

Punjab State Archives, Patiala
Chamber of Princes Archive

Rajasthan State Archives, Bikaner
Private Secretary's Records, Alwar
Records of the Huzur Department, Bikaner
Records of the Prime Minister's Office, Bikaner
English Records, Bundi
Council Records, Sirohi
Political Records, Sirohi
State Council Records, Karauli

History of the Freedom Movement Office, Karachi University, Karachi
All-India Muslim League Papers

Monash University Library, Melbourne
Microfilm copies of US State Department Records: India, 1945–48 (Decimal
     files 845.00–845.30)

3 Dissertations
Benichou, Lucien D., 'From Autocracy to Integration: Political Developments in
     Hyderabad State: 1938–1948' (Ph.D. dissertation, University of Western
     Australia, 1985)
Hurd, John, 'Some Economic Characteristics of the Princely States of India'
     (Ph.D. dissertation, University of Pennsylvania, 1972)

Nair, Janaki, 'The Emergence of Labor Politics in South India: Bangalore, 1900–1947' (Ph.D. dissertation, Syracuse University, 1991)

B PUBLISHED SOURCES

1 Official publications
Great Britain: *Parliamentary Debates*, 1930–47
India: *Legislative Assembly Debates*, 1933–4
Indian Round Table Conference, 12 November 1930–19 January 1931: Proceedings (London, 1931) (Cmd. 3778 of 1931)
Joint Committee on Indian Constitutional Reform: Volume I (Part I): Report (London, 1934)
Memoranda on the Indian States 1930 (Calcutta, 1931)
Proceedings of the Conference of Ruling Princes and Chiefs Held at Delhi on the 30th October 1916, 5th November 1917, 20th January 1919 and 3rd November 1919 (Delhi, 1919)
Proposals for Indian Constitutional Reform (London, 1933)
Report on Indian Constitutional Reforms (Calcutta, 1918)
Report of the Indian States Committee, 1928–1929 (London, 1929)
Report of the Indian States Enquiry Committee (Financial) 1932 (Calcutta, 1932)
The British Crown and the Indian States: An Outline Sketch (London, 1929)
White Paper on the Indian States (New Delhi, 1950)

2 Newspapers and periodicals
Harijan (Ahmedabad)
The Times (London)
The Times of India (Bombay)

3 Collections of documents
Grover, B. L. (ed.), *A Documentary Study of British Policy Towards Indian Nationalism 1885–1909* (Delhi, 1967)
Gwyer, Sir Maurice, and Appadorai, A. (eds.), *Speeches and Documents on the Indian Constitution 1921–47* vol. II (London, 1957)
Keith, A. B. (ed.), *Speeches and Documents on Indian Policy 1750–1921* (London, 1922)
Mansergh, Nicholas, Lumby, E. W. R. and Moon, Sir Penderel (eds.), *Constitutional Relations Between Britain and India: The Transfer of Power, 1942–7*, 12 vols. (London, 1970–83)
Philips, C. H. (ed.), *The Evolution of India and Pakistan, 1858–1947: Select Documents* (London, 1962)
Sever, Adrian (ed.), *Documents and Speeches on the Indian Princely States*, vol. II, (Delhi, 1985)

4 Memoirs, diaries and collected letters
Amery, L. S., *My Political Life*, vol. III (London, 1955)
Butler, Iris (ed.), *The Viceroy's Wife: Letters of Alice, Countess of Reading From India, 1921–5* (London, 1969)
Campbell-Johnson, Alan, *Mission With Mountbatten* (London, 1951)

Corfield, Conrad, *The Princely India I Knew: From Reading to Mountbatten* (Madras, 1975)

Das, Durga (ed.), *Sardar Patel's Correspondence, 1945–50*, 10 vols. (Ahmedabad, 1974)

Devi, Gayatri, and Rama Rau, Santha, *A Princess Remembers: The Memoirs of the Maharani of Jaipur* (London, 1976)

Fitze, Sir Kenneth, *Twilight of the Maharajas* (London, 1956)

Fitzroy, Yvonne, *Courts and Camps in India: Impressions of Vice-Regal Tours, 1921–1924* (London, 1926)

Forster, E. M., *The Hill of Devi: Letters From Dewas State Senior* (London, 1953)

Halifax, Earl of, *Fullness of Days* (London, 1957)

Hardinge of Penshurst, Lord, *My Indian Years 1910–1916* (London, 1948)

Ismail, Sir Mirza, *My Public Life: Recollections and Reflections* (London, 1954)

James, Robert Rhodes (ed.), *Memoirs of a Conservative: J.C.C. Davidson's Memoirs and Papers* (London, 1969)

Listowel, Lord, 'Further Reflections On the Transfer of Power', *Indo-British Review*, 11, 1 (1984), 46–57.

Lothian, Sir Arthur Cunningham, *Kingdoms of Yesterday* (London, 1951)

Mason, Philip, *A Shaft of Sunlight: Memories of a Varied Life* (London, 1978)

Minto, Countess Mary of, *India Minto and Morley 1905–1910* (London, 1934)

Montagu, E. S., *An Indian Diary* (London, 1930)

Moon, Penderel (ed.), *Wavell: The Viceroy's Journal* (London, 1973)

Munshi, K. M., *The End of an Era: Hyderabad Memories* (Bombay, 1957)

O'Dwyer, Sir Michael, *India as I Knew It, 1885–1925* (London, 1925)

Panikkar, K. M., *An Autobiography* (Madras, 1977)

Scindia, Vijayaraje, *Princess: The Autobiography of the Dowager Maharani of Gwalior* (London, 1985)

Simon, Viscount, *Retrospect* (London, 1952)

Singh, Karan, *Heir Apparent: An Autobiography* (Delhi, 1982)

Sreenivasan, M. A. *Of the Raj, Maharajas and Me* (New Delhi, 1991)

Templewood, Viscount, *Nine Troubled Years* (London, 1954)

Trench, Charles Chenevix, *Viceroy's Agent* (London, 1987)

Wakefield, Edward, *Past Imperative: My Life in India, 1927–1947* (London, 1966)

Zeigler, Philip (ed.), *The Personal Diary of Admiral the Lord Louis Mountbatten, Supreme Allied Commander, Southeast Asia 1943–1946* (London, 1988)

4 Monographs

Allen, Charles and Dwivedi, Sharada, *Lives of the Indian Princes* (London, 1984)

Ashton, S. R., *British Policy Towards the Indian States, 1905–1939* (London, 1982)

Batra, H. C., *The Relations of Jaipur State with the East India Company 1803–1858* (Delhi, 1958)

Bridge, Carl, *Holding India to the Empire: The British Conservative Party and the 1935 Constitution* (New Delhi, 1986)

Caine, P. J. and Hopkins, A. G., *British Imperialism: Crisis and Deconstruction 1914–1990* (London, 1993)

Campbell Johnson, Alan, *Viscount Halifax: A Biography* (London, 1941)

Cannadine, David, *The Decline and Fall of the British Aristocracy* (New York, 1990)

Chandrasekhar, S., *Dimensions of Socio-Political Change in Mysore 1918–40* (New Delhi, 1985)

Collins, Larry, and Lapierre, Dominic, *Freedom at Midnight* (London, 1975)

Copland, Ian, *The British Raj and the Indian Princes: Paramountcy in Western India, 1857–1930* (Bombay, 1982)

Creagh-Coen, Sir Terence, *The Indian Political Service* (London, 1971)

Crewe, Quentin, *The Last Maharaja: A Biography of Sawai Man Singh II, Maharaja of Jaipur* (London, 1985)

Darwin, John, *Britain and Decolonization: The Retreat From Empire in the Post-War World* (London, 1988)

Das, M. N., *India Under Minto and Morley: Politics Behind Revolution, Repression and Reforms* (London, 1964)

Dass, Diwan Jarmani, *Maharaja: Lives and Loves and Intrigues of Indian Princes* (Bombay, 1970)

Fox, Richard G., *Lions of the Punjab: Culture in the Making* (Berkeley, 1985)

Ghosh, S. C., *Decision-Making and Power in the British Conservative Party: A Study of the Indian Problem 1929–34* (Calcutta, 1972)

Gilbert, Martin, *Winston S. Churchill*, vol. V (London, 1981)

Glendevon, John, *The Viceroy at Bay: Lord Linlithgow in India 1936–1943* (London, 1971)

Gopal, S., *The Viceroyalty of Lord Irwin* (Oxford, 1957)

Haksar, K. N. and Panikkar, K. M., *Federal India* (London, 1930)

Hettne, Bjorn, *The Political Economy of Indirect Rule: Mysore 1881–1947* (New Delhi, 1978)

Hodson, H. V., *The Great Divide: Britain–India–Pakistan* (London, 1969)

Hurtig, Christiane, *Les maharajas et la politique dans l'Inde contemporaine* (Paris, 1988)

Hyde, H. Montgomery, *Lord Reading: The Life of Rufus Isaacs, First Marquess of Reading* (London, 1967)

James, Robert Rhodes, *Churchill: A Study in Failure 1900–1939* (London, 1970)

Judd, Dennis, *Lord Reading: Rufus Isaacs, First Marquess of Reading, Lord Chief Justice and Viceroy of India 1860–1935* (London, 1982)

Lamb, Alistair, *Kashmir: A Disputed Legacy, 1846–1990* (Hertingfordbury, 1991)

Lord, John, *The Maharajas* (London, 1971)

Louis, William Roger, *In the Name of God, Go! Leo Amery and the British Empire in the Age of Churchill* (New York, 1992)

Low, D. A., *Eclipse of Empire* (Cambridge, 1991)

Manor, James, *Political Change in an Indian State: Mysore 1917–1955* (New Delhi, 1977)

Menon, V. P., *The Story of the Integration of the Indian States* (Bombay, 1961)

Middlemas, Keith and Barnes, John, *Baldwin: A Biography* (London, 1969)

Montmorency, Sir Geoffrey de, *The Indian States and the Federation* (Cambridge, 1942)

Moore, R. J., *Churchill, Cripps, and India 1939–1945* (Oxford, 1979)

    Escape From Empire: The Attlee Government and the Indian Problem (Oxford, 1983)

    The Crisis of Indian Unity 1917–1940 (Oxford, 1974)

Mosley, Leonard, *The Last Days of the British Raj* (Bombay, 1972)

Nicholson, A. P., *Scraps of Paper: India's Broken Treaties, the Princes, and the Problem* (London, 1930)

Nicholson, Harold, *King George V: His Life and Reign* (London, 1952)

Panikkar, K. M., *His Highness the Maharaja of Bikaner: A Biography* (London, 1937)

    The Indian Princes in Council: A Record of the Chancellorship of His Highness the Maharaja of Patiala 1926–1931 & 1933–1936 (London, 1936)

Patil, S. H., *The Congress Party and Princely States* (Bombay, 1981)

Phadnis, Urmila, *Towards the Integration of the Indian States, 1919–1947* (Bombay, 1968)

Ramusack, Barbara N., *The Princes of India in the Twilight of Empire: Dissolution of a Patron-Client System, 1914–1939* (Columbus, OH, 1978)

Rangaswami, Vanaja, *The Story of Integration: A New Interpretation* (Delhi, 1981)

Reading, Marquess, *Rufus Isaacs, First Marquess of Reading*, vol. II (London, 1945)

Reeves, Peter, *Landlords and Governments in Uttar Pradesh: A Study of Their Relations Until Zamindari Abolition* (Bombay, 1991)

Rice, Stanley, *Life of Sayaji Rao III, Maharaja of Baroda*, 2 vols. (London, 1931)

Rizvi, Gowher, *Linlithgow and India: A Study of British Policy and the Political Impasse in India, 1936–43* (London, 1978)

Robb, P. G., *The Government of India and Reform: Policies Toward Politics and the Constitution, 1916–1921* (Oxford, 1976)

Robinson, Andrew and Uchiyama, Sumio, *Maharaja: The Spectacular Heritage of Princely India* (London, 1988)

Rothermund, I., *The Aundh Experiment: A Gandhian Grass-Roots Democracy* (London, 1983)

Rumbold, Sir Algernon, *Watershed in India, 1914–1922* (London, 1979)

Rushbrook Williams, L. F., *The Cultural Significance of the Indian States* (London, 1930)

Singh, Ravinder Pratap, *Geography and Politics in Central India: A Case Study of Erstwhile Indore State* (New Delhi, 1987)

Sisson, Richard, *The Congress Party in Rajasthan: Political Integration and Institution-Building in an Indian State* (Berkeley, 1972)

Smith, F. W. F., Second Earl of Birkenhead, *F.E.: The Life of F.E. Smith, First Earl of Birkenhead, By His Son* (London, 1960)

    Walter Monckton: The Life of Viscount Monckton of Brenchley (London, 1969)

Stern, Robert W., *The Cat and the Lion: Jaipur State in the British Raj* (Leiden, 1988)

Stewart, John, *Envoy of the Raj: The Career of Sir John Clarmont Skrine, Indian Political Service* (Maidenhead, 1989)

Tomlinson, B. R., *The Political Economy of the Raj: The Economics of Decolonization in India* (London, 1979)

Wainright, A. Martin, *Inheritance of Empire: Britain, India and the Balance of Power in Asia, 1938–55* (Westport, 1994)

Wasti, Syed Razi, *Lord Minto and the Indian Nationalist Movement 1905 to 1910* (Oxford, 1964)

Wilcox, Wayne A., *Pakistan: The Consolidation of a Nation* (New York, 1963)

Wild, Roland, *'Ranji': The Biography of Colonel His Highness Shri Sir Ranjitsinhji Vibhiji, Maharaja Jam Sòheb of Nawahagar* (London, 1934)

Young, Kenneth, *Churchill and Beaverbrook: A Study in Friendship and Politics* (London, 1966)

Zeigler, Philip, *Mountbatten: The Official Biography* (London, 1985)

5 Articles

Ashton, S. R., 'The India Office and the Malayan Union: the Problem of the Indian Princes and its Possible Relevance for Policy Towards the Malay Rulers, 1943–1946', in R. B. Smith and A. J. Stockwell (eds.), *British Policy and the Transfer of Power in Asia* (SOAS, 1988), pp.126–43.

Brasted, H. V. and Bridge, Carl, 'The Transfer of Power In South Asia: An Historiographical Review', *South Asia*, 27, 1, (1994), 93–114

Bridge, Carl, "Old Men Forget": Some Objections to the Templewood–Halifax Explanations of the Failure of All-India Federation, 1930–9', *Flinders Journal of History and Politics*, 6 (1980), 323–9

Brown, Judith M., 'War and the Colonial Relationship: Britain, India and the War of 1914–18', in D. C. Ellinwood and S. D. Pradhan (eds.), *India and World War I* (Delhi, 1978), pp.18–48

Copland, Ian, "Communalism" in Princely India: The Case of Hyderabad, 1930–1940', *Modern Asian Studies*, 22 (1988), pp. 783–814

'Congress Paternalism: The "High Command"' and the Struggle For Freedom in Princely India', in Jim Masselos (ed.), *Struggling and Ruling: The Indian National Congress 1885–1985* (New Delhi, 1987), 121–40

'Islam and Political Mobilization in Kashmir, 1931–34', *Pacific Affairs*, 54 (1981), 228–59

'The Baroda Crisis of 1973–77: A Study in Governmental Rivalry', *Modern Asian Studies*, 2 (1968), 97–123

'The Dilemmas of a Ruling Prince: Maharaja Sayaji Rao Gaekwar and "Sedition", in P. Robb and D. Taylor (eds.), *Rule, Protest, Identity: Aspects of Modern South Asia* (London, 1978), pp. 28–48

'The Hyderabad (Berar) Agreement of 1933: A Case Study in Anglo-Indian Diplomacy', *Journal of Imperial and Commonwealth History*, 6 (1978), 281–99

'The Maharaja of Kolhapur and the Non-Brahmin Movement, 1902–1910', *Modern Asian Studies*, 2 (1973), 97–123

'The Other Guardians: Ideology and Performance in the Indian Political Service', in Robin Jeffrey, (ed.) *Princes, People, and Paramount Power: Society and Politics in The Indian Princely States* (Delhi, 1978), pp. 275–305.

'The Princely States, the Muslim League and the Partition of India in 1947', *The International History Review*, 13 (1991), 38–69

Corfield, Sir Conrad, 'Some Thoughts on British Policy and the Indian States, 1935–47', in C. H. Philips and M. D. Wainright (eds.), *The Partition of India: Policies and Perspectives 1935–1947* (London, 1970), pp. 527–34

Darwin, J. C., 'British Decolonization Since 1945: A Pattern or a Puzzle?', *Journal of Imperial and Commonwealth History*, 12 (1984), 187–209

'Imperialism in Decline? Tendencies in British Imperial Policy Between the Wars', *Historical Journal* 23 (1980), 657–79

Haksar, K. N., 'Fiscal Interrelations of the Indian States and the Empire', *The Asiatic Review*, 24 (1928), 539–43

'The Salt Revenue of the Indian States', *The Asiatic Review*, 25 (1929), 7–16

Holdsworth, W. S., 'The Indian States and India', *Law Quarterly Review*, 46 (Oct. 1930), 417–35

Holland, R. E., 'The Imperial Factor in British Strategies From Attlee to Macmillan', *Journal of Imperial and Commonwealth History*, 12 (1984), 165–86

Jeffrey, Robin, 'A Sanctified Label – "Congress" in Travancore Politics, 1938–48', in D.A. Low (ed.), *Congress and the Raj: Facets of the Indian Struggle 1917–47* (London, 1977), pp. 435–72

'Status, Class and the Growth of Radical Politics, 1860–1940', in Jeffrey, *People, Princes and Paramount Power*, pp. 136–69

Kamal, K. L. and Stern, Robert, 'Jaipur's Freedom Struggle and the Bourgeois Revolution', *Journal of Commonwealth Political Studies*, 11 (1973), 231–50

Leonard, Karen, 'The Mulki-Non-Mulki Conflict', in Jeffrey, *People, Princes and Paramount Power;* pp. 65–106

Low, D. A., '*Laissez-Faire* and Traditional Rulership in Princely India', in Jeffrey, *People, Princes and Paramount Power*, pp. 372–88

'Sir Tej Bahadur Sapru and the First Round-Table Conference', in Low (ed.), *Soundings in Modern South Asian History* (London, 1968), pp. 294–329

Manor, James, 'Princely Mysore Before the Storm: The State-level Political System of India's Model State, 1930–1936', *Modern Asian Studies*, 9 (1975), 31–58

'The Demise of Princely India: A Reassessment', in Jeffrey, *People, Princes and Paramount Power*, pp. 306–28

Moore, R. J., 'British Policy and the Indian Problem, 1936–40', in Philips and Wainright, *The Partition of India*, pp. 79–94

'The Making of India's Paper Federation, 1927–35', in Philips and Wainright, *The Partition of India*, pp. 54–78

Mukherjee, Mridula, 'Peasant Movement in Patiala State, 1937–48', *Studies in History*, 1, 2 (July–Dec. 1979), 215–83

Nuckolls, Charles W., 'The Durbar Incident', *Modern Asian Studies*, 24, 3 (1990), 529–59

Patiala, maharaja of, 'The Present Situation of the Indian Rulers', *The Contemporary Review*, 134 (1928), 561–7

Ramusack, Barbara N., 'Congress and the People's Movement in Princely India: Ambivalence in Strategy and Organization', in Richard Sisson and Stanley Wolpert (eds.), *Congress and Indian Nationalism* (Berkeley, 1988), pp. 377–403

'Incident at Nabha: Interaction Between Indian States and British Indian Politics', *Journal of Asian Studies*, 28 (1968–9), 563–77

'Maharajas and Gurudwaras: Patiala and the Sikh Community', in Jeffrey, *People, Princes and Paramount Power*, pp.170–204

'Tourism and Icons: The Packaging of the Princely States of Rajasthan', in Catherine B. Asher and Thomas R. Metcalf (eds.), *Perceptions of South Asia's Visual Past* (New Delhi, 1994), pp. 235–55.

Richter, W. L., 'Traditional Rulers in Post-Traditional Societies: The Princes of India and Pakistan', in Jeffrey, *People, Princes and Paramount Power*, pp. 329–54

'Princes in Indian Politics', *Economic and Political Weekly*, 6, 9 (27 Feb. 1971), 535–42

Richter, W. L. and Ramusack, Barbara, 'The Chamber and the Consultation: Changing Forms of Princely Association in India', *Journal of Asian Studies*, 34 (1974–5), 755–66

Sherwani, H. K., 'The Evolution of the Legislature in Hyderabad', *Indian Journal of Political Science*, 1 (Apr. 1940), 424–38

Smith, Wilfred Cantwell, 'Hyderabad: Muslim Tragedy', *Middle East Journal*, 4 (Jan. 1950), 27–51.

Spodek, Howard, 'Urban Politics in the Local Kingdoms of India: A View From the Princely Capitals of Saurashtra (Kathiawar) Under British Rule', *Modern Asian Studies*, 12 (1973), 253–75

Talbot, I. A., 'Deserted Collaborators: The Political Background to the Rise and Fall of the Punjab Unionist Party, 1923–1947', *Journal of Imperial and Commonwealth History*, 11 (1982), 73–92.

Tomlinson, B. R., 'The Contraction of England: National Decline and the Loss of Empire', *Journal of Imperial and Commonwealth History*, 11 (1982), 58–71

Walia, Ramesh, *Praja Mandal Movement in East Punjab States* (Patiala, 1972)

Wood, John R., 'Indian Nationalism in the Princely Context: The Rajkot Satyagraha of 1938–9', in Jeffrey, *People, Princes and Paramount Power*, pp. 240–74

Wylie, Sir Francis, 'Federal Negotiations in India 1935–9, and After', in Philips and Wainright, *The Partition of India*, pp. 517–26

Index